DATE DUE

MODERN PUBLIC RELATIONS

MODERN PUBLIC RELATIONS

John E. Marston

McGraw-Hill Book Company

New York   St. Louis   San Francisco   Auckland   Bogotá   Düsseldorf
Johannesburg   London   Madrid   Mexico   Montreal   New Delhi
Panama   Paris   São Paulo   Singapore   Sydney   Tokyo   Toronto

MODERN PUBLIC RELATIONS

1 2 3 4 5 6 7 8 9 0 DODO 7 8 3 2 1 0 9

Library of Congress Catalog in Publication Data

Marston, John E
    Modern public relations

    Published in 1963 under title: The nature of public relations.
    Includes index.
    1. Public relations. I. Title.
HM263.M28   1979   659.2   78-7462
ISBN 0-07-040619-7

This book was set in Times Roman by Phoenix Publishing Services.
The editor was William J. Kane and the production supervisor was Diane Renda.
R. R. Donnelley & Sons Company was printer and binder.

49,214

Contents

v

2

PUBLIC RELATIONS AT WORK

Preface

Public relations constantly grows more important as public opinion is brought to bear on more and more issues. The fundamentals of its practice have not changed greatly in the past dozen years but its application certainly has.

Whole new fields such as environmental concerns and energy problems have opened up and others such as consumerism, race relations, government relations, financial relations, and sex and ethnic roles have become of new importance. Social attitudes and expectations have changed greatly. The place of America in the world has materially altered. It is quite apparent also that tomorrow will be different from today.

In this rapidly moving world the work of the public relations expert constantly becomes more demanding. It is no longer enough just to be a skilled communicator, although this is basic. The questions of "Why we communicate?" "What should we communicate?" and "What effect is it having?" also have to be answered—along with many others.

To do this requires an individual with broad understanding and wide experience; more understanding and experience than can be easily accomplished in a short time. This book is an attempt to help bridge that gap, although it can do so only partially. The study of many other academic subjects and experience, either personal or vicarious, is needed to produce a really capable public relations man or woman.

But a start can be made by studying well-tested public relations principles and illustrating them with actual working cases. The two need to go together since principles are abstract and easily forgotten or confused and cases without organization are not always meaningful. Both are necessary. Theory alters slowly, but its application is always new.

Like many other persons today, the writer *grew* into the practice of public relations because a number of years ago there were few, if any, academic courses in public relations or communication as we know them today. He engaged in aspects of public relations work on newspapers and in universities and businesses for many years without being consciously aware of the real nature of the activity or its importance. The evolution of a new field of work is often least observed by those taking part in it; they are like Molière's hero who discovered that he had been speaking prose all of his life without knowing it.

The writer's thanks, then, are due to many who contributed generously to his own education and experience and who could not have had any idea that their aid would help lead to the composition of a book on public relations. This includes teachers at the University of Missouri and elsewhere, fellow workers on *The Des Moines Register and Tribune* and *The St. Louis Star-Times,* many working public relations practitioners, business associates, and colleagues on the faculty of Michigan State University and at San Diego State University.

It also includes many whose help over the years has been quite intentional: members of the Public Relations Society of America and its staff; and members of the public relations departments of dozens of organizations both in the United States and abroad who have supplied examples, illustrations, information, and advice for this book. Nothing could have been accomplished without them. Credit must also go to the writer's wife, Jane, whose good spirit and willingness to explore new fields have been constant. Inevitably in such acknowledgments, many will be omitted who should have been included. Their consolation is that they have contributed to a new field of knowledge and that their aid is remembered and appreciated.

It is hoped that readers of this book will share some of the excitement of discovery and insight into the emerging new world of public relations that has engrossed the writer for many years. Nothing is more interesting than a new world and how people struggle to put it together. If this is accomplished, it will have served its purpose.

John E. Marston

Part One

The Nature of
Public Relations

Chapter 1

What Is Public Relations?

Public relations is as hard to define as religion or education. Everyone agrees that religion and education are important; yet no two people ever define them in exactly the same way.

You probably have your own definition of public relations. So do your friends and neighbors, if they have thought about the subject at all. Since an increasing number of people are interested in public relations nowadays, we shall all find it to our advantage to know what we are talking about. Making definitions acceptable to everyone is not easy. Perhaps, to avoid too much preliminary hairsplitting, we might start with a very broad definition, which we can sharpen later.

> Public relations is planned, persuasive communication designed to influence significant publics.

The key words here are "planned," "persuasive," "communication," and "significant publics." Public relations is not accidental, but is planned carefully. It is persuasive because someone wants someone else to do something or to believe something. It must communicate to particular groups of people rather than to scattered individuals.

The really important key word is "persuasive" because persuasion belongs to a very large and ancient family of human activity. The lawyer presenting a case to the jury, the pastor preaching a sermon, the salesperson selling machinery or shoes, the city school superintendent seeking support for a new building bond issue, and the United States senator running for reelection are all members of the family of "persuaders." All of them try to influence other human beings to believe as they do. The men and women who practice public relations are persuaders also.

Before trying to achieve a sharper definition of public relations, we may find it more immediately worthwhile to consider what it is *not*. It is not just being a pleasant fellow and glad-handing. Being friendly and making people feel at ease may be an important part of public relations, but personal affability is too limited in the extent of its influence to reach many people, unless, perhaps, it is projected to large groups by way of television, motion pictures, or the stage.

Public relations is more than simple publicity—getting news or feature stories into newspapers and magazines or on the air. Spreading acquaintanceship and information in this way can effectively improve public relations; but publicity is sometimes unfavorable or subject to various understandings, and frequently its very overabundance may cause bad reactions instead of good.

Public relations is not lobbying or legislative representation alone, although presenting a case well before the legislative or administrative branch of government is often an essential, persuasive, communication to a very significant public.

Public relations is not advertising, although its relation to this other form of persuasive communication is very close. Advertising generally has more immediate sales objectives and appears in paid space or time. Public relations usually attempts to influence opinions over a longer period of time in many fields, such as community or employee relations, in which conventional advertising would be unsuitable. But the public relations and the advertising programs of a company are obviously closely connected. Why do you have a certain mental image of a particular company? Because you know its products? Because you have met some of its people? Yes, but also because you have seen its advertising. A company whose advertising is misleading, crude, or in poor taste can hardly enjoy good public relations. In these days of keen competition many similar products, all good and all selling at similar prices, may be on the market. In this situation the public relations of a company, the sort of institution the public imagines it to be, may be an important factor in its sales development. Product advertising sells not only products but an image of the company which makes those products.

Nor is public relations the same as propaganda. This once-respected word, which originally meant simply the propagating, or spreading, of a belief, lost its neutral character during the two world wars; now propaganda has come to mean, for most people, false, exaggerated, or one-sided statements—often delivered under conditions of biased censorship. In a reaction against having been misled, some people now profess to believe nothing that they see, hear, or read; this alleged skepticism is a foolish attempt to escape the labor of decision and is as absurd as believing everything.

TOWARD A SHARPER DEFINITION

In an article in *Harper's Magazine* some years ago, Robert Heilbroner referred to public relations men as "a brotherhood of some 100,000 whose common bond is its profession and whose common woe is that no two of them can ever quite agree on what that profession is."

This confusion of disagreement is not so much an indication that the practice is confused as that it is varied. Within the framework of planned, persuasive communications, public relations people work in many different ways for different causes. Since the resulting concepts of their work differ, we get definitions like these:

Public relations is any situation, act, or word that influences people.

Not much here will help us to decide how to go about practicing public relations. The definition only approaches a statement of the standard operating policy for any intelligent organization which seeks to be liked by the public it deals with.

Public relations is the art of making your company liked and respected by its employees, its customers, the people who buy from it, and the people to whom it sells.

This definition goes a bit farther and at least specifies some of the various publics that might be addressed. The word "company" in a definition should really be understood to mean any "organization," since a church, a school, or a governmental department often has public relations problems as pressing as those of a business firm.

Public relations is the skilled communication of ideas to the various publics with the object of producing a desired result.

Getting warmer, much warmer! But is a definition which covers only the verbal communication of ideas adequate? Aren't deeds a factor in public relations also?

Public relations is finding out what people like about you and doing more of it; finding out what they don't like about you and doing less of it.

Here a new thought appears—research; and the need of action is well expressed.

Public relations is the management function which evaluates public attitudes, identifies the policies and procedures of an organization with the public interest, and executes a program of action [and communication] to earn public understanding and acceptance.[1]

Now the definition is becoming adequate! The elements of *research, action,* and *communication* are all strong. Note also the words "management function." They indicate that good public relations is a fundamental part of the nature of an organization—its people, its policies, its history, and its social enlightenment—and not just a bucket of whitewash to be splashed over an essentially ugly object. The words "with the public interest" are also significant, because an attempt to make actions counter to the public interest seem attractive to the public will not delude people long; a condition must not only be *said* to be right, it must *be* right!

THE GROWTH OF PUBLIC RELATIONS

If you were to look under the heading "Public Relations" in the Manhattan classified telephone directory of 1935, you would find just ten names; today the listing runs over many columns and hundreds of names. Among the top 300 companies in the United States in 1936 only one out of fifty had a full-fledged public relations department; today the propor-

[1]Definition from *Public Relations News.* The bracketed words "and communication" have been added by the author. Interesting additional definitions include one from Italy which translates as "Do well and make it known" and one from Britain: "Establishing mutual understanding between an organization and its publics."

tion is three out of four. General Motors had no public relations department or counsel until 1931, and Standard Oil of New Jersey had none until 1942. Today well over 5,000 corporations have departments or counsel.

This rapid development of public relations in business has been matched by its emphasis in welfare organizations, educational institutions, governmental bodies, labor unions, and trade associations, and by celebrities, political leaders, and assorted causes. An estimated 100,000 people work in public relations in the United States today in one way or another, and their annual earnings are more than a billion dollars a year. How much more is spent on public relations activities beyond these wages can only be guessed.

This growth is not confined to the United States. The seeds of public relations are always lying in the ground, ready to sprout when the right circumstances of freedom, easy availability of communications media, rising living standards, and important issues invite public discussion. Since the end of World War II, groups of professional public relations men have sprung up in Great Britain, France, Holland, Belgium, West Germany, Norway, Sweden, Finland, Canada, Australia, Mexico, Brazil, and other areas of the world. In many of these nations public relations practices and principles resemble those in the United States, with differences depending on local circumstances.

Even more, the rapid spread of communications and travel has now exposed millions of people in Asia, Africa, and Latin America to a vast array of persuasive influences from which they were formerly insulated by distance, poverty, and illiteracy. The result is a great outpouring of persuasion by national governments, and varied ideologies not only to retain the support of their own people but also to reach out beyond their borders. The persuasive efforts of Communist China or the Soviet Union, pan-Arabism, Israel's Zionism, and British and American government information agencies are all examples of a lively struggle to reach men's minds, now that new roads have been opened. At its best such persuasion may contain much useful information and new ideas; at its worst it may be false, inflammatory, and reckless. Some of the evaluation, of course, depends upon the person who is judging it, although real principles of truth and intent are involved. This new aspect of the struggle for men's minds will not soon disappear.

One thing is certain: Recent years may well go down in history as the time of the *communications revolution,* for never before have so many been so busy trying to say so much to so many. The prize for success is the right to shape the future organization of the world.

ADDITIONAL READINGS

No attempt will be made in this book to give a complete list of all the many books and articles which have been published on public relations and its related subjects. Only a few of the most pertinent are listed at the ends of chapters.

For a complete listing of more than 10,000 books and articles on public relations the reader is referred to four *Public Relations Bibliographies* which have been published under grants from the Public Relations Society of America. The first was compiled by Professor Scott Cutlip, then of the University of Wisconsin, in 1957, and the latest by Prof. Robert L. Bishop of the University of Michigan in 1974. All are carefully arranged by classifications of subject matter, annotated, and indexed. Their use will provide detailed directions to sources of public relations information in almost any area in which the student or practitioner may be interested.

Books in the General Field of Public Relations

Cutlip, Scott, and Allen Center, *Effective Public Relations,* 4th ed. (Englewood Cliffs, N.J.: Prentice-Hall, 1971.)

Moore, H. Frazier, and Bertrand Canfield, *Public Relations,* 7th ed. (Homewood, Ill.: Irwin, 1977.)

Newsom, Doug, and Alan Scott, *This Is PR,* (Belmont, Calif.: Wadsworth, 1976.)

Simon, Raymond, *Public Relations,* (Columbus, Ohio: Grid, 1976.)

Periodicals in the Field of Public Relations

To understand the expanding and changing public relations field, the student will find it necessary to read extensively and regularly both within the area and also in closely related areas. Among such periodicals are the following:

Immediate Field

Jack O'Dwyer's Newsletter, a privately published weekly newsletter.

Public Relations Journal, the monthly publication of the Public Relations Society of America.

Public Relations News, a privately published weekly newsletter.

Public Relations Quarterly, privately published.

PR Reporter, privately published.

Related Fields

Advertising Age, a weekly magazine covering changes in advertising.

Broadcasting, a weekly covering radio and television.

Business Week, a weekly general business publication frequently featuring news related to public relations situations.

Editor & Publisher, a weekly trade magazine of the newspaper field.

Journalism Quarterly, a publication of the Association for Education in Journalism, a university group, carrying occasional articles on public relations.

Public Opinion Quarterly, a scholarly publication which frequently carries articles of interest to public relations people.

The Quill, the monthly publication of Sigma Delta Chi, a national society of journalists, frequently containing articles of interest to public relations practitioners.

Background Knowledge

A public relations person needs to be well informed on important news and its background. Reading a good daily newspaper such as the *Wall Street Journal, New York Times,* or perhaps the *Washington Post* or *Los Angeles Times* is a necessity to keep up with employers and publics.

Reading publications such as the *Harvard Business Review, Business and Society Review,* and *Corporate Public Issues and Their Management* will not only aid in understanding what is going on in the business world but will also give advance knowledge of the things that are likely to be concerning progressive business leaders who also read these publications.

Chapter 2

Why Public Relations?

The rapid rise of public relations activity in the United States in the past generation is not an accident, nor is it a promotional bubble, destined to burst someday and leave us all in a simpler, quieter state. It is due to the great changes in our living and communications that have made new ways inevitable for people to work together and understand one another. Wherever such changes occur in the world today, public relations, unless prevented by other forces, can be expected to develop because it fills a modern social need.

CHANGES IN AMERICAN LIVING PATTERNS

The United States census of 1910 reported that this nation had about 92 million people, or less than one-half of today's population. The most striking fact in that census report, however, is that in 1910 more than

34 percent of all Americans lived on farms and many more in small towns; today fewer than 2 percent live on farms or in towns of less than 1,000 people. This trend to the city has been apparent since the first Federal census in 1790, when by far the largest part of the less than 4 million population was rural.

Pioneers moving westward, though they inspired many exciting stories, were actually a minority; most early Americans did not travel much. Farming demanded daily attention, cash was short, and transportation was limited. Of all the Union soldiers drafted in the Civil War, for example, only about 10 percent had ever been more than about 25 miles away from home before they joined the army.

Even at the beginning of this century, village and farm life was far different from life anywhere in the United States today. There were no automobiles, no paved roads outside the towns, no radios, no television sets, no motion pictures, practically no electric lights, few telephones, not much world news, and few travelers. People worked at their jobs long hours, six days a week, and much of the rest of their time was filled with farm or household chores such as stoking the coal furnaces, carrying out the ashes, washing, cooking, and baking.

Most Americans in 1900 weren't particularly unhappy, however. Times were much better than they had been; the country was growing; there were great opportunites (even if you personally didn't manage to seize them); and the United States was a big, happy, isolated land, securely resting behind its growing navy and well insulated from the shocks of the rest of the world. For entertainment people went on picnic excursions now and then by boat or train or carriage, had home visitors on Sunday afternoons, took part in parties and plays, sang songs around the piano, and attended fairs. In this orderly and progressive world you might not know a great many people or travel far, but you knew your friends well; you had had school days together, had lived at home in the same town, and had gone on into the companionship of old age. Issues of debate were few and comfortably black and white; indeed, it was the kind of world in which a man might feel at home and be of some stature. When older people today remember the Gay 'Nineties fondly, they are recalling a time that really existed for many—a time when a visit to the Chicago World's Fair was more of a thrill than a jaunt to Calcutta or Rio today.

Now most Americans live in large cities or their suburbs. They live in a far better physical environment, work less, travel more, are healthier and better educated. Their children are bigger and live longer. Americans today have more leisure and less cause to worry about old age or illness. But along with these advantages come occasions for uneasiness and frustration.

Most of the units in American life today are large. In populous cities the citizens may be just numbers, voting for people they do not know, taking little part in governmental responsibility, and being ruled by people they have never even seen. In huge businesses employees often work for men whom they have never met and never expect to meet; many do not even know their employers. People are separated by their occupations, of which more than 30,000 are listed in one directory alone. Distances are great. Workers may be employed in a plant or office and live so many miles away that home and employment are in completely different realms. Schools and churches are large. Keeping a sense of proportion is a problem. The whole world seems both large and small —large in its newly realized complexity in which America is but one unit, and small as a dot in the exciting concept of space.

Modern Americans are likely to be rootless. Today few city dwellers live and die in the communities where they grew up. As neighborhoods change, people move; when a job opportunity beckons, they may shift halfway across the country. When new types of work promise greater opportunity, people often change their trades or professions. Americans today meet far more people in the course of their lifetimes than their fathers or grandfathers would ever have dreamed possible, but they *know* far fewer of them.

Greater demands are made upon everyone. The swift march of science and human organization forces all of us to know and to decide many more things than our fathers had to consider. Today's citizen is expected to have intelligent, reasoned opinions on the merits of various plans to avoid social conflicts, on the nation's foreign policy, on avoiding business recessions, on the proper roles of management, capital, labor, and government in the American economy, and on the right portion of the national budget to spend on new energy sources.

One of the greatest changes since the 1930s has been the development of economic democracy in the United States. The old days when Commodore Vanderbilt, the railroad magnate, was reported to have said, "The public be damned," are now far past. The rise of powerful labor unions and widespread stockholding, among other factors, has caused many groups, including labor, management, stockholders, consumers, and government, to contend for the privilege of steering the nation's economic course and of sharing more of its benefits. Economic "laws" are no longer regarded with awe and felt to be fixed like the orbits

of the sun and the moon. Whatever most people want badly enough a
long enough they get; it thus becomes important to know what they wa
and why they want it. Whole new areas of economic discussion have been
opened up to public argument that only a generation ago were largely
reserved for experts.

In all this swiftly moving confusion, ordinary American citizens try
to be informed and to make correct decisions on the many issues presented to them, difficult and distant though they may seem. It is to their
credit they have done as well as they have. Except on occasion, and then
not for long, Americans have not given in to panic or thrown up their
hands in despair. They have kept their temper and wits, and although
somewhat slow to act (for democracy is always slow), they have generally shown that they understand the problems presented and are prepared to tackle them.

THE NEW COMMUNICATIONS WORLD

In coping with the depersonalization, bigness, and bewilderment of today's world, the ordinary American has been both aided and confused
by the media of mass communications. The ways in which the average
American gets information and opinions are as different from those of
the good old days as the physical world of the 1970s is from that of the
early 1900s.

Today's communications world is huge, complex, and omnipresent.
Modern men and women live in a sea of communications, deluged with
a rain of words, sounds and sights. Whereas a generation or two ago a
few newspapers, magazines, books, public speakers, and friends provided
the bulk of a rather limited communications system in which people
largely had to make the effort to get information by their own reading
or active investigation, today all sorts of communications thrust themselves at Americans continuously, free and unsought.

A person gets up in the morning and listens to chatter and song on
the radio while breakfasting and then drives or rides to work. Perhaps
he reads a morning newspaper at breakfast or on the commuter train.
Another person may watch television while doing household chores.
Numerous large, well-illustrated magazines come into most homes.
Paperback books are cheap and sold by the millions. The huge daily
newspaper is crammed with literally hours of reading for anyone who
wishes to spend that amount of time. Motion pictures are just around the
corner or on the late-night television show. There are numberless meetings to attend, activities to participate in, and places to go. Normal

citizens can spend so many hours daily receiving communications that they can very seldom be alone or quiet. It is estimated that the average American is exposed to 1,500 advertising messages each day as a result of a $35 billion annual expenditure by companies on communications.

Not only are these communications numerous; they also cover an extremely wide range of subjects, including the sciences, foreign events, and causes of worry ranging from the latest atomic missiles or the state of America's image abroad to the ups and downs of the stock market, new taxes, strikes, and riots. Occasionally, in the past, a newspaper was said to practice "Afghanistanism," meaning that it filled its columns with telegraphed reports of unimportant happenings in distant places while it neglected the harder and more expensive reporting of local news; today such an accusation would have little meaning because apparently almost anything in the world now has a bearing upon American daily life and is worthy of communication.

One effect of the pressure of modern communications has been to make it hard to gain people's *attention.* So much is presented daily that receivers have become adept at listening only to what they want to hear. This selectivity naturally concerns the commercial communicator (for example, the advertiser) because there are limits to how loud the enterprise can shout successfully for attention. At a certain point loudness collapses. Bigness and color in newspapers and magazines soon become quite expensive; shrillness and tricks and other devices to gain attention on radio and television, because they seem extravagant or domineering, are soon resented; yet the advertiser *must* be heard. For the public relations person, the advertiser's problem becomes even more acute, because the public is ready to condone a degree of blatancy in advertising that it dislikes in public relations. It wants to be informed rather than manipulated.

The public relations person who wishes to be heard today has arrived at several solutions—a more careful selection of audiences with which to communicate, more skillfully prepared communications, and greater identification of communications with the existing interests of the audience. A person who wants to promote boats, for example, tries to select an interested audience, say the readers of a boating magazine or marine column or watchers of outdoor-sports television shows; the message is presented as pleasantly and cogently as possible; and boat-minded people are appealed to about things close to their interests. If this is done well the message can scarcely say too much.

This applies to both advertising and public relations messages. The key to how much a person will read or listen to is the existing degree of interest in the subject matter. This is why it pays to select audiences as precisely as possible.

In addition, a public relations person who wants to promote some new scientific development by a company sends one type of story to *Scientific American* magazine and another type to a metropolitan Sunday newspaper, adapting the writing to each audience and relating the information to the degree of knowledge and interest of each group. Readers or listeners are usually willing to absorb a great deal about the things which concern them but easily ignore those not related to their lives.

Another problem is the present lack of *two-way* communication. People today are greatly talked *at* and get little opportunity to express themselves; a chance to ask questions or to challenge opinions would not only make them feel better, but would also clarify their thoughts. All mass media such as newspapers or television, no matter how excellent, are *one-way* means of communication; recipients listen, but unless they get sufficiently excited to write a letter or to telephone the newspaper or broadcasting station, they remain only receivers and are not participating senders. Very seldom does anyone talk back to a newspaper or to a television station. Recipients do not know the people who are writing or speaking, and realistically they expect little response; they usually prefer to mutter to themselves or to their friends and family, or to say nothing at all.

The frustration of listening helplessly while being "told" is heightened when the recipients are city dwellers with few close friends. Many people move often and do not know their neighbors. Fellow workers often live in widely scattered areas and know each other only on their jobs. Even next-door neighbors are not often real friends in modern life because today location contributes less to friendship than do common interests; and one just doesn't talk much to stray people on the street or to chance acquaintances.

The knowledge that many people in America today live in this loneliness of the crowd and the realization of their need for self-expression and participation are keys that the intelligent public relations practitioner can use in obtaining their understanding and good will. To change the metaphor, one of the biggest problems of modern society is building bridges of communication between large groups of people who are emotionally isolated, lonely, and frustrated.

THREE WAYS OF SECURING HUMAN COOPERATION

Ever since people first began to crowd together, to communicate, and to establish complex social structures, their leaders have found three main ways of getting them to make concerted efforts—*power, purchase,* and *persuasion*—although in actual practice all three are usually mixed.

Power, typified by the strong man with the sword, the despot, says, "Do this or I shall kill you, or beat you, or imprison you!" The chief limitations of power are the uncertainty of its duration, its difficulty of application, its wastefulness, its inability to progress, and its utter lack of moral principle, since the very essence of power is violation of the freedom of human will and choice.

Power has never ruled much of the world for long by itself; yet power, open or hidden, is found in almost all societies because some people cannot be governed otherwise. Between nations power remains dominant; yet we may wonder how long it will be so, since the value of power as a governing force varies with the nature of weapons. Between individuals, for example, the strong man with a sword was able to impose his will upon quite a number of lesser individuals until the invention of hand firearms. The rifle and revolver were great and deadly equalizers, and after their invention the tone of civil manners materially improved. Between nations, the so-called "great powers" with large armies and navies were once able to dominate their lesser neighbors with impunity because in war they could inflict more hurt than they could receive. Perhaps the coming of the atomic-missile age has changed all that.

Purchase says, "Do this and you will receive an advantage in money, goods, position, or honor," People can be purchased, of course, only by that which they value. The offer of a knighthood in the British Empire would probably have little attractiveness to a Chinese Communist, and offering a barrel of whisky as a prize award to a temperance union would doubtless also be futile.

But purchase is widespread. Those who work for money or other gain, or those whose work we hire directly or indirectly, are all engaged in purchase. A boss purchases not only the physical working time of employees, but also some of their interest and loyalty. The owner of stock in a corporation purchases the time and efforts of many unknown people.

Because purchase plays such a large and pervasive part in securing human cooperation in a money economy, people begin to think that they can buy anything, whereas in fact a great many things, like loyalty or love, are not for sale and can only be given. When Richard III, as Shakespeare tells the story, lost his horse in battle and dashed about the field vainly crying that he would give his kingdom for another mount, his plea was useless. Other fighters needed their own steeds too much at that moment either for battle or for flight, and Richard in that desperate time had no kingdom to give. Wealthy people, organizations, or even nations who think that they can buy good will and understanding are often mistaken. People are purchased by many things, but often seem to behave quite irrationally, "biting the hand that feeds them," preferring trouble and hardship to ease.

But purchase is more respectable than power, which always rests upon doubtful moral grounds. When purchase is a free transaction, the rights of human choice are not violated. Purchase may be obtuse and vain and it may degrade spiritual values, but it is not a negation of free will unless those who are purchased choose to let it become so.

Persuasion is the most complex method of obtaining human cooperation. Persuasion says in effect, "For these reasons which appeal to your mind or to your emotions, please believe and do these things." Religious or political beliefs have often been called persuasions; as St. Paul once put it, "I am persuaded [I believe] that neither death nor life . . . shall be able to separate us from the love of God."

Persuasion, in the sense of offering cogent reasons for belief, can be achieved only by communication. No words are necessary to explain the power argument of a gun or the purchasing power of a stack of coins, but people can be persuaded only by words, pictures, gestures, or other means of human communication. The world's great persuaders have been its teachers, preachers, prophets, writers, and artists. Through persuasion the religion of Jesus swept out of Judea and transformed the Roman Empire within a few generations; the writings of Marx, Engels, and Lenin animated the Communist third of the globe. Persuasion was the spark that ignited the Protestant Reformation, the American Revolution, the French Revolution, and the American Civil War.

There is an inescapable connection between persuasion, freedom, and democracy—because democracy is a system of government by persuasion. If enough people can be persuaded, rules may be changed in a democracy. For a democracy to exist, the right of free communication in order to persuade must be allowed, because otherwise nothing could ever change; gradual, orderly change is the essence and glory of a democracy.

In governmental systems depending upon power, whatever their disguise, the right of open persuasion is always carefully controlled or denied, and communication is a state monopoly. In a government depending largely upon purchase, economic weapons may be used to control persuasive communication; but the true test of democracy is its willingness to permit argument on many sides of issues. Obviously, public relations people can develop fully only in democratic societies.

A BRIEF HISTORY OF PUBLIC RELATIONS

In the past sometimes a combination of freedom and reasonably high living standards has allowed time for thought about important public issues, but widespread communications systems have been lacking until recent centuries.

Many of the small, ancient Greek city-states were political democracies in which the adult male population debated vigorously; yet the size of these democratic governments was limited by the persuasive range of the human voice. Since literacy rates were low, writing slow, and writing materials limited, public business had to be conducted in an arena in which a maximum of a few thousand participants might hear. These Greek cities produced some of the first hired persuaders and their teachers; they were the Sophists, or wise ones, who carefully studied the writing and delivery of speeches until their superior oratory could make their less sophisticated rivals sound tongue-tied and inept in swaying a voting assembly. Such capable Sophists were much admired, feared, denounced, and sought after by the would-be and actual political, military, and economic leaders of the day; they were hired to present causes before the assembly much as a lawyer or a public relations person would be employed today.

Republican Rome borrowed many Greek ideas, but the sterner ambitions of military power in Rome afforded less opportunity for the development of orators, although Cato, Cicero, Mark Antony, and others were noted for their eloquence. Writers could be persuaders. Julius Caesar's *Commentaries on the Gallic Wars* constitutes one of the most masterful propaganda tracts ever penned. But with the coming of the imperial power of the Caesars, the role of the orator and often of the writer declined to the dimensions of court lawyer, literary lion, and eulogist of the glories of the emperor. Roman despots, however, were not unmindful of the power of public opinion, whether in the well-financed ranks of the senate or in the roars of the street mobs. Simple forms of persuasion, such as triumphal parades, free grain, and free tickets to gladiatorial combats, replaced the soaring oratory or tight-clipped reasoning of Cicero or Brutus; banners, spoils, and pomp persuaded instead of words.

Rome's propaganda proved comparatively feeble a few years later in the face of the Christian saints and martyrs, who were among the world's greatest persuaders by letter, preaching, and example. The excit-

ing words of the Christian evangelists, despite vigorous persecution, sent
new blood coursing through the veins of a decaying empire which had
lost its ability to inspire men and relied primarily upon power and
purchase to govern; and they stole away the allegiance to the Roman
ideal from right under the noses of the emperors. Romans simply would
not believe any longer that the emperor was divine or that the imperial
regime was worth fighting for. When he adopted Christianity, the Emperor Constantine shored up the situation for a few generations by
removing the conflict between the church and the imperial power and
substituting a new alliance of persuasions. Then, with the coming of
massive barbarian invasions, the conditions of civilized living and free
communications which had made possible any public persuasive activities disappeared. Yet in the monasteries and among the common people
a body of scholarly and popular literature was being produced that was
to emerge a few centuries later to belie the apparent stagnation of mind
of Western Europe.

A New Communications Medium

Almost a thousand years after the barbarian invasions, a German named
Gutenberg invented movable type and printed a Bible in Mainz in 1456,
thus launching a new era of mass persuasion. New conditions of freedom
and prosperity, within walled trading towns and, by sufferance, in the
courts of some kings and princes, were ready to be united and strengthened by this new method of cheap communication. The world faced an
upset, the first of many since.

The first outflow of printed persuasion was largely in the field of
religion, which much concerned literate people in the fifteenth and six-
teenth centuries. Since the books were widely distributed and eagerly
read, their ideas proved inflammatory, and Europe was soon split by
religious wars.

Not all printed persuasion was about religion, however; some was
geographical, scientific, or economic; there were books on the new
worlds in North and South America, arguments over the ownership of
Brazil or the East Indies, journals of polar exploration, and trade reports.
Newspapers and newsletters began to appear, and an increasing number
of political arguments culminated in the writings of Voltaire, Rousseau,
and Thomas Paine—and, in due course, in the American and French
Revolutions.

But, exciting as this ferment of ideas was, it marked only the beginning of the change to be wrought by printing. When the communications
revolution was wedded to the industrial revolution, society was really
turned upside down. Setting type by hand, one character at a time, in

the manner of Gutenberg or Benjamin Franklin and then impressing the paper upon a page of type one sheet at a time by screw press is, of course, infinitely faster than handwriting, but it is still slow, clumsy, and costly. When in the 1830s the steam engine was commonly applied to printing presses, the cost of a newspaper fell from about 12 cents to 1 cent, and the size of newssheets was vastly increased. The result was that a whole new army of readers was informed, and popular democracy was greatly expanded.

With more and bigger newspapers came the rise of advertising and the spreading of many new ideas such as communism, nationalism, and other economic and political beliefs. Steam-powered railroads and steamships could take cheaply printed publications anywhere in a short time, and as a source of news the telegraph even outran them. Persuasive books and newspapers of the mid-nineteenth century look stuffy and dull in these modern times, but they burst like bombshells in their own world, which only a half century earlier had been more akin to the world of Julius Caesar than to that of today.

During the past two centuries, as the means of communication have increased, the types of professional communicators have continued to increase also, and many of these might be considered precursors of public relations practitioners. First were the politicians, because, of necessity, politics in a democracy is the art of ascertaining and molding public opinion upon a large scale. During the American Revolution, for example, Samuel Adams relied upon letter-writing committees of correspondence and copies of the *Boston Gazette* to tell the independence faction's version of the Boston Tea Party or the Boston Massacre or other such events. And in the early skirmishes for power in the young republic between liberal and conservative thinkers, Alexander Hamilton scored heavily with the *Federalist* papers, setting forth viewpoints favoring the moneyed class and a strong government.

When, in the 1830s, Andrew Jackson achieved power, the United States already had more newspapers and readers than any other country in the world, and Jackson owed much of his success to his adroit use of them. His "press secretary," Amos Kendal, a former newspaperman from Kentucky, was a member of Jackson's unofficial Kitchen Cabinet. He ghosted the president's speeches, wrote pamphlets and news releases, arranged the president's press interviews, and made it his business to ascertain public opinion, both advising the strong-minded president as to what to say and then helping him to say it.

Political press-agentry had become a big-time operation by the time of the Bryan-McKinley presidential campaign of 1896. At the headquarters of both conventions in Chicago, newspaper coverage was elaborate.

Then, in the 1930s, Franklin D. Roosevelt showed that he was a master of a new communications medium, the radio; and later Dwight D. Eisenhower and, even more, John F. Kennedy both showed great skill in handling an even more recent medium, television. Expertness in persuasive communication is essential in any political battle, and as the news media grow more complex, the need of professional help in their use also grows.

But showmen, no less than politicians, need to seek public attention. In politics ballots mean winning an election; in show business admission fees mean a fortune. In the long years of his lifetime (1810–1891), the prince of showmen was Phineas T. Barnum, whose publicity was so successful that he implanted in our language a number of words which are still in common use but whose origins have been almost forgotten. Consider "jumbo," for example. Everyone knows that jumbo is a synonym for something large; yet few today know that Jumbo himself was a large African elephant which Barnum exhibited in the circuses. Barnum had to have a name for his curiosity, and "Jumbo" had a nice African jungle sound well-suited to short headlines. Jumbo was so well publicized that the term remains in the language long after its origin has been forgotten. Or consider "Tom Thumb." Most people today associate the words with something tiny, but not many know of the real midget, Charles Stratton, called "General Tom Thumb," whom Barnum exploited, and who presided over a troupe of tiny people, drove in a little coach drawn by ponies, and was even presented to Queen Victoria, making a very proper speech for the occasion. Mention might be made also of the Siamese twins, recognized by everyone today as twins fastened together by an accident of birth, named after a pair which the prince of showmen exhibited.

Barnum was not averse to buying advertising space, but he also knew the news interest of his attractions and reaped a harvest of free publicity. With Barnum, and after him, came a host of other press agents whose speciality was getting into free public print the names of actors and actresses like Lily Langtry or Anna Held, and later of a host of motion-picture, radio, and television stars. The agents' methods were not quite so important to them as the results. All manner of stunts, such as fake jewel robberies, marital spats, and love affairs were reported; and a mine of misinformation about marriages, divorces, clothes (or lack of them), opinions upon any subject, and travels was constantly explored. Unfortunately, the public, or at least a large part of it, loved it!

Some of the stories were true, and some weren't. Sometimes news
tors let themselves be fooled and went along with the game for the
sake of a lively story; sometimes they didn't know; and sometimes they
were taken in. Being deceived hurt their egos; and newspapermen, de-
rided by friends and readers, occasionally became vitriolic about press
agents' morals. But none of this criticism stopped the press agents'
output, or its use, and the lurid or sentimental stories ran through the
papers in a great flowing stream. The racket reached an all-time climax
in 1926, when, at the New York funeral of the movie idol Rudolph
Valentino, some sixty to eighty thousand persons engaged in a near riot,
which was finally contained by the vigor of almost two hundred police
officers charging the crowds repeatedly on horseback.

There has always been a great difference, however, between the
publicity efforts of American politicians and the press-agentry of show
business; politicians are interested only in creating favorable public opinion, because this brings its reward at the polls; those in show business,
on the other hand, are often interested in any kind of public notice, since
the bad frequently pays off as well at the box office as the favorable (or
perhaps better). The two motives—desire for understanding and approval by means of public relations and desire for notoriety through
press-agentry—have been constantly confused. The misunderstanding
has impeded the growth of responsible public relations, and for many
years has needlessly embittered the feelings of newspaper editors and
other people involved in communications media toward public relations people. Today, fortunately, the differences are more widely understood.

Public Opinion and Big Business

In using public relations to reach people, American businessmen for a
number of reasons lagged behind politicians or showmen. Not until the
late nineteenth century did American business begin to develop on a
really big scale. Before that the small merchant or manufacturer often
knew his customers, employees, suppliers, business friends, and fellow
townsmen by name. His public relations were personal relations conducted by conversation, personal letters, and visits. The business institution was then indeed the lengthened shadow of a man—and the
nineteenth-century capitalist whose lengthened shadow it might be was
not going to engage in any folderol about influencing public opinion
unless a cash return could be anticipated. Business barons of the 1800s
tended to be authoritarian, satisfied, and serenely confident of the goodness of their work. Labor was voiceless; markets were constantly expand-

ing; and how the business was conducted or what it did was no outsider's concern.

But this freedom could not long endure, because as business firms began to become nationwide mammoths, far more people were affected, personal communications broke down under their own weight, and public opinion formed and began to make itself felt through the actions of government, which was sometimes more sensitive to votes than to dollars.

The first really big United States businesses were probably the railroads, whose spectacular growth was accompanied by scandalous construction frauds and government aid. Railroads, moreover, were monopolies in all parts of the country where competing lines did not exist, since neither paved cross-country highways nor the automobiles to run upon them had yet even been dreamed of. The lordly independence of railroad personnel all the way from conductors and country station agents to presidents was impressive to behold and quite indomitable, since if a man did not choose to ride or to ship upon the railroad, his only alternatives were to drive a horse and carriage or to walk. Perhaps one of the Vanderbilts did not say, in 1882, "The public be damned" in reply to a newspaper reporter's question about the public interest; but to many people the phrase seemed so in keeping with railroad-magnate character that the words stuck and have done harm to the railroads ever since. This in its way illustrates another fact about public opinion: Once established, it endures long after the facts upon which it was based have been forgotten. Railroads today may wallow in red ink and they may be strangers to an automobile-riding public, but the bad image lingers on.

Following the railroads came the gigantic growth of great national corporations in oil, steel, coal, meat packing, banking, and public utilities, whose proprietors, frequently lacking in humility, displayed an ostentation in turreted mansions, fashionably gowned women, huge steam yachts, and stables of race horses which became the constant preoccupation of the readers of the cheaper press.

Public reaction was two-sided. On the one hand, many people admired all business success. Exuberant bigness seemed to befit a booming America. The big good deeds of Carnegie's libraries and the little good deeds of Rockefeller's dimes were extolled; the flowing champagne of Newport-mansion wedding feasts, mirrored in Sunday newspapers, was vicariously lapped up by moon-struck maids and matrons; the scandals of a Jim Fisk or a Diamond Jim Brady met with a tolerant "Just what I'd do if I had the money"; and the solemn pronouncements of moderately educated millionaires upon the deepest matters of science, religion,

law, politics, and social and international life tended to be regared with
quite unjustified awe.

The Muckrakers

On the other hand, large segments of the public were uneasy and hostile.
Big business was feared because it seemed to have too much influence
upon big government; slums and rural poverty were contrasted with the
rich life of wealthy mansions pictured in the popular press; through
drought, depression, and change farmers and laborers found their lives
hard, their prices and wages low, and their independent futures obscure;
moralists yearned for a return to a simpler life; and even smaller businessmen, pressed or absorbed by their larger competitors, became embittered. In a time of change, of improvement, yet of distress for many, there
was too much one-way conversation by business to its employees, its
customers, its communities, and the people in general. Somebody was
about to talk back. The reply came from the muckrakers from 1900 to
about 1914 and has continued, with interruptions, ever since.

During the first years of this century, big business was under almost
constant fire from scores of magazines and newspapers intent upon
exposing its sins. Ida Tarbell's *History of the Standard Oil Company* was
advertised as "a fearless unmasking of moral criminality masquerading
under the robes of Christianity and respectability." Upton Sinclair's
novel, *The Jungle,* was intended to expose the mistreatment of meat-
packing-plant workers, but along the way painted so foul a picture of
slaughtering conditions that it resulted instead in a boost for the American Society for the Prevention of Cruelty to Animals and in a clamor for
better Federal meat-inspection laws. In 1903 "Frenzied Finance" by
Thomas Lawson in *McClure's Magazine* exposed Wall Street, and its
success fired many imitators.

There is no doubt that the muckraking writers struck a rich vein of
public response. Muckraking, considered both virtuous and profitable,
resulted in great literary reputations and soaring magazine circulations.
Nor were politicians, who knew a good thing when they saw it, tardy in
capitalizing on the clamor. Both Teddy Roosevelt's Bull Moose Progressive Republicanism and Woodrow Wilson's Democracy owed much to
the feelings expressed in the muckraking era.

Impartial assessment of the good and bad is difficult. One-sided as
it was, muckraking was a necessary corrective in American progress. But
affronted business barons, who sometimes seemed to consider *themselves*
the embodiment of American progress, reacted with more violence and

excitement than philosophy. A first impulse might be to sue, b
pany lawyers usually discouraged this response. Only a person
entirely innocent in all respects can afford to become involved in
suit; too much can be brought out in court and paraded for the
nation to see. And anyway, the truth of a statement is generally a full
defense against libel charges. Another reaction might be to threaten
advertising cancellation as a club to bring the offending journal back into
line; but often the newspapers might decide that exposure would be more
profitable than silence. Newspaper personnel were an independent crew,
as likely to fight back as to surrender. Bribery, another weapon, was
likewise limited.

The Beginnings of Public Relations

A final solution was whitewash. If you couldn't silence the opposition,
you could try to paint a better picture of yourself! Large corporations
began to hire former newsmen to set up news bureaus, which carefully
fed the press "favorable" stories by various means and rigorously tried
to conceal doubtful or bad reports. Gradually, through the influence of
Ivy Lee and other publicists who laid the beginning of a foundation for
modern public relations practice, this position was modified to the point
where companies would not only issue good news but would refrain from
impeding or would even facilitate the work of reporters covering controversial or unfortunate events such as railroad wrecks or strikes. The
millennium had not yet arrived when company public relations representatives would speak against their own cause, any more than company
lawyers would argue against their own case in court.

But the long war between many reporters and many corporate and
other organization public relations persons was nearing a truce. In an
increasingly complex world, news reporters now realized that they didn't
have the time and knowledge to cover all the details and developments
of great business organizations in which the public was seriously interested. They were now willing to give company public relations representatives a chance to supply factual, newsworthy stories. Those in public
relations, on the other hand, knew that they had to meet a high standard
of journalism, aid reporters in covering the bad as well as the good, and
beware of sheer puffery. During the boom years following World War
I, in which adulation of business came back strongly, exemplified in the
late *American Magazine;* in the dark years of the depressed 1930s, which
resembled the era of the muckrakers; and after World War II, the
understanding between news gatherers and news dispensers matured.

Each held a different allegiance, each had a different code, and yet on the common meeting ground of supplying news, each could respect and cooperate with the other.

The public relations problems of the United States government (or any lesser American government) are quite different from the problems of a politician trying to get elected in order to control that government; yet the two are so inseparably intertwined that to this day their conflict has not been resolved nor does it seem likely ever to be.

Democratic government, if it is to be effective, needs citizen cooperation and understanding. The police ask you not to weave down the highways at 100 miles per hour, slaying yourself or innocent drivers in the process; the forest rangers object to your walking away from a smoldering campfire in the dry woods or littering a campsite; the internal revenue collectors want the right amount of income tax on time; if you are the right age, the Army, Navy, or Air Force may wish you to enlist; and the post office always pleads with you to mail Christmas packages early. Some of these goals may be attained by the *power* of government, but much greater success in matters of safety, conservation, tax paying, recruiting, and post office aid depends upon understanding cooperation. Cooperation, in turn, requires public relations, and without it democracy may break down.

In wartime such citizen cooperation becomes even more important, because during a war the government wants citizens to give money, save food, drive less, work at different jobs, go out to fight, and if need be even die. How is this heroic attitude to be inculcated? Only by the concerted persuasion of public relations effort.

During World War I (1917–1918) President Wilson, with the aid of journalist George Creel, made a gigantic successful effort to enlist support for this nation's war aims. After the war the propaganda backfired. Some of it had been false, strident, or overdone; naïve Americans were inclined to regard the whole conflict as an unfortunate accident and wished to forget it as soon as possible. Wilson was defeated; isolationism returned; the League of Nations was rejected; World War II was made inevitable; and debunkers of idealism flourished in the material prosperity of the roaring twenties.

When America was catapulted into World War II on Pearl Harbor Sunday, 1941, government information programs were quickly organized, but on a more effective low-key basis under the direction of newscaster Elmer Davis. The American attitude now was much more mature than in 1917–1918. The absence of enthusiasm for the war caused some superpatriots who insisted upon brass bands and cheers to worry lest the national spirit had decayed. Instead of excitement there was a grim determination to win as soon as possible at whatever cost. America knew what had to be done, and four-minute orators, parades, and yellow paint smeared on German farmers' barns were deemed travesties of patriotism. The direct impact of on-the-spot reporting of the Japanese surprise attack on the American fleet, followed by the powerful words of President Roosevelt, showed the contrast between the communications methods of the forties and those which had existed two decades before.

But although the government had no difficulty in mobilizing the support of its citizens during a war, the problems of day-by-day understanding and cooperation by citizens in a democracy are still acute; these problems will be discussed later in this book.

In recent years, other major users of public relations have appeared. Beginning in the 1930s, large new labor unions began to seek support from the ranks of workers and wooed the general public through union publications, radio and television programs, speakers, and personal contact. Much development remains ahead. In these same years, welfare organizations, such as the Boy Scouts and the YWCA, and health agencies, such as the heart, cancer, and polio funds, as well as many local community united funds, became much more active in the public relations appeals upon which their success ultimately depended.

Other groups have also become much more active in public relations in recent years. Religious groups try to gain adherents, raise money, and support projects; associations represent activities as diverse as medicine, law, architecture, industries, trades, merchants, and tourism; and in education, city school systems try to obtain funds for new buildings, improved teacher salaries, and expanded programs, and universities ask for needed support in gifts and taxes. All kinds of activist groups seek to get public attention and support. One of the biggest new fields is international public relations, the effort of groups within a nation to reach abroad or of nations themselves to influence others.

This is the communications era. As more people have more common concerns and can communicate with one another more easily, it is inevitable that, for many reasons, attempts at widespread persuasion should increase. One cannot reasonably be for or against such a development, because changes cannot be turned back any more than the invention of television, the airplane, the steam engine, or even the printing press, or the discovery of a method of atomic fission can be done away with and forgotten. These things did happen, cannot be abolished, and will have their effects.

The important thing about modern public relations is not whether its development should be opposed or praised, but rather how well it is understood and used.

ADDITIONAL READINGS

The History of Public Relations and the Reasons for Its Development

Bernays, Edward L., *Biography of an Idea.* (New York: Simon & Schuster, 1963.)

Golden, L. L. L., *Only By Public Consent.* (New York: Hawthorne Books, 1968.) [How AT&T, General Motors, Standard Oil of N.J. and DuPont set up their public relations departments.]

Hiebert, Ray Eldon, *Courtier To The Crowd; The Story of Ivy Lee.* (Ames, Iowa: Iowa State University Press, 1966.)

Hill, John W., *The Making of a Public Relations Man. (New York: David McKay, 1963.)*

Pimlott, J. A., *Public Relations and American Democracy,* rev. ed. (Princeton, N.J.: Princeton University Press, 1971.)

Chapter 3

The Nature of Communication and Public Opinion

Businessmen, industrialists, educators, and government leaders all talk about communication. But do they know the essential meaning of the term? Haven't human beings always communicated with each other? In fact, isn't communication almost a definition of humanity's most characteristic activity? What's new? What is there to communication beyond the simple act of saying something to somebody?

There is something new, and that is the realization, within the past few decades at least, that in communication the *receiver* is at least as important as, and perhaps even more important than, the sender. Heretofore communication has been thought of primarily in terms of the sender and his message. The orator who made a speech, the author who wrote a book, the monarch who handed down an edict to subjects, were all communicating. But were they? Who read or heard the edict? What did they understand from it? And in what ways were their actions altered? These are questions which might be asked about almost any communication.

Because of this preoccupation with the sender and message, for a long time most of the study of communication centered upon the way the message was sent—whether the orator spoke loudly and distinctly, the printing was well spaced and legible, or the edict was worded in the best classical Latin and posted in all the important market places. These things are important, to be sure, and may alter the effectiveness of a communication materially; but they alone do not determine it. Much depends upon the receivers, since people usually cannot be made to listen or to understand or even to be interested in a communication except as it relates to their own concerns. When students of communication turned their attention to the receivers as well as to the senders of messages, they began to realize the unity of direction of all the different media and ways of communicating. Their discovery is of particular interest to public relations practitioners.

Different ways of reaching people, such as speaking, writing, and film making, though they require different technical skills, are all similar in that they may be addressed to the same persons. A public relations person may use any of these methods to communicate an idea to a receiver. This can be done with confidence only if the sender knows the nature of the receiver, and therefore the way in which the communication will be understood. A sender must realize that although receivers have various backgrounds of experience and various social contacts, they have much in common. On that common ground of shared life and thought the sender can meet them; and the meeting can go far toward solving the problem of conveying ideas.

We need to ask many questions about communication. Today, instead of defining the word very narrowly to mean only the means of communication, writers on the subject tend to call almost any act communication. Yet if people talk to themselves, is this communication? Are actions, such as buying a ticket to the zoo, communications of unspoken processes of decision making? Perhaps. It is true that gestures or actions do communicate; but we are concerned here primarily with purposeful, planned communication and not with introspection or actions designed to satisfy a person's personal desires, whose conveyance of a thought to others is largely incidental.

WHY DO PEOPLE COMMUNICATE?

It has been said that people communicate in order to *inform,* or to *persuade,* or to *entertain;* but seldom are these purposes clearly separated in the minds of the sender and the receiver.

Another school of thought holds that all communication is basically *persuasive,* that we always seek some response from others to even the most simple remarks, such as "Nice day, today" or "I think I'll get my hair cut."[1] Perhaps this is so; but often the connection between the remark or act and the response seems rather tenuous, especially among artists or writers who work primarily to satisfy some inner urge to express truth or beauty as they see it, and have little conscious thought about how others will respond. Is such communication persuasion, or is it simply an outflow of a personal thinking-through process?

Sometimes primarily self-expressive communication is referred to as consummatory; that is, it constitutes an end in itself. Communicators may hope that an audience will share their interest or they may not care greatly. When the chief purpose of a communication is to get an audience to do something, the message can be called instrumental. To illustrate the two approaches, consider spring as the subject of a poem and of a soap advertisement. The consummatory purpose of the poem is to express the poet's joy in the season of the year; the instrumental purpose of the soap advertisement is to sell more soap by reminding people that hot weather brings forth body odors. Both are on the same subject; both are persuasive; both express truth. One is not necessarily superior to the other; they are simply addressed to different ends.

HOW DO PEOPLE COMMUNICATE?

People may be said to communicate by words, by means of speech, writing, pictures, gestures, and so forth, or by radio or newspaper or other media; but none of these statements express the full truth of the matter. They center upon the sender of a communication and the physical aspects of the message, such as sound vibrations or letters of the alphabet. They lead to our next question.

WHAT ELEMENTS ARE NECESSARY FOR COMMUNICATION?

In his *Rhetoric,* Aristotle discussed speech under three headings: "the speaker," "the speech," and "the audience." There have been many

---

[1] Aristotle seems to have held that communication was basically persuasive.

variations and expansions of his thought; one adds two refinements to visualize the process of communication:[2]

Source—Encoder—Signal—Decoder—Receiver

The process may be illustrated by such simple statements as "I (source) see a cat." Encoding here simply means transmitting English words by vocal air waves to a decoding receiver who listens, understands English, and is acquainted with the concepts of "seeing" and "cat."

This simple pattern may also be applied to something as complex as a great metropolitan newspaper, both a source in itself for some statements and a collector of others, putting them all into print and sending them out to millions of readers. In each instance, simple or complex, the patterns are the same. As far as each item in the newspaper is concerned, the transmission is to an individual reader. Though mass newspaper circulations, the diffusion of many identical signals, certainly exist, there is really no such thing as a mass reader. Each reader of the *New York Times,* for example, reads alone as an individual. He or she does not sit down with others and read in concert, affected by their presence. When something a newspaper columnist says makes the reader smile as he reads amid the noise of the subway or a commuter train, a personal communication reaches him from an unknown individual. The fact that there are hundreds of thousands of readers makes no difference. Knowing this, wise writers always write to individuals instead of to a nonexistent "mass."

THE SOURCE OF A COMMUNICATION

Although objects such as scenes can express meaning to a person, the basis of such meaning lies in the mind of the perceiver and not in anything the objects have intended. Our real concern is with the intentional transmission of ideas from person to person, from a human source to a human receiver. When people perceive things, they combine the percepts with other remembered concepts in their minds (some of them the result of communication); they react and then themselves become sources of communication. Here we are coming very close to questions about the fundamental nature of thought itself. Perception is not necessarily limited to personal observation; it also comes from communica-

[2]The idea is similar to Aristotle's. In 1947 a Bell Telephone Company mathematician and an engineer, Claude Shannon and Warren Weaver, conceived of communication mechanically involving source–transmitter–signal–receiver–destination.

tions, in which the transmission of ideas from other persons can be highly varied and complex.

ENCODING A COMMUNICATION

An idea remaining in the mind of its source and not yet cast into a form which can be transmitted to others is not part of a communication; it must be expressed in some way that others can understand. We may even ask if it actually exists unless so expressed. Does a person have an idea if it cannot be verbalized? Words are symbols of things; can we be said to have a thought if we cannot reduce chaotic mind pictures and feelings into words? Or are we just unable to communicate?[3]

Language is a major step in encoding; and although a gesture, hum, or motion may convey meaning almost as precisely, complex encoding usually depends upon language. If we do not know what to call things, we find difficulty in communicating to others about them.

The manner in which a source encodes a communication is a reflection of a person's own personal or vicarious experiences, including his or her entire social background. In talking about the ring, a prize fighter doesn't use the same terms that a painter uses. Unless we try hard to do otherwise and are gifted with an ability to imagine other people's lives, we tend to shape our encoding in terms of our own social background.

Encoding also involves selection of a medium of transmission. An informal chat with a friend, a talk before a supper club, and a formal article on a technical subject are all encoded in different ways.

There are, of course, many ways of encoding messages other than verbal. A drawing, such as a cartoon, is a form of encoding. So is an insignia such as a cross or a star or a swastika. So is a gesture such as shrugging the shoulders or throwing up the hands. Playwrights and actors depend on these nonverbal forms to a very high degree.

Encoding is also the point at which "ghosts" (hired writers) usually first come into the picture. Persons who know what ideas they wish to convey but who do not have the time or ability to encode them well, may hire another to do it for them; a politician may need a speech writer and a manufacturer may need an advertising writer.

SIGNAL BREAKDOWNS

The signal (message) may suffer mechanical breakdowns. A page of printed type may be too smudgy to read; a radio broadcast may squeal

---

[3]S. I. Hayakawa, *Language in Thought and Action,* Harcourt, Brace & World, Inc., New York, 1949, will be found particularly interesting by those beginning to examine the relationship between words and thought.

with interference; a television screen may become filled with "snow"; a poster may be located where few pass by it; or a play may be performed in an auditorium with muffling acoustics. Professional communicators spend great energy in correcting such deficiencies, and this is as it should be, since an inadequate signal ends the communication; but questions of who should want to read the type, hear the broadcast, note the poster, or attend the play are less apparent than mechanical defects, so often go unasked and unanswered. Perfection in the mechanics of delivering a communication is quite important, because in a world crowded with messages, listeners are not likely to struggle hard to receive one message when others are more easily available. But deciding *what* to communicate may be even more important.

DECODING THE COMMUNICATION

Once the success of transmission has been assured, the primary question is: "Can the receiver decode the message?" The answer depends largely on whether the receiver and the sender have overlapping experiences. The requirement of a common ground is implicit in the Latin *communicatus,* meaning something shared.

A common language is itself a form of common experience and the first need in decoding a message. Similarity of language involves more, however, than a choice of English rather than French or Hindi; it is concerned especially with idiom and parallelism of expression within a given tongue.

The use of a common language breaks down for a number of reasons. Some well-educated people have as many as 30,000 words at their command, while many semiliterates have only a thousand or less. Even among people who have large total vocabularies, great areas of noncoincidence exist among the words that they do know. A Kansas farmer, for example, and a lifelong Manhattanite may each have a large store of English words, but those the farmer uses about weather, soils, crops, animals, and social institutions may not mean much to the city resident. The terms an atomic physicist commands differ from those of a jazz band leader; and a corporate treasurer's vocabulary (and hence set of values) is not like that of a lathe operator in the corporate plant.

The connotations of identical words constitute a problem, because meanings are understood in terms of differing experiences. Having a "good time" may mean one thing in Sauk Center, Minnesota, another in Las Vegas, and yet another in Harlem—and there will be considerable differences between individual good times within these places. A set of deerhorns means one thing to a hunter and another to a Frenchman; to an Eskimo rubbing noses has an affectionate social significance entirely lacking in the American wrestling ring; "reduction of the work force" gladdens the heart of stockholders but darkens the skies of employees; and "Republican" means one thing to a Kalamazoo banker and another thing to a Labor leader. Even "peace" has widely different meanings for most Americans and for many Russians or Chinese, and the Russian understanding of the word may well be different from that of the Oriental.

Lack of common experience can seriously affect the ability to communicate. Consider, for example, the well-bred child of a steel-company president, who has grown up in a fine home in an exclusive suburb, has had plenty of spending money and a car, attended the best schools, and associated with young people of similar wealth and position; he or she is given the job of editing a company publication which goes to hourly workers in the mill. How much will experience enable such a person to communicate to the readers? Can the new editor encode messages in terms the workers will decode? Or can this child of affluence even select the right things to try to communicate to them?

ACTIONS OF THE RECEIVER

Will the receiver try to decode the message? Much depends upon whether the receiver thinks such effort will be rewarded. The *reward* may be many things: satisfaction of sheer curiosity; a recognition or even deepening of previous experiences; strong motivational drives such as sex, fear, or pride; even hope of gain.

Effort involves the ease of decoding a message and the competition with other messages, other uses of time, and distractions. Decisions as to whether to expend such effort are often made quickly and almost unconsciously. A receiver leafing through the pages of a magazine decides in only a few seconds whether to flip on to the next page or to spend a measurable effort examining a particular message. To get more receiver attention, the reward for paying attention to the communication must be increased or the effort lowered—or both.

THE TWO-WAY NATURE OF COMMUNICATION

It is doubtful whether communication ever takes place without being two-way. When the master shouts an order and the slave silently obeys, an unspoken reaction has taken place; and when the radio announcer speaks into an impersonal microphone, there is feedback from distant listeners, although it does not reach the announcer directly. Lack of easily ascertained, immediate response is one of the most serious problems of modern communication through the mass media because, without visible response, a sender cannot know whether he has communicated or what effect his words have had. When the slave nods, the master knows the order has been received and understood; a radio announcer has no way of knowing unless letters or telephone calls show response. Two-way communication is quite apparent when two people are talking face-to-face. Gestures, facial expressions, eye focusing and verbal response show the receiver's response, and the sender may, if need be, alter the message accordingly; but the communicator is nonplused when the receiver simply looks blank and makes no response.

Two-way communication helps the senders express themselves, clarify their thoughts, and bolster their ego by the pleasant process of self-assertion. This is the pleasure of conversation. No matter how brilliant a lecturer may be, a time comes when listeners wish to reply. They answer directly or indulge in comments to their neighbors, or mutter, or perhaps go home and write letters to the newspaper. Listeners soon become bored in a one-way role; good conversations arise when the roles of sender and receiver are alternated, as most of us learn from experience. If you wish to be heard, you must listen at least part of the time!

DEMONSTRATING LISTENING

Listening is apparent (although sometimes feigned) in personal conversations; but when senders are separated from receivers by distance or time, as they are when communicating by mass media, then they must devise ways of finding out who is listening and how well they are responding.

There are two reasons for listening. One is to gain information. This motive is often so strong in the sender that communicators resort to tests, as in the scientific-opinion polling which has developed within the last few decades. Television advertisers want to know how many and what kinds of people listen to their messages, and therefore hire opinion surveyors to go out and ask people what they hear or install mechanical devices within television receivers' sets to keep a record of their listening. Magazine editors want to know what features are most popular in their publications; businesspeople or labor leaders wish to discover public opinion upon current issues.

Such listening is not really two-way communication at all and should not be confused with it. The action is taken simply for information, and only a few people are aware that their opinions are sought; yet even under these circumstances, polltakers are frequently surprised at the gush of information which spouts out in response to "yes or no" questions.

Another reason for listening is to give the other person a chance to talk. Public relations practitioners, politicians, educators, advertisers, members of the clergy, and others should realize that although the flow of communication today is mighty, *most of it is one-way!* Radio, television, newspapers, magazines, teachers, and preachers usually send out their messages with little opportunity for the receivers to respond. We are much talked at. Many messages are ignored, but those that are absorbed are still incomplete and frustrating because the recipients do not have a chance to express their opinions about them.

Perhaps this always being "told" may help to explain part of the extraordinary restlessness, frustration, and even violence of today's world. Everybody talks to young people, but few listen to them. The opinions of many other groups are little regarded. If we listened to them with understanding we might win their cooperation.

It is not enough, however, simply to say, "I am listening." Attentive listening must be demonstrated as well as proclaimed. Situations must be created in which receivers have the opportunity to return messages and to know that their replies have been received and understood. In mass media situations, such listening may be as complex and well organized as was the original effort to send out the messages.

For example, a company magazine editor runs an article expatiating upon the need for greater worker productivity within the plant because of foreign competition. The editor announces that readers' comments will be welcome (willingness to listen). Several letters come in. Replies are made by personal notes from top officers of the company (evidence of listening) which are also run in the magazine with appended editorial comment (widespread evidence of listening). Small group-discussion meetings are then held in which employees of various departments can discuss the subject (listening). At a company dinner special recognition is given to the most outstanding of these committee reports (listening), and some of the ideas are put into effect (final evidence of listening).

This kind of planned two-way communication causes company employees to say, "Our management really wants to know what we think," and makes them more receptive to all future company pronouncements of policy. In a small organization most of this interchange of opinion could be accomplished by a question from the boss: "Bill, Tom, and Mary, what do you think we should do about this problem?" But when there are thousands of workers in scores of plants, the necessity for two-way communication is likely to be forgotten.

WHAT IS PUBLIC OPINION?

Public opinion may be defined as the decisions of groups of people in connection with identifiable, stated issues. This differs from public *attitudes,* which are the predispositions, thoughts, or feelings of persons toward issues that have not yet materialized in a specific way. In New England, for example, prior to the Civil War, there were various public attitudes toward slavery, states' rights, the sanctity of the Union, and the Southern way of life, which were fused into public opinion upon the specific question of secession when Fort Sumter was fired upon. These attitudes had been long in the making and were molded by many communications, such as *Uncle Tom's Cabin,* the Lincoln–Douglas debates, reports on "bleeding Kansas," and the sermons of abolitionist ministers. Attitudes are opinions in the process of formation; once an opinion has been formed, such as that secession should be resisted by arms, it is not easily changed. Public relations efforts are usually most effective in dealing with attitudes which have not yet hardened into opinions, and the ability to foresee situations which may cause this solidification often leads to early and influential communication.

We often incorrectly assume that the opinions of a public are simply the sum total of the opinions of the individuals comprising that public. Public opinions may vary among groups because of the interaction of the individuals within each group. Conversations result in group communication and approval. The more the group becomes an interacting unit, the more the characteristics of cohesiveness, intolerance of dissent, and codification are magnified. Individuals within an interacting crowd differ in their behavior from isolated individuals, and the crowd itself differs from other groups of people that are casually thrown together without any reason for communicating or interacting with one another.

It has often been observed that in an interacting crowd individuals tend to shed their personal inhibitions, to respond to the crowd and to appeals which would scarcely move them or would even repel them if they were considered in solitude. The crowd itself tends to select lower common denominators of appeal and to respond with exaggeration or violence uncharacteristic of an individual. Such reactions account for the common experience of public relations personnel—that they may convince individuals of a viewpoint in private and then find that the same individuals will deny their previously expressed convictions when reacting with a crowd.[4] Within a crowd, communication is still made with the individuals comprising the crowd, but they are much altered individuals.

The term "public opinion" generally refers to individual opinions such as those which may be ascertained by questions or by secret ballot. Reasoned democracy depends upon solitary decisions by each citizen and is not to be confused with the aberrations sometimes apparent in crowds, parliaments, or legislatures.

A capable communicator knows the social backgrounds and pressures to which receivers are subjected, and realizes the stake that each receiver has in being an accepted member of a group. The communicator does not often expect a person to stand alone against peers and habits, but instead tries to obtain a more permissive attitude from the group or to seek paths of action for its members which do not run entirely counter to group norms.

COMMUNICATION AND PERSUASION

Whether or not all communication is persuasion, in public relations activities persuasion is almost always intended as a result of communication, and frequently the recipients are aware of the intent. Their awareness does not necessarily imply suspicion or hostility, but it means that the communicator should have some insight into the conditions which favor successful persuasion. The following sections discuss some of them.

Confidence in the Source of Persuasion

Emerson's line "What you are . . . thunders so that I cannot hear what you say" indicates how important it is to perceive the nature of a source if a listener is to evaluate a persuasive communication. Distrust of a source certainly makes persuasion more difficult, even though it is also true that listeners often remember *what* was said, even from a distrusted source, think about it, and then later accept it after they have forgotten where it came from.

The credibility of a source is enhanced if the communicator shares a common background or set of experiences with listeners. A political speaker who begins, "When I was a farm boy down in Carter County. . . ." is demonstrating this principle (*a*) if talking to farmers, (*b*) if in or near Carter County, or (*c*) if speaking to former Carter County residents. Testimonials or recommendations are another cause

---

[4]Herbert I. Abelson's *Persuasion* discusses this. See the readings at the end of this chapter.

of trust in a source. "I have known Congresswoman Smith for forty years and you can believe what she says. . . ." carries weight with an audience which trusts the introducer. Introductions are important, because they can greatly affect the way in which a forthcoming communication will be received. Tests have shown that a group of laborers who were shown a rather indefinite editorial upon wage rates and were told that it came from the *Wall Street Journal* scorned it, whereas another similar group who were told that the same editorial had been published in a union newspaper, felt that it was most worthwhile. Groups of businessmen tested with the same material had opposite reactions.

Confidence in the Message Itself

What makes a message credible when its source is unknown or *neutral?* Corroboration by the receiver's own experience and by the known or imagined experience of others contributes to his willingness to believe; and social atmosphere and accepted stereotypes add their influence.

Few people today believe in witches, not so much because no one has seen a witch (none of the people at Salem in the 1600s had seen a witch either), but because a belief in witches is decidedly out of step with contemporary opinion. It was decidedly in step in the seventeenth century to claim acquaintance with them. On the other hand, believing in invaders from Mars in 1938 seemed quite reasonable to thousands of people when Orson Welles's simulated broadcast of a Martian attack created panic in New Jersey. Though Welles's listeners had never seen a Martian, society was ready to accept the existence of men from another planet.

Testimony, evidence, and proof do little to persuade hearers of a statement's validity unless they also believe in the worth of the testifier and understand the meaning of the evidence. Although logical argument is a clincher to those who are disposed to believe, it is seldom in itself a cause of belief.

The education of the receiver, both in general and in the specific field of the communication is important because it affects the range of the receiver's vicarious experience, creating a greater area in which common response can exist. Receivers are likely to believe things which match their information and are likely to doubt things which run contrary to it. Their belief or skepticism is produced not by actual information but also by the deep ego involvement of their expertise.

Broadly educated people are likely to take broad standards for their beliefs and to turn for validation to national, world, or other distant authorities with which they are acquainted even if only by hearsay. Less well-educated people depend more upon the opinions of their neighbors and friends for validation, and testimony from high, but distant, authority may even repel them.

Benefit to Hearer

Persuasion must serve receivers' needs if communication is to occur. The benefits may be quite intangible, such as raising the social status of receivers by making them experts about a subject which their social group regards highly; or quite specific, like learning how to make money in the stock market. To a prisoner planning a jailbreak, any information about the hardness of steel bars or the time required to cut them with a hacksaw would be of sufficient benefit to justify careful reading.

Accordance with Value Systems

It is hard to persuade any person to believe in or to do anything which goes against the value systems accepted by his social group; and those most attached to the group and most prominent in it, who draw most of their ego support from it, are the least likely to be affected by such adverse persuasions. Those who "belong" have little tolerance for statements which upset them by contradicting beliefs which are socially acceptable.

Neither can people be persuaded easily if accepting the persuasion will cause receivers to lose face among their fellows because they have made a change. Perhaps the persuasion will have to be made to look like less of a change, or perhaps the norms of the group itself will have to be altered. Instead of persuading one person to change, it may be necessary to alter the whole group by means of discussion and the use of opinion leaders. If groups were always static, this would be a nearly impossible task, but in the flux of modern democratic society group change is common, and so individual beliefs can be changed too.

To persuade someone who is very strongly attached to a group, it may be necessary to change the attachment to the group or else be content with a lesser degree of persuasion.

Other Facts about Persuasion

When listeners are already well informed the greatest amount of persuasion is usually accomplished by telling both sides of the story; but when they know little about the subject or when (for various reasons) they can give their attention to only one aspect of the case, then a one-sided presentation is more effective. When opposing views are presented together, the one heard last will probably stick longer.

Stating conclusions in persuasion is more effective than leaving the audience to guess at them or to make up their own. When left to their own devices, listeners sometimes arrive at conclusions entirely different from those the speaker intended!

The more extreme the change of opinion asked for by communicators, the greater the change they are likely to produce. They can, of course, misjudge the temper of their audience; if the change conflicts too greatly with group norms, the speaker may be thrown out of the hall. But generally a weak request gets a weak response and a strong request, even if compromised, gets a stronger result.

But in persuasion, a mild threat seems often to be more effective than a more menacing statement. Hearers are repelled by a really strong threat and refuse to consider it or even to admit its possibility; but a little threat can be coped with and so is appraised. Americans, for example, could be sold to some extent on shallow atomic fallout shelters some years ago, because a minor fallout threat was within reason, but a program to build deep underground passages to avoid near hits envisaged a danger too serious even to be faced.

Persuasion Everywhere

In confronting the fact of persuasion, we find it easy to be superior or cynical and to laugh at the peculiarly gullible group of people we have around us. But we must remember that *we* belong to that group all the time. All of us have been persuaded, in one way or another, about most of the things we are sure we know and hold most dear—the things which give most meaning and depth to life. Religion, education, patriotism, and all altruistic enthusiasms are "persuasions" which can generally be realized only by persuading others in turn. The man who says that he has received nothing from persuasion is either densely ignorant, a recluse, or self-deluded. Despite its abuses, persuasion is a gentle art in which wisdom, patience, love, and friendly enthusiasm are by far the greatest elements and it is much to be preferred to the more brutal, crass forms of forcing or buying human cooperation.

ADDITIONAL READINGS

Abelson, Herbert I. and James Hanson, *Persuasion: How Opinions and Attitudes Are Changed.* 3rd. ed. (New York: Springer, 1976.)

Berelson, Bernard and Gary A. Steiner, *Human Behavior: An Inventory of Scientific Findings.* (New York: Harcourt, Brace and Jovanovich, 1964.)

Bettinghaus, Erwin P., *Persuasive Communication.* (New York: Holt, Rinehart & Winston, 1968.)

Lippmann, Walter, *Public Opinion.* (New York: Harcourt, Brace, 1922.) [A classic.]

Schramm, Wilbur, *Men, Messages and Media.* (New York: Harper & Row, 1973.)

Sereno, Kenneth K. and David Mortensen, *Foundations of Communications Theory.* (New York: Harper & Row, 1970.)

Chapter 4

Reaching Special Publics

What do you visualize when someone says "the public"? A cartoon character of timid little John Q. Public, perhaps, or a photo you recall of a crowd massed somewhere? Is it possible to communicate with such an abstraction?

It isn't, and for this reason people in public relations think almost always in terms of smaller, more specific *publics* drawn out of the general mass. Few people ever have occasion to communicate with the entire American public at one time anyway; only national political campaigns involve such an effort, and even these are largely confined to adult registered voters. The usual political campaign reaches toward many subdivisions of the general public, such as farmers, laborers, city dwellers, and old people. Even in such a local matter as a school bond vote, a public relations committee thinks in terms of groups of parents, teachers, real estate board members, civic clubs, retired people, religious groups, and other minor publics within the school district.

In fact, a public may be said to exist whenever a group of people is drawn together by definite interests in certain areas and has definite opinions upon matters within those areas. There are many publics, and individuals are frequently members of several of them which may sometimes have conflicting interests. In considering the school bond vote for example, a voter might be torn between feelings as a parent and as a member of a conservative economic group opposed to higher taxes; or an elderly couple, with no children now in school, might be the parents of a teacher. Conflicts of interest are common in America because we are great joiners; high economic status permits much varied individual activity; and the general high level of education creates wide interests. Americans, as compared to people in more static cultures, are hard to type into fixed social classes; they resent attempts at such typing and feel less ambiguity than most people of the world in belonging to numerous publics at one time.

INTERNAL AND EXTERNAL PUBLICS

Internal publics are the people who are already connected with an organization and with whom the organization normally communicates in the ordinary routine of work. The question is not "Shall we communicate with them?" but rather "How shall we communicate, and to what extent?" Typical internal publics in an industry are the employees, stockholders, suppliers, dealers, customers, and plant neighbors. In a school system they would be the employees of various types, students, parents, suppliers, and the general public divided into various subgroups.

External publics, on the other hand, are composed of people who are not necessarily closely connected with a particular organization. For example, members of the press, educators, government officials, or the clergy may or may not have an interest in an industry. The leaders of the industry cannot assume any automatic interest and to some extent at least, can choose whether these groups shall be communicated with or not.

But it is not possible to be silent in dealing with the internal publics, for a number of reasons beyond the fact that communication with them is inevitable in the ordinary course of doing business:

1 The cooperation, or lack of it, of internal publics greatly affects immediate operating activities. Employees who don't want to give a fair day's work for their pay, dealers who would rather work with another

company, or plant neighbors who would like to soak the company with
higher property taxes, all affect profit-and-loss statements directly.

2 Outsiders form their opinions of organizations, to a large extent,
by what those most closely connected with them seem to think. The
university student home on vacation who voices a low opinion of the
school's instructors may not be well informed or even unbiased, but
parents and friends listen to him. The customer who has had bad relations with a company from which she bought an automobile shifts business to competitors by her public complaints. The employee who runs
down his firm gets a ready audience: "He ought to know. He works
there!"

3 Growth itself, of an industry and of organizations, as John W.
Hill observes in his book, *Corporate Public Relations,* takes the leader-
ship-communication function away from management and puts it into
other hands. Unless planned efforts are made to remedy the situation,
management becomes big, vague, and distant. Orders and information
trickle down such a long chain of command that the internal public is
often not much better informed than the external public. The worst
situation exists when people outside the organization are actually better
informed, through the press or personal acquaintanceship, than those
who work inside; and this is not a rare occurrence!

In dealing with the various internal publics, public relations persons
soon find that their work runs into the domain of other departments of
the organization, such as industrial relations or sales, which are charged
with the main responsibility of maintaining employee efficiency or of the
profitable disposal of the product to customers. Even with such overlapping, a public relations person can help by remembering that the first
means of aid to other departments is excellence in communication methods. The public relations head does not have the responsibility for policy
or authority for personnel or sales. One in this position can suggest, but
not order, because the public relations function is to give staff aid rather
than to assume line command. If a personnel or sales policy is bad, the
public relations person should not promise to "communicate" it into
goodness by some hocus-pocus. Not every decision in an organization
can be taken primarily in terms of its public relations consequences.
There may be times when unpopular actions have to be taken or when
policies that anger the public have to be pursued.

When this occurs, public relations people have the obligation to give
useful advice, realizing full well that their understanding of the situation
may be inadequate or that the condition may be inevitable. They can help
straighten out public misconceptions arising from lack of information or

false information; and can explain motives and endeavor to ir
in management decisions.

Such public relations activities are a delicate and difficı
volving adjustment both to management and to the interיו. ,
which receive the communications. They demand sober reflection, great
patience, and confidence; and they must imply an enthusiasm in advancing the interests of the organization which will justify intrusion into what
some persons may consider their own private operating spheres. Behind
a tactful public relations director must also be a sympathetic and supporting management.

INTERNAL PUBLICS: THE EMPLOYEE PUBLIC

Large as this important internal public may be, it is usually divided into
many subsections which differ greatly from one another and which often
repay approaching in the ways best suited to their interests and reaction
patterns.

For example, among employees there are hourly paid workers,
salaried workers, and managerial staff—each group with its own special
characteristics and outlook.

Production-line workers may dress differently, spend their Saturday
nights differently, and often have different goals for themselves and for
their families than do their brothers or sisters who wear white collars and
coats in the offices and are equally or sometimes less well paid—although
the gulf between white collar and blue collar is not so deep as it once
was.

The supervisor, although called a member of management, is often
spiritually closer to the shopworkers than is the office worker; and supervisors themselves are often quite removed from the higher echelons of
management. In big industries the very nature of mass communication
by bulletin boards, employee publications, and the public press often
bypasses the foreman. Top management often speaks directly to assembly-line workers or negotiates directly with top labor chiefs without
following a chain of command. Summit conferences occur, and the
organization is like an army in which the noncoms know less of tomorrow's orders than do the privates with access to the scuttlebutt from the
general's office.

Employees often have few interests in common. For example, un-
skilled diggers, skilled crafts-workers, laboratory technicians, and scientists may all be engaged upon the same project for the same company,
and yet have little mutual liking or friendliness.

New employees may be little attached to an organization, often coming from distant places and having few close friends; they contrast sharply with veterans who have grown old at their work. Men and women employees look at things differently. In multiplant companies there is a distinction between headquarters employees, who almost always feel superior, and branch-location employees, who may feel left out of the communications stream and deprived of opportunity. Even the size of departments makes a great difference, because in some companies everyone knows everyone else by name and in others numbers would be more appropriate than names. In fact, in any but the smallest, most simple organization, it is dangerous nonsense to consider employees as a homogeneous type.

What do employees most want from their companies and their unions? *Must* there always be antagonism between employees and the company? A number of years ago, after living for more than a year in the stockyards district of Chicago and interviewing scores of employees in the strife-torn meat-packing industry, Father Purcell of Loyola University in Chicago[1] came to a not very startling conclusion which was yet a novel concept to many old-line businessmen and to labor leaders: employees want to have their cake and eat it too. Employee loyalties are divided; employees expect certain things from their unions, and they expect certain other things from their companies. They don't want to cleave entirely to one or to the other, and they dislike people or conditions which force them to make a choice.

Some of the things that employees of all sorts usually seem to want, although in differing degrees, are these: *Security.* Is the job itself secure? Is the company making money, or are layoffs and shutdowns possible? Is the business progressing or declining? More particularly: How secure am I in *my* job? What about automation or changes in processes? Seniority? Arbitrary or unjust dismissal? Personnel practices? And finally: What about retirement? What can I look forward to when age forces me to quit?

Respect. Am I recognized as a human being who knows something worth knowing? As personal skills increase, a worker's desire for recognition intensifies, and age also adds to this need for respect.

Participation. Am I just one cog in a big set of wheels, or do I know more of the process of which I am a part than just what happens in front of me? Not everyone has curiosity and ambition to the same extent—the

[1]Fr. Theodore Vincent Purcell, *The Worker Looks at Labor and Management,* Harvard University Press, Cambridge, Mass., 1953.

need to be part of a bigger, more meaningful whole—but a surprising number of people do. It's the difference between the two medieval stone masons who were asked what they were doing. "Cutting stone," one man replied sharply. "Helping to build a cathedral," said the other.

Consideration. Am I informed and consulted about what's going on (or at least informed in advance of outsiders)? Is there an opportunity for me to express my ideas when I have them?

Recognition. What rewards are given for good and faithful service? Do people know about such rewards both inside and outside the plant?

Opportunity. Are promotion policies fair? Is there a chance to advance? Can I do what others have done? If the road is open and I do not take it, have I anyone to blame but myself? Does the merit of those at the top justify their eminence? What are the opportunities for women or members of minority groups?

No organization can supply all these needs all the time to all its people; but the closer it comes to fulfilling them most of the time, the happier and more productive its work force can be if it is under efficient management.

Most employees expect management to manage. They understand that competent members of management should be reasonably rewarded for their services and risks. They recognize that investors deserve a return upon their capital and usually agree that the returns should be somewhat proportioned to the growth of the enterprise or the risks involved. The desirability of greater productivity is widely accepted. There is no great stampede in favor of government ownership, since most American employees have a distrust of government that makes them poor socialists and keeps them from being Communists. No one can impugn the intelligence or loyalty of the American employee public, but some major points of difference do exist between employees, ownership, and management.

Most employees, for example, think that business profits are much larger than they really are and tend to underestimate the risks of capital. They fear the effect upon themselves of automation and change. They sometimes do not have complete confidence in the wisdom or integrity of their managements. And, very often, they would like a bigger slice of the earnings pie distributed as wages.

In addition to these rather natural differences, almost all organizations have certain built-in friction points.

There is a conflict in all types of work between the old-line employees and the younger people, between old crafts-workers and younger. There are conflicts between skills; the highly skilled, brilliant

Figure 4–1 One of the world's smallest annual reports (each of the eight pages and both sides of each cover is shown approximately half original size), sent to Kroger Company employees, featured profits as a basis for profit sharing.

scientist chafes at seeing the administrator better rewarded. There are conflicts between departments; sales, shipping, credit, and production departments are constantly passing blame back and forth. There are even conflicts between workers in clean and in dirty surroundings, or between those of different racial, religious, or geographic origins.

Some friction is inevitable, but good public relations organization and communication to the Number 1 public, the employees, can modify much of its roughness and can direct natural energies into greater development instead of wasteful cross fire.

Downward communications from management to employees are typified by employee magazines and newspapers, newsletters, bulletin boards, announcement posters, films, reading racks, letters, and ceremonies. Such downward communication is often well developed, although it is not always well conceived.

Upward communications from employees to management are much more feeble, consisting usually of surveys, suggestion programs, group meetings, and a vague "open-door policy." Because of management's neglect, much of the upward communication in a company has become a union prerogative, and this, according to Fr. Purcell, is one of the main reasons for union popularity among employees.[2] Business must not only *assert* that it listens to its employees; it must show that it does so in ways which they can see and believe. At this point the supervisor and the lower echelons of management are the key persons.

The biggest challenge to understanding between employer and employee lies in mutual communication. In a talk some years ago Donald F. Carpenter, General Manager of the Film Department of the du Pont Company, observed:

> We utterly reject the idea that there is any inescapable conflict between the employer and the employee. To the contrary, we are convinced that the interests of employer and employee are more closely parallel than those of almost any other groups in our society. Among the more important of their common objectives are:
>
> To make a good product.
> To maintain low costs.
> To give good service to customers.
> To maintain good working conditions.
>
> For the employer this means operation of a prosperous business; for the employee it means steady employment, good wages, good working conditions, and self-respect. When an employee likes his job and gives it his

[2]Ibid.

best effort, both he and his employer benefit. When an employer operates his business profitably, both he and his employees benefit. When employers and employees work in harmony, the entire community benefits. . . .

The "frame of reference" is ideal. How can it be established?

The Employee's Family Public

The wife or husband, children, and relatives of an employee have interests in the organization similar to those of the employee, but dissimilar in scope and intensity. The world of the employee's family, though it impinges upon the plant or the office, is not a part of it, and the looser connection leads usually to a less intense interest and also to a greater opportunity for misunderstanding and distortion. The family may not know much about the employee's job, but they are seriously affected by it. Some of the keen interests of this special public, so vital to the happiness, productivity, sanity, and even the presence on the job of the employee, are:

Security. Often this is the first concern. How stable and growing is the worker's organization? Are its personnel policies fair? What does it offer in health benefits and retirement plans? How harmonious are the relations between management and labor? Are costly strikes a threat to family budget planning?

Opportunity. What are the employee's chances for advancement? Is there hope for more pay or higher social status? Is educational help offered or study encouraged? How long are regular paid vacations?

Information. Just what does the wage earner do anyway? What does the organization produce and how does it do it? Who runs the organization, and what sort of people are they?

There is a great lack of understanding of workers' jobs in modern American families, largely because an urban worker's place of employment is usually far from home. In earlier days, the village blacksmith's son had little doubt about what his father did for a living. He watched him work and as soon as he was able, he probably started helping him shoe the horses or hammer out the glowing plowshares from the hot iron. He knew his father's skill and brawn, his wisdom, and his weaknesses.

In modern industrial or office work, the father or mother disappears in the morning and comes back in the evening to a well-fed, busy family, whose questions about activities are largely for politeness' sake and are so understood. Many working people are poor communicators, and a few families are good audiences; and the higher and more abstract the activities may be, the harder it is to explain them, and the worse the family's misunderstanding. The mental pictures that a wife or child has of what a father does at his work are usually far from the truth. Sometimes this vagueness may be an advantage; more often it is a source of frustration and annoyance.

Employers can help to bridge this rift in the home, if they wish, by means of plant open houses, employee newspapers, letters, and other communication devices. But when they make the effort, they should be careful not to let the employee down, but to explain fully the importance of his or her work. In some highly automated industries, for example, an open house shows the wage earner fiddling with controls which seem unimportant unless their significance is made clear. We need some substitute for the image of the brawny, sweating, heroic laborer whom mural painters have loved to portray. In twentieth-century America, families need to know that the father's or mother's work often involves a high degree of intelligence. Employers can try to give them a lively sense of understanding.

Participation. The growing separation between the employee's family and the worker's job also poses some problems about the desirability of family participation in the social life of a plant or office. The job and the rest of a worker's life are usually rather closely connected in some small-town industries, among officers' wives on traditional military posts, and among faculty families on small college campuses. But increasingly in modern urban society, employee families have many other things to do than to hobnob with people at the office or plant. School and church affairs, voluntary groups of all sorts, gatherings of relatives, picnics, travel, and even television watching may all provide a more friendly and less caste-conscious social setting.

Some opportunities for employee family participation in social events may be welcomed, but if the company offers too many, they may seem an intrusion. Togetherness can be carried too far. Rare invitations are a treat, but frequent command performances become a worrisome chore. Almost unconsciously paternalism creeps in, even with management's best intent to avoid it. John or Jane Doe may be well acquainted with his or her various bosses, but their looks and mannerisms, which do not bother the employee because they are familiar, may utterly devastate a wife or husband who reads all manner of dire intent into them concerning Doe's future with the organization; and the activities of the bosses' spouses, whom Doe does not know, may also be baffling and alarming.

Perhaps semiformality on such occasions is the best answer. The top brass at an open house might well shake hands, make a speech, join in the refreshments briefly, and then—disappear. And when the pictures of the event are run in the employee magazine, one photo of the president at the event will be enough. Employee families desire participation and like to know the brass personally—but only to a degree.

THE STOCKHOLDER PUBLIC

After the employees and their families, stockholders are probably next most closely connected to a company, and there are many obvious reasons for cultivating their interest and good will:

1 In theory at least, stockholders are the ultimate authority of a company, electing the board of directors, which in turn appoints the president and other major officers.

2 Stockholders are often an important source of additional funds for expansion or acquisitions. Their word also carries weight with interested nonstockholders who might wish to invest.

3 Stockholders are important for their "political" support also. Their influence is particularly evident among utility companies, whose rates are fixed by public bodies and who wisely try to get their stockholding as widespread as possible within their service areas. Many local companies associated with larger national concerns try to overcome the stigma of outside control by encouraging local stock-ownership in the parent organization.

The stockholder situation of companies, of course, varies greatly. Until recent times a few industrial giants have been family-held without sale of their stock to the general public. Others are still largely held by a few people, often an original family or two and the friends of an early inventor. Others, such as the public utilities or large national industrial concerns, have many thousands of stockholders. The classic concept, however, of a large company as an organization in which a relatively small group of stockholders keeps in close touch and exercises effective control through personal knowledge of people and policies is generally far from the fact.

Types of stockholders vary greatly; they include insurance and investment companies, wealthy people and those of moderate incomes, widows and orphans, church and educational institutions. Very seldom do these diverse types of people ever get together in an effective stockholder revolt unless conditions are very much disturbed and some leadership is offered. The usual recourse of unhappy stockholders is to sell out and to cease their connection with the company; yet such is the volume of trading on many stocks today, that to assume that all who sell are dissatisfied would be quite incorrect. They may be cashing in their gains or easing their losses.

Companies are obliged by law to render annual reports to their stockholders. At first these annual reports were just tables of figures and the necessary explanations, primarily of interest to financiers; but in recent years they have become increasingly elaborate, and now are often highly illustrated, beautifully printed, well-written booklets, which are sent not only to stockholders but also to the press, community leaders, financial analysts, and frequently to employees also. Such annual-report booklets are often supplemented by films and stockholder meetings, depending upon the size of the company.

A movement toward "social accountability" in the United States and Europe has changed the nature of both stockholder annual reports and of annual meetings. Many stockholder reports contain extensive coverage of the good being done for employees, communities, the arts and the national welfare in general by corporate activities beyond the making of a profit and the production of products—although, of course, shareholders continue to be most interested in the return upon their investment. In shareholder meetings church or environmental cause groups, for example, need own only one share of stock to gain admission and frequently try to use such occasions as a podium to expound their causes, thus gaining much publicity despite the possible unpopularity of their views with other larger stockholders. Shareholder meetings which formerly were rather cut-and-dried affairs so long as the company's earnings continued to show profits have now often become contentious and heckling affairs lasting for hours. Since such meetings are in effect open to the public and the press and provide a good platform for cause agitators, it can be expected that this sort of activity will probably increase—thus providing another public relations problem in meeting all sorts of questions and getting fair news coverage.

Many employees now own stock in the companies for which they work and thus have a divided interest. Frequently companies encourage employee stock-ownership; they may lend employees money to buy stock and promise to buy it back at the original selling price if the employee leaves the company. (Some companies require that employees sell such stock back to the company.) Often such stock "buys itself" because dividends are larger than the repayment rate on the loan.

The stockholding public usually wants to know certain things: Why are the dividends down? (They usually will not ask why they are up.) What is being done by the company about reinvesting in its future? What

uture of the business? Why are the company officers paid so well
ered attractive stock options? And why are relatives or friends of
.gement on the board of directors or in key offices? When earnings
good, little may be said, but if they worsen, the questions may become
n..nerous and insistent. Some other aspects of stockholder relations will
be referred to under the discussion of external financial public relations
later in this chapter.

THE COMMUNITY PUBLIC

Generalizations about plant communities are usually as fruitless as those
about employees, since communities may differ from each other greatly
in their sizes, interests, and in their relation with plants. In some instances, a large plant in a small town may be the lifeblood and main
interest not only of that town but also of a half a dozen others near by.
Yet the identical plant in a city of a million people would be relatively
unimportant, only one among many.

Some plants which produce consumer products may look toward
their communities to absorb a large part of their output; others may ship
all over the world, their sales success being made far from the production
location. Some plants employ only less skilled or even transient laborers.
Even the differing social, religious, or racial attitudes of sections of the
country have an effect upon community relations, and large multiplant
organizations may find it difficult to install any single community relations program because of the variations in local conditions.

A community public is both internal and external; it includes the
employees, their families, their friends, and relatives; yet it goes beyond
these to include people who are closely connected by interest with the
organization and perhaps those who hardly know that it exists. Some
people may benefit much from the activities of a business within a
community and realize the advantage quite well; some will benefit and
not know the source; and others will not benefit, or at least will not feel
disposed to admit it. Yet, in all this variety, some natural contacts
between community and plant occur frequently, although their importance depends upon conditions.

Plants need services from their communities; they need streets,
sewers, water, lights, police and fire protection. Their employees need
these services also, plus schools for their children, shopping centers, good
homes, churches, and the other components of civilized life.

Plants get all or most of their employees from their communities,
and they may draw many of their customers from this source also.

Industry pays taxes and may give gifts to community needs. Yet industry may also sometimes make noise, look ugly, pollute the air and streams, dump unneeded workers on local relief rolls, and get involved in bitter strikes—all of which annoyances affect community relations.

What does a community expect of an industry?

Income. A community hopes that cash will flow in through wages to employees, perhaps from purchases from local suppliers, and from tax payments.

Appearance. A community hopes that the plant appearance will not be a detriment to life in the town and, preferably, that it may be an attraction. Plants can often be good-looking, and some care spent on grass, flowers, and paint pays greatly in community appreciation. Many plants which emit odors, such as stockyards or oil refineries, or which belch smoke or make noises may be tolerated because they are a reason for the existence of the town, but if the town ever grows enough so that they lose preeminence, they may find themselves in trouble. In any case, they may face environmental laws which are much more important than they used to be.

Participation. A plant is liked as an organization if it carries its load in necessary civic efforts such as school improvements, parks, welfare, and churches. Often this is done by individuals rather than by the company, and sometimes town leaders and company members may not agree as to how much is worthwhile, but willingness and interest are appreciated.

Stability. Fluctuating businesses sometimes bring more trouble than they are worth; the amount of trouble depends upon the size and nature of the town.

Pride. Many a city is on the map because it is the home of a nationally or even internationally known industry. Battle Creek means cereals; Rochester means Eastman Kodak or Xerox; and so forth. Civic pride in the town's industry can be fostered and extended.

From its community an industry expects adequate services, fair taxation, good living conditions for its employees, a good source of labor supply, and a reasonable degree of support for the plant and its products if they deserve it.

Sometimes one party may expect too much from the other, but the important thing is that they should understand each other. Some communities, hungry for business, are willing to subsidize industry by cheap loans, low taxes, free or almost-free building sites and even buildings, low-cost utilities, and acceptance of low wage rates. But any industry involving substantial amounts of hard-to-move capital investment and

ıtional advantages, would do well to consider such inducements care-
ıy, since the advantages may turn to losses if ill feeling should later
ıse.

Good community relations cannot be established overnight, nor can
bad opinions be altered easily. A sharp-dealing industry faces not only
local political dangers but also the votes and voice of its own community
people in state and national matters, over which it has no local control.
The city leaders of Jonesville may be willing to put up with stream
pollution, for example, but the other citizens of Jonesville and the towns
downriver, through their voice in the state or federal capital, may not
be so compliant. A plant which pays substandard wages may find its
workers pirated away by a new plant in an adjoining county a half-hour's
drive away. As this nation grows into a greater metropolitan complex,
local advantages tend to disappear, and community good citizenship and
reputation affect an ever-widening area and pay off increasingly.

THE SUPPLIER PUBLIC

The people who sell to a company also form an important part of its
internal public.

Many plants could not operate without suppliers of raw material:
the dairy farmers who sell milk to evaporating, butter, or cheese plants;
fruit-growers who sell to packing or canning plants; or farm wood growers and cutters who sell to paper or pulp-products plants. Such suppliers
are as necessary to the plant as the employees who operate the machinery
or keep its records, and the money paid to suppliers by the plant for sale
of milk, fruit, or logs may be even more important to the area income
than the plant's wage payroll.

Raw-material suppliers may also be very numerous. In some large
milk-processing operations, for example, from several hundred to several
thousand farmers may be selling milk to each plant—many times the
number of employees.

Suppliers also may have numerous choices of where they will sell.
In many areas a dairy farmer can easily sell milk to several markets, and
plant competition for supplies is keen; or the supplier may decide to go
out of dairying altogether in favor of raising beef cattle, or even to take
a factory job in the city. Both the large number of suppliers and the need
for their interest and loyalty create a field for good public relations. The
main responsibility for seeing that a plant receives a steady flow of raw
material may belong to the production department, but public relations

activities can assist greatly in obtaining valuable goodwill and understanding. Supplier publications, meetings, open houses, personal visits,
and public relations advertising are the usual steps taken along with plant
participation in city and regional events, to improve the community and
its resources.

Another important class of suppliers is made up of those who sell
component parts or materials to manufacturers who fabricate or assem-
ble more complicated machines. The automobile industry, for example,
draws upon hundreds of smaller manufacturers for items as diverse as
glass, fabric, plywood, paint, chrome-plated parts, tires, rubber mount-
ings, trim, springs, and screws. Frequently these subsidiary manufacturers will be scattered in dozens of smaller cities located near a large
automobile plant. Since such suppliers do not sell to the public directly,
their names often mean little to the public, and they are largely dependent for their orders upon one or two larger manufacturers who do sell
completed products to the public.

In turn, however, the larger manufacturers are also somewhat dependent upon these subcontractors for the quality of their goods and
certainty of delivery. A bad item in an otherwise good automobile causes
customer complaints and hurts the reputation of the whole vehicle and
its maker; and the inability of suppliers to meet demands may hold up
an entire production program.

Since the number of such suppliers is relatively small, broad-scale
public relations activities in this connection are not common. Many
companies, however, such as General Motors Corporation, have long
been aware of the public ignorance of how many smaller companies are
sustained under the supplier system to the benefit of smaller industry and
the widespread economic development of the nation. To combat such
ignorance, they have used campaigns of public relations advertising
showing the benefits of large-scale industry and sales and the manner of
their diffusion through the entire country by means of a multitude of
supplier contracts. The purpose is to affect public economic understanding as well as supplier goodwill.

There is yet a third class of suppliers, the local furnishers of office
equipment, linen, food, building construction and repairs, and other
services necessary to keep a large plant running. These people are such
clear beneficiaries of their business connection and are so much a part
of the community that usually no particular public relations activities are
necessary with them except fair treatment, passing the business around
somewhat evenly, courtesy, and information.

THE DEALER AND DISTRIBUTOR PUBLIC

The dealer and distributor public is primarily the responsibility of the sales department, but the special communications abilities of public relations persons may frequently be called into play, especially if the number of dealers and distributors is large, if they are widely spread out, and if personal communications need to be supplemented by additional contacts.

Public relations staffs may be called upon, for example, to help produce dealer magazines containing news about new products and their uses, sales and contest ideas, personal items about dealer accomplishments, and changes in company policies. Publicity help for dealers and manuals designed to enable dealers to get more favorable local publicity are frequently requested, as is also assistance in arranging sales-meetings programs and supplying special exhibits.

Because of the public relations department's special knowledge of public opinion, it may be called upon to arrange or to advise upon surveys of dealer opinion about the company or its products.

The dealer-distributor public is often very close to the company's heart, and any real assistance that public relations can offer, working in close conjunction with the sales department's goals and desires, pays off at the cash register and may be much appreciated. Such assistance is one of the best ways to demonstrate the value of good public relations and to gain greater internal appreciation for the portions of public relations work which may be less tangible or of less immediate benefit.

THE CONSUMER PUBLIC

The consumer public is also largely a responsibility of the sales department and of its right arm, the advertising department; but when consumers are numerous, or sometimes even when they are not, public relations methods of communication reaching beyond direct sales work or conventional means of advertising may become important. Here are some illustrations:

1   What creates the prevailing public attitude toward an organization? Though many companies in the United States today make similar products selling at similar prices, people often seem to prefer one of them to the others. What makes the difference? The product itself? Its advertising? The popularity of the manufacturing company—because of its good citizenship, enterprise, reliability, and the quality of its people? If public feeling is favorable, then how did people acquire their impressions?

2 How much does the public know about the product? backed by giant introductory budgets (and often not even then), ac ing usually does its best in selling a product with which the pι already familiar. Complete pioneering, creating a primary demand by advertising alone can be inordinately expensive, even futile. Yet since new products are *news,* they are well suited to public relations publicity, to films, exhibits, school contacts, and other unconventional ways of addressing audiences that usually result in a more active expression of interest than can be achieved in advertising in the mass media. Reaching opinion leaders and making friends are also especially important in introducing new products.

3 Actual events such as contests, award programs, and visits to plants or laboratories may bring customers. With the permission of school authorities, programs and contests for students are increasingly used to awaken interest.

4 Employees can often exert a strong influence upon sales through their own public relations activities. The company can encourage them, in many instances, by informal training and by suggestions designed to obtain better cooperation.

5 Careful listening to what consumers have to say through surveys, panels, and less formal means is the joint concern of the sales, advertising, and public relations departments. Since customers do not differentiate among these departments, their feelings affect not only sales but also the labor, community, and political relations of a company.

It is growing increasingly hard to separate the external aspects of a company into neat compartments such as sales, advertising, and public relations, because outside observers get their impressions from all three plus the product itself. Consumer reactions are of political importance when they affect pricing, licensing, and government controls as well as sales. The face a company presents to the public is really a unity, although it may be a composite drawn by different departments; and the time may come (indeed has come in some industries) when there will be but two main divisions, (*a*) *communications* and *contacts* with various publics and (*b*) *production.* Under the first heading would come sales, advertising, public relations, and parts of employee relations; under the second would come production, personnel (in part), and maintenance of plants. Finance, the legal staff, and other service departments would assist both.

THE EXTERNAL PUBLICS

The publics mentioned so far in this chapter—employees, stockholders, the community, and customers—are all more or less intimately connected with a company and come into contact with it regularly through their normal activities. But there are in addition some much larger outside groups which affect a company's welfare materially and with which the degree of its contact and the nature of that contact is more or less voluntary. Such groups include the press and the other communications media, leaders of thought, political forces, financial experts, and others.

Probably the biggest difference between an *internal* and an *external* public is that people, such as employees or stockholders, who are connected with an organization in some way will have a certain degree of interest in it, whereas to the outside world each company is just another organization, and unless some way can be found to relate its story to the interests of outsiders, they will probably not pay much attention to it.

There is, of course, interaction between internal and external publics. Yet it cannot be assumed that without effort good relations with insiders will ever be translated to outsiders. An employee who is quite happy on the job may be much more interested in bowling than in the fact that the firm has just opened a new branch in Australia. The firm must think of what interests the external public and not of what interests the firm. With employees and other internal publics there is a fair chance that all interests may coincide because all are connected with the same organization; with an external audience the assumption should be that the chance of such accidental coincidence of interest is slight.

THE PRESS PUBLIC

"The press" includes newspapers of all sizes and types, television and radio stations, general magazines, and trade papers. All of them serve as gatekeepers, opening the door to wider contact with a broad public through these media. The effective use of the media themselves will be discussed more fully in Chapter 8, "The Tools of Public Relations," but press staff people also constitute an important public in themselves, whose understanding and goodwill, regardless of their position, is well worth cultivating.

It is a mistake to think of news people as a peculiar group who demand special treatment. They are people like ourselves, who "live with bread" like us. They show a wide range of characteristics just as we do, from the conservatism of many publishers to the extreme liberalism of some young reporters.

Yet the nature of their profession does give them a few special traits or proclivities. In ordinary times the press exercises a tremendous influence over public opinion, and a news writer's words can affect the life

of a project or organization. Bad reviews have meant the death of
or book, and lack of publicity has prevented public interest in .
cause. Such power *can* corrupt in various ways. At the same time,
newspapers and journals need the financial support of advertisers. This
interdependence has tempted both advertisers and journalists to exercise
pressure or to court favors from each other by questionable means. But
such pressure is almost invariably a mistake and is resented by press and
public alike. Most newspapers can well afford to be independent, and
they value the traditional freedom of the press. The public, in the long
run, recognizes a biased presentation of news or causes. Public relations
people who want to get material into the press should avoid unwise
pressure just as they avoid blackmail or bribery. Honesty in straightfor-
ward stories that have genuine news value about good products is the
best policy.

It should be noted that the sharp distinction between advertising
space and legitimate news space does not always apply in the overseas
press as it does, almost without exception in the United States. In foreign
newspapers and magazines the use of public relations releases and pictures is often tied to the amount of advertising purchased. This is de-
plored in the United States and no first-rate publication in this country
would be guilty of it. In fact, such a request would be an indication that
the publication had little circulation or influence. But it is a fact of life
in many other countries of the world.

As a group, news people are intelligent—not only well educated but
well informed through wide reading and experience. They appreciate
direct, clear-cut explanations, since they themselves are experts in con-
cise exposition and are usually hard pressed for time. Their contacts with
many people and many political campaigns may make them mildly
cynical about people's motives. Their anxiety to "get the news" leads
sometimes to tactlessness and even callousness in its pursuit. But with
that side of their work the public relations person has little to do. He will
usually find news people extremely helpful, not only in getting stories
into the papers but, more importantly, in interpreting public feeling.
They know more about public relations than do people who get about
less; they are trained observers; and they are often happy to give their
impressions. In general, when treated with honesty and consideration,
the press public is friendly, helpful, and stimulating.

THE EDUCATOR PUBLIC

School people are another set of gatekeepers through whom messages
may be relayed to other people; in addition, they also serve as "legitimiz-

ers," in that their approval of a proposition carries weight. This is particularly true in the college or university field, where competence in special subject matter is recognized. If a teacher of engineering, for example, speaks favorably of a machine to a class, the recommendation is important to them. The support of teachers (again, particularly of those in specialized fields) is important, also in connection with recruiting employees. Graduating students often consult with their teachers about the choice of firms who offer employment; and teachers can direct company recruiters to promising students, giving them detailed information about the qualities of the young people.

The key to successful contacts with the educator public is *service*. Teachers are often willing to use commercially produced material in the classroom *if* it performs a real function which cannot be duplicated elsewhere or would perhaps be much more expensive. They are willing to read booklets or to attend meetings *if* they can get something of value out of them which they do not already know well.

Like members of the press, teachers are well educated and resent pressure, insults to their intelligence, or a waste of their time. They are independent-minded and perhaps equally suspicious of motives, but their pace is slower than that of journalists; they are less impatient and more willing to tolerate some dullness. Teachers are cautious about using material from an organization if they think it would expose them to charges of favoritism. They are pleased when others understand their educational ambitions, seek their advice, and offer to help make their work easier and more effective. Teachers are often willing to engage in joint efforts to improve education through award programs for outstanding students, summer internships for teachers, and public events such as science fairs. They resent being herded into "business-in-industry days," being marched through plants, and being lectured about the merits of the free enterprise system. They particularly resent attempts to tell them what they should teach in the classroom, although from fear or politeness they will usually express their resentment only to one another.

The best way to serve the teacher public (and the press) is to find out what it wants and then satisfy the need.

THE CLERGY PUBLIC

Churchmen serve as legitimizers of ideas and activities rather than as gatekeepers, since little direct speaking from the pulpit or in meetings can be expected from them except on moral issues such as support of welfare or educational drives. Their understanding and their good will,

Figure 4–2 Factual educational material; a 12-page bulletin produced by the American Petroleum Institute.

however, may be reflected in their personal conversations, in their presence at events, and in the use of their names upon letterheads.

Clergymen are interested first in moral issues and then in civic and area development, in education, in world affairs, in sociological problems, and perhaps in science, medicine, or economics. Church leaders look at the world in terms of people rather than in terms of dollars or material production. In many churches they avoid becoming involved too deeply in material matters, both from a lack of personal interest and perhaps also from a concern lest they awaken controversy among their own church members. Clergymen, however, appreciate the opportunity

informed about business activities and of being included in
nt plans or functions when their presence is appropriate.

AND BUSINESS CLUBS

Groups like the Lions, Kiwanians, Engineers Club, or the South Side
Improvement Association serve as platforms from which messages may
be communicated to the attending members and perhaps also, by mail
or by press reports, to those absent. Such groups act as gatekeepers in
so far as their members relay their opinions to others; they act also, to
some extent, as legitimizers from the simple fact that their acceptance
or appreciation or formal endorsement of a speaker indicates approval
in varying degrees. Such groups also furnish the occasion for a wider
dissemination of information through the press. They may not be large
in themselves, but they can be an important audience.

Business groups are usually inured to a reasonable amount of commercialism, at least within their own fields of interest, and do not resent
it if it is presented as necessary information or without undue emphasis.

Professional clubs, which include doctors, lawyers, architects, and
others, have a more precise focus of interest, and it does not matter
greatly, in many instances, if talks presented to them are somewhat
commercial as long as no disguise is attempted and the matter is genuinely germane to their professional interests. Indeed many talks must be
commercial, because professional associations provide a formalized way
of "talking shop." Skilled commercial presentations by experts, containing real information, well supplied with visual aids and demonstrations,
are often welcomed because they improve the professional competence
of each man present.

Membership within these groups, if it is possible for a member of
a firm, helps public relations, since it usually indicates his or her willingness to be of personal service in advancing the interests of the profession,
business, or area involved. Such personal generosity is particularly important in highly specialized fields or in small cities where group membership may be limited.

Clubs directed mainly to women are similar to other civic and
business organizations, except that they tend to be in suburban locations
and to be more concerned about cultural subjects, children, gardens,
welfare, and matters of particular interests to women.

Social Groups

Informal social organizations, such as city or country clubs or dance
clubs, exist largely for the pleasure of the members, and admission to

them almost always depends upon personal popularity. To a degree they are gatekeepers or legitimizers among the people who know of them. But since they are private groups, they are most valuable for the opportunities they afford for improvement of strictly personal relations. Often the leading social groups in a city together constitute a field which can be worked by the boss and friends rather than by the public relations person.

GOVERNMENT AS A PUBLIC

The government publics are primarily neither gatekeepers nor legitimizers, but rather groups of persons whose attitudes often have very concrete and direct effects upon the fortunes of many kinds of business and other activities. With the great expansion of government functions in this country within the past fifty years, the power of anyone associated with the government has tremendously increased. Government—city, state, or Federal—now affects big and little businessmen, farmers, laborers, teachers, transportation firms, merchants, scientists, and almost everyone else who can be named.

Work among such government publics differs somewhat from political activity as such, or from "economic education," or from the formation of pressure groups (although all are somewhat related), in that it involves the fundamental problem of fostering good relations with a large public associated with government—administrators, employees, and legislators.

Government administrative bodies—state highway departments, food and drug commissions, health authorities, and police forces, for example—often concern themselves directly with a business or organization; they may make regulations about such things as purchases of materials; may require statements about products; and may set standards of performance.

Government legislative bodies make the laws under which business and other activities operate. The process of legislation involves constant bickering about items as diverse as the size and weight of highway trucks, aid to dependent children, beer taxes, regulation of the practice of medicine, and the amount of money to be spent upon tourist promotion—all of which matters are of deep concern to certain business and professional groups and to the public relations people who represent them.

In a democratic government there is no question of the *right* of a business or interest group to present its case before a legislative body. It is part of the citizen's constitutional right of petition—the right to present facts before laws were made, hard-won hundreds of years ago from tyrannical kings. Nor is there any question about the *necessity* of such petitions. Government actions which may put a business out of operation or greatly reduce its earnings, which may beggar or enrich whole sections of the population, and which may pass the public's tax money around for better or for worse effect, are important. All persons whose interests are strongly concerned, including those who fight for causes, would be doing their organization an injustice if they did not do their best to present a case before government.

Lobbying isn't the sinister activity that it appears in the public eye, yet the word itself has become a smear term, suggesting all sorts of selfish people exerting undue influence, bribing and generally corrupting honest lawmakers and government administrators who would be paragons of wisdom and uprightness if only left alone. Actually, the activity of lobbying today springs out of the same big changes that have affected all communication and business in the United States within the past few decades. Lobbying, legislative representation, or whatever it may be called, is a natural outgrowth of bigness and great social interdependence. If it existed in the past only in the form of corrupting influence, that was because the dissemination of information was less needed.

Today a great many people are closely affected by many proposed laws and regulations about which they cannot pass a well-reasoned personal judgment. The doctor seeing patients, the architect at a drawing board, the farmer plowing fields, and the college teacher lecturing in a classroom are all so busy with their increasingly complex work that they do not have enough time to study and evaluate proposed new laws, and to decide to support or not to support them. Many scores of bills affecting business or professional activities are introduced at each session of a typical American state legislature. (For example, 1,200 bills are introduced at each legislative session in one typical large midwestern state, of which perhaps 100 will in some way affect the practice of medicine.) Someone must be the watchdog of these bills for each interested group —must read them, recommend positions, and present views—or otherwise no views will be heard, and the issue will be left to chance or to other pressures. This is lobbying.

In any matter of importance involving the continuing interest of government, someone has to be hired to watch changes, or to introduce them, and to know the ropes—who legislators are, where they come from, what their beliefs and interests are, what the nature of their legislation is, and what they are responsive to. Such representatives also have to know what the group that they work for really wants, what the opposing interests are up to, and what the general public's reaction may be. This is obviously no job for a part-time amateur—although often people on the fringe of politics can help. The line between public relations and lobbying is a thin one; lobbying might be defined as the practice of public relations directed toward one very specific and important group.

There are, of course, crooked lobbyists, those who offer bribes, who pander in various ways, and who appeal to ignoble, narrow interests in a manner harmful to the general welfare. Corruptible people will be found also in many other human activities when the stakes are high and the temptations great. There are also honest, well-informed lobbyists who perform a valuable information service for legislators, their supporters, and the public. Many of the complaints about lobbying arise from groups of people who have no adequate representation for their own interests or who were defeated and seek a good excuse to explain their failure to their followers; some complaints come as a political smoke screen to explain legislative failure or inactivity; and still others come from genuinely concerned citizens who are afraid that underpaid, insecure, and sometimes naïve lawmakers may not continue to be honest and independent.

But the right of petitioning government is undeniable as long as democracy endures, and although the ground rules may be altered from time to time, the principle must be preserved. Government and political parties in the United States are supposed to reflect the popular will and do not themselves decide it. Government cannot and should not insulate itself from listening to public opinion between election dates.

Lobbying, however, is an area of great sensitivity and subject to quick criticism. How, then, should the important government public be approached?

Low pressure is the key in dealing with government administrative people. For example, fact and study reports, truthful and with the sources well identified, are good material. No one can criticize a public relations worker for making such reports available or an administrator for looking at them, since government is supposed to be well informed and to hear all sides before acting. Reprints of speeches by prominent or qualified people are also acceptable, although they may not be so well read as is desirable.

Bolder general publicity in a newspaper published in a state capital or upon radio or television might reach the persons at whom it is aimed along with the rest of the general public; but it might also reveal such pressures to public view and hence must be used with care if it is not to bring forth complaints from the opposition. Most big issues have several sides and several sets of lobbyists, acting sometimes in opposition to each other, sometimes in concert. The more apparent one effort is, the quicker and greater the opposition it may arouse and the greater the danger that government will be itself subject to attack if it supports a side that has been too well proclaimed.

Actually, nothing succeeds better with government people than personal contact. A lobbyist may establish contact with no immediate purpose beyond "You may want to know me. I represent so and so," and sometimes one may achieve it in the course of belonging to the same groups or of being helpful in other matters. In relations like these no one fools the other very much; the reason for the contact, like that of a sales person with a customer, is admittedly commercial. Yet, oddly enough, genuine liking between people often does spring up in these ways over the years and endures long after its original purpose has been lost. People would, of course, prefer to be liked for themselves alone rather than because of their positions, but motives are often hard to untangle and often it does not pay to examine them too deeply.

Public relations activities with legislative groups in government are more lively, difficult, and dangerous than dealings with administrative departments where tenure is more secure, action slow, and the chief fear often that of offending someone important. When the chips are down in a legislative vote, issues will be either passed or scuttled, with resulting rewards or brickbats for the lobbyists who have won or failed. Like elections, these are what public relations people call hard issues; one either wins or loses, and there are no consolation prizes for second place. Legislative actions are so close to the limelight of publicity, that overzealous or effective lobbyists may be spotlighted by their competitors or by legislators upon the losing side who seek to explain their failure by shouting that they were swamped by undue influence. Success is never to be counted on; the tide of public opinion turns without warning; and all manner of extraneous issues and deals have a way of swimming into the scene suddenly, turning "sure things" into failures overnight.

The first problem of the legislative lobbyist is to know what's going on—to read, to understand, to be familiar with committee structure (the most important work is usually done in committees), to see the right people, and to present the case, usually not too formally. If a legislator is from a cotton-producing area, for example, a few accurate figures upon the effect of a proposed bill upon the cotton-crop income in his district might be pertinent and enough. These might be given at lunch or over a drink, neither of which should be considered entertainment big enough to constitute bribery (but in some places are). In some cases the presentation might be more formal, as at a public hearing. Frequently the heads

of schools or professional groups or other organizations will be (
by committees for information, often at their own petition. At t
ing the executives must do the talking, but very often a public
person will have assembled the material and ideas that they present.

Some lobbyists come out of the ranks of capital-city newspaper
people, whose acquaintanceships and observations are useful; others are
former government officials or legislators; and others, like educators,
come from the professions which maintain them. Some approach the
public image of a lobbyist, being obviously well financed, effusive, and
friendly; others, equally effective in their fields, may be quiet and conservative in their appearance.

Another way to influence legislative actions—one full of danger—
is to take the case directly to the public in order to put pressure upon
their elected representatives. Of course public relations activity makes
this sort of appeal all the time anyway, but when it starts publicity in the
heat of impending legislative action with the obvious intent of building
a fire under a legislator right in his or her home district, it sometimes
amounts to a declaration of war. As Emerson once said, "If you strike
at a king, you must kill him."

A legislator, however, has no right to expect immunity from phone
calls, letters, or visitors; he is hired to listen. But if he rightly questions
the integrity of those who exert such pressure, or if he doubts that it
represents the sentiment of constituents, and if calls are critical or threatening, fear may naturally turn to anger. Honest, calm pleas, truly representing the wishes of the constituency, raise no question about the right
to petition, but excited pressures are upsetting. Legislators are just like
other people, only perhaps a bit more sensitive, egotistical, and excitable,
because it takes a certain hopeful, enthusiastic, warm temperament to
enjoy and endure the perils of politics. A legislator may react too violently and illogically to the provocation of pressure, even to the point of
endangering his or her own future. But we cannot expect legislators to
be a cold logicians: people act as they will, not as they should.

PUBLIC RELATIONS WITH THE FINANCIAL WORLD

Dealings with the financial world skyrocket rapidly as more and more
companies feel the necessity of telling their story to stockholders, banks,
investment houses, security analysts, and other groups which might be
of financial assistance at some time. Stockholder relations, discussed
earlier, are only a part of financial relations, because cash may come from
many other places. Companies need an active market for their securities

to improve the corporation's position in mergers or in acquisitions, to create a market for future stock issues, and to broaden the base of stock ownership. A newsletter from the Public Relations Board, a Chicago counseling firm, put it well by telling this story:

> This is a true story. Only the name of the company has been changed.
>
> The Smith Company had been listed on the New York Stock Exchange for nearly thirty years. Two years ago its stock sold at $12 a share, a price which allowed the high yield of 6.6 per cent on the regular dividend. Interest in the stock was slight, despite the company's increasing sales volume and earnings, diversification of operations, and expansion into more profitable areas. Only about four hundred shares were traded each week.
>
> Independent counsel conducted a survey among one hundred New York security brokers and analysts. Eighty-five men had never heard of the company. Twelve remembered the name but did not know one fact about the company. Three knew that the company was listed on the "big board" —and nothing more.
>
> The Smith Company engaged . . . financial public relations counsel. The company's shares subsequently sold for more than $36 a share before a recent two-for-one split, a price that reflected a sharply higher capitalization of earnings. Volume rose to nearly four hundred shares a day.
>
> A new survey of analysts showed one of the reasons why: 86 percent were well informed of the company's performance and prospects, while the rest at least knew the company's name and where the shares were traded.
>
> Here are some surprising statistics behind the growth of financial public relations:
>
> 1   Nearly 50,000 publicly-owned corporations are bidding for the attention of investors through newspapers, financial publications, and security analysts.
>
> 2   Fewer than thirty daily newspapers carry more than one full page of financial news. Local corporations, of course, gain precedence for their news. That leaves nearly 50,000 other companies competing for space in perhaps a remaining half page.
>
> 3   The same 50,000 companies compete for the time of the security analyst, the backbone of the brokerage business. It is he who researches a company and reports on its value as an investment. His decision is passed along, verbally or by market letter, to his firm's customer men and to investors.
>
> 4   The average analyst covers a minimum of three hundred and fifty companies. As many as one hundred pieces of mail cross his desk daily. He is besieged with inquiries about individual securities. And he must still research, evaluate, and write up hundreds of companies annually.
>
> 5   Nearly 50,000 companies issue Securities Exchange Commission-required annual reports which they hope will attract the attention of investors and analysts.

The solution? Better news preparation and better cooperation with newsmen. Better liaison with security analysts. Better annual and interim reports. In short, financial public relations.

The consensus of the sophisticated investment world is that (business) managements will continue to broaden their use of financial public relations as an effective corporate tool. And much credit is given management now for the role it has played in bring more investors into "people's capitalism," as it has been called by the head of the New York Stock Exchange.

When people buy stock in a company, of course, they also become members of another of its publics (an internal one), but material aimed at the outside financial community then serves them too.

Financial public relations has become a specialty in itself and to practice it well requires an understanding of accounting terms and procedures, financial laws and regulations, and corporate financial methods, among other things. It is a highly skilled field and one in which amateurs may get both themselves and their companies into serious trouble quickly. Public relations writers, for example, are not at liberty to say just anything that seems to be a good notion, but must meet strict standards of both accuracy and of timing. The important thing for the beginning public relations person to be aware of is the existence of such requirements and to get good legal and accounting advice before touting stocks or issuing reports of new discoveries, for example.

THE TRADE ASSOCIATION PUBLIC

Every business or occupation in this country has its trade or professional associations. Lawyers and engineers, rugmakers and hornblowers, railroad operators and plasterers, to mention only a few, band together, all finding it worthwhile to be in association with each other, though they may often be competitiors within their own ranks. Sometimes an association's goals are to police its own activities or to present a united front to government or to labor, but often there is also a very good public relations or sales reason.

Carpet or rug manufacturers do not compete with each other alone, or perhaps even mainly with each other, but rather with alternate ways of covering floors (or not covering them), such as plastic tile, wood, or linoleum. When people choose these products, they do not buy woven carpet material, except perhaps for throw rugs. Since no single carpet manufacturer can afford to spend all his advertising effort in bucking a problem which is common to all, the obvious procedure is to get together. When all chip in, they can make a concerted effort to encourage the use of carpeting instead of a substitute. Only by helping to increase carpeting's total share of the floor-covering market can each carpet manufacturer acquire more business.

The same story lies behind programs in which clothing manufacturers supported an effort to make American men more conscious of the importance of dressing well; of the American Music Conference, which encouraged the buying of horns or pianos to creat homemade music; and of the National Highway Users Conference, which wanted to increase the amount of highway travel and shipping in the United States. The clothing-manufacturers group bucked a trend toward informality in clothing; the musical-instrument makers faced the competition of listening to radio, television, and records; and the highway users faced the competition of other forms of transportation.

Group promotions like these are hard to organize because they demand complete participation by all in an industry so that no single firm will get a free ride upon the general promotional effort of all but must contribute its just share. Getting a consensus of agreement from a group upon what shall be done once the money is available, is also often hard. Sales problems are sometimes baffling; there is no guarantee of success; and neither advertising, for which there is seldom an adequate amount of money, nor the most ingenious public relations can overcome a really deep-seated social trend. The most inspired advertising of the American Federation of Musicians couldn't halt the disappearance of costly pit orchestras when sound films arrived in motion-picture houses in the late 1920s; and in more recent years the hatters have been having a hard time trying to stem a tendency to go hatless, first among men and then among women. But when public opinion is neutral and even more when it seems to be swinging toward the course advocated, group efforts can often have a marked effect.

In this way trade associations themselves constitute a special public for many businesses. Exerting influence within them is a means of reaching a larger public than any one company could manage to speak to without undue expense and too evident self-interest.

THE FARMER PUBLIC

More than a generation ago, when hardly any public relations activity existed, there was a great gulf between city people and their rural neighbors. Farmers were isolated by mud roads, lack of communications, long, hard work, and a necessary absorption in their own interests. But beginning in the 1920s, this division largely disappeared as roads were im-

proved, radio and then television became general, schools were
consolidated and improved, and a revolution occurred in farming practices through the introduction of new machinery, new crops, fertilizers,
and better agricultural methods. Today the farmers who produce the
bulk of the nation's crops are in big business for themselves, often with
capital investments worth hundreds of thousands of dollars, and with
bookkeeping, tax, and farm-science problems far beyond the comprehension of the average city wage earner.

Yet old farm stereotypes still exist, and many urban people still
regard farmers as country bumpkins, apple knockers rolling straws in
their mouths and speaking a quaint dialect. In spite of the misapprehension, it is true that most farm people *do* differ from city people in the
way they respond to attempts to influence them—recognizing, of course,
that cotton farmers, corn-hog farmers, fruit farmers, and truck garden-
ers, for instance, are all quite different from one another. The alert public
relations person will do well to take into account the differences between
farmers and city people to speak to the farmer most effectively. Various
media, such as farm magazines, smaller newspapers, rural radio and
television, and direct mail are available to reach farmers. The important
thing is how to approach them.

Despite automobiles and more travel, farm people are more isolated
in one sense than city people, less so in another. Farmers see fewer people
in the course of a week, but they also see fewer strangers. The inhabitants
of a very large city seldom look closely at the faces of the people they
encounter upon the street, because they do not expect to know them.
Farmers almost always look, because if they failed to recognize and to
greet their friends, they would be considered snobbish.

Prosperous, well-established farm people move about less than city
people and are more deeply rooted in their neighborhoods, although
because of drifting renters, factory workers who live on farms, and
suburbanization, there are a lot of newcomers in many farm areas today.
Farm work is less pressured than many city jobs, allows the farmer to
be more independent, but requires longer hours. Farmers have more time
to think, and in these days of widespread communication their thoughts
cover wide fields; they tend to think more deeply and to hold convictions
more strongly than do city folk, although perhaps over a narrower range.
Farming is usually a big personal business today, involving much careful
calculation. It depends upon the weather, general prices, and political
actions which are beyond any one individual's control. Farmers are
classical capitalists who yet find it necessary to use government to unite
and control their prices and production.

Because of these facts, farm people tend to be much attached to their own organizations—to farm groups, community-improvement clubs, youth groups such as the 4-H Clubs, to schools, and churches. Such connections are often deep, and the opinions of fellow members of these groups and of other neighbors count for much in the attitudes taken by farm people. The higher the scale of living and education of the farmer, the more likely he or she is to draw opinions from a wide range, including those presented nationally in the mass media; the smaller and less educated the farm operator, the more likely he or she is to seek opinions from immediate neighbors and relatives.

Because they are property holders, farmers tend to be conservative unless driven into radicalism by force of circumstances, to distrust fast and flashy approaches, to count their dollars carefully, to say "no" the first few times that a new idea is presented, to resist pressure, and to move more slowly than city people, who often prize novelty for its own sake. Farmers also tend to be less affected by new ideas and to retain longer those which they have made their own. The better farmers are intelligent, have thought deeply, and often have broader national or world outlooks than city people who are immersed in municipal affairs.

SUMMARY

A list of "publics" could be extended indefinitely. The public for a state conservation department, for example, consists primarily of sportsmen, farmers, foresters, and others; for a pet-food manufacturer it consists of dog and cat owners; and for another manufacturer the public might be just the broad group of men or women.

Almost all public relations practice is specific. It selects publics, analyzes them, plans its actions in relation to their needs and desires, and then aims its communications directly toward these specific publics by whatever means are most suitable and effective. Success depends largely upon how well each of these steps is planned and executed.

ADDITIONAL READINGS

Since each special public is only a portion of the general field of public relations, few book-length works are produced on each one. Most material appears in magazine articles, of which there are scores of entries in the PRSA Public Relations Bibliographies listed at the end of Chapter I, or as chapters in omnibus handbooks such as the following:

Darrow, Richard W., Dan J. Forrestal, and Aubrey O. Cookman, *The Dartnell Public Relations Handbook.* (Chicago: Dartnell Corp., 1967.)

Lesley, Philip, *Public Relations Handbook.* (Englewood Cliffs, N.J.: Prentice-Hall, 1971.)

Stephenson, Howard, *Handbook of Public Relations,* 2nd ed. (New York: McGraw-Hill, 1971.)

Complete Books

Newcomb, Robert, and Marg Sammons, *Employee Communications in Action.* (New York: Harper & Row, 1952.)

Purcell, Fr. Theodore Vincent, *Blue Collar Man.* (Cambridge, Mass.: Harvard University Press, 1960.)

Roalman, Arthur P., *Investor Relations Handbook.* (New York: American Management Association, 1974.)

Chapter 5

Some Special Users of Public Relations and Their Needs

Public relations efforts sometimes fail because their originators are not adequately grounded in the fundamentals of research, action, communication, and evaluation; but they may also fail because the practitioners are ignorant of the particular characteristics of a given type of business or organization. Hence, it is instructive to examine the peculiarities of some of the special areas of public relations practice and to begin to develop skill in their analysis. One of the things that makes public relations so interesting is that it largely consists of using actions and communications to solve problems of human understanding and cooperation in special cases. If there were no problems, there would be no need for public relations.

At the same time, it should not be forgotten that the practice of public relations is always a *unity*. While the circumstances of their application may vary, the fundamental principles of reaching and influencing people remain the same. Good public relations people can tackle the problems of a bank, an educational institution, or a retail store with equal success—*if* they learn enough about the nature of the organization whose problems they are attempting to solve. The advantage of specializing in public relations for particular types of accounts is accompanied by the big disadvantage of so identifying oneself mentally with an organization or type of business that one becomes incapable of seeing how it looks to outsiders. Loyalty and concern are sometimes bought at the price of blindness.

There is no need to learn a different kind of public relations for each separate business, occupation, and cause. With diligent effort, the skilled practitioner can readily adapt his or her work from one area of practice to another, because the fundamentals are always the same. The successes of the great public relations counseling firms constantly demonstrate this unity of principle. Their comparative unfamiliarity with particular fields of action is generally quite offset by their understanding of basic processes of communication and of the nature of the publics involved, and by a wealth of varied experience in many similar fields. Skill in analysis will dictate the application of principles to specific needs. Long exposure to new ideas is often a highly effective catalyst because it directs thinking toward the important receivers of communication rather than toward its self-conscious senders and results in greater ability to see both sides.

THE PUBLIC RELATIONS OF RETAILERS

Smaller Retailers and Service Establishments

The size of a business is often a faulty basis upon which to generalize about its public relations needs. For example, the problems of a small grocery supermarket in Brooklyn, New York, are quite different from those of a store in Algona, Iowa (population 5,000) with the same yearly receipts; and a small hobby shop just off State Street in Chicago is obviously serving a public unlike the customers of a drugstore in Jackson, Mississippi, although both may have approximately the same annual total sales. These smaller stores have in common only a tendency toward more personal relations with their customers, smaller staffs, less opportunity for specialization of personnel within the business, and less money than larger establishments.

Activity that might be formalized public relations within a large institution becomes simple personal relations and standard operating procedure for everyone in a small organization. It goes without saying that clerks should be polite and interested, that the proprietor should try to remember the names and needs of good customers, and that the store should be clean and attractive; but these things should be done anyway. The real problem is to find ways to develop memorable, distinctive qualities in the business and to communicate them in some way to the people from whom trade may reasonably be expected to be drawn.

In a specialty shop, even in a large city, this kind of communication may not be impossible. A list of customers can be compiled and direct mail used to reach them. Small advertising can be placed in specialized parts of large publications, such as sports or garden sections of newspapers. The shop can participate in exhibits and special events. Despite intense news competition, it might hope for occasional publicity from the press, especially in suburban or neighborhood newspapers. Talks might be given to appropriate groups or award programs arranged. The main limitations are the operator's time and money, but the vehicles for public relations communication are often available if the operator has sufficient ingenuity and time to develop them.

In nonspecialty stores, such as the retail grocery in Algona, Iowa, the problem of reaching people can be mastered more easily because of the small size of the market. Advertising space is readily available at a reasonable cost in the local newspaper which goes to everyone; publicity is easily achieved; time can be bought upon local radio stations with excellent coverage opportunities; and establishing personal connections with customers is easy. The main problems are to give the store a personality, to provide good products at competitive prices, and to sell ideas about good eating instead of concentrating on peddling staples. Such small, unspecialized businesses often do best in small communities where their size is commensurate with the size of the mass communications media available. The grocery store in Algona, for example, can perhaps buy a page in the local newspaper at a cost of $100 or more; but in a large city the same $100 spent by a grocery store would buy only a very small ad, sandwiched in between more imposing neighbors like a minnow among whales.

The problems of the small supermarket in Brooklyn, part of a great metropolitan city, and of the ordinary drugstore in Jackson, Mississippi, are the most difficult and challenging. Perhaps the difficulty of communicating with people through the mass media is the chief reason why this type of small proprietorship has almost disappeared in big cities within the past generation. The small store is at a disadvantage in prices, variety of merchandise, and advertising opportunities. If the owner cannot establish valid points of difference and distinction and communicate them to the proper publics, he may fail in business. His limited capital, credit, and supply sources, usually do not allow him to make economical use of the mass media of communication in a large city, such as the daily newspapers, radio, and television.

The problem of division of human abilities also enters in. A proprietor who has to run all aspects of a store usually has little time left for effective public relations and only rarely competes in this field with large organizations which can hire those who are skilled in planning communication and make it their sole business. Yet such skill in promotion, advertising, and public relations is vital to the small proprietor to prosper in the face of competition. Otherwise the proprietor's chief dependence is likely to be upon employees' acceptance of longer hours and lower wages, or upon poorly paid self-employment, convenience goods, and area growth or fortunate location—all of which are likely to be transient advantages.

There are, of course, additional ways in which the small proprietor's problems can be eased, such as specializing within certain areas and engaging in cooperative effort, but they are not easy. They constitute a retailing subject in themselves, which should be studied elsewhere by those interested.

Larger Retailers and Other Businesses

Among larger retailers the competition is usually no less intense than among small businesses, but the available resources in time and money are more commensurate with the modern media of mass communications and the large concentrations of customers in modern urban areas.

In these large retail stores and service establishments, the employees properly become the first concern of the public relations department because the owners can no longer know personally all their employees well and supervise their activities. To the store's customers, the employees *are* the store.

Polite, capable employees contribute most importantly toward establishing a good image of this type of business in the minds of customers. But such men and women are hard to attract and keep. The selection, payment, and control of employees usually come directly under the

responsibility of the personnel management department; but the workers' desire to enter the business, their willingness to accept training, their
information, activities, and encouragement are closely related to public
relations because they are basically communications problems. Employees are people of the community and do not magically adopt different minds and personalities when they walk into the store every morning.
Many of their ideas have evolved before they became employees; many
of their special concepts of the store are formed by their outside contacts.
People try to live up to whatever standard of conduct seems to be
expected of them by whatever groups they value.

Large stores also advertise their merchandise extensively in local
daily newspapers and by other means. Advertising is primarily the responsibility of top management and of the advertising department, which
works closely with merchandise experts. Such advertising not only tells
what the store has for sale but also expresses its personality. In tests, for
instance, a group of Chicago women, shown advertisements from an
Atlanta, Georgia, department store with which they were quite unfamiliar and from which the store name had been removed, were still able to
describe the nature of the store quite accurately from the appearance of
the ads alone. Readers associate certain printing types, layouts, and
illustrational styles with certain kinds of merchandise and store patterns.
Management must decide what image the store has or wishes to have,
and then choose an appropriate physical advertising style. Projecting a
proper and favorable public image of a store through its advertising
demands the constant cooperation of artists, writers, and advertising-
layout people, as well as those who select and price the merchandise to
be advertised.

However, good advertising alone cannot create store identity, because any large city may have several stores which have nearly the same
types of merchandise, price range, and advertising. Besides, in recent
years store loyalties have weakened because of customers greater exposure to many communications media, their extreme personal mobility by
automobile within an urban area, their change of residence from city to
city—a tendency that brings large numbers of new, unattached customers—and a tremendous growth of population. The problems of downtown stores, in particular, have been rendered so difficult by suburban
movements of population which have placed customers at constantly
increasing distances from the central stores that many of them have
closed.

The changes have led to the increased importance of at least three types of public relations activities in the retail field which are directed toward the establishment of store personality—institutional advertising, community services, and storewide promotions.

None of these are new, but in a time when it is hard to find any exclusive merchandise, lower prices, or favored locations, the feelings of customers about a particular firm because of its people, its record of reliability, or social responsibility, may be more important than ever before. Unless all department stores are to become discount houses, the background of a store, its projects in aid of young or old people, its interest in public education or health or recreation, its support of national goals or needs, its concern with the spiritual side of life as well as the material goods in which stores primarily deal are elements of more importance than ever before. None of these can overcome poor location, bad pricing, unattractive merchandise, or poor advertising. A good store image can assist success; it can make 100 into 120 but cannot stretch 40 into 80.

Among the public relations activities which become of increasing importance today are the storewide promotional events which give new reasons to go shopping at old places. Shopping should be an adventure, an education. If it isn't, what would attract people to one store rather than to another except convenience and price?

A good illustration of a storewide promotional campaign was the program staged a number of years ago by southern California manufacturers and tourist interests. They made up a complete California store promotion, including merchandise, window displays, menus for store restaurants, fashion shows, motion pictures, historic photos, paintings, maps, mission bells and reproductions, and well-known California personalities. Another good example are the many international two-week programs held by Nieman-Marcus of Dallas. This type of promotion elevates a store for a few days above and beyond being just "Scott's Department Store" and makes it exciting, glamorous, and interesting— a genteel combination of sideshow, boardwalk, museum, and travel-bureau window.

Such good storewide promotions are not easy to find; the danger of disappointing the buying public is worse than no event at all; and such attractions cannot be spaced too close together. The fact remains, however, that many big stores are commonplace, offering familiar merchandise at routine prices, in a competent but dull way; and if this is true, the customer is likely to buy where the prices are lowest (or at least where he or she thinks they are lowest) and where the parking is easiest. Most stores could do much more than they have in developing interesting special promotions.

In small stores the personality of the store is primarily the "lengthened shadow" of the proprietor; large businesses, with far more resources, can and should develop a planned image and project it to customers through the mass media by way of public relations techniques.

THE PUBLIC RELATIONS OF INDUSTRY

The fundamental difference between an industry and a retailing or service establishment is that, in most instances, the problem of dealing with a mass of customers is one step removed from the manufacturer rather than his first, constant, and most immediate concern. Industries primarily make things, and retailers sell to the public what other people make.

Small industries usually sell to larger industries or to sales organizations, perhaps moving their goods to distant locations over a wide area. The close relations which small industries need with both their suppliers and their markets are brought about often by personal contact, salesmanship, and perhaps a limited amount of specialized trade-paper advertising. Small industries usually do not need the wide public patronage which is the lifeblood of a retail or service establishment.

There are hundreds of small industries in every large industrial city, specializing in all sorts of products. Each may have from a few dozen to a few hundred employees, and the disappearance or the doubling in size of any one of them would hardly be felt by the city as a whole—crucial as it would be to those directly involved. Their main problems are technical, financial, and personal; and the big currents of general business climate, major labor relations, government actions, and national public attitudes are beyond their control except, to some extent, through associational efforts. Bosses in this type of industry succeed because they know the right people to buy their products, because the supervisors get along well with the employees, the engineers are ingenious in finding ways to pare costs, the bookkeeping office is diligent, everyone says "Good morning," and everyone can apparently be induced to turn out slightly more than a day's work for a day's pay. All these idyllic conditions contribute to success under conditions of sharp competition.

Small industries also have their important communications problems. Sometimes public relations and publicity can be applied to selling their products if they are at all noteworthy or unusual, and may catapult obscure little firms toward success or profitable mergers. Sometimes their problem is just to be known, and even usual public relations efforts may achieve this. Within themselves small industries seldom have the staff resources for specialized public relations development, but they offer a fruitful field for the work of small public relations counseling firms or for the public relations arms of advertising agencies which may also handle their limited trade-paper business. In fact, public relations counseling firms tend, on the one hand, to serve these small organizations which cannot afford to support internal public relations staffs, and on the other hand, tend to give high-level, objective counsel to larger firms whose main need is for new thought and good advice.

Since the problem of the small specialized industry often is visibility in a field of production where it is but one among many, seemingly unrelated ideas in cultural areas such as art, music, or history should not be rejected out of hand simply because they do not seem to be product related. People have varied personal interests and such public relations activities might get their attention and approval. Perhaps, for example, an art exhibit would interest not only professional artists, but also some of the general public and in addition some persons in the industry, as well as getting favorable publicity. The wider experience of outside public relations counseling firms might suggest such ideas where product-centered management would be unaware of them or even hostile.

What we have called a small industry, however, when located in a small-town environment, gains both in stature and responsibility. In a town of 3,000 people it is probably the leading employer, "the plant," usually eagerly welcomed with offers of land, low taxes, and low wage rates. Its small payroll makes the difference between profits and stagnation for local merchants, supports school systems, and upholds town income.

With this prestige, however, a small industry in a small town finds that certain things are expected of it, such as reasonable cleanliness, modest participation in civic affairs, local purchasing when possible, some employee information and activities, and a certain amount of social contact with the townspeople. Laborers may be cheaper in smaller places, but they are also limited in numbers and in skill; and since they have the great automobile-based mobility of all American people, they may always be lured away to distant places by greater opportunities. A firm's cultivation of good will and its reputation as a good place to work may be much more important than it seems. Such public relations functions in small-city industries are usually the responsibility of the general manager, an assistant, and the superintendents, and often involve employee committees and other participation.

Small chain industries in small towns have the additional problems of transient management and of the habit of local personnel to pass the buck to distant headquarters whenever anything is wrong or unpleasant—sometimes to forestall the wrath of unconsulted managers, sometimes to avoid responsibility for unpleasant actions at home. Such chain industry may be respected and feared because of its national connections and financial power, but it may also be less liked than a local plant and so may need additional promotion if it is to become a part of the community. In many cases ideas and inspiration for this will be a part of the job of the chain's national public relations headquarters.

Large industries, employing thousands of people, since they constantly face a breakdown of personal communications, find planned communication programs with many publics a matter of great importance. The old days when the boss could know and talk to everybody are long gone. Employees need to be informed, encouraged, and listened to; the support of stockholders and financial sources becomes vital; the good will of the community is involved in such matters as the recruiting of new employees, fair treatment in regard to local taxes, costs of utilities and services, police and fire protection, and even sales of merchandise. Large industries have much more to give to their communities; but they also have much more at stake, since their capital investments are greater and often not easily moved, and their labor problems may also be more acute.

Large industries are a part of the national or even the world scene. National public opinion, as reflected in Washington, may determine their profit-or-loss statements, and competition exists not only with other similar industries within the nation, but also overseas. Big industries are not necessarily helpless in the face of national and world trends; sometimes alone, and often in association, they have the power to help direct and channel them. Large industries were among the first to recognize the importance of public relations to their growth and prosperity, and they are now among the major employers of public relations specialists in the United States.

THE PUBLIC RELATIONS OF BANKS

Imagine being in a business in which all the merchants operate in about the same way and have the same goods to sell at almost identical prices! Bankers are in just such a business. All banks look much alike, offer much the same customer services in the same way, lend money at the same interest rates, and then pay depositors the same returns upon their savings. This being the case, why should customers prefer one bank to another? Yet they do!

Banks are in competition, not only with each other, but also with savings and loan associations, cooperative credit unions, consumer small loan companies, and the credit departments of all sorts of businesses from automobile dealers to department stores. There are many ways to save or borrow money besides using banks. Investing in stocks and bonds helps corporations—and even the government—to compete with banks for the public's funds; and other uses of money, such as simply spending it, which is attractive in inflationary times, offer a kind of competition.

In addition, the public has a bad image of banks, which is a legacy from a previous generation, compounded out of folk tales of flinthearted bankers and unhappy memories of the great crash of 1929–1933 in which many American bank depositors lost a great deal of money despite the solidity implied by heavy bronze name plates, granite pillars, marble halls, and impeccably dressed bank officials.

To many people money is a strange and corrupting influence, understandable only in small amounts and to be spent for immediate benefits. The ancient stigma against moneylenders clings to "filthy lucre"; its power and use as a measure of success is resented; and the very Greek-temple architectural glory of the typical old-style bank, intended to reassure and impress the small citizen, also frightens and depresses him. Such an awesome temple is obviously intended only for doing business with the demigods and not for such trivial human wants as borrowing money for a new car, refinancing an elderly mortgage, or saving for travel or for a Christmas fund. And in talking about money matters, most people are somewhat abnormal anyway.

Another problem of banks arises from their relations with government. Thanks to the Federal Deposit Insurance Corporation and to closer regulation, bank depositors no longer fear for their savings, but they are often inclined to favor yet more regulation and control. If this amount has worked well, more would work better. Today there seems to be little popular drive toward government banking, as it existed once here in the postal savings plan or in the systems now favored in some other countries, but there might be sometime. And in addition, banks are also involved in many places in the consideration of projected laws about branch banking, taxes upon bank deposits, regulation of hours, interest rates, and limitations upon their fields of lending. Regulation of bank mergers is also often a major issue.

What steps do banks usually take to improve their public relations?

1   The place of business is more important to the image of a bank than it is to many other institutions. Since banks deal in a service, the location must be convenient, primarily to business people. Downtown, this means a prime corner in a good block location: in the rapidly expanding suburbs, it means drive-in facilities and parking.

Since, to uninformed customers, the manifestation of the bank itself is found in the bank building rather than its balance sheets or the integrity or ability of its staff, bank atmosphere presents a problem in public impressions. On the one hand, a bank has to seem substantial and efficient. It can be modern in its architecture or colonial (to suggest sturdy early American virtues of thrift), but in no case can a bank afford to look jerry-built, temporary, or insecure. On the other hand, a bank's atmosphere should be warm, somewhat intimate, and home-like. It should have a floor space large enough for traffic movement, necessary safety features, and private consultation facilities. All these requirements present a problem to the architect which is still only partly solved.

Because the bank buildings are so much a personification of the bank itself, they frequently appear in advertisements and upon letterheads. The modern symbolism for banks is yet to be fully developed; the devices adopted by Chase Manhattan and others are of interest. Meanings come to be attached to symbols quite apart from the nature of the symbols themselves, if indeed they have any meaning alone.

2   Employees are particularly important in service institutions such as banks because their attitudes, competence, and appearance do much to determine public reactions. Unfortunately, the public stereotype of a bank clerk tends to run to an underpaid, meticulous slave who occasionally breaks into the headlines by embezzling a million dollars and running off to Brazil with the spouse of the teller in the next cage. Examining the employees of any modern bank or keeping a statistical check upon the frequency of embezzlement will quickly show that these beliefs have little foundation; but the persistent image shows that public means of communication, such as institutional advertising, news, and feature publicity, as well as actions, might be used more than they are to contradict the impression.

3   As substantial institutions, holding the keys to financial undertakings, banks are expected to lead in community progress. Bank people are expected to work on Community Chest drives, to be active in Rotary and Kiwanis, and to lead in city-planning commissions. Unpaid as it is, this service has its own reward by bringing bankers into contact with many important people with whom they may also do business, and it results in much good publicity.

4   Since thrift is still preached as a virtue in America, banks have a ready entry into the schools with savings plans, personal-budget advice, and economic information.

5   Bank advertising has increased steadily in volume and in quality in recent years. Its tone is particularly important since a bank deals in an intangible service.

6   Minor stunts and activities (always properly dignified) can be of service in establishing the personality of a bank, such as returning all change on a given day in freshly washed and polished coins and newly printed bills, holiday music in a bank lobby, or special tours and receptions.

7   But, above all, since a bank depends upon service, the greatest asset a public relations person can have is a lively, sympathetic, imagination that will enable him to put himself constantly into a customer's place and to think: "How would I feel about that treatment of an overdraft?" "Would it be embarrassing to ask for a loan?" "Why were my check charges $2.50 last month and only $1.80 the month before?" The imperatives in bank public relations are to anticipate questions before they arise and to provide a reservoir of good will against inevitable moments of misunderstanding and dispute.

PUBLIC RELATIONS PROBLEMS OF UTILITIES

The public relations staffs of the telephone companies, the electricity companies, the gas companies, and a smaller number of privately owned city water companies, have often been among the most highly developed in the nation, with the longest experience and the most carefully planned courses of action looking far ahead.

The attention that public utilities pay to public relations is not an accident. Public utilities sell a largely intangible but vital service, and the whole functioning of civilized urban life depends upon their constant watchfulness. No one notices the gas or the electricity or the water until it stops coming, and then everything goes to pieces—homes grow cold, babies cry, hospitals are plunged into blackness, thieves prowl the streets, fires rage unchecked, and even bridge-club arrangements may be seriously interrupted. Public utilities are monopolies regulated by the government, and they hold their monopolistic position by virtue of their promise to give good service efficiently and courteously. If they fail to do so, a clamor for government ownership is always ready to burst forth.

In arguing for a system of private ownership, the utilities contend that because they are business-managed, they operate more efficiently and are more interested in progress, that they pay taxes, give low rates which have been relatively reduced over the years, are good employers and good citizens, and earn only a reasonable profit. Their continued existence is evidence that most Americans believe these things to be true.

They are attacked by those who would like to see more government ownership of public services. They are charged with too high profits and sometimes with refusal to extend their service into unprofitable areas. Critics remember that some private power companies were slow in supplying remote rural areas and that their recalcitrance encouraged the development of the federally financed Rural Electrification Administration. Water-power developments, also, have usually fallen into Federal hands, since the multiplicity of river uses—flood control, irrigation, navigation, and the like—often seem to justify the cost of high dams which would be uneconomical for power production alone. Water power, however, is often seasonal, depending upon varying river flow; when the need arises, as it did in the case of the Tennessee Valley Authority electrical system, to add steam-power generating plants to help balance the load, private power companies complain bitterly that their domain is being invaded by subsidized competition.

A big, unsolved struggle was precipitated by the atomic generation of electric power. The wartime birth of atomic energy and the related government control of fissionable matter gave a running start to the advocates of public power in this field, and the challenge was not refused by the private power companies. Various atomic reactors and associated electric generating plants, both private and public and of several designs, have been built, many of them at a much greater cost than could be offset by any present savings in generating electricity by conventional coal plants. Construction costs have also often proved higher than anticipated. In addition, there has been a constant dispute about the safety of atomic power and the ultimate disposal of spent but still radioactive fuel. But the need for electricity increases and oil as a source of fuel grows more expensive.

An additional public relations problem for electric and gas public utilities has been a sharp increase in their prices to customers since 1973, brought about by increased prices for gas and oil on a world-wide basis. In addition, the extremely cold winter of 1976–77 resulted for the first time in widespread shortages of natural gas for industries. From trying to sell more use of electricity and gas, utilities have had to switch their advertising and promotion to conservation. The problem has become not one of sales but of supply and retaining independence.

The extent of public ownership of utilities varies. Water plants are usually owned by the city or by a water district, perhaps because water is the oldest utility, most common in its supply and need, and is thought of, along with air, as a general good. Although predominantly in private hands, the electric power industry is often city-owned, or is federally owned in connection with most major water power production, or is cooperatively owned in rural REA areas; in one state, Nebraska, it is entirely publicly owned. Gas, because of its distant sources of supply, is usually privately owned. Telephone systems, with the exception of a few small-town or rural systems, are almost entirely privately owned, largely through the American Telephone and Telegraph Company and its many Bell Telephone Company subsidiaries. (In England, the telephone service is operated by the Post Office.)

The private utility business has had its historic problems, also. During the 1920s Samuel Insull and others pyramided holding company upon holding company, only to see their unreal empires collapse with the ruin of many small investors in the 1929 crash and give the whole utility business a bad name. The conspicuous expenditures of some utility heads in this period upon big homes and estates, company-financed parties, and hunting lodges were poor public relations also; but these tycoons were not alone in their extravagance.

Because utility services are a necessity, the public feels a sense of helplessness when faced with a rate raise because it can secure no alternative supply. Increasing the price of butter a few cents provokes no great outcry, because people feel that using margarine or using less butter is an answer, whether they actually do so or not. But it is not easy to get along with less electricity, less gas, less water, or less telephone service nowadays; in fact, modern living demands more and more of these services all the time; automatic controls and labor-saving devices multiply as suburban living expands. Despite more efficient production, rising costs caused by general inflation and increased fuel prices have forced utility costs upwards (even though the advance has been perhaps less than for other cost-of-living items); and, in any event, more services used mean higher bills. Every one of these rate raises and higher bills involves potential political danger.

The public relations solutions to these problems attempted by private public utilities have been numerous and largely successful.

Employees are carefully selected and are trained and promoted from within the ranks. Long service, steady pay, and resulting loyalty are the rule. Employee information services are excellent, and good citizenship is encouraged and rewarded.

Utility stockholders are sought from local service areas where their interest in dividends and in company growth will help counter their customer interests in the lowest possible rates. Stockholder information services are excellent.

A complete financial picture is presented to the employees, the stockholders, and the general public. Since utilities are semipublic institutions anyway, and are required to report their affairs in detail, a complete report is a natural step, not revealing anything that would not be generally known.

Plans for expansion and the continuance of good service are always well publicized. The many benefits obtained from good public utility services and the need for conservation are stressed.

Good citizenship and the boosting of local service areas are continuous. Typical activities include advertising campaigns advocating the location of business in a certain state, and the erection of large highway poster boards outside service-area towns telling about their outstanding advantages and welcoming visitors. Awards may be given for civic improvements or for the use of modern agricultural methods; schools may be aided and worthy causes assisted generally. Many of these efforts could also be performed by local chambers of commerce, by service clubs, and by other groups of interested citizens, but the fact is that often no such responsibility would be assumed if the utility company did not take the lead.

Both from necessity and long practice, public utility companies have become among the nation's best practitioners of public relations.

THE PROBLEMS OF PUBLIC TRANSPORTATION

Trains, buses, airlines, ferries, and a few steamer services are public utilities also, but the conditions under which they operate are very different from those prevailing among the gas, electricity, or telephone service companies.

A public bus line in a city may have a franchised monopoly, and a suburban railroad may enjoy a similar privilege; yet in these days of automobile travel and decentralization, both companies probably face low profits or losses. Many people have alternatives to using their services, and such transportation companies are no longer the sole suppliers that they once were.

In intercity travel the competition can be even greater. Railroads, buses, and airlines compete with other similar ground or air services and with each other, and all battle the private automobiles for passenger trade and the trucks and waterways for freight haulage. They undergo regulation, but except in isolated instances, have no monopoly. Also, in contrast to the services of electricity or gas utilities, those of a transportation company are visible and differ in quality: This airline is felt to be better than that one; this train has a more convenient or scenic routing; the flight attendants are more polite; or the meals are better on that airline. Although feelings may not be so keen as they once were, people develop strong attachments or dislikes for particular lines and for types of transportation service, such as buses or subways. Public transportation has character, color, and occasional accidents—a physical being and public presence not shared to the same extent by water, gas, or telephone services. Travel plays a great part in customers' life experience as is shown by rail-fan clubs, steamboat buffs, the tears shed at the departure of the last streetcar, and transport museums maintained by enthusiastic amateurs.

Public carriers have two main problems—getting customers and obtaining government approval for adequate routes and rates. The private business of transportation is hopelessly intertwined with government through the public interest, the use of publicly built or maintained highways and waterways, postal and other subsidies, a qualified right of eminent domain in the construction of routes, and a great effect upon the "public interest, convenience, and necessity." On the highways and waterways, government shares its routes with private operators ranging from yachtsmen and small-car owners to farmers' trucks, fleets of Great Lakes ore ships, and foreign-flag shipowners who also ply the inland seas, rivers, and harbors.

The main contacts which the public has with transportation companies come in the fields of equipment, employees, and information.

Modern attractive equipment, well cared for and publicized, is fundamental to good public relations in transportation.

Employee courtesy and efficiency also contribute to favorable public reaction to a transportation system. They can be developed through

reful selection of employees, training, rewards and recognition, a sup-
ly of general background information, and specific informational help
as needed. A breakdown on a railway commuter line, for example, may
make thousands of office workers late getting home for supper and is
certain to result in scores of inquiries addressed to conductors and brake-
men the following morning. These employees should have answers or
should at least know what to do or say if they do not have the answers.

The public has so much interest in transportation that it should
always be fully informed. It should be told particularly about accidents
and their causes, changes in equipment, and route changes. Press relations should be open, and informative publicity releases and advertising
should be used frequently.

THE PUBLIC RELATIONS OF THE MEDIA
OF MASS COMMUNICATIONS

Newspapers, radio and television stations, and magazines are generally
thought of in connection with their own communicatory content—their
news stories, entertainment, and advertising. Yet they are also institutions in their own right and have public images of their own. Readers
may feel that one newspaper is reliable but dull, and that another,
perhaps less trustworthy, is more interesting. A listener may criticize a
television station for making lots of money although it contributes little
to the community. One magazine may seem to speak with authority
while another is ignored. Why? In the past two or three decades, progressive publishers and broadcasters have become aware of these differences,
and public relations departments, or promotion departments which concern themselves to a large extent with public relations, are now almost
standard on all larger American newspapers, broadcasting stations, and
magazines.

Newspapers

Most American newspapers today are published in only one locality,
usually a city, and most are also monopolies in their home territory—
largely because publishing two big newspapers in any but the very largest
cities would be as economically wasteful as supporting two light companies or two telephone companies. Although newspapers provide an information service almost in the nature of a public utility, they cannot be
regulated as utilities are, because they have the right of free speech—
"freedom of the press." Newspaper employees come into contact with

the public frequently. If the news staff turns out a good publication, if the circulation department distributes it well, and if the advertising people are accurate and enterprising, what more does the publication need to do than to be satisfied and to count the dollars?

Quite a bit! Readers expect their newspapers to do the expected things well and complain sharply if they don't, but to achieve the greatest public respect and liking, a newspaper must go much above and beyond the ordinary call of duty. A newspaper is a personality, and a planned public relations effort helps to invest it with the strongest and most attractive character. A newspaper speaks for itself only to a degree; it also needs to be spoken about and to act. People do not necessarily know all about a newspaper because they read it and because the paper itself is a medium of communication. Readers usually ask certain questions:

1   Who works for the paper? What kind of people are they, and why should a reader feel confident in relying on them for information?

2   What does the paper do to better its community, the nation, and the world, beyond distributing news? Vital as this function is, it should imply an obligation of leadership, provided it is not carried to the point of domination.

3   What is the history of the publication? What is its personality?

Such major needs of newspaper public relations go far beyond the best standard operating procedure of simply producing a good product and selling it well.

But why attempt newspaper public relations at all? Won't virtue (in a communications medium) be apparent and speak for itself? The best answer is to engage in research. Get public-opinion surveyors to go around the streets, stores, and homes of a town talking to people. Find out how many are suspicious of newspaper motives, convinced that news is being suppressed or altered, resentful of the power of the newspaper, and unaware of its citizenship and service. Ask the same questions of young people in high schools or colleges. Talk to their teachers.

A newspaper cannot expect to be popular with all of the people all of the time. Publishing the news in itself brings out enough unpleasant facts to make enemies, and errors and mistakes inevitably creep in; but there is no good reason why a newspaper's vices and failures should always be apparent and its virtues unknown. It might profit by trying to be understood and respected.

A good newspaper is expected to report the facts as fully, accurately, and completely as its own income and area of service allow it to do; to express its editorial opinions but to keep them in plainly recognizable editorial space; and to present also the reasoned opinions of others upon various sides of important current issues. Then it is expected to go an extra mile or two by aiding others to achieve community and world betterment in many ways and by being a unifying force and speaking for its constituency, the readers.

Newspapers today no longer operate in the news vacuum they occupied almost alone in the early 1920s. Readers can listen to or look at many other conveyors of information, and the advertiser can usually spend money in a wide variety of ways. A newspaper today, though it can succeed without planned public relations, cannot be so well read, so much respected, so influential, and so profitable as it might be with it.

Radio and Television

Radio and television differ from newspapers in that they usually face heavy competition from other broadcasting stations; they have no physical being which people can look at and feel as they do a newspaper or a magazine; and they are usually largely devoted to entertainment. In addition, the content of radio and television is principally sponsored by advertising and can frequently be heard or seen on several stations in the same form by the same listeners; even news and public-service programs frequently come from national-network sources rather than from a local source. Most stations, also, do not express editorial views, and both their function as a common carrier and the FCC regulations make this reticence more the rule than the exception.

For these reasons, establishing a vital personality for a local broadcasting station is somewhat more difficult and perhaps less immediately necessary than for a newspaper; but it is often vigorously and sometimes successfully attempted. To the listener or viewer, however, the personality of the station lies to a great degree in the content of its broadcasts, and public relations faces a problem influencing this public image and in going beyond it. The main problem is to make a nonmaterial broadcasting signal into a real personality by means of visual devices, background information, public activities, and promotions which demonstrate effectiveness and service. The more "real" a popular station can be, the easier it is to sell advertising and to exert local influence. Getting listeners, however, depends primarily upon good programming and promotion.

Magazines

Magazines are usually directed toward special reader audiences and are not rooted in a place as are newspapers, or even so localized as broadcasting stations. A fishing magazine, for example, selects a sportsman audience from over a wide area; a farming magazine goes to farmers; and a machinists' magazine goes to machinists. Like newspapers, magazines have a certain physical being; they look and feel a certain way. No one is likely to mistake *Fortune* or *Business Week* for *Successful Farming* or *Playboy*. Each is right for its audience.

Because of these specialized audiences, magazines should by nature have more personality than any of the other printed media. With the exception of the few large weeklies of truly general national circulation, magazines should express themselves more fully and be more active within their special fields than other journals. Their public relations should be an extension and personification of this magazine character in visible ways, so that readers and advertisers can be aware of its personality. It should create reader loyalty and interest, aid renewals, and prepare the way for the constant problem of successful direct-mail solicitation of subscriptions over a wide area—a matter which grows increasingly expensive and difficult as competition increases. Yet surprisingly little is done in effective public relations by many magazines, perhaps because of the diffusion of the audiences or perhaps because of the hard struggle for circulation which absorbs all their energies.

Magazine public relations often takes the form of reprint books of previously published content, award programs within the magazine's field of special interest, and general publicity about writers and articles. Much more could be done—for example, sponsoring seminars upon problems suggested by the magazine's preoccupations, aiding the education of young people, and developing new areas of interest or of profit for readers and advertisers.

THE PUBLIC RELATIONS OF AGRICULTURE

The phrase "public relations of agriculture" does not refer to the problem of how to reach and influence agricultural people, which was discussed in Chapter 4, but rather to the problems of relations with the general national public shared by American agriculture and its associated activities, such as food processing, the manufacture of agricultural machinery, and agricultural education.

American agriculture today is far different from what it was only a generation ago. The great changes affecting the practice of public relations in the United States in that period have also greatly affected farming. As machinery, new crops, and new fertilizers have increased yields and lessened the need for manpower, farms have become fewer and larger, subsistence farming has diminished, and its operators have drifted off to the cities to become factory hands or gasoline service-station operators. Many farmers are now part-time factory employees themselves, with divided interests. Cities have penetrated rural areas, and new highways have brought city and country close together. The amount of capital required to establish a large farming operation has become so huge (perhaps hundreds of thousands of dollars, if a farmer starts from the beginning in a typical Midwestern corn-hog operation, for example) that it is no longer possible for a young couple to begin real farming with a few thousand dollars, build their own house, and raise a family to grow up on the land they have cultivated.

Farming has become a large and complex business, as efficient, in a less apparent way to city people, as the impressive automated factories which have been so much discussed. Every year fewer farmers turn out more crops, and the percentage of farmers in the United States declines. In 1910, for example, there were 32 million farmers in the United States. By 1970 there were only 2,730,000 farms in the United States. In 1976 there were only eight million Americans living on farms.

Farm operation is a continuous, long-term program. If a dairy farmer has a surplus of milk, he cannot just close down the factory, lay off the hands, go into another line, or wait for better times. He has to keep producing (in fact, he is driven into producing more at lower cost) or go out of the dairy business entirely, sometimes at considerable loss —as many have done. A cow factory is geared to nature, and production depends upon rainfall, temperature, and other factors which the farmer cannot control. Moreover, many American farm products compete with those from other parts of the world which supply identical quality at sometimes lower production cost. Farming is an atomistic business, composed of many millions of operators who, unlike a smaller number of industrialists, would find great physical difficulty in getting together to agree upon what prices to charge and what amounts to produce. The farmer's wages are the profits.

Under these circumstances, American farmers early turned to political ways of bettering their lot and getting what they considered to be a fairer share of the national income.

Alliances between farmers and labor groups have succeeded very little, since farmers want higher prices for the food they sell and lower prices for the farm labor they buy and for the many manufactured products—the tractors, fencing, or fertilizers—which go into farming; and laborers want lower prices for food, higher wages, and perhaps less of their taxes spent upon farm-price supports. Many industrial interests are at variance with farmers' goals also, preferring lower prices for food or raw material, and higher prices for manufactured goods. Often labor and industry have combined to raise wages and prices together, at the same time complaining about government efforts to regulate farm production and to keep up farm prices.

Thus the agricultural problem in the United States increasingly involves public relations and public understanding. City people are often ignorant of the changes in modern farming, of its efficiency, and the size of its investment. The conditions of individual farming force American farmers to engage in political action for the regulation and pricing of their production which is comparable to that possible in many industries through the actions of large companies and industry-wide unions. The facts about American farming are not well told and are little understood, and a farm stereotype arises in the public mind in which a robber baron succeeds the bucolic hick, with resulting danger for the future understanding of the national economy. Even if farmers today constitute only a small percentage of the population, they are important and mean much more than this figure would suggest in total purchasing power, stability, and influence upon the national well-being.

THE PUBLIC RELATIONS OF TRADE ASSOCIATIONS

Every important type of businessperson in the nation from furrier to plumber, from dog breeder to small retail merchant, belongs to one or more trade associations, each with its secretary and staff, its publications, meetings, and goals. The fact that trade associations exist in such profusion indicates that they serve a need in a modern democratic economy which could not be met in any other manner.

Trade associations exchange information, promote the sale or development of products, establish standards, regulate the activities of their members, and enable their membership to speak with a united voice on economic, social, and governmental problems which may affect their general welfare.

In many cities, for example, when charity solicitors approach a merchant for a donation, they will be referred to the secretary of the

Retail Merchants Association, who will then give them an amount that the members have previously decided upon, take the matter under advisement, or say "no." In this way, individual merchants avoid being whipsawed by implied threats of pressure against their businesses. Or an association, such as the California Fruit Growers Association, may become famous for developing a high-quality orange produced by its members and then advertising and promoting it so well that oranges become a standard breakfast food and the brand name "Sunkist" achieves national acceptance.

Much of an association secretary's time is taken up in public relations activities, both internal among members and external. An association secretary has to keep members informed and enthusiastic about the organization's progress and activities. This internal publicity requires meetings, presentations, booklets, letters, perhaps motion pictures, and usually magazines or newspapers to communicate to the membership what is going on. Recruiting new members is often also a major activity, because some members are always lost through deaths and resignations.

Externally, the work of an association may be even more important, since often only an association can do the big job of telling the public about the merits of a general type of product.

Associations also busy themselves with less immediate public relations activities such as awards programs, exhibitions, general publicity, and a mixture of product and institutional advertising. In small associations the general secretary has many jobs, including public relations; in large associations, several people specialize in areas such as membership, legislative representation, labor relations, and public relations. But however handled, public relations, involving research into public attitudes, actions, communications, and evaluation of results, either formally or informally, is an important associational activity.

ADDITIONAL READINGS

Most special-use fields of public relations change rapidly, such as the problems of electric or gas utilities. So most current information in areas of practice such as this will be found in the scores of references to magazine articles listed in the latest volumes of the public relations bibliographies rather than in book form.

Belden, Clark, *Public Relations and Association Executives.* (Washington, D.C.:
    American Society of Association Executives, 1959.)
Jacobs, Laurence W., *Advertising and Promotion For Retailing.* (Glenview, Ill.:
    Scott, Foresman, 1972.) [Closely related.]

Miller, Robert W., *Profitable Community Relations For Small Business.* (Washington, D.C.: U. S. Government Printing Office, 1961.)

Roalman, Arthur R., *Communications For Savings Institutions.* (Chicago: Savings Institutions Marketing Society of America, 1974.)

Rucker, Frank W., and Bert Stolpe, *Tested Newspaper Promotion.* (Ames: Iowa State University Press, 1960.)

Sullivan, Frank C., *Crisis of Confidence.* (Canaan, N.H.: Phoenix Publishing, 1977.) [Deals with public utility public relations.]

Chapter 6

More Special Users of Public Relations

The motivation for public relations activities by profit-making organizations is quite clear. Many other groups, ranging from doctors and architects to union heads and from government bureau chiefs to public school superintendents, are equally interested in public understanding and appreciation because the fortunes of each member of a group rise and fall, to a considerable extent, with the prestige and success of the fellowship. While perhaps two-thirds of all public relations activity is practiced in behalf of the area generally called "business," a large and growing proportion is practiced in behalf of professional associations and labor, welfare, religious, and governmental groups. Some of these groups are discussed in this chapter.

The fact that public relations is not exclusively a child of business should occasion no surprise, because its uses in the fields of religious persuasion and the support of governments, although somewhat obscured in modern American society, are historically among its oldest and strongest manifestations and are today more important abroad than in this country.

THE PUBLIC RELATIONS OF THE PROFESSIONS

What is a profession? There is no easy answer, because with the proliferation of specialized knowledge, the number of highly skilled and learned
human occupations has increased so much in recent years that the former simple listing of the professions as the clergy, law, medicine, the
military, and a few others has become obsolete.

There are, however, several hallmarks of a profession. One is its
possession of an organized body of special knowledge which cannot be
acquired except by long and difficult study. A layman seeks the services
of professional persons—a lawyer or doctor, for example—because of
what they know that the ordinary layman cannot know: the rights of
citizens under the law or the effect of medicine upon disease. Another
hallmark is the requirement of a recognized standard of competence to
practice. Sometimes this may be schooling alone; often it includes examination and licensing or certification by the state or by an association of
the profession involved. Another professional characteristic is independence. Professionals do not have to work as part of an organization. They
carry their assets primarily in their heads and can practice anywhere that
their services are in demand, either as an independent practitioner or as
a hired part of an organization. Finally, the professional person under-
takes a responsibility to use his or her talents for the public welfare. The
doctor vows to assist whenever aid is needed in an emergency. If she
makes a discovery, instead of hiding it, she shares it with her fellows and
with the world by reporting it in a medical journal or elsewhere.

The independent professional person, say the lawyer, is free to take
clients or to reject them; yet it is a rule in the courts that everyone should
be helped to obtain legal counsel if needed in criminal actions. Although
the clergy are usually closely organized into associations, they do not
strike as a means of protesting and fixing their compensation, but instead
negotiate individually. Often, too, "good form" prevents professional
people from advertising their merits directly; they must become known
by their good works and by actions which might be called public relations.

What are the goals which the professions usually seek to attain by
means of public relations?

Two of the most common are the attraction of new capable entrants
into the profession and the provision for their proper education. Obviously, the profession must not die out or be unable to provide adequate
service. British lawyers (solicitors), for example, were concerned at one
time because the number of young men wishing to enter the practice of
law in that country was about the same as it was in 1914, despite a great

increase in population and fields of practice. To attract promising young men, pamphlets were issued, meetings, and scholarships arranged, and members showed their keen personal interest in candidates.

Professional groups are also concerned with legislative actions which may raise or lower their standards. What qualifications should be required of those appointed as government "engineers," for example? Or who should be legally eligible to practice pharmacy?

Definitions of the proper boundaries of practice are also of concern. Prescribing and making eyeglasses was done by optometrists. But who would be responsible for contact lenses which fit directly over the eyeball? The ophthalmologists (doctors of medicine) felt that the latter prescriptions should be their function because contact lenses may exercise an actual physical effect upon the eye itself. A law or legal decision might be needed to embody the answer.

Freedom of private practice, as against government-controlled medicine, is a goal in dispute. Tax laws, to equalize the advantages and privileges of professionals and business people in computing income tax deductions and payments, are much desired. General public esteem, which will cause their services to be more sought after and better rewarded, is another goal of professional groups. All these can be obtained largely through public relations methods.

An illustration of the ways of creating greater public appreciation of services is the work of the many chapters of the American Institute of Architects. Many of the new stores erected by businesses in a middle-sized Western city, for example, were ugly because of their unimaginative cracker-box lines; not only were they unsightly but they were destined to last for years. How could the business community be imbued with a desire to make a better-looking city? How could builders be made more aware that good architecture is a business "plus," attracting favorable attention and conferring personality upon the stores which are well-housed? How could church or school groups be led to plan not only beautiful buildings, but also to make the greatest use of available space and sites and to plan for expansion? The architects' answers to these questions lie largely within the field of public relations. In one western city, for example, the architects held an "orchids and onions" contest for the best and worst buildings finished during the year.

THE PUBLIC RELATIONS OF LABOR UNIONS

Outside of the ranks of their own membership and those closely connected with it, American labor unions notoriously suffer from extremely poor public relations. Why? The truth seems to be that their publicity creates a worse rather than a better impression. In a strike, for example, by the nature of events the union is usually cast in the role of the aggressor, wanting more money or other benefits; its demands are news. The company merely says "no"—an attitude which is somewhat less news. If a strike begins, the inconveniences of a great many people provide even more news; and if any violence occurs, the news reaches the headlines. Finally, if the strike is won and pay raises are granted, the company may promptly increase its prices, and the higher cost to the public is news again. In an inflationary period it may be necessary for a union to seek wage increases, but the actions needed to get them usually result in a very poor press.

Electioneering for office within a union also creates a press problem because the campaigning is conducted in the limelight, with a publicity that corporation managements seldom meet except when dirty linen gets washed in a proxy fight. To get elected, a union official may have to make promises loudly, plainly, and belligerently, often expressing more hope than the final settlement will justify. These extravagant statements may all get into the news, while company counterparts, working quietly with a small board of directors and officers, are seldom heard by the public except in prepared statements.

Racketeers have also disfigured the faces of several unions, and the evil and arrogance of these unsavory parasites gets more than their full share of attention.

Many nonunion citizens fear the political power of unions or regard them as special-interest groups, solely out to benefit their own members at the expense of society. Unions have, for the most part, done an excellent job of selling unionism to their own members; they are often still feared and disliked by other segments of society. What can unions do about this problem? In many cases they supply their side of information about economic matters fairly well, but their arguments fall far short of persuading many citizens that unions are interested in improving the products of industry, in greater productivity, and in other contributions to the general welfare. If they are thus altruistic, they should demonstrate their good intentions.

Unions have a difficult course to steer. They can hardly control government and are in danger of being further controlled by it, to the detriment of their freedom to bargain. Although public understanding and liking are essential to union freedom, unions have not fully accepted the fact. The public relations of business are ahead of union public relations because business understands the value of communication with the public and is more willing to pay what it is worth. Unions frequently incline to pay hired intellectuals only what average union members would regard as right on their own scale—something below the market price. This parsimony, coupled with insecurity and lower social status, has not attracted many of the best public relations experts to union representation.

As American economic life grows more complex and more influenced by world events, constantly greater government intervention may be expected. This means that take-home pay may be decided at the ballot box rather than at the bargaining table, and that therefore public support is vital. Both unions and business see the handwriting on the wall, but their reactions thus far have not always been in line with their awareness.

CAUSE GROUPS

One development of recent years has been the increase in the number of public pressure or promotional groups seeking to advance various causes —often by very capable public relations techniques and employing, sometimes as volunteers, public relations professionals as sophisticated as those formerly found only in large corporations. Environmental, consumer, race, and sexual equality groups would be examples. The first problem of such groups often is simply to be known and to be taken seriously, a need in which they are often assisted by the news media because of their use of controversy, attack, and visual demonstrations. This step is often fairly easily accomplished because of the nature of the media concept of news. In many ways the news media allow themselves to be easily manipulated by such action groups and the result is to give an impression of much greater public support than they actually enjoy which may give them unwarranted political influence. But cause groups need to be taken seriously because frequent repetition of ideas, even if unsupported by many facts, gives them credibility and in time may result in real influence unless countered. Being too proud to reply leaves the field to those who are talking.

THE PUBLIC RELATIONS PROBLEMS OF SOCIAL
WELFARE

The Red Cross, the Cancer Society, the League for the Hard of Hearing, the local United Fund, the YMCA, and a host of other organizations which minister to the needs of the American people depend for their

support entirely upon successful public relations. Big donors are important, but thousands of little donors and volunteer workers actually carry
forward the activities of these organizations. When the public is informed, urged, and encouraged, it gives to the tune of about a billion
dollars a year in drives alone. Nowhere else in the world is there a
phenomenon comparable to this American charitable instinct.

The public relations men and women who promote these causes are
in an enviable situation in many ways. The worthiness of their goals is
usually beyond question. Everyone wants less cancer, better hearing, or
the development of youth, and the promoters find great personal satisfaction in assisting these causes. It is usually easy to find good friends and
willing allies in the work.

The American press is also unusually kind to the publicity which
emanates from social welfare sources, sometimes almost too much so;
usually all that editors or broadcasters ask is that the stories approach
reasonable standards of news interest, and often the standards are somewhat bent. The suspicious eye that greets commercial news releases is
largely absent, and often the welfare personnel's chief problem, particularly in small cities, is to find time to supply all the news and pictures
that the papers are willing to print and all the story aspects that television
can handle.

A great deal of advertising for welfare causes is frequently available
through donations of unsponsored time on radio or television and of
billboards by outdoor-advertising companies. Portions of their regular
advertising space or gratuitous notices are frequently given also by business firms in their newspaper ads. Show windows are easily obtained if
there is good material with which to fill them. City authorities are lenient
about the use of posters, banners, and other street decorations. In fact,
publicity is so readily available that many people who inform the public
about social welfare are inclined to depend upon it too much, forgetting
that being known is not necessarily the same as being understood or
being liked.

As business and labor organizations and professional groups have
become more conscious, in recent years, of the value of public relations,
they have also become very willing to lend their manpower to welfare
efforts for the sake of the public goodwill which this type of activity
returns to them. This is particularly true of show people, of the utilities,
of large department stores, of local big industries, and of large service
organizations such as insurance companies, in which someone from the
large staff can be assigned to help without too much loss in operating
efficiency.

Unpaid volunteers are the backbone of all welfare drives. They come from the local welfare groups and from other people whom they are able to contact through clubs, civic associations, women's groups, schools, churches, and similar organizations. Almost always a sponsoring "letter-head committee" of the leaders of these organizations is used to give validity to the group's participation.

With complete penetration of factories, offices, and professional organizations, American welfare drives frequently resemble a voluntary system of taxation, having quotas, offering payroll deductions, and exerting considerable social and business pressure to ensure compliance. It may be argued, of course, that such voluntary taxation is better than that imposed by government.

The resemblance to taxation is particularly marked in United Fund or Community Chest efforts, in which the business and other interests of the city get together to limit the nuisance and ineffectiveness of a large number of separate drives by combining them into one major effort which they and their employees pledge to support. "Tin cup" street-corner collections every other day dull the edge of charity to the point where only nickels and dimes are collected, whereas payroll deductions, pledged once a year, get dollars. In united drives, the less glamorous but useful welfare organizations, such as the rehabilitation of injured workers or aid to broken families, tend to get a fairer share, while the tear-jerking drives for the relief of human ailments which excite the most sympathy are perhaps somewhat handicapped, since their stronger human interest appeals are submerged in the general effort.

Yet united drives, although logical, also face some serious public relations problems.

Because united giving bears some of the marks of taxation, it lacks the spiritual uplift of more personal donation to specific causes or needs in which a more personal interest may be involved. How can such satisfaction be supplied?

Unpaid volunteers may make zealous fund solicitors, but they can also be clumsy and hard to control; they have been known to apply open pressure or even to insult those whom they ask for gifts; sometimes they are not well informed as to the uses of the money and show their ignorance. Obtaining, educating, and rewarding volunteers is a big job, closely related to the public relations success of the organization involved.

The public frequently misunderstands the activities and goals of such voluntary welfare organizations. Part of this misapprehension springs from garbled stories given out by aid recipients who may be

ignorant or emotionally unstable; part arises from the natural ↑
ness of human nature, which likes to report evil or folly in those s↑
to be doing good; and some is a compensation mechanism. Th↑
do not wish to give often excuse themselves by saying that the cause to
which they have been asked to contribute is not worthy anyway, charging wastefulness in the collection of funds, carelessness in their use, or
even misappropriation. Frequently the very size of charity budgets is
misunderstood because they look so huge that small-money thinkers
have difficulty in accepting them. There are also critics who persist in
transferring charges of government-welfare wrongdoing to the private-
agency field.

To meet these problems, public relations people in voluntary social
welfare organizations must:

1 Conduct valid and adequate research studies to determine public
attitudes which may affect the success of their efforts—studies which are
often more complex and difficult than those required by industry.
2 Interpret the work of their organizations in human terms both
to inform the public and to give a feeling of satisfaction to those who
participate in its support.
3 Whenever possible, correct misconceptions immediately.
4 Develop and support their campaign organizations, both the
small paid staff and the large number of unpaid volunteers, with information and with aid in meeting the public by such assistance as plans for
open houses, meetings, and informal conversation.
5 Be alert to changes in basic public attitudes.

THE SPECIAL PUBLIC RELATIONS PROBLEMS OF HOSPITALS

In recent years American hospitals have unfortunately had to depend for
their necessary growth almost completely upon the goodwill and understanding of the public under conditions which have tended to make their
public relations bad more often than good. The dice have been loaded
against them for several reasons.

Hospitals are not profit-making institutions. Few, if any, have stockholders, and they are not in the habit of declaring dividends. Operated
as a public service, hospitals have usually been established by churches,
welfare associations, or communities, and are dependent upon gifts or
taxes for all of their expansion and often for much of their daily operating
costs. Although a growing national population has made necessary continual expansion of facilities, bed capacity has sometimes lagged behind

needs. The result has been long waiting lists, worry, and ill will. Sometimes hospitals have been overbuilt and expensive equipment duplicated. Hospital rates are high—disastrously so for people of moderate or small incomes who may be caught without the help of hospital insurance. Both inflation and increased services have contributed to much higher per day costs, although because of better treatment, the average patient spends much less time in a hospital now than formerly, when hospitals were largely "lying-in-bed" establishments.

The turnover of hospital help has been high, and training has been a serious problem. Patients and their friends and relatives are often in an abnormal state of mind, prone to be upset at even minor faults and inclined to take the word of anyone from a sweeper to an orderly as the latest medical gospel. There are also some inevitable losses of life and even some errors in hospital procedure, and these lamentable occurrences are magnified out of all reason and remembered while the high percentage of success is accepted as commonplace.

A natural friction exists between hospitals and the press, which wants to know facts about patients that doctors may not wish to release or seeks interviews that administrators are not willing to permit. Photographers wish to take pictures that hospital administrators feel interfere with their work or invade the patient's right of privacy. The press is usually ready to magnify hospital errors to the entire public.

Finally, behind each private hospital lurks the possibility of government control, either through a take-over made necessary by financial collapse or through public dissatisfaction with its operations or simply to lower costs. The possibility is particularly distasteful to the medical profession.

It is fair to assume that if things are left to themselves with no planned effort, the public relations of most hospitals will at least be somewhat ineffective. This unenviable condition hospitals share with such diverse bedfellows as labor unions, police departments, public utilities, and public education. What can be done about it?

Obvious first steps in hospital public relations would include analysis of the opinions of important publics, public information about goals and methods, careful employee selection and training, staff indoctrination with the principles of public relations, constant efforts to achieve good relations with the press upon a basis of mutual understanding, efforts to give patients greater participation in activities, and the favorable involvement in the work of the hospital of as many persons and groups in the community as possible. Because of the turnover of the staff and patients, this continuous program should be as much a part of standard operating procedure as cleanliness.

THE SPECIAL PROBLEM OF CONVALESCENT HOMES

There are a great many old, infirm, ill, or senescent people in the United States today. The expectancy of longer life, the spread of social security payments and of pensions which give at least small amounts of money for support, and the changed housing and living habits of the younger generation have all altered the picture from that of a half-century ago. Then, when grandfather became infirm, he usually got the northwest corner bedroom in the big white wooden house of the son or daughter who was least burdened with a large family. Other children contributed to his support, if need be, and he was fed and cared for to the best of his family's ability. Low-cost, readily available domestic help often eased the burden. But since today's houses have almost no room and little domestic help is available, other solutions must be found.

The chief answer is to be seen all over the country in the many old hotels, mansions, and more modest houses which have been converted into nursing or convalescent homes. In addition many new buildings have been built just for this purpose. Some are run well and some poorly; the costs vary and so do the degrees of efficiency; and all share the same serious public relations problems.

Many of the relatives who place their kin in these homes suffer feelings of severe guilt because they are not personally taking care of the older people, and they may take out their feelings upon the home management. The inmates themselves often complain to their relatives when they visit, out of the need for human sympathy or because of illness. When things go wrong in these homes, when cases of mistreatment, injuries, or fires occur, they always make the headlines. Worst of all, because life in such a home leads to the unhappy end of the road that all people dislike so much, the bitterness of human mortality and decline overshadows the whole atmosphere of nursing homes.

What can be done—not to meet the whole problem of care for the aged of which the present rather haphazard system of nursing homes may or may not be an adequate solution—but rather to obtain the best public understanding and support for those nursing-home operators of today who are doing an adequate job? There is, of course, no substitute for adequacy, trained skill, kindness, and a sincere desire to do the best with the resources at hand.

Standards of practice might be adopted by nursing-home associations and made public, so that they come to mean something in the identification of well-run nursing homes. Homes which cannot or will not adhere to these standards could be excluded from the association. The interest of local communities in nearby homes should be enlisted through contacts with churches, schools, women's groups, and civic groups, so that elderly people will not feel forgotten and also so that the public can see both the good and the bad of the system. Further, community interest should be enlisted by feature stories about interesting people in the homes or about their present accomplishments and needs. Some kinds of open houses might be arranged, and better plans for excursions or visits by patients off the grounds might be worked out. A system of regular communication between patients and home management and also between patients and their relatives and friends should be provided as needed.

THE PUBLIC RELATIONS OF CHURCHES

"Aren't the activities of churches already pretty much public relations?" some may protest. "Aren't churches concerned with attracting members, creating a favorable public reception for their messages, and doing good in their communities and the world? What more can they do?"

It is true that these typical public relations activities constitute a large part of church work, but many churches carry them out only on a word-of-mouth, person-to-person basis. As far as any single individual is concerned, the personal approach is most effective; but in these days of large, mobile populations, some more modern methods of general communications might well be added. In a way, the minister, an assistant, or lay people making personal calls may be likened to salesmen calling upon prospects; and they will be much more effective if the product which they are selling is already well known and respected.

This introduction can be made by disseminating information about the beliefs, activities, staff, equipment, and program of the church, and by working hard in the community to attain desirable social goals. If the minister of a church is elected to national office in a denomination or to another post of responsibility, or if a new program is established within the church, the local newspapers should be supplied with a story. Much, of course, depends upon the size of the city. In a small town almost any activity of a church will be news; in a big city, only the most important. Letters, illustrated folders, and news bulletins can be mailed; and many other ways of reaching large groups of the public are familiar to good ministers. None of these media will do the job alone. They are simply preparation, in most instances, for personal contact; but as parishes grow larger and more fluid, the extension of communication through public relations methods becomes both necessary and helpful when handled fittingly. The apostles, after all, used the best means of communication they had at hand in their day, and church evangelists in the twentieth century can well do the same.

A Word about Interfaith Movements

Despite their differences, all branches of the Christian and Jewish religions share many things in common—a belief in God, common standards of morality and justice, ideals of the brotherhood and sanctity of man, and social idealism. The likenesses among their members are much greater than the differences; yet only a few short centuries ago the whole Western world was convulsed by religious wars, and only a few decades ago the Jews of Europe were being slaughtered in the gas chambers of Dachau and other horror camps.

We are all now much concerned about freedom of religion, mutual respect, and a common social morality, because we know that what benefits one, benefits all. Attaining respect and cooperation is a public relations problem which has been vigorously tackled in the United States by the National Conference of Christians and Jews and other organizations.

PUBLIC RELATIONS AND RACE RELATIONS IN THE UNITED STATES

The race relations problem in this nation is not a legal problem but a public relations problem. Without question, all citizens of the United States have equal rights under the Constitution. These legal rights have been demanded, as they should have been, and are being attained; but even after they are won, there remains the problem of obtaining the *human* rights and respect of members of minority groups, which court actions cannot give and which policing systems cannot enforce.

No laws can be passed which will make people friendly, willing to give others a fair share of good employment, advancement, or promotion, willing to vote for the candidate instead of for his or her color, and willing to be good neighbors. The bestowal of human rights cannot be entirely enforced; it can only be given because of understanding, a sense of fairness, and the honest desire of a majority group (influenced by its leaders and by its own social pressures) to do the right thing. The race relations problem of the United States today is rapidly passing into this stage if, indeed, it is not already there. Enforcement by public action will still be needed in certain places and at some times, but the big problem of minority groups in the future is to convince the majority of their high standards of personal worth, their value to the common society, and their loyalty; and also to lead the majority to recognize the justice of fair and generous treatment.

This obligation puts a great burden upon a minority group. It is asked to be much better than the majority in many ways, to see that the majority is aware of this merit, and yet to steer a careful course between assertiveness and subservience. Every time that members of a minority group do something well in any field—sports, music, art, the Armed Forces, education, business, or science—they advance the respect in which all their fellows are held; and every time that they do something bad, they hurt all their fellows, because unobserving majority publics may not readily distinguish among individuals. To gain public esteem, the members of a minority group require more wisdom, self-control, social control, and cohesiveness, plus a better public relations sense, than do the members of a majority which is not forced to work uphill.

Such progress, hard as it is, can be made because Americans have a conscience, take their vows of government seriously, and, when encouraged and reminded, are always generous to those who need help. But progress in public relations requires good sense and planning, followed by a program of deeds. The next best step for groups interested in the advancement of minority groups in the United States will be to utilize more frequently thoughtful and experienced public relations counselors.

THE CONTINUING PROBLEMS OF LOCAL PUBLIC EDUCATION

Once there was an elderly school-system superintendent who had been in the same town for forty years and who had done the job by the simple expedient of spending almost no money and continually assuring the taxpayers that they had the best schools in the country (whereas in fact they had almost the worst).

That same person, using the same technique, would hardly last more than a few years in the job today, for a very good reason: Rising operating costs would force the superintendent to go to the voters for building bonds or operating millage votes with regularity whether he wanted to or not, and if he couldn't get more money, the whole school system would start falling to pieces! The modern school head's situation is something like that which the grocer would face if every time she wanted to raise the price of butter, he was forced to seek approval at a public vote; yet it is inescapable, because in inflationary times the cost of teachers' salaries, custodial wages, repairs, supplies, and new buildings goes up and up; the number of students mounts in new suburban areas because of an exodus from the older cities and in central cities the tax base erodes. Bussing has added to the turmoil.

But rising costs are not the only problem facing American public schools today. The school is not only expected to teach; it is also expected to overcome juvenile delinquency, to act as a baby-sitter and to provide a social hall in a period when, often both mothers and fathers work and when more youngsters drive their own cars and there is less parental supervision than ever before. Parents gladly turn more and more of the load over to the schools and then complain if it is not always successfully handled.

There is a constant dispute over what should be taught in the schools. Parents' groups are full of advocates of greater emphasis on the sciences, foreign languages, or English; but at the same time they cannot agree on what should be thrown out to make room for the additional hours to be spent on these fundamentals. The less academic activities, such as basketball, football, swimming, music, sewing, woodworking, and senior plays, all have their own ardent advocates. Not many have agreed so far that the school day should be expanded, say from 8 A.M. to 12 noon and then from 1 P.M. to 5 P.M., with corresponding increases being made in teaching staff, and time-and-a-half pay provided for teachers who do night work or lunch-time work—for instance, supervision or grading.

Local school districts find themselves in a lively (and losing) competition for tax money with the U.S. Internal Revenue Service and other major tax agencies, which go around like vacuum cleaners, sucking all before them. After income taxes, sales taxes, and excise levies have exacted their due, the remaining local property tax cannot easily be increased. It is about at the limit of toleration. In some suburban, nonindustrial areas, each new home is so full of new children that the cost to the community of their education exceeds the household's tax payments. Yet at the same time, when local citizens have a chance to vote "no" on a local school bond issue, they often do so, because this is the only chance that they ever have to vote "no" on any tax—the Federal and state taxes usually being beyond their reach in Congress or a legislature.

Schools must constantly compete for parent and student attention with television, social events, bridge, bowling, magazines, newspapers, worrying about the Communists, appointments at the beauty parlor, and a host of other bids for interest and time.

Under these circumstances, able public school superintendents do not have a choice of whether or not to practice public relations; it must be employed. At the same time they have to deny that they do it; they are usually not well trained in the subject; they are hindered from spending any public money on really expert assistance; and they have a host of needling and conflicting volunteers at their elbow.

The school's publics are (1) the teachers, who must be informed, encouraged, and advised on how best to contribute their efforts to the common cause; (2) the students, who are often enthusiastic but sometimes fractious and shortsighted; (3) the parents, who increasingly seem to know all the answers which have escaped the educators thus far; (4) the press, which can be a good ally but sometimes lacks understanding; (5) business groups, which often have a decided leaning toward paying lower taxes, teaching the three R's, and producing many brilliant scientists, all at the same time; (6) professional groups, which are interested in making good future lawyers, doctors, nurses, engineers, or accountants; (7) sports fans, who demand that the home team win all the time; and (8) the general public. The last group consists of all groups not previously named. It gets its information secondhand through the mass media and word of mouth, distortedly remembers school as it was thirty or forty years ago, is vaguely anti-intellectual, and gets tired of being constantly asked to vote more money for a cause in which it often has no direct, apparent stake; but for which out of the goodness of its heart and the great American belief in education it often does much of the time anyway.

To reach these publics, the superintendent can use both personal and mass media methods. Personal methods include home visits by teachers, notes, conferences, open houses at schools, parent assistance in school affairs, and parent-teacher and other meetings. Mass media may include newsletters to the staffs, school newspapers sent to students and parents, yearbooks, annual or quarterly reports to taxpayers, broadcasts, news releases, and speeches.

Typical news stories, for example, might include accounts of graduations, curriculum and program developments, new staff members, retirements, enrollment and financial figures, pupil and project activities, honors, and interviews with successful graduates. One of the biggest needs is for the warm, human type of feature which shows how lives are changed by education, a fundamental task which we are now all likely to forget since free public education has become almost universal.

HIGHER EDUCATION—THE TROUBLED
HALLS OF IVY

American colleges and universities faced not only a doubling of population within the past fifty years but also a great increase in the percentage of young people who went to college. Whereas in 1900 only about 4 percent of high school graduates entered institutions of higher learning, in 1970 the national average was about 40 percent and the average in certain sections of the country was much higher. In 1960 total college enrollment was about three million; by 1977 it was estimated at 11 million and still climbing.

At the same time, we have seen a great proliferation of the desirable subject matter to be studied and a change in its nature. Compared with the same subjects as studied in 1900, today's chemistry, physics, biology, medicine, business administration, foreign languages, social sciences, and journalism, are not only more complex in content and theory but bear little resemblance to the simpler college subjects of a generation earlier. A few years ago a great university expected to turn out experts in only a few fields, but today it must prepare for many, because in our expanding universe many more areas of knowledge must be explored.

In early days, widespread public support for American colleges and universities was not so important as it is today because only the elite planned to attend college and they expected to pay for it, but today, when a college education is increasingly necessary for many higher-level job opportunities, most higher education has become state-supported. Private funds handle less of the educational load; the states themselves find their sources of revenue increasingly absorbed by the Federal government; and the problem becomes one of gaining popular support for the increased costs of a higher education that almost half of the families in the nation now expect their sons and daughters to have.

At the same time an obsolete, stereotyped image of college education lingers on in the popular mind, compounded out of the good old Siwash stories of years ago, when college was nothing but a great big happy lark for many well-to-do undergraduates—old-graduate tales, sports pages, and exaggerated reports of riots and general subversion. Why should anyone wish to be taxed for this—or to contribute to it?

Obviously, a considerable communications job needs to be done, and to accomplish it, college public relations personnel resort to various means.

News bureaus supply the press and broadcasters with complete coverage of events at institutions of higher education. Such coverage is necessary because most newspaper staffs are not big enough to deliver a complete report from a university without aid, and left to themselves, would often cover only the student indiscretions, football victories, and trustee squabbles which regularly seem to rise to the top.

College news bureaus are often well staffed with able and dedicated people, but the results of their earnest efforts are not necessarily good promotion. They may not report objectively on the whole work of a vast institution or create a generally favorable public image. Communication between college and public cannot be established by reliance upon the naturally haphazard selection of stories released to newspapers or the equally peculiar ways in which their readers snatch impressions out of the melee of daily events. Such publicity is sometimes valuable, but it is not public relations, because while people will certainly learn from it, they will not necessarily like universities better or admire them more.

Alumni work is another common approach, probably most useful in small, long-established homogeneous institutions where alumni bonds are tight and can be reasonably maintained. With the great recent growth of all colleges, their varied curricula, and the dispersion of their graduates all over the world, communications to alumni in many large schools are not so effective as they probably once were.

Events such as anniversaries, graduations, conferring degrees and honors, speeches by notable persons, concerts and art shows, and engineering or science exhibits are other ways of personifying the work of an institution.

Involvement of parents, friends, professional groups, government groups, and others in the activities of the university as guests, visitors, conference attendants, lecturers, and advisers furnishes another opportunity for contact and communication.

But these rather standard approaches are obviously not going to be enough to accomplish the enormous public relations task which must follow upon the great expansion of American higher education today, both because of the number of students and the diversity of their needs. The aim at the publics to be reached must be more sure; the means employed to reach them must be more refined and more intelligently used; and greater effort must be expended, more commensurate with the greater task.

Effective new approaches may include greater concentration upon the specific publics of which the general public of higher education is composed and greater personal contact with individuals. Only certain groups or persons have the motivated interest to listen to and to understand the complex messages which must be conveyed; others will either ignore or misinterpret them to suit their own desires and preconceptions. All too often educators bask in the delusion that they are communicating with important publics when, in fact, they are only talking to other educators (who admittedly constitute an important public in themselves).

It is important to consider some of the specific publics closely related to higher education

Students of the callow freshman type of the good old Siwash days are still to be found upon American campuses, but they are exceptional. Most students today are older and more sophisticated; many of them are married and are parents; frequently they have extensive military or work experience; and often they are engaged in graduate study for advanced degrees in highly specialized areas. Student support can be enlisted both in representing their particular institutions and in speaking for higher education in general. To convey a message to others, students need information, participation in university affairs, and a knowledge that freedom is inevitably accompanied by responsibility.

Parents may or may not have been to college. (If they have, they probably share many old-graduate delusions.) Since many parents are under severe financial strain and are making sacrifices to send their children to college, information about the work of the institution, personal reporting, and recognition at some time other than the end of a term or graduation day seems only their due.

University faculty members may be assumed to be competent within their own disciplines, but also sometimes incompetent and, unfortunately, vocal in other areas. Academic freedom, like other freedoms, has its concomitant responsibilities to society, its fellows, the nation, and world. A discharged professor once remarkedly bitterly (and with some truth) that a university teacher had less freedom of speech than a ditchdigger. The limitation is inevitable; few people expect much of a ditchdigger's statements, but a professor carries a much heavier load of responsibility.

The fact that university faculty members are highly intelligent does not mean that they will be well informed upon the whole state of the university and the role of higher education in society today. Many teachers might be more confident, more tactful, more kindly, and more closely connected with the mainstreams of economic, social, and cultural life flowing through the world if they were better informed about subjects beyond their specialties. The old stereotype of the university professor as a hopelessly underpaid recluse is quite out of date, but the full potential of today's new-style teacher has not yet been enlisted upon many campuses. There is need for closer links between campus and the outside world.

High school contacts are increasingly important as larger numbers of high school students seek admission to colleges.

Professional and occupational groups are interested, not only in the development of their own successors, but also in their own professional updating on campus. Since they can both learn and contribute, continuing education offers many public relations opportunities.

New alumni provide an opportunity to show what higher education can do for individuals and for the public welfare. Concrete illustrations will reassure a public that is not in danger of being swamped in statistics and vague generalizations.

The communications media, such as the press and broadcasting stations, must be considered carefully. A spate of minor items or an overwhelming preponderance of sports news may now be of less value in creating public understanding than it used to be. Today's need is for appreciation of educational efforts in human terms, and this can be achieved only when the editors, reporters, and broadcasters themselves are in full rapport with the institution they are discussing. If *they* think of university news primarily in terms of protest marches and touchdowns, the case is almost hopeless. How many major universities, for example, take key news people individually through their establishments so that they may learn the work of the institution and meet faculty members informally?

Government is of primary concern to the tax-supported majority of higher educational institutions. How well do government people understand educational problems and aspirations? How outdated or distorted are their stereotypes? How responsive are they to the needs and wishes of their home constituencies in regard to education? Could they be more sympathetic? Although personal connections influence political action, the fundamental university problem is one of public support; it is imperative that the public supply information on how it feels about the value of higher education to its elected representatives in government. Last-minute, put-out-the-fire campaigns are often useless, or even harmful, unless a sound foundation has first been laid.

Groups such as business corporations and labor unions (or smaller groups), civic organizations, and churches are examples of special areas of interest which have their own terms of reference in relation to the work of a university and can be approached in appropriate ways.

The list could be multiplied, and if the huge public relations task of higher education is to be accomplished, help will be needed not only from college public relations staffs but also from the administrators, faculties, the students, and their friends. No public relations task was ever larger or more continuous in modern times.

THE PUBLIC RELATIONS OF THE MILITARY SERVICES

Wars, past, present, and future, are the American people's biggest government investment, accounting for about half of the Federal budget. Not only do the military services ask support from taxes; they also seek men and women for active service, and, in time of war, all the life of the country.

With the great need of recruitment and of citizen support during the past two world wars, and with continuing heavy financial demands and constant changes in weapons, the United States Army, Navy, Marine Corps, and Air Force have all developed large, effective public relations machines totaling perhaps 3,000 persons and spending several million dollars a year to place their needs before the public to which they look for support. They direct most of their efforts toward certain sections of the public.

Those now serving in the Armed Forces. The understanding and approval of men and women in the service are the keys to the reactions of their parents, relatives, and friends throughout the country. Good treatment, good food, adequate information, opportunities for recreation and advancement are primary, of course, in determining attitudes. A sound public relations program in which the members of the armed services serve as ambassadors of good will for their organizations can be built only upon the facts. With the end of the draft, large sums are now needed for advertising to attract new recruits into volunteer military forces.

Reserve forces need recognition and encouragement for the hours they put in, without much public appreciation, in times of peace. When they are called to active service because of an emergency situation short of war, their reactions may present many problems.

Civilian employees of the military forces (such as those in the many river and harbor projects of the United States Army Corps of Engineers) need to be considered just as are groups of industrial employees.

Communities near military posts offer many special problems. Soldiers in uniform on leave arouse the herd instincts in both civilians and their own military brethren. Each group can be distinguished by its dress, and Tom, or Joe, or Mary in civilian clothes are magically transformed into "those damned soldiers" when wearing their country's uniform. Special forbearance is necessary to prevent friction when traffic and civil police are involved.

Near big bases, schools, housing, and sewage become problems; near air bases the public worries about loud noises and falling objects. All these inherent problems provide much opportunity for the local staff PIOs (Public Information Officers) to practice their foresight and skills in public relations.

Industry is another major public of the military services because it furnishes most of their supplies.

Higher education is almost a prerequisite for the recruitment of many officers and enlisted men. ROTC programs have had many public relations problems.

The press presents a continual problem, because it is not only a gatekeeper to broad public contact, but itself wants to know everything that goes on, especially accidents or other trouble, which unenlightened or fearful base commanders would sometimes like to hide. Because the boundary line of real military-defense secrecy is hard to draw, and because it is frequently drawn too fine, newspapermen often feel that national security is being used as a cloak for incompetence or errors.

The Congress of the United States is the ultimate military public because it determines which branches of the service will get how much money and for what purposes. Only a few people at the top levels at the Pentagon in Washington work directly with Congress, but the efficacy of the general public relations programs and the activities of all military operations with which Congress may come into contact, including those within the member's home territory, may do much to influence their attitudes.

THE UNITED STATES GOVERNMENT AND POLITICS

Within the past generation the United States government has grown so large and so complex that its scope is now beyond the comprehension of all but a few American citizens. Like the sands of the sea, its personnel and functions are numberless, and its costs are calculated in figures like those of interstellar distances. Some conservative citizens violently oppose this development as a matter of principle, but it does not seem very likely to change, and in view of the great number of services which the people now expect from the government, probably most voters really do not wish it to change very much.

In a democracy in which citizens are called upon to understand and to direct their government from time to time, this swollen size presents many communications problems. How can an individual citizen know what is going on in government? For that matter, does the press know? Most newspaper and wire-service staffs are hopelessly inadequate to report much beyond the activities of a few key persons. In addition, the citizen is often called upon for willing and intelligent compliance with government requests instead of being forced by law. Conservation efforts, assistance in preventing forest fires, and even proper payment of taxes are all greatly aided by willing citizen effort.

The need for public information about government activities and for public cooperation with government projects has given rise to the development of public relations practice within government; but for a number of reasons the activity is hedged about with fear, and people engaged in publicity are often disguised under other titles, such as "assistants" or "service bureaus."

The basic trouble is that the power to communicate is a great asset to political success in a democracy, and those who enjoy this power, particularly through being in office, have an advantage which their opponents abhor—until they attain the same position. In our form of government, such public relations communication is usually an arm of the executive branch (the President, Cabinet officers, and bureau heads) and is much less attached to Congress; official communication is therefore frequently attacked by congressmen because the executive uses it to maintain public favor. In fact, in these days of wide newspaper coverage and of instantaneous television communication, an appeal to the people can be the American President's strongest weapon. The built-in feud between the American executive and legislative branches of government finds its most painful point of contact in government public relations.

The American press itself has an ambivalent attitude toward government public relations sources. On the one hand, the press realizes that internal news releases are necessary, because no newspaper or news service could possibly be equipped to cover the vast machinery of United States government, at all levels, without material assistance from the inside. But, on the other hand, such open dependence is often felt to be contrary to the best traditions of the press in that it exposes the press to possible omissions or distortions at the source of the news. (It is hardly to be expected that a government agency will go to any great effort to dig up facts about itself which may be adverse to its own interests.) Secrecy, also, may be used to hide governmental ineptitude, and as America's foreign involvements grow increasingly complex and secret, often the mantle of state security is, rightly or wrongly, thrown over an ever larger area. The press's right to know is increasingly confronted with questions as to the ability to know or the wisdom of telling. Boundaries between right and expediency are uncertain, and surely no one will ever be satsified in such a fluid and complex field. The Watergate affair of the early 1970s provided evidence of the abuses to which official secrecy could be put.

Political public relations may be defined as getting candidates or parties elected, or perhaps obtaining public vote support for specific objectives such as bond issues, referendums, or constitutional changes. These activities are difficult for nonpolitical public relations people because their prestige is laid squarely on the line; if an election is lost by only one vote, it is just as much a public failure as if it had been lost by 10,000 votes, except in giving reason for future encouragement. Time to work for political issues is limited, and a single campaign is a promotional rather than a developmental effort, often played by ear, and all too seldom with long-range planning. The haste is unfortunate because the real build-up of a political issue or figure involves careful planning and time in which to work, as well as the arts of publicity and showmanship. Too often the ballyhoo is applied long after most minds are already made up. Political campaigning is a specialty in the public relations world for which special firms or teams exist.

Pressure groups of all sorts (for better schools, less pollution, mass transit, and different labor laws, for example) employ general public relations methods in addition to their special efforts directed at lawmakers personally. The way to attain a major political or economic goal in the United States seems to be to organize strong citizen support outside the framework of a political party. When the cause gains sufficient strength, either the party in power will adopt the program in order to stay in or the party out of power will adopt it in the hope of attaining a majority. (Sometimes both adopt it.) The rise of pressure for a U.S. Constitutional amendment to prohibit alcoholic beverages in the early 1920s and its subsequent repeal in the 1930s is a case in point. When success has been achieved for their particular demands, such citizen groups tend to melt away and do not remain behind to clutter up the political landscape as voter attention moves on to new issues and needs. In this way American political parties become *registers* of public opinion rather than *creators* of it. The system has many advantages because it avoids freezing party loyalties and platforms to long-outworn issues and allows for fluidity in crystallizing and facing new problems. The common criticism of American political parties for not "standing for anything" may well be somewhat beside the point; perhaps they are not supposed to stand for anything, and it may be better that their platforms are expressed in very general terms.

A SUMMARY OF CHAPTERS 5 AND 6

With the increasing complexity of modern life, the list of spe
of public relations practice becomes greatly extended, and it
tinue to grow as more and more groups find such planned pu sudsive
communication necessary to their existence and progress. But although
each of these special areas has its own particular problems, the fundamentals of successful public relations practice remain the same. There is
no need, at least to begin with, to learn one type of communication for
banks, another for schools, another for railroads, and so on. The best
evidence of the essential unity of principle in this field is seen in the
manner in which the big public relations counseling firms of the United
States handle many types of accounts with success; they obviously have
the advantage of greater general experience and a fresher viewpoint than
those that specialize too narrowly.

For the future practitioner, a study of the list of possible applications of general theories and techniques is valuable because it indicates
the wide scope of communications problems in today's rapidly expanding and complex world and stimulates thinking toward further applications. But before expertness within any area is attempted, mastery of the
basic principles of public relations practice which are covered in later
chapters is essential.

ADDITIONAL READINGS

Baus, Herbert M. and William B. Ross, *Politics Battle Plan.* (New York: Macmillan, 1968.)

Cochran, Charles L., *Civil-Military Relations.* (New York: Free Press, 1974.)

Cutlip, Scott M., *Fund Raising In The United States.* (New Brunswick, N.J.:
Rutgers University Press, 1965.)

Engstrom, W. A.: *Multi-media in the Church.* (Richmond, Va.: John Knox
Press, 1973.)

Gilbert, William H., *Public Relations in Local Government.* (Washington, D.C.:
International City Management Association, 1976.)

Heibert, Ray and Carlton Spitzer, *The Voice of Government,* (New York: Wiley,
1968.)

Kelley, Stanley, Jr., *Public Relations and Political Power.* (Baltimore, Md.: Johns
Hopkins, 1956.)

Kobre, Sidney, *Successful Public Relations for Colleges and Universities.* (New
York: Hastings House, 1974.)

Kurtz, Harold P., *Public Relations for Hospitals.* (Springfield, Ill.: Charles P.
Thomas, 1969.)

McCloskey, Gordon E., *Education and Public Understanding.* 2nd ed. (New York: Harper & Row, 1967.)

Napolitan, Joseph, *The Election Game and How to Win It.* (New York: Doubleday, 1972.)

Schmidt, Frances and Harold N. Weiner, eds., *Public Relations in Health and Welfare.* (New York: Columbia University Press, 1966.)

Sumption, Merle R. and Yvonne Engstrom, *School-Community Relations.* (New York: McGraw-Hill, 1966.)

Woodress, Fred A., *Public Relations for Community/Junior Colleges.* (Danville, Ill.: Interstate Printers & Publishers, 1976.)

Chapter 7

Images—Corporate and Otherwise

The word "image" implies to most people something unreal, illusory, or transient. But Webster's *New International Dictionary* (second edition) offers as one definition of the word: "a mental representation of anything not actually present to the senses; a revival or imitation of sensible experience, or of sensible experience together with accompanying feelings; the reproduction in memory or imagination of sensations of sight, touch, hearing, etc.; as, visual, tactile, auditory *images;* a picture drawn by the fancy; broadly, a conception; an idea."[1]

The definition leads us away from illusion. There is nothing unreal at all about the image of a corporation because to the person who has the image in mind, it *is* the corporation. Whether the image be true or

[1]By permission. From Webster's New International Dictionary, Second Edition, copyright 1959 by G. & C. Merriam Co., Publishers of the Merriam-Webster Dictionaries.

false is quite beside the point; the person who has it thinks it is true and will act accordingly. Images exist; they are more or less forceful according to the degree of contact and interest which the holder has with the organization image; and they can be measured and changed, although such change is often a slow process.

The more usual meaning of the term "corporate image" would be that given in the third edition of Webster's NID as one of the definitions of image: "a mental conception held in common by members of a group and being symbolic of a basic attitude and orientation toward something (as a person, class, racial type, political philosophy, or nationality)."[2] The word "corporate" would refer to the group holding the image in common rather than to the *object* of their thinking. (See Webster's definition of "corporate" as synonymous with "aggregate.") But the phrase has been ambiguously applied so that it seems often to mean, at one and the same time, an image *by* a group and *of* a group (a corporation). The latter meaning had by 1958 reached a point of acceptance which prompted the Opinion Research Corporation of Princeton, New Jersey, to engage in a study of corporate images and of their possible development and change. Writing in *Public Relations Journal* in September, 1959, Dr. Claude Robinson and Dr. Walter Barlow of Opinion Research said:

> Our thesis in this article is that the corporate image is a bright new concept that is extremely useful to thinking about company communications; that the usage of the image concept will grow and become common in the language of communications; in short, we submit that the corporate image is by no means a conversational fad. It is, in fact, the *real McCoy*.
>
> Words have no inner or inevitable meaning, but are devices for communication. They are carriers both of meaning and of feeling tone. And, as all of us know, the cargo of meaning carried by any one word is constantly shifting and undergoing change. The test of the acceptability of a word or concept is very simple. It is this: Is the word or concept useful in visualizing, or as we might say, mentally imaging the world?
>
> The idea of the corporate image passes this test with high marks. It is a convenient and helpful way to visualize people's ideas about companies. It lends itself to measurement and analysis. A corporate image situation can be diagnosed, programs can be worked out to deal with it, and results can be measured. Or, in other words, the concept of the corporate image fits very practically into the working day world of operations.

[2]By permission. From Webster's Third New International Dictionary, copyright 1961 by G. & C. Merriam Co., Publishers of the Merriam-Webster Dictionaries.

By corporate image, then, we mean simply the mental pictures that people have in their heads about companies and corporations. These mental pictures may come from direct or indirect experience. They may be rational or irrational, depending on evidence or hearsay, appear in an infinite number of patterns.

The fundamental reality of mental pictures in people's heads is evident to all.

Columbus practically had to shanghai men aboard his three-ship convoy to the New World, because of the belief that the world was flat, and that if you sailed far enough west, you would drop into the Abyss.

Standard Oil Company changed its name in part because Ida Tarbell fastened upon it the mental picture of monopoly.

A major eastern employer still has difficulty in recruiting top-flight labor because the idea is still afloat in the community that it is a "butcher shop" despite the fact that old hazards have been so successfully removed that the company has won industrial safety awards.

The railroads today are being regulated on the basis of their "monopolistic position" despite the emergence in recent years of strong competition from other forms of transportation.

Even in the above explanation two definitions compete for acceptance. The fourth paragraph is clearly slanted toward the object imaged —a corporation; the sixth paragraph, toward the tendency of people to hold an image corporately.

The word "image" is similar to the term "stereotype" and is associated with "prejudice," which in its Latin form simply means prejudging a matter before the evidence is in. It is obviously impossible to have an image of something with which one has no contact, and images about remote things are generally quite feeble and susceptible to change. The concern about images in modern times springs from the fact that people today are supposed to have valid images of a great many things—the United Nations, Soviet Russia, African Nations, labor union B, or corporation X—about which they really know very little at first hand. Persons find that these images, once established, are often very hard to change. They have to make a distinct effort; they are likely to upset other closely held values; and such independence of thought may alienate them from friends who are to some extent friends because they hold the same opinions. Altering images is a painful, wrenching process, often leading to great unhappiness. Many persons, under certain conditions of age, health, or emotional conflict, simply give up even trying to alter their images; they have even been known to stone or to crucify those who persist in disturbing them.

ASCERTAINING THE NATURE OF THE CORPORATE IMAGE

In the study referred to earlier, Opinion Research Corporation sought to find out about corporate images by the following means:

1   Motivation research using lengthy taped interviews to see how closely connected people are with corporations and to determine what image areas are real enough to justify measurement.
2   A pilot test consisting of 307 interviews.
3   Depth interviews nationally to examine the effect of distance upon perception.
4   Tests upon a panel of persons.
5   Field testing scattered over the United States to see if the survey method really worked in practice.

In the completed survey itself, respondents were first given a pack of twenty 3- by 5-inch cards, each with a company name on it, and were asked to sort the cards into five different piles according to their degree of familiarity with each company. The choices were: "Never heard of company or company name," "Heard of company but know practically nothing about it," "Know just a little bit about the company," "Know a fair amount about the company," and "Know the company well."

The names of companies which were totally unfamiliar were discarded, and overall favorability and unfavorability were then checked by the same method. Following this came a more detailed survey in which respondents had the opportunity to express their reasons for opinions in fifty different ways. More than 3,000 interviews were conducted in respondents' homes.

Among the major findings about company images flowing from this study were the following:

The bigness of a company does not ensure a widespread or favorable image.

Better-known companies are almost always more favorably known.

The public is quite selective in what it considers good or bad about a company.

Companies manufacturing consumer goods have an advantage in image building; but producer-goods companies can also use advertising in print or on television to achieve a better-than-usual response.

A company may be profitable yet unknown to the public.

People may praise a company's products, yet consider it a bad citizen.

Employee opinion contributes greatly to reputation, but often only as an employer and not in relation to products.

CONGLOMERATES AND MULTINATIONAL COMPANIES

In recent years two types of companies have become much more prevalent and have developed particular public relations needs.

One is the conglomerate, a company which has many operating divisions engaged in making varied products or is in different lines of business. Often conglomerates have long, uninformative names which have been condensed into initials such as TRW, ITT, or LTV or the names may simply not tell you much about what the company does such as "Northwest Industries," or "Kiddie," or "Transamerica." With the financial and diversification advantages that these companies have also goes an impersonality that organizations engaged in making fewer products do not face to the same degree. Gaining public and investor recognition of the scope and business of a conglomerate presents special public relations problems of which there are a number of examples later in this book.

Large companies, also, frequently operate within many nations of the world. These multinationals face public relations problems both in their home countries and within the host nations in which they do business. In the United States, for example, mutinationals may be accused of exporting capital that is needed at home, of importing manufactured goods in competition with American labor, or of engaging in bribery of foreign rulers (although this may be the customary way of doing business in those places). In host countries American multinational companies may be accused of paying too little for raw materials, taking too much profit out of the country or of favoring American managers over local people. There is always the danger of restrictive legislation at home or of limitation of earnings or even seizure abroad. So there is a public relations need to present the case for multinational operations both at home and abroad.

DOING SOMETHING ABOUT THE CORPORATE IMAGE

In effect, "doing something about the corporate image" is the whole point of this book (if we expand "corporate image" to include images of many kinds of organizations). The recommendations of Opinion Research after further analysis of the survey are therefore of special interest.

1   Map out the strengths and weaknesses of the corporation's existing image. This obviously calls for valid study and also some questions about what publics one is most concerned with.

2   Consciously plan and write out a definition of the corporate image which it is wished to project. Here some soul-searching may be necessary, because if the image desired is too far away from the facts, its projection will be difficult or even self-defeating. Questions such as "Who are we?" "What do we stand for?" "In what ways are we distinctive?" and "How would we wish to be thought of?" are in order.

3   Create selling themes for projecting this image to the publics. One problem is to refine a whole list of qualities and goals to a few simple things which may be understood. Depending upon the degree of their existing connection, publics are only *somewhat* interested in what one has to say, since they are exposed to a great many competing messages.

4   Utilize *all* means of contact to build an image—advertising, employees, salesmen, letterheads, product, slogans on shipping cases, everything possible. The favorable image increases with the number of contacts.

What Can You Expect from a Favorable Corporate Image?

A conservative (and realistic) answer to the above question might be: to be better off with it than without it. An unfavorable image is more of a handicap than a favorable image is an assurance of success, because numbers of companies have reasonably favorable images. An organization with an unfavorable image may find it hard to get good new employees and may have more sales problems, more labor difficulties and more governmental friction. It may have more difficulty in obtaining money and enjoy less stockholder satisfaction.

But while an unfavorable corporate image may rightly be thought of as a handicap, a favorable image is no substitute for good products, good selling, progressive research, and good all-round company management. Favor will not ensure that a firm will never have a strike, never be investigated by a Senate committee, or never face a falling sales curve. Favor is simply money in the bank against the time that these things may happen, and it is also capital upon which an enterprising management may build more soundly.

THE PUBLIC IMAGE OF "BUSINESS" VERSUS SPECIFIC BUSINESSES

An interesting point in the public-opinion surveys referred to earlier (and still true today) is that while people frequently feel quite well disposed toward individual companies, many still fear and dislike "big business" in general. Apparently the efforts of individual concerns, even the very large ones, to be understood and liked often meet with considerable success, but the group efforts of business people as a class have been far less successful.

The explanation probably lies in the fact that every time business attempts to speak as a social group, it sets itself off from (and in opposition to) other American social groups. The phenomenon is not new and applies equally to other American groups, such as farmers or laborers; yet for many reasons, business people feel it necessary to engage in political activity and often talk a lot about their own virtues. Increasingly their business success is determined by political factors, and in the climate of the economic democracy of the 1970s politics can scarcely be ignored.

The Proper Role of Businesses in Political Activity

At the close of the nineteenth century, in the days of Hanna and McKinley, it was accepted as a matter of course that business should have a strong influence in politics. In getting a street-railway franchise approved, arranging for a tariff boost, or fighting against an eight-hour day, the purse counted heavily, and there were frequently close and only slightly concealed alliances between business bosses who could deliver the cash and political bosses who could deliver the votes.

With the coming of the trust-busting and muckraker days, however, and with political upheavals and politically strong labor unions, the pendulum shifted, and business firms eschewed open political activity as if it were poison. Known business support became a "kiss of death" for many candidates, and company sales managers preferred that their firms should not take sides for fear of retaliation in the market place.

In a way, this divorce from politics was something of a relief to many business people because the plain fact is that, for a number of reasons, most people in business are not very good at politics. Because of necessary advertising and sales promotional activities, large businesses are usually well known to the public. They are assumed to be rich, powerful, and interested in money. By comparison with the relative obscurity of the individuals who may oppose them, their motives are shining targets.

Business people themselves are often singularly obtuse when it comes to dealing with other people who are not in the business world. They often do not take into account the fact that other groups of people in the world may have quite different value systems, and they may consider other value systems wicked, lazy, or impractical.

Even worse, business people have a great propensity to associate only with other people of the same standing in industry; their exclusiveness leads to a mental inbreeding which soon causes them to believe that the opinion of this peer group is the true voice of the people.

It is not easy for typical business executives to engage in politics, even if they want to. They have little time; they are accustomed to issuing orders and having them obeyed, rather than to palavering and compromising; and if they run for office and should be so unfortunate as to get elected, there is a good chance that while they are away for a year or two serving their state or nation, the ranks of the organization will close behind them and upon their return they will not find their original position open; someone else has moved up the company ladder while they were absent. And frequently they may find their fellow corporation members practically forbidding them to seek offices which might implicate the firm even by indirection.

For these reasons, most United States legislative bodies are about two-thirds filled with lawyers, who find their value enhanced when they return to their firms or partnerships after a tour of duty in the state or national capitals, and by an assortment of other people whose activities permit them to campaign and to serve. Major business people are conspicuously absent.

Yet this abstention from politics today leaves business in a dilemma. In the bad old days of the nineteenth century, business was often in unashamed, direct control of government to its own advantage. In the past few decades, business has been largely cast out of the governmental fold, where votes count more than money (although money is needed to buy media time and to seek votes), and has contented itself with concentration upon technological improvements, expansion, and a struggle with labor organizations. But this no longer suffices. With inevitably increasing government control business will be influenced by political actions more and more, whether or not it makes any endeavor to influence them. And, in addition, self-interest is not always wrong simply because it *is* self-interest.

The question for business interests is, what to do.

In most instances, when business openly, and *as business,* enters the political arena, it gets licked. Although a profit motive may be unimpeachable, it makes a poor platform from which to campaign, unless large groups of people outside the business can also be shown to benefit. It may be argued that labor or farm groups are also interested in a profit motive (their own profits), but their case is somewhat different, because these numerous groups of people easily succeed in convincing themselves that their motives are disinterested and for the good of the country.

Besides, they have many votes, while major business executives are few in number, and with the expansion of the size of corporations every year, the ranks of proprietor-owners continue to diminish and the proportion of wage or salary earners to expand. If business people wish to win political battles, they must take with them into the campaign a sizable proportion of wage earners or other groups who can see their advantage also in management's goals. The problem is, how to do it. A strictly "business party" in the United States can hardly expect to get to first base, and by arousing strong antagonism might bring about the very trends toward greater government controls which it wishes to avoid. Business people might with more wisdom penetrate deep into the ranks of existing political organizations, where issues are fought out at the primary or at a previous level before they ever see the light of public vote.

This idea of infiltration into political parties is not new; it gained ground under the leadership of the United States Chamber of Commerce in the late 1950s.

In 1961 Earl P. Johnson, Director of Industrial Relations of Frederick & Nelson Department Store in Seattle, Washington, said:

> (We) also have a responsibility to encourage the staff members, as individual citizens, to participate in the political party of their choice. . . . In the field of politics there has recently been a great hiatus. In the past, there was an unwritten law in most businesses that perhaps it was best not to get into politics too much because it is a controversial area. If it is controversial an individual might find that top management would be unwilling to let him participate because he works in a company that caters to the public. . . .
>
> We have now said that it is not only our responsibility to encourage staff members to become active in the party of their choice, but that as a company we will do what we can to assist them to become effective.
>
> With this statement of policy, we have assured our staff members that their political activities are the same as though they were active in some charitable or cultural program where some time away from the job is needed, that we would work out a program whereby time would become available. . . . We would not draw the line if someone decided they wanted to become a candidate for office. We would take a good look at the dilemma in which the individual might find himself and would try to work out a program for him. If a company is to encourage its staff members to get active in the political party of the individual's own choice, then the company must go into the program wholeheartedly.

The Frederick & Nelson program not only included encouragement of staff members and time allowance, but also contained an indoctrination course in the free enterprise system (United States Chamber of Commerce material) and in the operations of the department store itself.

Another program upon a large scale was that of the Ford Motor Company, which in 1950 established a Civic Affairs Office and in 1959 greatly expanded it to include eight regional offices. Here the program stressed encouragement of political participation, an eight-session Effective Citizenship Course, setting up a voluntary political contribution plan for all employees, promotion of voting, and coverage of political contests in plant newspapers. Particular attention was paid to the relations between plant and city and between plant and state, to tours by public officials, to presentation locally of company views on current issues, to a service-awards program for employees who made exceptional contributions to civic and governmental affairs, and to presenting to employees a record of legislative activity as it affected the company and business in general.

The success of such programs depends upon the individual's freedom to act as he or she sees fit and upon the company's stressing issues rather than parties. If these conditions can be met, and if business groups can be imaginative enough to think in terms of human reactions instead of dollars, then there is a good chance that, over the years, business people may again exert considerable influence in political decisions; but they will do so primarily as people and only secondarily as representatives of firms.

The "Corporate Image" Is Not a "Corporations Image"

The building of a corporate image which may work so well for a single company often breaks down when thoughtlessly transferred to "business" as a group interest. Most people see individual companies primarily as sources of benefits—employment, payrolls, products, and the like. They see business groups as a menacing form of control.

Perhaps the best public relations for a business group is to forget its self-consciousness as much as possible. Its members should stop gathering in clusters at luncheon and country clubs; they should include students, scholars, farmers, laborers, and homemakers in their social structures without condescension, should stop talking about what is good for business and instead concentrate upon what is good for the nation or the world, and above all should stop making pronouncements upon subjects in which the businessman's competence is neither greater nor necessarily less than that of many other persons. The attempted deification of any group in an outspoken, individualistic, democratic society is likely to have adverse results and should not be sought but rather avoided. Business organizations would frequently be well advised to be inconspicuous (except among their members and by their good works) while their members become well known by many segments of the rest of the public through activities that all enjoy in common, such as recreation, education, welfare, religion—and politics! Business has many good ideas to present and a vital role to play; but it does not have the voting power or the attractiveness to be dominant by itself.

This discussion has been going on for almost a generation now and the latest public opinion polls show "business" held in low esteem along with government, education and many other American institutions—but business-supported ideas about the best conduct of government and the economy have often made progress. Perhaps being understood is more important than being loved.

ADDITIONAL READINGS

Brayman, Harold, *Corporate Management In A World Of Politics.* (New York: McGraw-Hill, 1967.) [Written by a former DuPont public relations head.]

Bristol, Lee H., ed., *Developing The Corporate Image.* (New York: Scribner's 1960.) [A book that had a great influence upon popularizing the idea of corporate image among business people.]

Epstein, Edward M., *The Corporation In American Politics.* (Englewood Cliffs, N.J.: Prentice-Hall, 1969.)

Chapter 8

The Tools of Public Relations

One reason why the practice of public relations may be called an art or perhaps even a science is that it requires knowledge and expert skill to use the tools of mass communication effectively. Since most people are not proficient in the field, such knowledge sets those in public relations above the amateurs whose winning personalities can charm a few persons at a time in face-to-face meetings. Charm is always useful and often highly desirable, but even applied during a whole lifetime, would scarcely be enough to change the image of a big corporation, to succeed in a major welfare drive, or to win a big election.

This chapter, therefore, will concentrate on an explanation of the effective use of the mass media—press, radio and television, motion pictures, and other means of reaching large numbers of people at one time. Those who work in the mass media fields spend their lives becoming expert in the use of these tools of communication, and a single chapter in this book can do little more than point out how to begin. Many good detailed books are available upon the nature and uses of the mass media. The serious student is referred to the short list at the end of this chapter and to many other books which can be found in any good library.

What Is Said Is Most Important, but It Must Be Well Said

Expertness in the use of the mass communications media such as newspapers, posters, booklets, or motion pictures is not, in itself, enough to ensure success in communication. *What* is said is as important as *how* it is said. But expertness is still essential; we know that a surgeon's capable diagnosis must be accompanied by sufficient skill and dexterity to enable the doctor to perform the operation successfully. A poorly written news story never gets past the desk of a keen editor to see the light of day in a daily newspaper's columns; a poster which attracts no attention carries no message; a badly designed booklet may repel and discourage a reader; and an ill-planned, poorly produced motion picture is a waste of time, money, and opportunity. Skill in handling these media does not lead inevitably to communication, but it makes it much more possible!

Once, before people were bombarded with so many messages every day of their lives, their tolerance of dull, clumsy, or even ugly communications was reasonably high. They are no longer so patient. Readers, listeners, and viewers have become sufficiently sophisticated, from wide exposure to good techniques, to demand excellence without even being conscious of the basis of their judgment. Readers may not expect a company magazine to look like a major national publication, but they do expect it to be well designed and illustrated, colorful, lively, and interesting. To offer them less is to court rejection as a rank amateur. Viewers may not expect an industrial motion picture to meet the most lavish Hollywood production standards, but it must be well photographed, well written, and well paced. Amateur film scrambles belong only in the privacy of family reunions.

But expertness in the mass communications media can be its own trap through "the illusion of communication," which develops when a publicity worker totals up the many inches in the press clippings file without asking, "Who read these?" and "What did they think?" or when a board of directors of a firm departs, oozing congratulations after seeing the preview of a new motion picture about their company, without asking coldly, "Why should a stranger be at all concerned with this?"

The best writers, magazine editors, artists, and graphic-production experts are often the most likely to suffer from these illusions of communication because, to them, a well-written story, an attractive magazine, a beautiful picture, or an award-winning film are often ends in themselves, whereas to a public relations person, they are a means to the end of conveying thought to other people. This is why a good newspaper writer or a good broadcaster may sometimes fail to be a good public relations person; he or she may be too easily satisfied with the high quality of methods and not enough concerned with their real effects upon people.

In fact, the very phrase "mass communication" is in itself a trap. There is no such thing as *mass* communication; there is only the mechanical multiplying of single messages by mass means—by the printing press or broadcasting station—to produce many identical messages which go to many single persons at the same time. In each such mass communication the writer or speaker tries to communicate with individual receivers at the other end of the line. Very seldom do receivers get together in interacting groups to receive communications. They might do so at a pep meeting or in a mob, but usually receivers read alone, listen alone, see alone—even in the midst of others.

THE NEWS FAMILY OF THE MASS MEDIA: THE PRESS AND PUBLICITY

American newspapers, because of their size, frequent appearance, and universality, provide probably the best way of reaching large numbers of people at the same time. They are not so useful in many other countries where a large proportion of the population is illiterate, newspaper circulations are scattered, the papers are small, and the standards of journalism are low. In the United States, until broadcasting came along in the 1920s, the press was the only large medium of news communication. American public relations first sprang out of press-agentry, which was the practice of supplying newspapers with free stories in the hope that they would see fit to print them.

Since it was natural for firms that wanted press agents to hire those who were already skilled in press methods, most early specialists in communication were former newspapermen, and even today a majority of the public relations people in this country still spring from newspaper backgrounds. The percentage is diminishing, but it may always remain high because press experience, entirely aside from the fact that it makes a person expert in news writing, also develops qualitites of alertness, enterprise, and good judgment, which are valuable to a public relations worker under any circumstances.

American newspapers have certain special characteristics. They are issued locally; they tend to play up local news to a relatively greater extent than national or foreign news (although this tendency has changed); they are read by most of the people within their circulation areas; and though they differ in many ways, they all use similar wire services, syndicated features, and much the same formulas and patterns of editing.

Advantages. As a medium of communication in public relations, newspapers have certain advantages.

They are timely. Stories can be taken to them, mailed, or wired, and then released very quickly.

Newspapers are inexpensive to use. Almost all American newspapers are honest and would scorn an offer of pay for running genuine news coming from public relations sources. Such news, in fact, is of advantage to both promoter and paper, since it supplies the material which a newspaper is in the business of selling. The only cost to a public relations person of such newspaper publicity is the time in obtaining, writing, and delivering the news.

Newspapers are precise. Their facts are detailed carefully in a manner which readers can study at the time or refer to later.

Newspaper news implies belief in its importance because in running it, a good newspaper says to its readers, "We believe this to be true, or we shouldn't have presented it to you."

Disadvantages. Newspaper stories must be brief and of wide appeal. Long, complicated reports, of interest to only a few people, cannot be carried in most newspapers and should usually not even be submitted.

News stories are subject to editing. The editor has the full right to change them as desired, and their size may be cut or the emphasis of the contents changed.

News stories may not be used at all even if submitted. All big newspapers and many of the smaller ones are deluged every day with far more stories than they can print; the best, in the editors' judgment, are used and the rest are thrown away.

News stories may not always be read or understood. Readers are not expected to read *all* the items in a large newspaper every day, and a story which scores 20 percent recall is doing very well. But in a daily of 500,000 circulation this percent would mean at least 100,000 readers (and really far more than that, since newspapers are usually bought one to a family), which is quite a large figure.

However, just because a news story runs and is reasonably well read, we cannot conclude that the important readers have seen it. Those who are hostile or little interested—and they may be the very ones whose attention is most sought—will probably ignore such a news story. A whole battery of similar stories would not affect them much more; they could ignore them all.

"Thinking like the editor" is the key to success in writing news and feature stories for American newspapers. This adaptability often comes naturally to those who have been reporters or editors, but even persons without this practical advantage can try. The way to start is to forget the kind of stories *you* want to run and, instead, consider what the editor might want to run.

Good public relations people make a habit of reading and understanding the newspapers to which they send releases. Nothing is more insulting and exasperating to a newspaper editor than for a public relations writer to try to foist off stories which are obviously not suitable to readers' interests. The kind of stories that a newspaper wants in every department is plain for anyone to see in every day's issue. Editors are naturally flattered when those who offer them news stories give evidence of having read and appreciated their paper. Stories should be written, for example, for readers with the special interests of people in the editor's own town or area.

Knowing the editor and being a friend cannot fail to be of some help, simply because the friendship creates better understanding, if for no other reason. At the least, the editor would like to know who is responsible for the public relations news, how capable he or she is, how reliable, and where he or she may be reached for further facts or for verification of a story.

Our advice, then, is: Send the editor the kind of story that is most likely to be used—accurate, timely, and in the best news style. *Accuracy* is always the first requirement; when an editor accepts a news story from a public relations source, he trusts that it will be correct to every last name, address, or minor fact. If it is wrong and if readers complain, they will complain to the newspaper, because they do not know who supplied the story in the first place. An editor receiving these complaints isn't likely to forget where the blame belongs and may be little inclined to do business in the future with that source of misinformation.

News is news because it is *new* and timely. If a company's president is to make an interesting public speech and the public relations person has a text of what the president is planning to say, it is a good idea to give the text of the speech to the newspapers a day or two in advance, especially if the delivery of the speech is slated to be close to their news deadlines. (Afternoon papers usually go to press from 11 A.M. to 3 P.M. and should have news items by at least 9 A.M. on the day of publication and usually much earlier if possible. Morning papers usually go to press between 6 P.M. and 11 P.M. and should be supplied by at least noon of the previous day. Sunday papers often close some of their sections several days in advance, and weeklies may close a day or more before publication date. It is always well to ask newspapers when they would like material, if there is a choice.) Make sure that the speech was *actually* delivered as scheduled. Telephone the paper if there are any changes; if the speaker departed materially from the text or, worse yet, didn't even appear, the people who were in attendance might be highly amused by a newspaper report of an event which never happened—although the editor wouldn't share their amusement!

If the date of a coming event is known, a release date can be placed upon a story submitted well in advance. This gives a paper time to think how the story may be used. Play fair with news releases. If there are morning and evening newspapers in one city (not a common situation today), be sure that first release dates are divided somewhat equally between the two papers except, of course, for spot-news happenings that cannot be controlled. When a daily newspaper is surrounded by weeklies, which are usually issued on Wednesdays or Thursdays, don't always release stories for the daily on Friday, for example, leaving the weeklies to wait for a whole week while the news spoils. Above all, don't expect a newspaper to print stale news; get it to the editor quickly.

Anyone who can write the English language well can write a decent, even if not an inspired, news story if he or she tries. To do so, read many good news stories analytically and study a good basic journalism text for style. Remember that news stories are distinguished by the following characteristics.

Brevity. How long a story should be depends somewhat upon the publication. The story of a new-plant dedication in a small town might run a column in length or might even occupy a special section or page; in Chicago, it might be worth only two short paragraphs if run at all. Length also depends, on any given day, upon the local importance of news in relation to other items and also upon the total news space available. But in any case, a good news story keeps on the track, avoids long-windedness, and does not wander or digress. It has an informational mission to accomplish and is not a literary essay.

Inverted order. Newspaper readers are skimmers who want to get the essence of what happened as easily as possible. Hence the writer should put the main news facts into the first few sentences—usually the answers to the ancient questions of who, why, what, when, where, and how.

Objectivity. The writer's opinions generally do not belong in news reports because the reader is paying to learn the facts, not to hear what some reporter thinks about them.

Timeliness is, of course, essential.

Accuracy, as mentioned earlier, is fundamental in every respect.

Mechanical conformity. A news story should always be typed (or duplicated similarly), should be double- or triple-spaced with ample margins, usually on white or light-colored paper. The source's name, telephone number, and address should appear in the upper left-hand corner of the first page. The word "More" should appear at the bottom of the first page if the story is continued and should be repeated at the bottoms of any other pages preceding continuations. Second and subsequent pages should be numbered in the upper right-hand corners and should also be identified by a slugline based on the essence of the news, such as "Jones's speech" or "fire." The end of the story should be identified by a crosshatch (#), "30," or some other indication of conclusion.

Don't beg or carp in dealing with editors. If a single story fails to appear, you may have misjudged its news value for that publication, or competition for news space may have been unusually intense on that particular day. Such competitive news pressure arose when the president of a leading American university died just before Pearl Harbor Sunday in 1941. Two days earlier his obituary would have been worth a column, but on that particular day most newspapers considered it worth only one short paragraph. But if a string of submitted news stories fails to appear, it is time for you to check. See if the material with which the paper is being supplied is of genuine news interest. If you think it is, then perhaps you should ask the editor whether it is being prepared in the right way and sent in at the right times. Never, however, make the mistake of insinuating to an editor that you know better than he or she does what readers need and want.

In dealing with reporters, it pays to shoot square. Getting news is reporters' business; you may help them, but you must not expect too many favors. Don't ask reporters to suppress a news item, because their first duty is to give it to the newspaper. Generally, don't ask an editor to suppress a story either (although you may discuss a possible change of timing to avoid anticipation of a bigger story or to prevent injury to someone); the decision of the press is final. If you have a complaint about the way a story has been written by a reporter to whom you have supplied the facts, tell the reporter before you run to superiors. If you have a valid complaint about the distortion of a mailed or wired release, then see the editor to whom it was directed.

There are right and wrong times to see newspaper editors. Getting out an afternoon daily newspaper is a periodic crisis which in times of stress becomes almost theatrical. Generally, the critical period is from midmorning until press time, and then for about a half-hour thereafter, while the debris and the mistakes are being cleared away. (Any large paper which runs tens of thousands of words daily is certain to have errors in its first edition.) Finally, later in the day, comes a period of relative bliss in which long-range efforts (for tomorrow, perhaps) can be thought of. This is the best time to see an editor or a reporter in the news room.

There are all sorts of editors on large newspapers—city editors, responsible for local news coverage (the "editors" generally referred to thus far), sports editors, business editors, financial editors, family living editors, school editors, real estate editors, church editors, editors of the editorial page, and editors in almost any other field of particular interest in which the paper specializes. A publicity release concerning a new food usually should go to the family living or food editor, if there is one, but if it refers to the expansion of a local plant, it might well go to the city editor, or to the business editor; a charity football game would, of course, be reported to the sports editor, but the story of a benefit ticket-selling tea in connection with the game should be directed to the family living editor or society columnist, if there is one; a company's annual financial report is destined for the business or financial editor. It pays to get acquainted with all the special needs of these editors, because they all value good news sources which help them in their coverage and make them win the approval of the managing editor, who is in charge of the entire news department and is usually immediately under the publisher.

The news standards of these various newspaper editors and their departments may differ considerably. The city editor deals with important items of general local interest and may not be at all interested in an item concerning a new use of plastic sheeting in covering building excavations. He would either throw it away or send it to the real estate or financial editors, to whom it should have gone in the first place. They might, perhaps, welcome it, especially if they were struggling to fill a quota of news space on a dull day or if they faced the production of a big special section devoted to one of their areas of interest.

Editors also usually welcome knowing about the availability of helpful authorities in news related to their fields. Frequently a person handling public relations news releases for an oil company or chemical firm knows (and should know) more about oil or chemicals than the business or perhaps even the science editor of a newspaper. One public relations man for a French oil company had not only become an expert in his field but had also assembled a great library of facts and pictures about world petroleum production and processing. When an oil crisis breaks out in the Sahara or in Iran or in Venezuela, reporters for many French newspapers call upon him first for factual material.

A public relations person is ill-advised to attempt to use advertising as a club to "persuade" a newspaper news staff. On most good newspapers the news staff is well insulated from such attempts to bargain with advertising. Editors and reporters resent any attempt to apply pressure and will often punish those who try to do so by ignoring even good material later. In fact, advertisers sometimes need the use of space in monopoly newspapers more urgently than the newspapers need the money of the advertisers.

A public relations person will do well, too, to be careful about gifts and lavish entertainment of the press. Newspaper people are busy, and free cocktails or dinners are no novelty in their lives. They do not usually mind being fed or being given a few drinks when business is to be done, but they will not be bought in this way. On the other hand, it is not a bad idea to give a press party sometimes, just to get better acquainted. It should be purely social, with no suggestion of commercial motives.

If minor gifts, such as a fifth of whisky at Christmas, have been customary, the habit might be continued; but if you start giving away fifths or cases more often, consciences will start hurting and relations will be impaired rather than improved. Major gifts arouse the suspicion of news heads, who understandably want their staff's first loyalty to be to their newspapers and to honest reporting rather than to a set of personal benefactors. In general, giving gifts to the press is a dubious practice which has not been favored greatly in recent years and is entirely forbidden by many good papers. It should be looked upon with suspicion.

Press Conferences

There are a few occasions on which an organization may legitimately wish to invite the press to send representatives to hear an important announcement or to interview an important person. The inauguration of an outstanding new company president, with whom news reporters might wish to become acquainted, or the announcement of an important new product which requires considerable explanation would warrant an invitation. The main advantages of a press conference from a newspaper's point of view (which is all that should be considered) are that it permits each publication to develop an individual story, facilitates questioning, and releases a news opportunity to all at the same time.

It is customary to prepare complete press kits for everyone at a press conference in order to save time. For the inauguration of a new president, for instance, such a kit would probably include a biography, a picture, a prepared statement, facts about any other staff changes, and perhaps material upon the retiring president and the company as a whole. A kit on a new scientific discovery might be almost a book in itself and might be sent out several days in advance with a "hold for release" date, which the press will honor.

If, from the newspapers' viewpoint, the news given out at a press conference could just as well have been obtained from a prepared release, then the press conference probably should not have been held. Reporters are busy, and once having been fooled by a newsless press conference, they do not tend to return to the scene of their disappointment.

Another question to ask in considering the desirability of a press conference is: Is the organization really willing to answer all questions which might be asked at such a meeting? A person who holds a press conference offers to tell the whole truth, as if taking the witness stand in a court; if one has anything to hide, the suspicious circumstance will be brought to light.

Handling Bad News

Some bad news is just the report of an unfortunate occurrence for which no one is to blame. An oil-refinery fire, for instance, does not necessarily reflect unfavorably upon the efficiency of the company which suffers the loss nor does light wire damage in a sleet storm or a hurricane. In a case like this the company public relations staff should be well prepared in advance to help the press do the necessary job of covering the major news break. The company must have the basic facts ready to give out to reporters; must designate company spokesmen to describe accurately the damage, dangers, time needed for repair, and other details; must provide space in which reporters can work, typewriters, and telephone facilities; must supply guides and perhaps also special aids for photographers; must provide transportation around the scene—and perhaps even food. These arrangements must be mapped out well in advance and should be filed as carefully as a battle plan, since there will be no time to improvise coverage once a disaster strikes. The rewards of foresight and helpfulness to the press can be a chance to get across the company's side of the story, that is, to emphasize the smallness of the loss, the continued solvency of the company, the brief interruption of production or service, the assurance that orders will continue to be filled, the humanity of the company in caring for its workers and for volunteer helpers, and expressions of thanks. A final reward may be the expectation that those who help the press to do a good job in their work of covering the news at one time will most likely themselves receive somewhat more consideration (or at least a hearing) from the press some other time.

Bad news, however, may also be somewhat disgraceful—as, for example, the absconding of an insurance-company official with a large amount of money, or carelessness in the manufacture of a product which results in death or injury to users. In these instances a company public relations representative will hardly seek out the press and call the unhappy facts to their attention. Yet bad news is often passed to the press for two reasons:

1   Auditors' reports, customer suits, or government orders will often bring such matters to light before the public soon, and it is better to be sure that the whole story comes out at one time.
2   Complete honesty with the press, even when it hurts, is much respected by news people.

In any event, there is no use trying to deny the facts or to cover up bad news. Public relations persons, in effect, work for the press as well as for the organization which employs them. They cannot expect to lie to the press and still preserve usefulness as a source of news. The very least they can do is to say, "I don't know" (and this is not very satisfactory because they should know, and if ignorant, the esteem of the press is lost). Or they can say, "I can't tell you" (which is taken to mean "Yes —but you'll have to dig higher"). In *no* case can they say, "The truth is this," when really it is something entirely different.

Nor can reporters be easily kept from a story once they are on the scent of it. At one time the airlines, following the theory that accident news was bad for air travel, tried to keep newspapers from getting or running pictures of air crashes, and the personnel of the United States Air Force has covered up news of disasters, sometimes alleging security needs when none existed. Company guards at strike scenes have been known to rough-up photographers and break their cameras, and labor goons have done the same. But the press always has the last word, and it is better for an organization to accept inevitable news coverage with grace, since it cannot expect favorable treatment at one time if it makes reporters' work harder another time. The press has a long memory.

Publicity Photographs

Paradoxically, photographs are both easier and harder to get into large daily newspapers than are news stories. Photos encounter more difficulty because the competition for pictures is great on a large paper. The picture editor of a big metropolitan daily may be able to run perhaps forty pictures in each issue as compared with several hundred news stories. Some of these forty pictures are "mug shots," plain face-pictures of people involved in crimes, accidents, political campaigns, speeches, honors, and other events; others are necessary news shots of fires, floods, and so forth; and society and sports photos account for many of the rest. Not much room is left for publicity.

Photos are *easier* to get into a newspaper than stories because many news pictures are so routine that anything unusual or interesting in itself is welcomed. Every spring, for example, the city editor says to the picture editor, "I think we ought to run a spring shot." Then the photographers try to think of something "different" for a spring photograph. Lambs? No. Flowers? No. Little boys wading in the rain puddles without their galoshes? No. Young couples walking down a farm lane hand in hand? No. All these have been worked to death.

On one large Detroit newspaper a photographer, confronted with this annual problem, reasoned like this: "What does spring suggest? Romance. What does that suggest? Love-making. What creature could do the most necking? A giraffe." So he went out to the zoo to get a picture of necking giraffes. When the zoo keeper told him that giraffes had never seemed to find necking romantic, he decided to try for kissing giraffes. He started two giraffes eating simultaneously at the ends of a tasty green vine, and when both reached the middle—click! The kissing giraffes made a most unusual spring shot.

Not everyone can be so ingenious, but because *good* news-feature pictures are hard to come by, newspapers often use them when available. Standard ordinary subjects which may or may not be used include new buildings, new products, new personnel, and newly promoted employees. These have value "for the record"; but their use depends upon the size of the city and the importance of the organization. Beauty, babies, and animals are subjects which are more interesting in themselves and though much overworked, are still popular. Since the public pays attention to newspaper pictures and remembers them, public relations will find them well worth working for.

A few mechanical points should be noted about supplying pictures for newspaper use. Photographic prints for newspaper use should have good, but not extreme, black-and-white contrast and clear object outlines, since printing reproduction is only fair in quality and the pictures may be reduced in size. Busy backgrounds should be avoided. Hotel lobbies, for example, seem always to be adorned with floral wallpaper. When the president of a company is photographed against this background, flowers may seem to be growing out of his or her ears. Even amateur photographers should know that a contrast between object and background is important.

Waste space should be avoided in planning the original composition of a photograph. When one person hands another an award scroll, for example, both people should be pictured standing shoulder to shoulder instead of at arm's length. In a picture of a house a great foreground of lawn is needless, unless the lawn has something to do with the story.

Most large newspapers want 8- by 10- or 5-by 7-inch size photos on glossy paper so that retouching, if necessary, may be done more easily. Exactly square or very tall pictures or pictures wider than they are tall are hard to fit into a newspaper page, although size may not be a difficulty if the subject and print are excellent.

Weekly newspapers are likely to have relatively more picture space available than larger dailies and they welcome pictures of local interest or simply attractive, not-too-commercial feature pictures. Good pictures, supplied in the form in which the paper needs them, are often most helpful in livening up the content.

Just as all public relations people need to be able to write a competent news story, so they also need to be able to judge and perhaps to obtain adequate news pictures or feature pictures by their own efforts. Some kinds of photographs, however, are better left alone. Taking personal portraits is a specialty outside the province of the amateur public relations photographer. People are sensitive about their appearance and it is better to let them supply their own photos themselves or to get the pictures from a professional portrait photographer. Fashions, food, architecture, and large groups of people also need special photographic methods, and the amateur should not attempt them. But excluding these and perhaps a few other types of pictures, one may experiment at will.

Reasonable mastery of a reflex or 35-mm camera is a skill well worth attaining, if for no other reason than that it frees the public relations worker from the necessity of depending upon the services of professional photographers all the time, and from the resultant problems of expense, travel, and arrangements.

However, it is wise to keep out of the darkroom, since developing and printing photos takes an inordinate amount of time which might better be spent otherwise. Arrangements for handling developing and printing may be made in any large city by working with a good commercial photographer who will not only save time and do a better job but can also give the amateur much good advice about exposure and composition.

Feature Stories Yield the Greatest Reward

The difference between a news story and a feature story is easily illustrated. Suppose that a company is having an award dinner for its employees who have had more than twenty years of service with the organization. The fact that the dinner was held, that certain persons attended, and that so-and-so spoke is news, though not very important news, perhaps, except in a small town, because these dinners occur all the time. But suppose that one of the persons receiving an award has been with the company for forty-five years, is the inventor of a process upon which the company of 20,000 employees was founded, and is going to retire next week. Her history is surely the basis of a feature story. What sort of person is she? What does she recall of the early days, and how have things changed now? What does she foresee in the company's future? What does she plan to do after she retires?

Such feature stories are usually longer than news stories. They start with an interesting point instead of trying to cram their essence into the first paragraph, trot along pleasantly, and then try to end with a "twister." Feature stories are almost always illustrated, and their purpose is to entertain and inform the reader at the same time.

Since no newspaper can carry many feature stories (perhaps two or three a day at the most and several more on Sunday), they must be well written and must justify the considerable expenditure of work and space they demand. At the same time, because of their length and usual human interest, features can make a strong impression upon readers. In today's great flow of communication, features may perhaps be read less often than formerly, but they make a deep impression upon those who do go through them, and they are remembered more vividly than many small news stories just because they are less usual. Features, thus, are big game, well worth stalking with great patience and care.

A first rule about features might be: Don't write them yourself. In *news* stories, except for the comparatively rare press conference, the best procedure usually is just to write down the facts in proper news style and then to take or send the story in to the paper. Unless a public relations writer is an expert *feature* writer, he or she would do better just to jot down the facts, add photos and supporting evidence, perhaps suggest a lead, and then submit the whole effort to the editor, a reporter, or sometimes to a free-lance writer. Doing this well in advance for possible future use often makes it possible to tie the feature into a handy news event. Several feature ideas may be suggested to an editor for each one that is accepted; but when an editor does once assign a reporter to handle a feature, the story will probably appear. Too much effort and money will have been invested to warrant scrapping the product.

As we remarked about press conferences, the proposer of a feature should be sure that he *wants* the subject to be investigated. If, for instance, a major newspaper or magazine is persuaded to do a feature upon a corporation president, once the investigative process has started, the company has little control over it, since reporters will ask their own questions and write in their own ways. The company may be permitted to check upon factual accuracy, but when this supervision is granted it is a courtesy and not a right.

TRADE-MAGAZINE PUBLICITY

Just as every profession and occupation in the United States has its associations, so it also has its trade or professional magazines and news-papers which serve the needs of specialized reader interests. There are many thousands of such trade publications, ranging in size from large weekly magazines such as *Business Week,* which takes as its field the whole business world, down to the *Pigeon Breeders Journal.* Some are the size of very large magazines, well written and profusely illustrated. Others are flimsy little publications, struggling to make a living, and printed on cheap stock in inexpensive country printing shops. Some have news standards as high as any in the world, pay well for their stories, and hire first-class staff men. Others exist on a precarious advertising income from small, poor, or overcrowded fields, are easily subject to pressure for free news plugs, and may even solicit such material for a fee. A few are strictly puff sheets with no legitimate circulation to speak of, playing upon the vanity of space-hungry tycoons, and the gullibility, carelessness, or venality of public relations people who wish to make a good impression on their superiors by exhibiting a large number of column inches published rather than by choosing a reputable vehicle.

Good trade papers, however, represent an excellent outlet for public relations news and features. Such stories can be aimed directly at interested audiences and can go into a degree of detail which general-interest publications could hardly allow. In many highly specialized fields, such as scientific products or office machinery, general mass publicity is of secondary value only, since the general public is not a direct purchaser of these items; but good trade-magazine stories, catering to scientists' or businessmen's own interests, may result in immediate, recognizable sales. Trade-paper stories are much easier to place than general-magazine stories because their audiences have much more exact information and are good critics, whose opinion can often be important in their fields.

The editorial content of trade papers, like that of most magazines, is usually planned well in advance. But since some of the weekly and even daily trade papers pride themselves upon the speed with which they rush trade news to their readers, it well to inquire carefully about deadlines. Pictures, particularly those of a technical nature, are more likely to be wanted by trade journals than by more general publications. Trade-paper printing quality may be so good and technical interest in detail so keen that much more intricate photos may be submitted than would be suitable for general newspaper use. Editorial staffs, accustomed to dealing with public relations people in their special fields, often welcome help because of the complex job they face in covering large, rapidly changing industrial, commercial, or professional projects.

GENERAL MAGAZINES

There are only a few truly general magazines in the United States, such as *Reader's Digest.* The rest of the many hundreds of American magazines are aimed at specific audiences—at hunters and sports enthusiasts, those who are interested in homes and household furnishings, hot rodders, boat enthusiasts, and almost any interest group large enough to support circulation and attract advertising. Most of these audience appeals are apparent in the magazines themselves. A writer should stick to their patterns, because the chance is small that they will use anything unfamiliar. If America's daily newspapers represent the *places* where they are published, most American magazines represent their *audiences.*

In writing for a magazine, a public relations person will find that it pays to study its readers and how its editors try to appeal to them. The larger and more general a magazine becomes, the tougher is the competition it offers to writers. Not only do more writers attempt to sell to it because of its fame and higher rewards, but when its circulation reaches several million, it can and should be quite selective in using only material of interest to its subscribers. If a half dozen stories have to be thrown away in the process of selecting one, the waste (in the author's opinion) matters little to the editor, faced with the absolutely vital task of interesting and holding readers.

But if breaking into the large general-magazine field is not at all easy, the rewards are correspondingly great for products, services, or causes which can benefit from such widespread publicity. Articles for large publications are often written either by staff members or by free-lance writers. Whereas for smaller trade magazines it may be a good idea to submit whole articles and pictures already finished by a public relations source, the approach to a larger publication may need to be less direct; the magazine may want to write or to buy its own stories. A writer engaged in publicity work may do well to offer an idea for a story, completely outlined or roughly sketched, to a free-lance writer who may be interested because of the opportunity for a story sale. The practice of some free-lancers of getting paid twice, first by a public relations source and then by the magazine to which they sell their stories, is not unknown; but such dishonesty sometimes results in the ending of relations between the magazine and the free-lancer.

Since most of the nation's larger magazines are published in New York City, connections there, including feature-placement bureaus, can be most helpful.

RADIO PUBLICITY

Most radio stations today stress local interests in the content of their programs, thus offering a useful medium for local publicity. Radio news is shorter than printed news and should be of more general interest than expanded newspaper accounts, since the radio listener does not have the same choice of selection that the newspaper reader enjoys. Listeners can turn the set on or off or switch stations, but cannot select what they hear or do not hear when the station is on.

Broadcast news is even more timely than printed news. It can be put on the air rapidly and is of value in emergencies. Radio news people cannot be ignored at press conferences and other events, but their ability to disseminate news ahead of press deadlines is irritating to print news people, who have to move more slowly. Radio is always in a position to make a "scoop."

Radio can be especially useful for special features such as short on-the-spot recordings, longer news reports like those describing ski-resort snow and weather conditions, and brief interviews with interesting persons.

In smaller places, because of their low production costs, radio stations may tend to resemble local weekly newspapers and to carry all sorts of localized material so long as it is reasonably rapid-paced. But as stations get larger or are located in larger cities they must become more selective and carry only material that is of interest to large numbers of their listeners or face a loss of audience and advertising. In very large localities radio stations frequently become specialized, some seeking audiences of classical music lovers, others rock and roll fans, or devotees of country-western. Some stations may carry only news and others appeal to ethnic groups, sometimes in foreign language broadcasts. All of these offer publicity and advertising opportunities to the public relations person having very specific target audiences in mind.

TELEVISION PUBLICITY

The amount of time available for television news is even more limited than that for radio news, since there are fewer broadcasts, and fewer items can be used in each broadcast. But television's great need for *visual* material in its news broadcasts opens up many opportunities for public relations entry.

Events which make *good pictures,* although perhaps of only modest news value, may attract television newsmen when they are informed of them far enough in advance to schedule a crew. Activities involving children or animals or sports would be examples. Sometimes, if the station cannot cover the events, they might use short bits of film. A talk with station news managers in advance will give an idea of what they want and are prepared to carry or cover.

It is particularly easy for "public service" causes such as civic and cultural organizations, schools, health agencies, and youth organizations to get both publicity and free commercial spots on radio and television because, as a condition for maintaining their broadcasting licenses, stations are required to give a certain amount of their air time to this purpose by the Federal Communications Commission.

Longer "sustaining" films of a low-key, feature-service caliber are sometimes welcomed by stations to fit into unsold time, to provide substitutions in the event of sudden cancellations, or to help fill the odd intervals of time left after sports events and other irregularly timed programs. High standards of production are expected, in contrast to the jerky or overexposed shots tolerated on local news broadcasts. Resort-area promotion, interesting processes and people, sports, and social activities are typical subject matter. The commercial angle should be almost nonexistent, or at least not very apparent; when promotion is obvious, the station properly feels that it should be paid for the time.

There can be no doubt of the great impact of television and it has not been used as extensively as it might be by public relations people. Perhaps this is because so many of them are former print news people and are not really familiar with the medium. Perhaps, also, it is because it is harder to keep a record of what has been done on television and to show it to management. Perhaps it is because of the restricted nature of television news broadcasts. Whatever the reasons, the power of television which has been so much used by product advertisers and in political campaigns has been applied to public relations primarily in low-key sponsorship of worthy programs by large corporations and by institutional advertising, commercial spots promoting corporate identity or viewpoints. There seems to be a recognition that television is a powerful but difficult medium with somewhat unpredictable effects and there remains plenty of potential for public relations pioneering in its best use for persuasion and information.

MERCHANDISING PUBLICITY FOR THE GREATEST RESULTS

All public relations practitioners who engage in publicity work also keep a scrapbook of clippings, not only to see how they are doing but also to impress employers. Often these clippings are duplicated and circulated to other company officers or to salesmen to show them how much attention is being paid to their organization by the various media. This useful aid in buttressing public relations's value to the organization also has its perils. Superiors may say, "This is fine—now get us lots more!" and if the press becomes aware of such a trophy bag, it may think it is being imposed upon and curtail the number of news items and other stories. A sounder public relations procedure is not to display every single clipping but instead to select significant typical stories to serve as demonstrations of "This is what they're saying about us." A deeper danger is that public relations people may oversell the value of publicity (always easy to do), which is only part of the job, sometimes not even the major part, and then find themselves chained to their organization's impossible expectation of more and more mentions. In fact, clippings, rather than the achievement of understanding or good will, may become the managerial measure of success.

Another aspect of merchandising of publicity is found in the advertising pages of *Editor & Publisher,* the newspaper publisher's trade-paper Bible, and in other magazines devoted to the mass communications media. Here the public realtions department of a company or other organization may offer its informational services to the press in whatever field of expertness its experience encompasses. "If you want to know about space communication," it may say, "call us up. We're glad to help." For those who have a genuine store of expert aid available, this is a worthwhile practice and also reflects credit upon all releases which proceed from such a source.

Publicity, however, can never be considered the equivalent of all public relations activities; while publicity can make an organization known, publicity alone cannot determine what people will think of it.

THE ADVERTISING FAMILY OF THE MASS MEDIA: PUBLIC RELATIONS ADVERTISING

Any advertising not aimed at the reasonably immediate sale of a product or service can be called public relations advertising. It is fairly common and has increased greatly in recent years.

Advertising, in contrast to publicity, appears in space purchased in a newspaper or magazine or in time bought on the air; in it buyers say what they wish—as loudly, persuasively, wisely, or foolishly as they wish. Such space or time is expensive, but it often provides the quickest and surest way of speaking to many people at once. Large space in a daily newspaper can reach almost all the people reading the paper within its circulation area, and in a magazine it can reach all the types of persons who constitute its reader audience.

Public relations advertising may be used to make an *announcement,* for example, of the position of a company in a labor dispute; to make a statement about a new product or a merger with another company; to contradict rumors; to thank those who helped in case of a disaster; to dedicate a plant; to invite to an open house; or to announce a closing because of the death of an official.

Advertising may be used to build a *corporate family image.* The du Pont Company, the General Electric Company, and General Motors Corporation make many products and advertise them all as individual items. But these companies do more; they also sponsor quality television shows and printed advertising designed to make customers think better of the company and of all its products because they come from that company. As many similar products develop, made by many other companies, this institutional type of advertising becomes more and more important because real, valid, individual product differences are constantly harder to find. Also, although people will refuse to buy a product whose maker is not known to them, they will take a chance on buying one of which they have heard.

In the discussion of high-quality products, particularly, the boundary between *sales* advertising and *public relations* advertising tends to blur. In a Steinway piano advertisement, for example, the objective of the advertisement is not to sell at a price or perhaps even to sell immediately but to create an image so favorable that the eventual goal of a piano purchaser will be to own a Steinway.

Advertising which is used to promote *causes,* such as opposition to taxes, anti-inflation drives, fighting foreign competition, seeking a larger share of the market (as when railroads compete with trucks), or presenting economic viewpoints and governmental philosophies, is also definitely public relations advertising. In today's increasingly complex world, where many arguments seek to influence public opinion, this advertising abounds and will doubtless spread still further. A question of tax deduction enters in at this point, however. Sales advertising, regarded as a necessary part of doing business, may be deducted from a corporation's profits before taxes are levied. But often a similar allowance will not be made for an electric power company which takes space in a paper to argue against the desirability of public ownership. Or how about a machine-tool-products company which constantly uses space to preach the virtues of the American free enterprise system? Or an oil company which buys advertising space to try to influence laws which may be passed against it—such as requiring it to sell its holdings in coal mines? The question is far from settled because it is related to the American constitutional right of freedom of speech. Can different rules be applied to organizations, whether profit or nonprofit, than are applied to persons?

Community understanding and goodwill are often the objectives of public relations advertisements. They may seek to explain the economic contributions of a business, to humanize the image of its management, and to recognize the good work of its employees. Even brief forms of annual financial reports are often published in this way.

Influence upon legislation is sought by many ads which run in state capitals and in Washington as well as in some other large cities.

Financial public relations goals are often sought by advertisements in newspapers such as the *Wall Street Journal* or magazines such as *Forbes* or *Business Week*.

Many other public relations advertisements are run as *consumer services*, for example, the noted magazine series on health by the Metropolitan Life Insurance Company of New York or the career series of the New York Life Insurance Company.

Public relations advertising not only appears in newspapers and in magazines, but is perhaps even more important on television, as is illustrated in its use by firms such as the United States Steel Company and Aluminium Ltd. of Canada.

Large, well-designed outdoor posters on highways announcing that a nearby city is the home of a certain factory also are a common form of public relations advertising. When an electric light company erects poster boards at the edges of its service-area towns telling passing motorists about the histories and merits of the towns, there is no doubt about the public relations slant, nor is there at the other extreme when an organization sponsors an "attend church" or "support the Community Chest" board with only its name below as sponsor identification.

TOOLS OF DIRECT APPROACH

In both press publicity and in paid advertising space, the primary vehicle for a public relations message is operated by someone else. A publicity story in a well-respected, widely circulated newspaper owes some of its effectiveness to the newspaper itself. A public relations advertisement in a magazine directed to physicians, for example, is effective only to the extent that the magazine reaches doctors and is read and believed by them. Both the originators of publicity releases and the buyers of advertising space can judge the vehicles that carry their messages, but they do not control them. However, when an organization starts making speeches, showing motion pictures, taking visitors on tours, constructing exhibits, mailing out company magazines, erecting plant reading racks, designing pamphlets, or writing letters, the public relations source assumes full responsibility for both the message *and* the vehicle that is to carry it. The very list of possible media conveys an idea of the complexity of the job of public relations people. They need not be expert in all these fields (although they will be in at least several), but *must* be able to judge their good and bad points—their beauty, suitability to the message, and effectiveness—and to hire people who can best do the job of preparing or using them. They must be skilled in the use of the graphic arts, including typography, photography, color, and design; must know good radio and television material from bad; must be able to originate an exhibit which will stop the crowds streaming through a bewilderingly large fair and tell its story; and must do well in many other means of communication.

COMPANY OR ORGANIZATION MAGAZINES AND NEWSPAPERS

Nobody knows how many organization magazines and newspapers there are because no complete census has been taken and because they keep constantly springing up and disappearing, but estimates indicate that there are perhaps 8,000 in this country with a combined readership of perhaps 20 million people and an annual publication cost of more than 150 million dollars.

A publication is the most common form of organizational communication and may range in size from a single-page mimeographed sheet to a large, elaborate, four-color magazine resembling the best general commercial publications on the market. Editing organization publications is almost a profession in itself, and company magazine editors are nationally organized into a strong professional association.

The greatest number of these publications are known as *internals* because they are aimed chiefly at reader audiences already closely connected in some way with the organization, such as employees, stockholders, dealers, or suppliers, and on the outer fringes, perhaps community leaders and friends. A smaller number of publications, called *externals,* go to customers or possible customers, leaders of general opinion like educators and legislators, and have as their objects selling company products, informing readers of product uses, and creating general prestige, good will, and understanding.

Whenever an organization of any sort gets so large that spoken communications are no longer sufficient, it publishes printed literature of some kind. People will always communicate, since humans inevitably think and talk, and there can be no such thing as a communications vacuum among employees or stockholders, or in any other group. These people will think about their vital concerns, and they will get impressions and information from one source or another. The organization has no choice as to whether it will or will not communicate; it can only decide how it will communicate, to what extent, and about what.

There is no single right way in which a company publication should be designed, since what is proper for one organization may not be fitting for another. Publication appearances and contents may properly differ greatly, but there are certain basic principles common to all good editing, and the right way is to apply all these properly to the particular situation of the organization in question.

Internal publications have among their frequent objectives:

1 Informing and persuading readers about company policies and goals, ranging from efforts toward better safety records to more productivity, lessened absenteeism, or conservation of materials. A publication should not only tell readers the facts or hand down management edicts, but should also find and explain points of coincidence of interest between employees and management. For example, both employees and management share an interest in greater productivity; better production of goods may preserve jobs because it enables the company to maintain competitive prices with foreign products in American overseas markets and at home.

2 Encouraging good work by recognition. Because of unionization or other causes, many workers draw identical paychecks and are classified in the same jobs; yet some of these employees do much better work than others. How are they to be rewarded and others encouraged to emulate them? Public recognition in the form of pictures and stories in a company publication is one form of reward which may be unusually important in a big city. In a large metropolitan daily newspaper, for instance, the ordinary citizen is fortunate to get even three lines of type in his obituary notice. Only the quite famous or infamous, or those who end in some spectacular way, such as jumping off the World Trade Center building, are much more noted. Yet even in a faceless world people still crave recognition and personal warmth.

3 Preventing interdepartmental friction. Built-in feuds are common in too many organizations. The sales force could always sell more if it had a better product; the production staff could make a better product if it had more money; there would be more money if there were more sales, and so forth. Such disputes are natural, and to a certain point the ambition and aggressiveness of each portion of an organization are beneficial; but when too much energy is expended upon bickering, the resulting rash of accusations, excuses, and alibis, the shirking of forward thinking, and the general unhappiness leads to a cessation of company progress. Better personal understanding of the whole program of the organization can be provided by a company publication, and is often a partial answer to the problem of creating greater cooperation and enthusiasm.

4 Diminishing labor turnover. It takes both money and time to train new help, particularly skilled workers or executives; it is therefore worthwhile to find out what makes employees think well of a company and want to stay with it. Among the causes of goodwill certainly are information, confidence in the future, both for the employee and for the organization, and a realization of the advantages enjoyed, the social life, work benefits, and pensions.

5   Aiding company public relations. What do employees tell others about their organization? Ill-informed or little-regarded employees are likely to be gripers, more so than those who are taken into the confidence of management. "I call you not servants; for the servant knoweth not what his lord doeth: but I have called you friends," said Jesus to his disciples.

6   Aiding sales. When numbers of employees in a large area are engaged in making general consumer products, they are a major market in themselves, and their work carries weight with many other possible customers.

7   Gaining acceptance for the division of earnings. Every company slices its earnings pie at least four ways—*wages* to employees, *salaries* to management, *dividends* to stockholders, and *plow-back* into the business for expansion or development. While most people agree that profits are necessary and desirable, their proper amount and uses are often subject to dispute. Employees often have an exaggerated idea of profits, and think that they should receive a larger share of the total income. If a company has a good case to present to its employees, it should publish the facts.

8   Protecting private industry. Among the public utilities or transportation companies, the need to protect private industry may be urgent. Public ownership of utilities is common in many places in the world and also in this country. Urging the merits of private ownership as a basic economic philosophy is necessary in any event—certainly to industry and probably to the country as a whole.

Such a list of objectives might be extended, but it should be noted that these objectives are all primarily those which belong to the organization issuing the publication and are not necessarily those of its readers. Company objectives will be listened to only insofar as the interests of the organization and the readers can be made to coincide. There is no such thing as a captive audience for a company internal publication; the magazine may be issued and mailed free to the homes of employees, but there is no assurance that it will be read or will have any effect. Its influence depends upon the skill of the editor and the wisdom of superiors, usually including the public relations director. Their work will decide whether the publication will be respected and liked or whether it will sound pompous, pushing, and careless of the employees, perhaps doing more harm than good. Nothing can be more important than selecting a good editor, since a publication is no more than the thinking of its editors and writers compressed into print, and cannot possibly be any better than its origin.

The editor must have the technical skill and training to write well and also have a good understanding of photography, art, layout, and printing. The ability to interpret a company and its management to employees requires intelligence and a desire to understand both the company and its people. In a large company which makes many specialized products in plants all over the country and employs people ranging from Ph.D. scientists to barely literate millhands, such adaptability and impartiality are not at all simple. An editor needs poise and study to be able to talk to the president or the production manager in their terms, to mingle with the country-club set one day and then to cover an employee picnic at plant Number 9 tomorrow with equal grace and friendliness. He or she needs wisdom to avoid offending people by making mistakes and humor to take well-meant but often oblique advice; patience to understand complex situations and humility to realize that *comprehension* of someone else's work is not the same as being able to perform it well. And, above all, the editor's post requires unfailing accuracy, zeal, and the determination to put out such an interesting publication that readers cannot possibly avoid going through it from cover to cover.

Finding such an editorial paragon isn't easy. In most companies an editor cannot be trained easily from the ranks of salesmen or production workers because good editing is a specialized art. In a very small organization, a secretary might do the job under good leadership, but in a large company a trained editor is a necessity. A young college-journalism graduate might work as an editor's assistant and eventually take over the job. A news writer might be hired, and if he or she could change from the objectivity required of a good newspaper reporter to the persuasion expected of a company editor, they might do well. Or an editor might be hired from a smaller company publication. In any case, a new person will take months to learn enough about a large company to be able to speak authoritatively. The editor has to be given freedom, encouragement, patient guidance, and proper payment. The work, though highly instructive and enjoyable, has a natural wage ceiling, and the upward route for the company editor is often into broader public relations practice itself, for which publication editing is an excellent training.

Getting Out the Publication

It is important that the format of a publication be suitable for its audience and main objectives. A small plant, located under one roof and with limited funds, would probably find an offset-printed, monthly, informal newspaper or semimagazine about right, probably set in typewriter type or something similar. But a bank, with the same number of employees in a large city, would perhaps want to issue a small pocket-size magazine, more formally edited and set in regular printing type with a more dignified appearance. Perhaps neither of these publications would be exactly "right" for the most effective communication, but they would be what readers and onlookers would expect. A huge, elaborate publication for a small industry, or a breezy gossip sheet for a bank might well be criticized for not properly mirroring the character of the organization. Informality is fine for Smith's Machine Works but would be out of place for the City First National Bank.

A large company with 20,000 workers under one roof might well find that a five-column tabloid-size newspaper on coated stock, appearing every two weeks, with plenty of pictures would best fill its needs; another company with four widely scattered plants of 5,000 workers in each might find that a single magazine and four modest monthly plant newspapers was the right prescription; and a shoe company putting out an expensive line of women's shoes would probably want to send its dealers a brief, but very finely designed and printed monthly or quarterly publication which would reflect the high fashion of its product.

The really important thing, however, is not how a publication looks but what it says. A good appearance may gain an audience, and a hard-to-read, uninviting appearance may drive it away, but only good content can satisfy readers and keep them returning to absorb the ideas which the organization wishes to convey.

Among the important factors in such content are news, pictures, and human-interest features. But what, for example, constitutes "news" for a company publication?

News is anything of timely importance or interest which affects a significant portion of a reader audience. Election of a new company president is obviously news, but the fact that a new mechanic has joined the maintenance force in plant Number 3 is not news to the same degree; the mechanic may be just as good a human being as the president, but his hiring does not affect as many people. The retirement of the mechanic in plant Number 3 after twenty years of service, however, is much more news than his first employment because after twenty years many more people know him and are interested in him.

When an employee goes on a weekend fishing expedition, hooks three fair catfish, and the employee's spouse takes a picture and sends it to the company paper, the editor has to think twice before running it; if the picture does run next month a half dozen employees are likely to bring in pictures of similarly undistinguished strings of fish and expect these photos to appear also. A possible working rule might be that if the employee catches a 60-pound catfish, the picture will appear because that is sufficiently unusual to be news anywhere.

In a small plant where people know each other fairly well, trivial items may be legitimate news, just as they are in a small-town weekly newspaper, where a child's birthday party may be worth at least three or four lines of type. But for large, scattered plants, news standards must be more restrictive because people do not know each other so well. An editor makes a dull paper for most of the readers when trying to please everybody by filling it with trivial personal items which interest only a few individuals and their friends. More genuine news should have a broader appeal. Reports of outstanding personal achievements, service records, promotions, transfers, and new company developments would be of general interest. A standard news policy should be adopted and maintained so that the editor does not favor one person's report over another's. News may be run to please people, to recognize their achievements, and to get reader interest, but the question must also be asked: "How much does this item benefit the organization which is paying the costs of producing this publication?" Answers should be in terms of information, good will, and more direct benefits, but there should be answers.

Where does internal publication news come from? Certain sources can be organized for regular coverage; the records of promotions, transfers, retirements, illnesses, hiring of new employees, and vacations are available in company business or personnel offices. Other news items can sometimes be obtained through department heads, who will know about new production equipment, sales-drive plans, and advertising programs. Other news items may be obtained through a network of departmental or plant correspondents, whose work can be rewarded with recognition, an annual dinner, and perhaps Christmas gifts. All news items must be carefully checked for accuracy, and clumsy attempts to be funny (and certainly to play malicious pranks) must be guarded against. With all its great power for good, a company newspaper also has the capacity to hurt individuals.

Photographs and other illustrations are an important part of almost every company publication. When an item in type is hard to read or does not seem particularly interesting, the reader will ignore it completely; but a picture is at least always looked at, and viewers take meaning from it according to their abilities and interests. A photo of a complicated piece of chemistry laboratory equipment will cause the average person to say simply, "What a complicated gadget!" while the scientist will grasp every significant detail. But if a verbal description of the same equipment is presented, the layman will understand exactly nothing and even the scientist may be somewhat baffled. Most potent, however, is a *combination* of words and pictures, because readers first look at the pictures and then read the type under them to learn the meaning of what they are seeing. Many a story can be told in pictures and cutlines which would get absolutely no attention in straight type.

Many pictures, however, can be as dull as poor prose, and their dullness often lies, primarily, in the way in which they are displayed in a magazine or a newspaper. A common failure is to run too many pictures in such small sizes that the many details in each cannot be seen or appreciated. This crowding may be excusable in a series of service-anniversary-dinner group photos because these are "record" pictures. But in covering a company picnic, the editor often commits the same sin, trying to please everyone by cramming in six photos showing ten people in each, rather than by using one or two decently large pictures and omitting or playing down the rest. If many pictures have to be used, at least they should not all be of equal size. Even though company magazines and newspapers are usually printed on good paper stock with good engravings and can usually reproduce crowded small pictures successfully from a mechanical viewpoint, good reproduction still does not make them interesting.

Very often, also, the company-publication editor will have to be a photographer also. He or she will need to follow the general rules about photo taking previously mentioned in connection with other newspapers or magazines. Photo negatives cost so little that it pays to shoot a great many pictures. An editor should be careful, however, not to lead people to expect that every picture taken will be used. Remember, too, that people are sensitive about their appearance; and give them a chance to look their best. Personal portraits, such as those for service-award photos, are usually better left to professional photographers, as are also large group shots in which adequate lighting and negative size are important. The editor's camera, however, can be a great icebreaker, getting people to talk and cooperate more quickly than any other means.

Artwork is important to lighten a publication and to give a change of pace; the soft grays of many photographs tend to become visually monotonous and to blend in with each other. Drawings such as humorous cartoons can add greatly to reader interest.

There are numerous good books on company-publication planning and layout, and a public relations person should be familiar with them. If, to other duties, must be added that of an editor, one will find that a good magazine designer, a good printer, and a good photographer can do a great deal. But the real test of ingenuity and purpose will come in what is put into the publication.

Features constitute the third main part of the content of company publications. They are relatively more important than in commercial publications because they frequently achieve great success in getting across the information about an organization which can be illuminating and persuasive to readers. Suppose, for example, that an editor wishes to convince employee readers that the company has a good pension plan. What better way could be chosen than to interview several recent retirees, taking their pictures and finding what interesting things they are doing? Such a feature not only is full of readable human interest in itself, but since many present employees know these people, it also shows indirectly the merits of the company pension plan. Or a company might wish to encourage its employees to take a leading part in civic-improvement programs in plant cities. For example, an employee who has just served as chairman for the local United Fund drive, might be mentioned and his work described; and perhaps, incidentally, information might be given about the types of people assisted by the United Fund and the reasons why the company supports it.

Some interesting features, of course, may have no direct purpose of any sort. A story about an employee who takes an unusual vacation, or a service feature on how to prepare your income tax, or on how to tan while avoiding early summer sunburn may have a place. Although a company has good reasons for spending money on a publication, not every item should have an overt purpose or the paper will be like a friend who can discuss nothing except business.

Soft Sell versus Hard Sell

By sound tradition, most company publications try to build goodwill and understanding by example and encouragement rather than by direct exhortation in which their self-interest is quite apparent.

There is a difference, however, between avoiding preaching and ducking the mention of facts because they are unpleasant or controver-

sial. Labor union papers are often filled with exhortation and controversy. Because of legal restrictions, the company press must be careful
not to tell employees what to do in a labor controversy or to seem to
threaten them under such circumstances, but this does not mean that the
company press must be silent. Dignified, factual reporting of news of
such keen employee interest as an industrial dispute would seem to be
a part of necessary coverage of what is going on.

But even so, the strongest statements might best be left to direct
letters, to bulletins, and to newspaper advertisements, where they will get
the greatest immediate attention anyway. A long-established company
publication has often become a friendly institution. It is sometimes the
most popular project undertaken by the company, and its readers may
enjoy it better and continue to depend upon it longer if the most bitter
elements of economic controversy are not introduced. They may prefer
the usual run of stories of babies, vacations, old pensioners, and company
progress. Issues come and go, but organizations and their publications
can go on indefinitely. The respect and friendship which have been
earned over a long period by a good company publication should not be
sacrificed in the heat of perhaps one day's conflict.

A really successful internal company publication is not only read
and accepted by the employees; it goes to their homes and is read by their
families and friends as well. It is consistent, friendly, reliable, and frank
in its purposes. It is edited from the viewpoint of those who read it. Its
editor needs a good sense of communication, and the ability to understand "what I should like if I were in my reader's shoes, with his or her
background, interests, hopes, and problems."

External Publications

External publications differ from internals because their readership and
their purposes are different. In general they are better-looking magazines, directed at customers or leaders of opinion outside of the organization. They may exist to further sales or to obtain good will in influential
quarters. Since their readers have less direct connection with the issuing
organization, the publications must compete for their attention with
more commercial publications and do so without the advantage of personal contacts. Readers compare external publications directly with big
general magazines or newspapers. For that reason their news must be of
compellingly wide interest, as are the presentations of scientific or financial subjects in any semipopular magazine; their features must approach
National Geographic or *Reader's Digest* quality; and their pictures must

be noteworthy in themselves. Sometimes external magazines are so well edited and successful that they outgrow their original purpose and become almost general national publications, as have *Arizona Highways* and *Ford Times.*

External magazines can be of great value to a company dealing in specialized products whose use must be explained in detail to customers too widely scattered for the salesforce to reach personally; to an organization making many varied products which it wishes to group under a single sales banner; and to an organization which needs goodwill because of its political or social situation. An external magazine, as a rule, should be well done or it is better not attempted, because its reading public gives it no quarter.

OPEN HOUSES AND TOURS

Surprisingly, many of the spouses and children of employees have never been in the plants or offices where workers of the family earn their living; farmers selling wheat or milk to a processing plant have never seen what goes on inside of it; users of electricity have never seen a generating plant; and parents of school children have never been inside a schoolroom. Such a separation of life and work makes for easy misunderstanding. Those who do know something about where people work and what they produce have a personal interest in their industrial environment and an intelligent comprehension of it.

Setting up a good plant or office visit, however, is not simple. Some factories are too noisy, too dirty, or too dangerous to be suitable visiting locations. Other places offer little to see because the machinery is hidden or, as in company offices, because the work is largely mental and clerical and there is nothing to observe except people at their desks. It may sometimes be necessary to set up exhibits and pictures to show what cannot be seen.

Since people give their time and attention to a tour of a plant, the conduct of their visit should be perfect. Guides must be courteous and well prepared, routes carefully laid out, explanatory signs posted as needed, rest and refreshments provided. An opportunity to make friends can easily be soured by thoughtlessness. Among the most common tour groups are employees and their families, townspeople, and special groups composed of students, scientists, salesmen, dealers, and suppliers.

Some visits to a plant are handled en masse on special occasions. For example, an open house might be held in connection with a new-plant opening or a plant-addition dedication. Such a program might include three days of tours—an opening day for employees and their families, a second day for opinion leaders, and a third day for the general public.

Tours may be arranged to other places also upon special occasions. When Pet, Incorporated, a large national food company of St. Louis, Missouri, reached its seventieth anniversary, for example, it was decided to hold an open house for all office employees and their families of the St. Louis headquarters and of a nearby plant, at the farm home of the original founder of the company, Louis Latzer, about 35 miles east of St. Louis. Several hundered people attended, most of them coming in their own cars, although buses were provided without charge for those who wished to use them. Because Louis Latzer had come from Switzerland, a busload of employees from the Pet Company milk processing plant at New Glarus, Wisconsin, a Swiss settlement, attended, dressed in traditional Swiss costume, to put on a program of yodeling, flag throwing, and alpenhorn blowing.

Staging a visit like this required a planned tour route, road maps, road signs, directed parking and policing, guides along the route of the tour through the big old farmhouse, large tents for luncheon and refreshments, another large tent for rest and shelter in case of rain, hundreds of folding chairs and tables, favors for the children, first-aid facilities, insurance, fire protection, printed programs, and extensive coverage in the next issue of the employee magazine. The inside of the house had to be rearranged to enable hundreds of people to walk through it. A small museum of exhibits was constructed. Its preparation included collecting objects, labeling them, and placing them in suitable glass cases which had to be built for the occasion. Every contingency was anticipated and adequate volunteer and paid help provided for. The reward was that the people who participated enjoyed themselves and got an idea of the history of the company and of the nature of the people who founded it which could have been obtained in no other way. In these days when all of us receive a constant flood of vicarious experience through many mass media, the two words "I saw" are stronger than ever. Every plant open house should have a reason. Such events cannot be held very often, but when held, they should be perfect and memorable.

Regular visitor tours through plants are another problem and opportunity. Large plants, making well-known products, located in or near major cities and on main highways, have the greatest opportunity to attract visitors. The flow can be stimulated by plant identification signs, highway billboards, and promotion in other company advertising and communications. Almost any reasonably interesting and important plant can obtain many groups of visiting students and members of clubs or of professional groups, if it makes an effort to do so. Such tours can be either perfunctory or meaningful.

A number of years ago a newspaper for which the author then worked discovered that about 6,000 students a year were touring its downtown St. Louis office and plant. Since conduct of the tours had been haphazard, steps were taken to improve their management. Young men and women from the circulation and want-ad departments, located on the first floor near the building lobby, were trained as guides. To help them in their task, a tour route was laid out, areas in which guides could stand and talk to groups were marked, and a script was prepared for them.

At the conclusion of each school tour, the guide gave the students' teacher a tour booklet, then showed it to the children, and asked if they would like to have a copy mailed to their homes. Those who wanted it (almost all, as a rule) then filled in a small gummed address label which was later affixed to the envelope in which the booklet was mailed. A duplicated letter of appreciation for the visit accompanied the booklets, which were received at the homes of the children and were probably read by several family members. Thus the memory of the visit was revitalized. Previously, booklets given to children at the newspaper plant were frequently found in nearby street gutters.

After obtaining the teacher's approval, the guide would also announce that if the members of the class wished to write brief essays on the aspects of the visit which interested them most and would send them in to the newspaper as a group, a large world globe would be awarded to the class in the name of the student who submitted the best essay. On a plate at the base of the globe the student's name and the date of the visit would be inscribed. There was no obligation to write an essay, and the announcement was never made unless the teacher agreed in advance. Reading the essays not only gave the guides a good idea of what most impressed the students, but also led to improvements and served as a check upon the guides themselves.

The values of plant tours can be endless. In one company, a new public relations person discovered that new salespeople coming into headquarters for their initial two-week training period had, until then, never been taken on a plant tour to see the manufacture of the product they were supposed to sell. In fact, many veteran salespeople had never been inside a plant, although they had been selling for many years and had many times visited headquarters, near which a plant was located. A plant visit was immediately made a standard part of introductory training, since the process of production was excellent and gave increased confidence in the product itself.

In another case, farmers who had been selling milk to a processing plant had had no opportunity to see what happened to their daily output once it left their farms. Since the size of their checks partly depended upon butterfat, bacterial, and other plant laboratory tests, it was well worthwhile to plan tours which would enable dairy farmers to see the careful scientific testing and the expensive laboratory equipment, and to satisfy their natural interest in other aspects of milk processing.

EXHIBITS

There is little doubt of the communications value of well-edited company magazines or of carefully planned open houses and tours, but exhibits such as those at fairs or professional meetings present a greater problem to the public relations planner. What should be told? How can there be any assurance that adequate traffic will justify the investment? How can viewers be stopped and an exhibit be made memorable even if there is such traffic? In many instances the cost of an exhibit per viewer is extremely high, not only for the exhibit space, which is often sold upon a charitable or sandbagging basis, but also because the competition for attention is intense, the costs of construction high, and the labor costs of manning an exhibit much beyond the probable benefits.

But these problems do not constitute reasons for giving up the attempt to get the utmost value out of every dollar which must be spent. The ideal exhibit is colorful, pictorial, and unusual. If possible, it includes action and participation on the part of the spectators. Can the viewer push a button, for example, and see something happen? Can he get an answer to a question? Can she see a step in a process or distribution on a map? People remember best what they take part in.

Some years ago the *Des Moines Register and Tribune* purchased a new airplane which could fly from Des Moines, the capital of Iowa, to any major city in the state and bring back news in a few minutes. To dramatize this fact, the newspaper used Iowa State Fair exhibit space that year to install a huge map of Iowa with all the main cities of the state indicated by opaque glass circles on the map. "How long does it take to fly to your city for *Register and Tribune* news?" said the overline. At the rail in front of the big map was a row of push buttons labeled with the names of the towns and a sign: "Push the button. See how long it takes for the airplane to fly to your home town." When the button was pushed, the correct number of minutes lit up in the correct glass circle on the map, and an illuminated white line indicated the flight course. The only flaw in the exhibit was that the buttons were pushed so hard during the day that the electricians had to replace them every night.

On another occasion, at the same state fair, the newspaper used a group of instant photo cameras for the week of the fair. An enlarged copy of the front page of the newspaper was made, with the headline CELE-BRITY VISITS FAIR and a blank space, as if for a picture, cut out beneath it, into which a visitor could stick his face from behind. This was set up at the exhibit, and as soon as a visitor's picture was shot, it was ready and the visitor could depart with a photo showing his or her picture, supposedly, upon the front page of the state's largest newspaper. This exhibit, which combined participation with selling the newspaper, was a great success; crowds lined up in a block-long queue, and the exhibit produced about 15,000 pictures in the five days of the fair.

If a public relations employee knows that his or her organization is going to be called upon for numbers of small exhibits which may be of questionable value, it may be worthwhile to prepare colorful, pictorial, but unattended displays for certain locations and to concentrate most money and effort upon exhibits at the events which are likely to be well attended, and where prestige may be gained or lost.

Several other types of display activity are related to exhibits, including parade floats and exhibit museums at construction scenes or at historic sites. Parade floats, like outdoor advertising in general, should be attractive and confined to the impact of one single idea. If other organizations in a parade spend money to look attractive, your organization must do so also, but the actual public relations value of these expensive floats in relation to their cost is often dubious.

Informative signs and museums at building construction sites are another matter, because there is usally keen public interest in what is happening, and signs, plans, and preview photos can capitalize upon it. If a new electric power plant is being built, for example, a small museum may be constructed on a nearby highway containing models of the completed plant, pictures, facts, and perhaps push-button questions and answers to inform visitors who, for safety reasons, cannot go through the construction itself. A similar program could be followed with a factory or a new school. At the very minimum signs and drawings should be used to tell passers-by what is going on and when completion is expected. This is not only a courtesy but also offers a chance to get across a message when interest is naturally keen. In big city construction, which is usually walled off from pedestrians by high board fences for safety reasons, viewing windows are often provided and sometimes even viewing platforms.

MEETINGS

Getting a group of people together and talking things over is one of the oldest communications medium in history, yet one which is often neglected today because it seems so simple. Because it is a personal experience, rather than a secondhand sensation, a meeting has great power for either good or ill.

One plan is simply to get everyone together and then tell them something in lecture form, perhaps enlivened by visual aids. An annual-report meeting for stockholders or a mass meeting of employees to announce a new policy is an example of a lecture meeting. Its weakness is that it is one-way communication. The audience's interest cannot be assumed unless attendance is entirely voluntary, and achieving two-way communication in a large meeting of this sort is not easy because questions are likely to be long, trivial, and digressive; yet denial of questions is not a good policy either. It is even worse when no one has a question.

One alternative is a number of small group meetings, such as those used by du Pont and described in Chapter 12, "Communications Cases." Here two-way communication avoids the sense of rebellion caused by the imposition of one-way lecturing. Although the cost in training time and hours of work lost is great, perhaps the effort is worthwhile if communication is well established.

Another type of meeting is the voluntarily attended lecture on some subject related to the business or simply of general interest. The employees, their families, and friends are invited, but it is made clear that attendance in no way affects an employee's job. At a chemical plant, for example, the visit of a noted scientist might provide the occasion for such a semipublic lecture. On a newspaper, the Washington staff correspondent might report to the home-town people every year. Promotion of the business can be touched on lightly in the remarks of the moderator and in questions from the audience. An informal social hour may well be combined with this type of meeting. Here again the problem is: What if nobody (or almost nobody) comes? Common sense suggests a little sounding-out and advance organization to check the pulling-power of an idea before making a public invitation and putting the prestige of the public relations person and the organization on the line.

ORGANIZED SOCIAL ACTIVITIES

Company picnics, Christmas parties, bowling leagues, and golf tourna-ments may not, at first, be considered communications devices; but to a large extent that is what they are because they say something about the people who put them on and take part in them.

The question as to how much togetherness is desirable in running a business or an organization depends on the size of the organization and the city in which it is located and also on the expectations of the persons involved. Generally, in larger American cities, the separation between the job and social life is virtually complete, and here a few well-produced formal events with a pleasant atmosphere, to which *all* employees (or those within a certain area) are invited, convey the impression that the management is thoughtful and interested. In big organizations people don't know each other very well anyway. More frequent (or wilder) parties are better left to the employees themselves. The development of political cliques based upon prowess in company card playing, golf, or bowling can be disruptive to the morale of other employees who may want to get on with the business but also to run their own lives at the same time.

In small places, especially in the South, work and private life tend to run into each other more indistinguishably, and a greater amount of planned social activity may be expected of an organization. But the dangers still persist, and management must be careful not to seem to play favorites or to be too paternalistic. Social arrangements are often better left to the employees themselves with only cash and blessing bestowed by management.

The entrance of a company into the social activities of an employee's family is of even more uncertain desirability. In this area of half knowl-ege on the part of spouses and other relatives, strong feelings may be aroused or explosions set off by the most trivial things. The company is invading a very sensitive region, like that in which political jealousies abound or like the mined fields on faculty row in college campuses.

PARTICIPATION IN LOCAL EVENTS

How much should a company take part, or encourage its employees to take part, in efforts for community betterment? Should employees be encouraged to serve on local school boards, to lead charity drives, to be elected deacons in their churches, to head the local Kiwanis or Lions Club, to lead farm youth groups, to help neighborhood-improvement associations, and even to engage in politics?

The answers depend upon the nature of the company. An organization which sells service, as does an electric light company or a bank, should pay more attention to these local activities than a shoe manufacturer. Often American business has encouraged its people to be active local citizens, often at considerable cost in lost time to the company and even, on the part of some employees, in lost interest in their jobs.

More than this, companies often supply speakers and contribute heavily from their own funds and time to local efforts, in which the public relations director is usually the prime mover. When such activity says something about the nature of the company which supports it, it is a justified form of public communication.

Action Programs

Not strictly a communications medium, "doing things" is closely related to communication because actions sometimes speak louder than words, and they provide the material which can later be communicated to others by speech or writing. Actions are discussed more fully in Chapter 11, "Action Cases," but it may be noted here that the fundamental nature of many public relations actions programs is communicatory. Awards for town betterment or for accomplishment in work demanding expertness reflect the interests of the donor; giving scholarships and aiding schools in the development of their curricula communicate an attitude toward education; and holding seminars in which scientists can discuss their problems is an act of leadership.

The Motion Picture and Its Uses

One of the most complex and expensive means of communication, the motion picture, offers a great opportunity to influence viewers in a way which no other medium can match—and also to waste money and time prodigiously. Next to its uses in entertainment and in education, the motion picture finds its greatest value in public relations, and the development of television in the past few decades has greatly extended its possible influence. Books have been written upon the successes and failures of motion pictures in public relations endeavors.

Advantages of motion pictures. Appealing to the eye and ear simultaneously, the motion picture is the most powerful communications medium short of direct experience. Films can hold the sustained and exclusive attention of receivers for long periods of time and can show motion, sequences of development, and details of actions in a way that cannot be seen by the unaided human eye. Time can be collapsed, objects enlarged, and cartoons made to move. The motion picture can convey ideas quickly and lastingly with subtle emotional overtones, and in today's television era people are getting more and more used to receiving their information this way. Motion pictures can be beautiful and exciting works of art in themselves.

Disadvantages. Motion pictures are primarily limited to showing external aspects and often become insincere when trying to portray ideas. In many processes of importance, for example, legislation or scientific thought, little appears on the outside, and in the absence of concrete evidence, the motion-picture maker is tempted to resort to oversimplification and undue dramatization. Not everything makes a good visual story or spectacle. As we said earlier, television news broadcasts frequently suffer from the same deficiency.

Motion pictures proceed at a set pace, allowing the viewer little opportunity for reflection or questioning while watching the film. The viewer often wants a clarifying two-way conversation after "The End" is flashed on the screen, but this desire is usually not satisfied. Nor is there ordinarily much opportunity to review what has been seen and to ponder its significance.

Problems. Despite its power, the public relations motion picture is an expensive medium for the small organization, with a median production cost of perhaps $1,000 to $2,000 per minute of running time, or about $30,000 to $50,000 for the average 26-minute noncommercial film. A good rule of thumb, also, is to budget about as much for extra prints and for distribution costs as the original cost of the film; these additional expenditures would bring the total cost to perhaps $60,000 to $100,000 per film. Since the life of a film would have to be at least five years to amortize this cost (except in special instances), the subject matter is usually limited to relatively undated activities.

After a film is made, who is going to see it? Distribution may be handled by the organization itself, but only very large organizations handling many different films find it economical to prepare catalogs and mailings to tell possible users of their films of their availability and to maintain a film mailing and repair service. Smaller organizations, and many of the larger ones also, often use the services of commercial film distribution companies who publicize films, receive orders for showings, mail the films out, render their clients a report on the audiences each month, and charge for these services.

A survey by one of these distribution services showed that the biggest audiences obtained were from schools, for which 89 percent of such films were intended. Eighty-two percent were also intended for clubs and the general public, 80 percent for business and industry, 62 percent for employees, 61 percent for churches, 57 percent for company managements, 52 percent for television, 41 percent for social agencies, and 12 percent for stockholders. These figures seem to indicate that an organization should ask some precise questions before venturing to produce a public relations film. Who wants it made? Is this the best communications medium to do the job, considering the film's cost and its distribution possibilities? Is the story it tells good film material? At whom should the film be aimed?

Several conclusions often emerge. The public relations film with a general aim at a broad market and expectation of a long life is a blue-chip proposition, best suited to the long-range public relations objectives of a large organization. To be used on television, except in paid time, and in the schools, its "sell" must be subtle or almost nonexistent. Film production standards must match Hollywood's best, and subject matter should be of keen public interest. Such a film will also be useful in giving general information, explaining a public-service concept, or recounting history rather than in promoting a specific firm or product.

There is also often good use for the lower-budget, more specific type of motion picture which seeks to present to a more compact technical or special-interest audience material which could not be conveyed so well in any other manner. For example, several years ago the Baden Street Settlement House, serving poor people in a mixed neighborhood in Rochester, New York, decided to get out a motion picture showing the work of the House. Since no money was available for professional help, a highly skilled amateur on the staff of the agency planned and shot the 16-mm picture. The film, musical scores and recording, printing, lights, and many other items were contributed. All in all, perhaps three hundred persons helped. The roles of the persons shown in the film (settlement-house workers and a black family) were all played by the actual people portrayed. The consummate artistry of the film moved its audiences and told the story of the work of Baden Street Settlement House better than any speech, printed brochure, or even tour of the facilities could have done.

A number of years ago the Dow Chemical Company of Midland, Michigan, spent a great deal of money installing equipment to end the pollution its wastes might be contributing to streams in the area; yet, because it is a large and well-known chemical manufacturing establishment (and therefore an obvious target for criticism), it still found itself being blamed for downstream pollution. Much of this contamination was actually caused by a combination of circumstances, among them waste from other industries and untreated city and town sewage. Instead of taking a defensive and useless attitude of simply denying guilt, several Dow employees produced a good 16-mm color film showing how such stream pollution arose, illustrating Dow's successful efforts to remedy the situation in its own watershed, and urging, over the sound track, that other industries and cities, nearby and all over the nation, join in a clear-streams effort. The film received wide showing in the Midland area among engineering, industrial, and conservation people, as well as the general public; and it was also in demand all ᴜver the United States. This story could have been told as well in no other way; in fact, it is doubtful if duller methods would even have held many audiences.

In the early 1970s The Burlington Northern Railroad decided to make a film showing the activity of the railroad. It would be aimed at the broadest popular audience because a western railroad has great scenic possibilities, but would also be of great value in employee and investor relations.

The public relations head of the Burlington Northern budgeted $50,000 for the film, though he felt that he could perhaps go as high as $65,000. Then he talked to film makers and started getting prices of from $80,000 to $500,000. Finally he received a bid of $150,000 from one of the best industrial film producers in the country. With this sort of cost (the film eventually cost $165,000) it would have to have a wide audience over a considerable period of time to justify the expense.

Production took nine months and resulted in a 26-minute version for use before clubs, social groups, employees, investors, and others. There are numerous "commercial" references to the railroad company in this longer film which is in 16 millimeter. Then a 20-minute version on 35 millimeter film was produced for theater and television use. This shorter version had no "commercials" in it except the closing credit but the name of the railroad appeared on the cars and elsewhere.

The film making company was paid 10 percent upon agreement, 5 percent upon approval of the script, 30 percent at the start of filming, 20 percent at the end of filming and the balance upon final completion of the long and short versions. During the production of the film the public relations director and the line's head made the final decisions of its content, working with the professional producers. One danger in making a film is that too many chiefs from the sponsoring organization will tell the film producers what to do, confusing them and resulting in an aimless, inartistic film.

The film was completed in 1973 and three years later 85 prints had been seen by 7 million people in hundreds of theaters as well as by more

Figure 8–1 Railroad operations provide good photographic material for a motion picture, but some idea of the cost required to make a good movie can be gained by noting the equipment needed. Shown here is the shooting of Burlington Northern's *Portrait of a Railroad,* a 26-minute award-winning film. Courtesy Burlington Northern.

closely connected groups. Television usage was still to come. Distribution had been handled by a New York-based company which specialized in this service. The picture was a winner in the 1974 Venice Film Festival.

A third general use of motion pictures is communication, at an admittedly high cost per viewer, to very specific groups such as stockholders and to limited regional publics. A power company, for example, might find it advantageous to show its industrial-development activities to groups of business people, or a concrete-paving association to show progress in new concrete state highways before engineering, political, or news media gatherings.

Sometimes a film must be made to do the job simply because the use of a film is expected. The necessity was apparent in a United Fund drive in a midwestern city some time ago. The success of the drive hinged upon the way in which the employees in one large industrial firm would contribute, and a film had been shown as a part of the solicitation drive in this plant for several years previously. Since no one was willing to take a chance on using an old film over again or on abandoning a film entirely, a new one had to be made. If it had not been made and if the drive had failed, the lack of a film would have been blamed.

The biggest thing to remember about public relations films is that they must be well made. Since few public relations people are expert film producers, it is the part of wisdom to obtain the aid of someone who is. Examining past work and talking to past clients will serve as a guide in selecting the right film producer for your needs.

SUMMARY

A great many other communications tools—direct-mail letters, booklets of all sorts, bulletin boards, posters, information-booklet racks, suggestion programs, speakers bureaus, and meetings—are often used by public relations people in talking to various publics. Each one is a tool which the skilled practitioner handles as a matter of course, always using the right means of communication in the right place, in the right way, and at the right time. The tools themselves should be perfect and their employment without a flaw. But excellence in their use is simply a means to an end and not a goal in itself.

The public relations person is not satisfied with asking, "Wasn't that a beautiful motion picture?" or "Wasn't this a handsome booklet?" Instead, real public relations people are more concerned with those who saw the effort and what they thought as a result of their experience. Mastery of tools is but the beginning of success.

ADDITIONAL READINGS

There are so many books and articles about the tools of public relations that only a sampling of some of the most useful books can be given. For more detailed listings see the Public Relations Bibliographies referred to earlier.

Arnold, Ed, *Ink On Paper: A Handbook of the Graphic Arts.* (New York: Harper & Row, 1972.)

Baddeley, Walter H., *The Techniques of Documentary Film Production.* 3rd. ed. (New York: Hastings House, 1973.)

Baird, Russell N., and Arthur T. Turnbull, *Industrial and Business Journalism.* (Philadelphia: Chilton, 1961.)

Daubert, Harold E., *Industrial Publicity.* (New York, Wiley, 1974).

Dover, C. J., *Effective Communication in Company Publications.* (Washington, D.C.: Bureau of National Affairs, 1959.)

Golden, Hal, and Kitty Hanson, *The Techniques Of Working With The Working Press.* (Dobbs Ferry, N.Y.: Oceana Publications, 1962.)

Hall, Babbette, *The Right Angles, How To Do Successful Publicity.* (New York: Ives Washburn, 1965.)

Hilliard, Robert L., *Writing for Television and Radio.* (New York: Hastings House, 1967.)

Muse, Ken, *Photo One*. (Englewood Cliffs, N.J.: Prentice-Hall, 1973.)

Schoenfeld, Clarence A., *Effective Feature Writing*. (New York: Harper & Row, 1960.)

Schwartz, James W. ed., *The Publicity Process*. (Ames: Iowa State University Press, 1966.)

Strunk, William, Jr., and E. B. White, *The Elements Of Style*. 2nd. ed. (New York: Macmillan, 1972.)

Part Two

Public Relations at Work

Chapter 9

A Formula for Successful Public Relations Practice

The distinguishing mark of successful public relations people is that they know where they are, where they want to go, and how to get there. Like explorers, they have a map of the terrain always in their heads. They know that far more time, money, effort, and opportunity have been wasted through lack of an objective or unfamiliarity with the route than through inability to travel.

This map, or plan of action, can be reduced to a formula. Red Motley, once president of the United States Chamber of Commerce, said that "no man is smart enough to remember all he knows." This is the justification for the existence of formulas: They remind us of what we ought to know but often forget. They are an aid to thinking, not a substitute for it.

In the advertising world an ancient formula called "AIDA" has served many beginning direct-mail or other ad writers well by reminding them that they ought to get *Attention, Interest, Desire,* and *Action* into their copy for surest results at the sales till.

In the public relations world a new formula using the letters R-A-C-E can accomplish the same result. These letters stand for a sequence of words used in attacking a public relations problem—*Research, Action, Communication,* and *Evaluation.* Remembering these words won't make a dull person bright, but orderly consideration of them will prevent many mistakes and omissions. Detailed one at a time and illustrated by actual cases, they form a large part of the content of this book.

RESEARCH IN PUBLIC RELATIONS PRACTICE

When called into public relations responsibility, a person must first ascertain the expectations of those who have asked him to do the job. What does the organization want? What are its resources? How much time will he have? Can its wants be fulfilled by public relations aid?

Some years ago, an Englishman went to work as public relations director for a large British industry. He stayed there only about eighteen months. "I failed to ask the right question," he explained to a friend later. "When I was being interviewed for the position, I answered all the questions that were put to me satisfactorily, and then the pause came which meant that it was my turn to ask questions. I should have said, 'And Mr. Doe, what would you say that public relations is?' Since I didn't ask this, it took us many months to find out that our understandings of the subject were really quite different."

Often employers have unrealistic expectations. They may think that in some magical way public relations can gloss over bad situations and by much favorable speaking make them seem good; they may simply desire widespread publicity regardless of its effects; and sometimes, although they will seldom admit it, they may simply seek a sop to their vanity by getting their names and pictures into newspapers and magazines or onto programs. Or they may have only the vaguest picture of what they want. Public relations, they think, is supposed to be a good thing; others are doing it.

Sometimes employers are unwilling to allot adequate resources to attain the goals they have in mind. Brains and enterprise in public relations cannot be bought by the pound as one would buy steel scrap or sugar, and a public relations person who is too burdened by necessary routine tasks will probably not be so fully productive as one more adequately subsidized, who has more time to think. And again, an employer may expect results too quickly. A public relations campaign composed of a flood of news releases, booklets, speeches, tours, exhibits, and motion pictures may look huge to the company president, who sees it all outward bound; but dispersed among millions of people and scattered into millions of competitive messages, it is usually reduced to a trickle when it reaches its public. But that trickle may still bring a flood of results if given time.

The *first* step in necessary research is for public relations employees or counselors to look into the minds of those who plan to employ their services. Often one of the biggest helps that can be given to prospective employers and to themselves is to enable those who retain them to clarify objectives and to understand the role that public relations can play in attaining these goals.

The *second* step in research consists in assembling all the existing available information on the situation. This might consist of careful inspection of all newspaper and magazine clippings over a long period of time, of examining an organization's correspondence files, of reading sales and promotional literature and advertising, of reading the minutes of past meetings, and of having conversations with people who know the story well.

Such research often goes even further into examination of the history, economics, and sociology of the business, area, or institutions involved. Personalities, politics, and feelings have to be known well, since before public relations people can do anything wisely, they must know and assess all the facts. This sounds like a big assignment, but it can be easily accomplished with a little work.

The *third* step in public relations research is more difficult. It consists in finding out the opinions or attitudes currently held by the groups of people toward whom one wishes to direct persuasive communication. This investigation is vitally necessary, because if practitioners do not know how people stand on important issues, they may find that they are needlessly antagonizing some persons, trying to convert those who are already converted, or even wasting effort upon others who are not really concerned. Many good books have been written on opinion research, and the reader can become informed in greater detail at any good library. At this point it is worthwhile to examine two aspects of the manifestation of public opinion.

1   *Existing evidence.* This might consist of press clippings about an organization, comments in letters received in the normal flow of correspondence, the reports of sales people, staff members, and others, and the opinions of friends and relatives. Such informal evidence is pertinent and often gives highly significant tips, but it is too haphazard to be representative, and it is usually highly subjective. We remember

what we like to hear, and our friends (if they wish to remain friends) tell us what we like to hear, although occasionally a confirmed pessimist will make a point of recalling the damaging evidence. Only a very well-balanced observer can arrive at truth through hit-and-miss surmises about existing public opinion.

2 *Planned investigation.* Planned investigation usually means sampling, by some reasonably scientific method, the opinions of groups with whose thought one is concerned. Such sampling might take the form of a cross-sectional survey, a survey panel, depth interviews, mail surveys, or other methods—each with its strengths and limitations. There are numerous possible sources of error in such samples: Questions or interviewers may be biased; answers may seek prestige; returns may be inadequate or unrepresentative; and since opinions change frequently, time also may invalidate such a survey. The investigator should be aware of the limitations of opinion research and of its proper use. In a large involved program it is usually better to hire the services of a firm which specializes in opinion research; yet even so, much of the burden of answering "Is this valid and significant?" and "What does this mean to us?" remains a public relations responsibility and cannot be escaped.

Scientific opinion research can do much to clarify management thinking as to needs in public relations and to obtain support for a program in a manner which no amount of personal persuasion could ever accomplish. In addition, it may help by enabling the investigator to pretest communications media and appeals before they are launched on a grand scale.

But opinion research is a foundation for creative thinking rather than a substitute for it. It measures public opinion of what *has* been done or *is* being done, but cannot ordinarily tell one what *might* be done! Respondents can tell how they feel about existing conditions but can hardly anticipate their reactions to some possible future event. One cannot expect them to vote intelligently about what should be done, nor should one always be guided by what they seem to wish. Public relations is not to be confused with gaining favor at any cost, and public relations people must sometimes try to promote unpopular or unpleasant programs.

The Importance of Sound Research

The things that you don't know, or the things that you think you know that aren't so, usually have the capacity to hurt you most. Public relations people are naturally enthusiastic, and natural enthusiasts are often inclined to get on with their jobs without any critical appraisal of *how* or *why*. Influencing human opinion by means of public relations is a serious thing because it is indelible. A mistake can't just be erased and a fresh start made. If an impression takes root at all, it may remain in the minds of its receivers for many years to come, perhaps for their lifetimes.

Large companies frequently spend a great deal of thought and money on opinion research. In Chapter 10 you will see how some organizations found out what their public really thought. None of these things could have been accomplished without first ascertaining the facts by the use of shoe leather, planned, persistent questions, and a notebook —all three, synonyms for research.

The best-laid plans concocted in an office far away from the reality of the assembly line, the town council chambers, or a parent's struggle to feed, clothe, and corral youngsters are often wide of the mark, and only down-to-earth research can set them right again. Only after the true situation is really *known* is the public relations planner ready for *action,* the next step in the R-A-C-E public relations formula.

ACTION IN PUBLIC RELATIONS PRACTICE

We sometimes think of public relations as primarily a process of telling people about an institution, but before we can discuss something, we must be sure that it is there to be discussed; if things aren't happening, they may have to be made to happen.

Sometimes actions already exist. Consider the public relations efforts of the United States Marine Corps, for example. The bright uniforms and the stirring band music of the Marine Hymn are present realities, and the tradition of gallantry represents a history of continuing action. If these things did not exist and one faced the problem of popularizing the Marine Corps, they (or some equivalent) would have to be created.

Action may take the form of changing a situation. If a bus company is getting complaints about slow service on a commuter run, it is useless to argue that the service is really fast. Before the public relations problem can be fully overcome, the service must be speeded up, and the riding public must be informed of the change.

Actions, too, may be contrived to express externally in some way an inward quality which is abstract or invisible. We do this all the time in our daily lives. An American who once visited Argentina came back with a new word, "exteriorization." In the Spanish language this means simply to show on the outside how you feel on the inside. Latin Americans are somewhat better at exteriorizing than most North Americans, whose Anglo-Saxon tradition makes them regard "stoicism" as a point of honor. But North Americans must learn that exteriorization is practical in public relations. How may a company that makes high-quality merchandise *demonstrate* this high quality instead of just telling about it? How can enterprise in scientific research be shown in actions as well as in words? These are practical questions.

Another opportunity for action lies in giving evidence that one is *listening*. As will be shown in the discussion of communications in Chapter 12, most organizations are fairly adept at telling things to people and then in *saying* that they are listening to their responses; they know that two-way conversations are the most effective means of gaining conviction and cooperation. But how does one *show* that one is listening? What actions can be taken to organize channels of communication upward as well as downward? Organized listening should be dramatized in much the same way that outgoing messages are frequently dramatized.

Finally, actions in public relations are frequently needed to make news and to gain public attention. The safe operation of an airline for ten years without an accident is only minor news because this is the way airlines are supposed to operate. The papers will hardly give such routine safety a line, and this treatment is negligible, compared with their coverage of one crash. But what sort of action could be organized to make safe operation *news?*

The insistence upon *action* as a vital element in public relations practice is one of the main things that has made public relations into what it is today—a broad-gauge art, or profession, far-removed from the old-style press-agentry which simply tried to whitewash events and never took a hand in their development. Action makes public relations a part of management, because action is primarily a management responsibility. Actions not only speak louder than words; they also provide the basis upon which many words can properly be written.

It is not an accident, for example, that in recent years the word "demonstration" has come to have a renewed meaning in our language. Groups put on demonstrations today to show by *actions* such as marching, singing, or shouting how they feel. Sometimes they engage in dramatics such as burning something in effigy or laying down on the highway to block traffic. Sometimes their actions pass all bounds of legality by engaging in fights with police or smashing windows. Sometimes the demonstrators wind up in jail or provoke unproductive counterfeelings by their actions. But in any case they do more than speak about their feelings—they show them by their actions. Such actions make *news* and can be reported and photographed. By way of coverage in the mass media, they reach much wider audiences than would be possible in any other way.

This is not particularly new. In the days before mass communications media even existed, mobs and shouting often expressed what passed for public opinion, as when in the 1600s, for example, a throng assembled in London to protest the arrest and imprisonment of a clergyman named Trelawney with the shouted doggerel rhyme:

And shall Trelawney die?
Then twenty thousand Cornishmen will know the reason why!

What *is* new about demonstrations is television. Unusual visual actions are almost automatically news for this medium. It reports best those things that can be seen and move very quickly. So many causes find that they can get instant publicity on television—much more so than in the more selective print media. Television news is a prisoner of its own nature and can easily be manipulated. Indeed, television news people sometimes aid in the manipulation by visual exaggeration of the numbers engaged in a demonstration or of the intensity of their feeling. This can be easily done by focusing the camera on a portion of a crowd which may not be very large and letting the viewer add to its scope by imagination. Intensity of feeling can be exaggerated by picking those in the group who show their feelings very visibly and photographing them only. The viewer concludes that they are typical.

It is common for viewers who have been greatly impressed by seeing a televised demonstration to be disappointed when the morning newspaper relegates it to six inches on page three—but this is the editors' judgment of its importance in relation to other news of the day. Nor is it uncommon for demonstrators themselves to be disappointed when a public vote on their issue goes overwhelmingly against them, as often happens.

But it must be admitted that the magnification of demonstration actions, primarily by the broadcast media and to some extent the printed press, has enabled many causes, which otherwise would have been unknown for years to get instant publicity. Translating such necessary publicity into favorable public attitudes is another matter—one which sets a real public relations thinker apart from amateurs who see no further than simply being known. People deeply committed to a cause are likely to think that if their cause were but widely known, public favor would automatically ensue; but if their cause goes strongly against the beliefs or interests of other groups, the opposite may follow. Before engaging in actions to get publicity, it is well to think of their effects which cannot easily be changed.

Chapter 11 presents many examples of effective actions engaged in by various public relations people. In all these cases what a public relations person could have *said* about the organization on its own behalf would have been weak compared with the statements made by others because of what it *did*.

Public relations planners thus become experts not only in saying, but in doing. They influence the course of events by instigating action as well as by writing about it, and sometimes such influence can be very great indeed. This broadening of the concept of public relations adds interest to its practice. It is not just a mirroring of events but actually a creator of them. As researchers, public relations practitioners delve into reasons and causes; as communicators, they tell about them; but as activators they are persons of affairs who know the thrill of setting up events and gambling upon their success or failure, of making policy, and of personifying organizations by their deeds.

COMMUNICATION IN PUBLIC RELATIONS PRACTICE

When the average person thinks about public relations practice, the first thing to come to mind is *communication,* and the instinct is right, for facility in spreading information is still the backbone of publicity efforts. Ability in communication alone, of course, isn't enough to make a person qualify as an expert in the profession; certainly a capacity for research, for promoting action, and for evaluating the results is also vital to the practice of public relations upon an executive level. But the fact remains that communication is the one area in which a working public relations practitioner *must* be good, and that is why so much of this book is devoted to the communications aspect of the R-A-C-E formula.

There is very little chance that communications will be underemphasized. Yet there is a chance that the essential ability of the good communicator may be overlooked. He or she is not just a spokesman or mouthpiece; but is also highly skilled in at least two ways:

1   Understanding the nature of the many communications media which may be used.

2   Understanding the communications process itself, not to confuse the transmission of a vast amount of material with its successful reception—not to fall victim to the "illusion of communication" that

regularly trips those who are sure that their "much speaking" has made them heard and understood.

Both of these simple-sounding aspects of communication have commanded the lifetime attention of very capable thinkers; scores of books have been written about them; and we are still far from understanding them well. The subject of communication is not at all simple!

Yet, despite such complexity, communication is often quite well accomplished, and in the detailed discussion of communication cases in Chapter 12 you will find varied examples.

There is very little danger that anyone engaged in public relations will forget to attempt to communicate, but there is a good chance that he or she will omit the final step in the public relations formula, which is *evaluation*.

EVALUATION

When actions have been taken, when messages have been sent out, what has happened in people's thinking? Who listened? How much did they listen? What did the message mean to them in their own terms? What effect did it have upon their attitudes? Their actions? These are questions which could be asked in evaluating the results of public relations. They are important to the practitioner not only because they measure success, but also because the answers provide the basis for the next moves.

Yet important as evaluation is, it remains the least developed and most tantalizing of all the areas of public relations work. Trying to estimate the results of efforts to change human attitudes and opinions is within the province of the social sciences, whereas the effort to change material things belongs to the physical sciences. Controlled experiments are possible to solve many problems of the physical sciences. If, under known conditions, a chemical is added to a substance and change occurs, there is some reason to suppose that the new factor was the cause of the change, especially if the experiment can be repeated numbers of times. But human beings are much more complex than the physical elements which compose their bodies. One cannot know exactly what natures and experiences they bring to an experiment; no two of them are alike; and in any complex civilization people are exposed to many influences, while an experiment is going on and also immediately afterwards while a scientist is trying to measure the results. The methods of estimating opinion change are crude at best compared with the weights, measures, and litmus papers of the physical sciences.

It is no wonder, then, that social sciences have progressed much more slowly than physical sciences; they started later, and their field is much more complex. Public relations, through its kinship with the social sciences, shares their tardiness and uncertainty. This difficulty sometimes causes scientists or hardheaded business people (both of whom are accustomed to dealing with exact measurement) to decide that a statement about something which cannot be measured easily is either unimportant or mumbo jumbo; and it must be confessed that some public relations people have taken advantage of this difficulty in measurement to peddle rather vaporous wares themselves, clothing their lack of exact knowledge in vehemence and big words.

Many public relations people, faced with the difficulty and cost of evaluation, forget it and get on with the next job, relying upon common sense, which often serves well enough, to assess their results. In this they have been joined by employers who are willing to take results for granted. Perhaps their confidence is fortunate, because if all important human efforts had to await exact definition and substantiation, then not much would be accomplished. One may not be able to see the wind, but any intelligent mariner knows that it is there and that it can be used to sail.

As a rule, only large companies with continuous problems engage in persistent evaluation; some of these efforts are described later in this book.

Closing the Circle

But evaluation is important because it is evidently very close in its nature to the first step in the public relations formula, *research*. It *is*, in fact, another form of research, conducted at the end of a job instead of at the beginning. At this point the R-A-C-E public relations formula will take on the appearance of a spiral. Each step leads to the next, and the conclusion leads to renewed action.

EXAMPLES OF THE R-A-C-E FORMULA IN USE

Re-enacting "America's First Victory"

Fort Ticonderoga is a massive military structure famous in the colonial history of the United States. It was established by the French in 1755 under the name of Fort Carillon and captured by the British in 1759. But its real fame in history arrived in the before-dawn darkness of May 10, 1775, when Col. Ethan Allen with eighty-three "Green Mountain Boys"

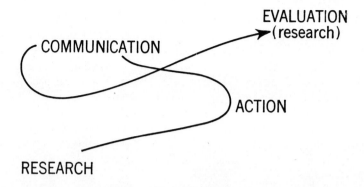

Figure 9–1 In ongoing public relations programs the R-A-C-E formula is really a spiral leading to the next step, since *evaluation* also serves as *research* for future programs.

from Vermont surprised the strong British fortress while its garrison was largely asleep and captured it without firing a shot.

The great stone fort in upper New York State commanded the entrances of Lake Champlain and Lake George. For more than a year it barred any attempt by British troops to come down from Canada and subdue the rebellious colonists. It was full of military stores badly needed by the colonists. But most important were its big cannons weighing more than 60 tons which were dragged about two hundred miles over the snow in sledges the next winter to be set up on Dorchester Heights commanding Boston where their menace forced the British troops there to take to their ships and evacuate the city forever.

In later years the abandoned fortress was largely torn down by neighboring farmers who mined it for stone and timbers. Then in the early 1800s it was acquired by a family named Pell who started restoring it over several generations. Today, aided by others who have joined in the Fort Ticonderoga Association, it stands very much as it did two hundred years ago. Its beautiful wooded setting overlooks the lake and it is a striking example of an eighteenth century military work of great historical value.

The Fort Ticonderoga Association as a client retained a New York public relations firm to aid in making May 10, 1975—the two-hundredth anniversary of the fort's passing into American hands—a memorable event to attract attention to the fort and increase its flow of visitors for years to come. The national bicentennial of the United States was approaching in 1976 and the event would be a precursor of that celebration and gain from its association.

Figure 9–2 Fort Ticonderoga, high above Lake Champlain, was considered impregnable in the eighteenth century but was captured by American revolutionary soldiers in their first victory. A public relations program commemorated the bicentennial of the event in 1975.

Approaching this problem with the R-A-C-E formula in mind, a public relations practitioner might ask a series of questions:

Research. What is the history of Fort Ticonderoga and its restoration? What is to be seen there today? Where will most visitors come from? What will interest them? How will they travel? How may they be reached? (The Association is a nonprofit organization without extensive funds for advertising.)

Action. Merely announcing a two-hundredth anniversary of the capture of the fort by Ethan Allen will not make news. Something needs to happen to make news and pictures. What can it be?

Communication. How would such an event be communicated to people who might become visitors? What media are available? What will people want to know? What support and materials would the media need to cover the event?

Evaluation. How did the media respond to the event? How did readers or listeners respond? What were the attendance figures at the fort before and after the event and its associated publicity? How much additional support for further restoration and improvement of the historical site had been attracted?

These are just a few of the questions that might be asked under the R-A-C-E headings. The actual public relations program developed somewhat as follows.

Research into history led to the production of booklets and folders as well as providing the facts upon which an event could be built and communicated. The *action* decided upon was a re-enactment of the 1775 capture of Fort Ticonderoga using many of the actual descendants of the men who took it then—costumed and armed with muskets of the day as

Figure 9–3 A descendant of Ethan Allen, commander of American troops that surprised Ticonderoga in 1775, re-enacts his ancestor's role at the restored fortress-museum on May 10, 1975.

were the defenders. The time of the original surprise was about four o'clock in the morning so this was adhered to in the first re-enactment. A descendant of the original Ethan Allen banged on the door of the room of the sleeping British commander. Asked by what authority he demanded surrender, he shouted as his ancestor had: "In the name of the great Jehovah and the Continental Congress." For the benefit of those not willing to get up at 4 A.M., the event was re-staged at 10:30 A.M. and at 2:30 P.M.

Other actions during the day included a fife and drum corps marching, a ceremonial flag raising, firing demonstrations by cannon and muskets, a muzzle-loading shooting contest, a military encampment, an ox roast and chicken barbecue, and speeches.

All of this was announced by an informational folder for the press and advance news releases for better *communications.* News of the event was covered in advance by area newspapers and nearby big city newspapers and was also carried on AP and UPI wires. It appeared on CBS-TV and on WOR radio in New York as well as in *Time* and *Newsweek* magazines.

Over 150 press representatives came to the fort on May 10 and reports and pictures of the re-enactment and other activities during the day were also carried by NBC-TV, French National TV, PBS-TV and Reuters, the British wire service. There were a number of large feature stories in New York City newspapers and additional magazine stories. Later at least four educational television stations developed documentary programs on Fort Ticonderoga which have been shown extensively throughout the country. It was estimated that total coverage in all media was more than 400 million impressions.

The *evaluation* of such an event-centered program can be seen in its immediate response as well as in the more long-range effects. Police estimated that 40,000 people attended the May 10 anniversary. In 1975 visitor attendance at Fort Ticonderoga increased more than 50 percent compared to 1974. Bookings for tours in 1976 rose to a record high within a few months.

The public relations effort was a success for a number of reasons. The product being promoted was excellent and the biggest elements were timeliness and dramatization. Timeliness arose from picking the exact day two hundred years later even to surprising the fort at four o'clock in the morning. The dramatization came through re-enacting the event using many of the descendants of the original revolutionary soldiers. Timeliness was further enhanced by acting in 1975 when the national independence celebration of 1976 was already being discussed widely in the news. With these elements ample news coverage was assured.

The Drinking Driver Problem

The preceding case was a pleasure to work with but the following one is more grim. Statistics in a 1968 report to Congress from the U.S. Department of Transportation showed that drunken driving accounted for half of the nation's traffic deaths and that two-thirds of these alcohol-caused traffic deaths involved chronic problem drinkers who were killing 360 people a week on our highways. As a result the Department of Transportation funded thirty-five Alcohol Safety Action Projects as community level demonstration efforts. These attempted to reduce drunken driving deaths by building support for alcohol-related traffic law enforcement and identifying and rehabilitating people who drink excessively and then drive.

The public relations objectives of these projects were to increase public awareness of the amount of alcohol involvement in traffic deaths, to inform people what excessive drinking is and how to recognize it, to aid individuals in dealing with excessive drinking in others through better hosting and intervention, to untangle drinking myths and facts, and to increase awareness of alcohol and traffic laws.

One of these projects was set up in Hennepin County, Minnesota (Minneapolis and vicinity). The budget was small and the public relations staff consisted of only one person.

This, obviously, was not an easy public relations assignment. *Research* already existed in traffic figures but much more would be needed to determine public attitudes and to see how they could be changed. *Action* would be necessary to make news. Preaching about the subject would command little attention. The big problem in *communication,* would be to get people to pay attention to the message. Unpleasant subjects and those which go counter to people's desires are often ignored. *Evaluation* would be needed to show progress being made in public knowledge and attitudes and, hopefully, in diminished accidents and deaths.

Tools used were public-service television and radio announcements, news releases and news conferences, exhibits, a speakers bureau, newsletters, films and other methods. The efforts were directed at the general public, at younger poeple who are most often killed in such driving accidents, at businesspeople, law enforcement officers, lawyers, doctors, and city officials.

Figure 9–4 Working on a low budget, exhibits and booklets distributed at the Minnesota State Fair were one method of communicating with the public used by The Hennepin County Alcohol Safety Action Project.

In 1975, for example, a speakers bureau gave slide talks to 4,891 people in schools and community groups; a monthly newsletter reached 2,600 readers, primarily police officers, judges, driver education teachers, and opinion leaders in this field. Testing leaflets and slide-rule alcohol calculators were distributed to 35,000 people. Exhibits reached 16,000 persons. Several hundred radio and television spots were aired and there were numerous news and feature stories.

Such a volume sounds impressive, but it must be measured against the million population of Hennepin County and also against the thousands of other messages to which people are exposed every day.

Elements of action were gotten into the program by a voluntary roadside breathalyzer test and an exhibit at the state fair in which participants could punch buttons to see if they knew how many drinks of various liquors were needed to sustain a drunken driving charge.

In two telephone surveys of a thousand people each made in 1975 56 percent of those replying said they felt that drunken driving was more of a problem than street crime or drug abuse. In another telephone survey one out of three persons said that during the past year they had been in a situation where someone who had been drinking too much wanted to drive. Of this number 69 percent said they had taken some action to prevent the person from driving and 85 percent said they would do so in the future. This was a significant improvement in response from a similar survey taken four years before.

Driver deaths were down and drivers were drinking less. Some of this resulted from increased enforcement and better training of police officers, for which funds were also provided in the program. Some of it was related to the alcoholic rehabilitation programs which were also being followed. But a good deal of it was public relations—which also supported the other programs.

It is hard to enforce unpopular laws and a good portion of success must lie in self-policing by individuals in stopping drinking before they have had too much and in the efforts of their real friends to stop them from driving when they have drunk to excess. All elements depend upon public support and understanding. Final success will never be won, but real satisfaction can be taken in the thought of each life saved.

Moving an Automobile Manufacturing Plant[1]

In the 1930s, Ford Motor Company built an assembly plant at Edgewater, New Jersey, across the Hudson River from New York City. It was a multistory building in the middle of town, which in time became inefficient. As the demand for cars increased, it could not be expanded easily; as assembly-line techniques changed, large horizontal in-line plants were found to be much cheaper in operation than buildings with stories piled one on top of another. Ford found a larger new plant site in Mahwah, New Jersey, some 26 miles away. Ford public relations people were called in to help plan the move.

[1] *Public Relations News,* Sept. 19, 1955.

Research showed that many of the 2,900 Ford employees at Edgewater had spent years with the company. Their skills were valuable, and the company wanted to keep them. The loss of the Ford plant would hurt Edgewater, but not too badly since there were many other industries in the area and the old Ford building might be turned to some other purpose. Besides, Mahwah was within commuting distance, and many older Ford employees with homes in Edgewater would probably continue to live there, especially if they were within a few years of retirement. The main problems were to expedite the move, to keep employees, to build goodwill in both towns, and to cash in on the publicity value inherent in such a major industrial shift, for it was not intended to shut the plant down in the process of moving.

This plan for continuous operation provided a basis for a special *action*. Why not publicize the unique feat of moving tons of machinery and thousands of people 26 miles without skipping a beat in the production of Ford automobiles? Surely this achievement would be spectacular and newsworthy. Plant whistles could blow farewell to the factory at Edgewater; a welcoming delegation could be at Mahwah; and in between, a caravan of trucks and railroad cars escorted by police could be seen hauling the machinery. The move would get the attention, not only of the towns involved, but also of the New York metropolitan area and the nation as a whole!

Of course there were many other actions to be taken—a new plant tour for employees in advance of the move, open houses for opinion leaders in Mahwah, and a campaign to find new occupants for the plant at Edgewater. The oldest employee was to drive the last car off the line at Edgewater (and when it was discovered that she could not drive, the town's mayor drove instead). The first car off the new line in Mahwah was specially fitted for amputee use and was given to a hospital. But the action inherent in the move itself lifted the change to regional and national importance.

Communication flows naturally in a situation like this. Employees must be informed before anybody else. Provision must be made for listening to their problems and aiding them. Management must know the story and carry it to opinion leaders in the area. The local public must know what's going on. The press must be kept aware of events and supplied with material.

Evaluation was carried out in many fields. Only ten out of 2,900 employees left the company because of the shift, and these were elderly persons who decided to accept accelerated retirement instead of moving. Coverage in various media all over the New York metropolitan area was of outstanding quality. Many people doubltless admired the enterprise of the Ford Motor Company in its smooth transfer of production and by implication valued Ford products more highly.

Many other examples of the use of the R-A-C-E formula in solving public relations problems could be cited, and other, perhaps equally useful, formulas could be devised. The most important thing is to develop an orderly pattern of thought, to face the truth squarely, and to think not about what you would want to hear, but about what others would find interesting. Then with a dash of the unusual, you have the beginning of a good public relations program.

Chapter 10

Research and Research Cases

Suppose a person goes to a doctor and says, "I don't feel well, but don't bother about making a diagnosis. My relatives and friends all assure me that my symptoms are exactly the same as those which my Uncle Otto had when he suffered from an inflamed appendix. I know that you're a good surgeon, so get busy. Take out my appendix and send me the bill later." If the doctor then operates, you may rightly conclude that he or she isn't much of a physician, but rather some kind of charlatan.

But in public relations, many may try to practice the art who are often shockingly inexperienced. Some people are quite willing to admit that they may not be able to write a really good magazine feature article, prepare a well-paced television script, or produce a good motion picture; few will claim to know how to produce an attractive exhibit for a great world's fair or even how to plan an effective youth-talent show; but a great many people will assume, without second thought, that they are completely competent to identify public relations problems, decide their weight and severity, know what other people think about them and why they think it, and then prescribe all sorts of effective remedial communications. Sometimes they may be right; often they are not.

A FRAMEWORK FOR PUBLIC RELEATIONS RESEARCH

The general objectives of research include probing basic attitudes, measuring actual (not supposed) opinions, identifying leaders of opinion, reducing costs by concentrating upon the most valid targets, testing themes and media, timing, discovering the strength of antagonistic views, achieving two-way communication, revealing trouble before it develops, and using opinion research as a communications tool in itself.

Much research is done by amateurs, but even amateurs should know its limitations and be able to judge rightly the validity of what they are doing. Mistakes made in amateur research are quite often serious because whole sets of plans are built upon the foundations laid by research, and a user who is convinced of something untrue is worse than an ignorant user. In addition, since amateur researchers are often responsible for the selection and hiring of professional research firms and for judging the value of their findings, some knowledge of the research field is absolutely essential, even for those who have neither the time nor the desire to become really expert.

EXAMPLES OF BASIC PUBLIC RELATIONS RESEARCH QUESTIONS

In approaching a public relations problem, any organization might ask itself some fundamental questions.

Who are we and why do we exist? What do other people think of us? Who are these "other people"? The image that an organization has of itself may be quite confused, and before much can be communicated to anyone else about that image, perhaps the possessors of it need to engage in some objective introspection—if that paradox is possible.

Can others be criticized for not having an accurate image of an organization if it has done little or nothing to communicate it to them? We must always remember that as far as others are concerned, their image of the organization *is* the organization in their own minds—even if it does not happen to coincide with the facts.

Often the problems of an organization are really not what the people of the organization think they are. For example, when an industrial plant was being enlarged in a Southern city, the work had to be held up temporarily because of the objections of nearby residents to the noise. Since these complaints did not appear to represent a valid criticism, a survey was made to determine whether noise or some other reasons lay behind the efforts to block the proposed expansion.

In the survey-research interviews, only 5 percent of the respondents volunteered any criticism of the noise at the plant. When those being interviewed were questioned directly about their reaction to noise, common answers were, "The noise doesn't bother me" or "It's sometimes noisy, but that doesn't happen very often." Several volunteered that the noise from nearby railroad trains was much worse than any noise from the plant construction. "We have forty-four trains a day pass by here, but I never notice any noise from the plant," was a typical remark.

It seemed apparent that the criticism of noise at the plant was not serious, but further probing brought out complaints that the company should "do something to cut down the dust on the street leading to the plant." Accompanying these complaints were more practical suggestions: "The company should sprinkle or oil these two streets that go from the highway to the plant, especially when they are hauling materials, because the dust is simply fierce," or "The trucks and traffic are terrific; our streets will be all broken up and we shall live in a cloud of dust all summer." There were also complaints that better provisions should be made for parking the cars of construction workers, which had to be left on the street in front of homes all day.

When action was taken to meet *these* complaints, objections disappeared, and it was possible to proceed. What had prevented people from complaining openly about the parking and the driving before? Probably they were reluctant to be critical of the construction workers who were of their same social and economic class.

When the Hospital Association of a midwestern state wanted to find out the opinions of twenty-nine of the editors of the state's leading newspapers, who constituted a small but very important public, an experienced newspaper reporter was hired to make the interviews.

He found that twenty out of the twenty-nine editors thought that the most important hospital public relations problem was costs and that nineteen of the twenty-nine felt that access to information from hospitals by newspapers was the second most important problem. The two major problems observed by the editors were entirely different in character. In mentioning the cost problem, the editors were reporting on community feeling. The information problem, on the other hand, was one with which they were professionally concerned as newspaper professionals. To solve the problem of public irritation with costs, the editors suggested such things as simplified annual statements released to the newspapers, more information and breakdowns on statements given to the patients, greater emphasis in releases to all media on the fact that payrolls (what the patients paid for services by others) were a big cost in hospital operation, explanations that a hospital is a community-based service and that the biggest part of a dollar spent in a hospital returns to the community, and using hospital personnel in an enlightened way to tell the hospital-cost story.

On the problem of getting information for the press from hospitals, the suggestion was made repeatedly that an educational program be started inside the hospitals to inform the personnel on how to give out information while at the same time preserving the traditional privacy of the patient. One frequent suggestion was that someone on the hospital staff should be empowered to serve as a press contact 24 hours a day to provide coverage when the chief administrator was not present.

There was nothing startling in the information gained by either of these simple forms of research. Yet if the company which was building the plant addition had assumed that the complaints of noise represented the real trouble and had tried to correct it, while at the same time neglecting the dust and parking problems, the hostile feeling would have continued; and if the hospitals had assumed that their main public problems (in the eyes of the press, at least) were poor quality of service and lack of public confidence in their skill or facilities, they also would have spent much time solving unreal problems.

Public relations research is nothing more than planned, carefully organized, sophisticated fact-finding and listening to the opinions of others. It becomes necessary when human relationships exist upon such a big scale that some form of organized, scientific feedback is necessary to find out what is in the minds of other persons. When one person talks to another or to a small group, he or she can get some idea of reactions simply by watching other people's faces and by listening to their comments. But when public relations practitioners, addressing an audience at long distance in news stories, booklets, or television programs, want to know what impression they are making, they have to devise some planned mechanism for listening and to establish ways in which two-way communication can be achieved. Otherwise their efforts to communicate are likely to be misdirected and ineffective.

COMMON OBJECTIVES OF RESEARCH

To Probe the Basic Attitudes of Groups   What predispositions exist to accept or to reject ideas, and to judge favorably or unfavorably the sources from which they might come? If a railroad, for example, wishes to talk to Kansas wheat farmers, it will profit by knowing in advance what these wheat farmers think about railroads in general and about their rates, practices, and history in particular; and by knowing what feelings they have about road building, trucking, gasoline taxes, and anything else pertinent. Our own estimates of what others think are often misleading, because we project our opinions into their minds. The old saying "If I were in your shoes, I should do so-and-so" is not so useful as "If I were in your shoes and had your background and interests, I should probably do so-and-so."

To Measure the True Opinions of Groups   How can you tell what a group of people really believe? This is often a complicated question because the loudly expressed opinions of a vocal minority within a group may not be at all the same as those of a silent majority. Who within a group holds certain opinions? How intensely do they hold them? And how are trends shifting?

Identification of Leaders of Opinion   Where do people within a group get their ideas? From immediate friends and neighbors? From those a notch or two above themselves in the social scale? Or from the top brass which they read about in newspapers or see on television? Who spreads opinion? Who are the first to adopt new ideas or practices, and how much are these innovators then copied? What is the role of gate-keepers—editors, broadcasters, teachers, and preachers, who pass on information and opinions to others, although their own viewpoints may or may not be reflected in such conveyance?

Reducing Public Relations Costs By Concentrating Upon Valid Targets   Trying to reach too many people and reaching them ineffectively through a poor medium of communication may both be extremely costly efforts. A number of years ago, a California company began the manufacture of pepper mills. They made pepper mills easily and placed them in the hands of retailers by the hundreds. And then nothing happened. The buying public did not know what pepper mills were, and they did not want them. So a public relations campaign was entered into, concentrating upon the food editors of newspapers and magazines who controlled space in which the public regularly expected to find new ideas about food. This was a natural alliance, because food editors are constantly pressed for something new to present. Pepper mills appeared in pictures of table settings, in motion pictures of famous restaurants, in descriptions of salads; and after a time, when people had learned about the purpose of pepper mills by seeing them, reading about them, and hearing about them, the contrivances could be sold by means of regular small-space advertising which had previously failed.

Testing Themes and Media Before Placing All Bets Upon Them Public relations advertising may cost hundreds of thousands of dollars for magazine space or broadcasting time. Often it is only prudent to test public response through a representative sample before risking all on a major effort. A company magazine may be costing thousands of dollars for each issue. How well is it being read? What items are most read or least read? What ideas do readers gain from the magazine? The best way to know is to ask questions in a scientific manner. The answers may not be complete or final, but at least they will be a guide.

Timing The American commander at the Battle of Bunker Hill warned his untried troops to hold their single-shot musket fire until they could "see the whites of their eyes." This good advice prevented scattering musket fire at ranges too distant to be effective and ensured that every bullet would count when the concentrated blast came. But in public relations conflicts, withholding fire often doesn't work. People are usually much more susceptible to persuasion *before* the battle has been clearly joined. Later, when they have chosen their side, they tend to stop listening to anything which might shake their faith, and their ears are closed to reason. Rapid opinion research can often tell whether thoughts have solidified upon issues and to what degree, and in this way can separate areas in which appeal may be vain from other areas which still may be cultivated.

Ascertaining the Strength of the Opposition In the heat of a political campaign, for example, a certain idea injurious to your side may seem to be catching on. Should forces be diverted to answering it right away, or should they continue with their original plans? A quick survey might show that the apparently widespread strength of the idea has been greatly exaggerated. Some newspapers and strong partisans of the opposition may be giving it great play, but the great balance of the public may be quite apathetic. Changing communications strategy at once to meet this minor threat may dislodge the adherents you have been gaining upon the present tack and profit nothing.

Achieving Two-way Communication Simply finding out what recipients think is not really two-way communication; such research is done for the benefit of the sender, and if only a small segment of the recipients are sampled, very few of the total number will be aware that their opinion is being sought. A small cross-sectional sample may be adequate from a scientific viewpoint, but a large well-known survey can also become a means of two-way communication for the respondents who are interviewed, giving them a chance to express themselves and to talk back.

Revealing Trouble Before It Happens   Effective public relations work often never shows itself openly because it consists of ascertaining difficulties before they ever come to the surface and in correcting problems before they ever break out into public view. Opinion surveys, especially those taken at intervals to show trends, constitute one of the most effective ways of raising warning flags, since before people act in a certain way, they must first have done some thinking. The strike that didn't happen, the plant changes that were accomplished without a protest, the stockholders who regularly returned a management to power, were probably the result of intelligent actions and communications which were themselves preceded by careful public-opinion research; without the research nothing might have been communicated because the need for it would not have been so clearly realized.

Opinion Research As a Weapon In Itself   Showing valid evidence of public opinion upon an issue can be very effective when used in groups outside of an organization. A survey, for example, taken by an impartial research firm showing fairly the opinions of a city population, might be a decisive factor in the decision of a city council.

Inside an organization, fact-minded people such as treasurers or production personnel frequently dominate company boards of control. These people sometimes need to be shown the reality and true nature of a problem. Frequently public relations directors, because their antennae are more attuned to outside human contacts and reactions, may see danger or opportunity in a public attitude and yet be unable to move their colleagues who do not have a similar responsiveness. In such a situation it is both difficult and dangerous to insist upon action solely upon a basis of unsupported hunch; more evidence is needed, and this is best supplied from the findings of organized opinion research, to which the hardest-headed will usually listen.

THE HISTORY OF MODERN OPINION RESEARCH

Trying to find out what people think about things is certainly as old as democracy itself. Putting issues to a vote is the ultimate test of public opinion, and although from time immemorial monarchs and tyrants have snooped about by means of agents to discover the sentiment of their subjects, the final revelation takes place at a general public election.

Modern public-opinion research, however, using samples of public opinion before the formality of a mass vote, is largely a creation of the past few decades—a period which seems almost absurdly recent. In the 1930s, for example, public-opinion research methods moved from the inaccurate system of taking big "chunks" of popular sentiment (samples which, no matter how large, were not necessarily representative of the whole group from which they were drawn) to a serious effort to ascertain mass opinion by cross-sectional samples which would truly reflect the feelings of various groups and might thus safely serve as a basis upon which projections could be made about the entire group.

One fiasco which helped to kill unscientific chunk sampling as a serious research device was the *Literary Digest* poll of 1936 involving some two million responses from users of telephones or similar upper-economic-level lists and predicting a landslide sweep for Alfred Landon, the Republican nominee for the Presidency, just before Franklin D. Roosevelt, Democrat, in fact mopped the floor with the remains of the Republican party. There were several reasons for the failure of the *Literary Digest* poll.

In the midst of the Depression, when every dime counted, telephone service was more largely restricted to the upper classes, who would be likely to vote for Landon, than it is today. At that time also, as George Gallup, later to wrestle with some polling problems himself, noted:

> Before 1936 you were as likely to find Republicans among workers as you were among people who owned telephones. The controlling factor was still the Civil War; my grandfather was worse than any Southerner, only he'd fought for the North. He was an immovable Republican. Social class bias in your sample made no difference—until the New Deal stratified the people of America politically.

In other words, an inaccurate chunk which had fortunately served well enough as a sample previously had ceased to be at all representative.

To avoid the trap in which the *Literary Digest* had been caught, Gallup and the other polltakers developed "quota sampling" to a point of some refinement. Each interviewer was given certain types of people to query, the combination of types being planned in all *important* aspects of the whole universe to be surveyed. The problem still remained, however, of what was important.

Even quota sampling had its limitations, for a number of reasons which will be discussed in more detail later, such as last-minute shifts in opinion and the inability of respondents to tell what is really on their minds. This inaccuracy made necessary further development, and the very late 1930s and 1940s saw the beginning of "motivational research," an attempt to probe by psychological means not only what people *say* they believe, but also whether they really believe it or something else, and why they believe as they do.

TYPES OF RESEARCH USED IN PUBLIC RELATIONS

1 *Fact gathering.* Much of what a public relations person may need to know about audiences is available just for the gathering from the United States Census reports, publishing company surveys, and other sources. One can easily find answers to such questions as: How many cars do people have? How far do they drive? How do they vote? What is their race, age, and sex? How much do they spend for different varieties of merchandise?

In addition, many newspapers, broadcasting stations, and magazines are prepared to give more or less reliable profiles of some other characteristics of their audiences, such as where they shop, go on vacations, send their children to school, and (of course) what they say they read or listen to.

The interpretation of the facts is up to the person who assembles them, and the proper conclusions are not always so obvious as they seem. But carefully chosen sources of information can be relied on. If one has something to publicize to boat owners, for example, boat registrations and the readership of a boating magazine would seem to be pretty good guides to interested personnel; and if one has a resort to promote, the people who habitually visit the region would seem to be worth following up and questioning.

2 *Opinion research* is at least two steps deeper in complexity (*a*) because opinion research concerns itself with what people say they think rather than with the much more easily verifiable record of what they do and (*b*) because an opinion survey almost always must depend upon a sample and is misleading unless that sample is representative of the whole. Some dangers will be noted in the paragraphs following. One of the best uses of opinion surveys is to show trends rather than absolutes.

3 *Motivational research.* As we have mentioned before, motivational research attempts to probe into the reasons why people believe and do things, often seeking reasons which they cannot, or will not, tell an interviewer in response to simple questions.

Motivational research takes a variety of forms, including *depth interviews,* in which those interviewed are encouraged to talk freely and seemingly almost at random, although the interviewer has in mind a planned pattern in the conversation; *thematic apperception* tests, in which respondents are asked to write or speak freely about situations imagined in pictures; *projective techniques,* such as asking people to describe an imaginary scene glimpsed through a keyhole; *psychodrama,* in which people are asked to take part in and to interpret plays; and a variety of multiple-choice tests including the *semantic differential,* by which degrees of response toward pairs of polarized words can be expressed.

A weakness in motivational research efforts to peer into the human mind sometimes springs out of the necessity of creating hypotheses, both in setting up the studies and in interpreting their meanings. A number of years ago the author witnessed an instance of such misinterpretation. A number of Cadillac owners and De Soto owners (a car then built by Chrysler) were asked to tell their reactions to a picture which showed a car passing another car on a hill; just over the crest of the hill, on the passing side, could be glimpsed the upper works of a large truck. The question was: "What does the passing car most need to do?" Most of the Cadillac owners said, "Step on the gas and clear the car being passed to get back into line." Most of the De Soto owners said, "Stand on the brake and fall back into line behind the car alongside."

From these answers the researchers concluded that Cadillac owners as a class were more dashing and venturesome than De Soto owners. This may very well have been so, but the test did not prove it. The De Soto model that year was an extremely underpowered car with a "slushy" transmission, and any De Soto driver knew that when caught in such a passing trap there was no solution except to fall back into line as quickly as possible. Whether De Soto owners as a class were more cautious by nature in advance of purchasing their cars was not shown by the research. It was clear, however, that they soon became so after a little experimentation with their vehicles!

RESEARCH PITFALLS

Mark Twain once referred to a man "who knew more things that weren't so" than anyone else he'd ever known. Despite the great and necessary use of research, the unreliability and gullibility of the human beings who express opinions and of those who employ opinion sampling and motivational research as a basis for public relations practice still make the basis shaky and dangerous. The typical public relations worker seldom becomes a formal research expert (this particular vocation seems to be more of a "calling") but will certainly be involved in buying opinion research and in judging its validity. For this reason he or she needs to understand the chief pitfalls, without flying to the other extreme of being antagonistic to well-conducted research or feeling that in some way it hampers creative intuition.

Nonrepresentative Listening   All of us tend to associate with people who are similar to us in their tastes and habits and in their wealth and social positions. Business people tend to spend their spare time with others in business at clubs, professors with other faculty members, and laborers with other laborers, each of the same rank and type. Furthermore we tend to remember only what pleases us, and other people tend to tell us what they feel we would like to hear. Even more, we hear only what is spoken, and the louder and more persistently it is spoken, the more we note it. If ten people are silent and one is speaking, we are likely to assume that the speaker expresses the sentiments of the other ten, although there may be many reasons for their silence.

All these tendencies make random, unplanned observation of popular feeling highly unreliable. We are all familiar with the businessman who is convinced that everyone is as conservative as he is (or that they would be if only they had the "facts") and with the liberal who is appalled by the conservatism of the "masses." As the poet, Robert Burns, once said:

> Oh wad some Power the giftie gie us
> To see oursel's as ithers see us!
> It wad frae monie a blunder free us,
> An' foolish notion . . .

But the probabilities are that even if we were to receive this gift, we would be inclined to discount such insight heavily in favor of our preexisting feelings.

The Advisory Committee   "Letterhead" committees are one of the oldest devices used by drives and causes. Sometimes keen individuals within such committees are able to feel the public pulse; but the main function of advisory committees is to give support and testimonials and to create involvement. An advisory committee is always drawn from the ranks of those who are at least somewhat favorably disposed toward a cause, because otherwise they would not be willing to serve. In addition, they are usually drawn from the top ranks in whatever groups they circulate among, and since they are thus more aggressive, vocal, and wide-ranging in their interests, they may be helpful; but they are not typical. They are not chosen for their valid reflection of public opinion.

The Representative Panel The representative panel reflects an attempt to set up a somewhat permanent cross-sectional body from which, at intervals, a realistic sample of opinion can be obtained. The device is not a bad one in some respects, since it permits deeper probing than can be done in offhand interviews and also enables a researcher to have greater knowledge of the peculiar characteristics of the panel members. Its weakness is that the longer a panel is kept in touch with a given situation, the less it becomes really representative, because familiarity with the subject matter alters the panel's reactions. As the old saying has it, "No one can step into the same river twice."

Field Reports "Our salespeople say so-and-so" is one of the most frequent and invalid clichés that research-minded public relations people encounter. It's worth knowing what salespeople think (sometimes it's all-important), but they are necessarily favorably disposed toward the company which they represent or they wouldn't be its representatives, and in any case, they are usually prudent enough to tell the boss what they think he or she would like to hear. Nor is there any assurance that the outsiders they contact are at all representative of the whole group whose opinions are sought. This applies also in the case of their reports upon dealer opinions, since the sales force prefers to call upon and listen to dealers who like them and who receive them well. Even when field reports are not intentionally misleading, the reporters are often self-deluded.

Improper Sampling Improper sampling may be of serveral sorts: inadequate, unrepresentative, or badly timed. Although huge samples are not necessarily representative of the whole, tiny samples involving only a few people are likely to be misleading because they may easily have happened upon nontypical persons. The danger is particularly great when an adequate large sample is broken down for analysis into smaller subsections, some of which may include only a few respondents; the inadequacy of the subsections may be masked by the adequate size of the main sample.

Unrepresentative sampling can occur, for example, when telephone checks on broadcast listening are made only within the city limits because of the cost involved in reaching rural listeners by long-distance telephone. In this way the differences in taste between rural and urban listeners may be obscured, and with some programs, such as mystery dramas or church music, their true ranking with the total audience is altered.

Timing errors arise when something happens to alter the validity of a sample between the time it is taken and the time it is used. In the 1948 presidential election, for example, one of the major national sampling polls predicted a victory for Thomas E. Dewey on the basis of a poll taken in September. The actual vote in early November came out quite otherwise, and the pollsters believed that the trouble lay, not in the sample, which was accurate enough, but in the voters' last-minute unrecorded swing to President Truman. The fact that results of periodic sampling polls may show definite, consistent variation over a period of time indicates that changes do occur in public opinion and that plans based upon outdated research may be inappropriate and dangerous.

Biased Interviewers   To biased interviews we might add careless, lazy, and dishonest interviewers. Fortunately, this error is usually easily checked by comparing the work of one of several polltakers against that of the others. Any undue variation in what should be adequate subsamples will bear careful investigation.

Foggy Response   This may spring from the respondents' simple inability to understand what is being asked, often accompanied by a cheerful willingness to make a stab at answering anyway so as not to lose face by an admission of ignorance. Akin to this is the common desire of those interviewed to look good in the eyes of the interviewer.

Some years ago, when a soap company's researchers went about asking people how many baths they took each week, a prodigious amount of bathing was reported. Taking frequent baths has social prestige, and those who seldom went near a tub could scarcely be expected to admit the fact. A similar prestige response occurs when people are asked whether they read the editorials in a newspaper or whether they subscribe to certain high-class magazines. Many respondents will answer "Yes," but will fall down on further specific checks of readership of the exact contents of yesterday's editorials or last month's magazine.

Often related to this desire for prestige is a simple desire to please the interviewer. "The young lady obviously wants me to say that I use Blotzos, so I'll say that I use Blotzos." There is also, sometimes, a fear or caution reaction. "This fellow is asking me about my reading the company magazine. He *says* the survey is anonymous, but how do I know that he won't tell the boss if I say I don't read it much? So I'd better play it cool and say that I read it most of the time." Or: "How do I like the *Tribune?* Well, it's the town's only newspaper, and if I ever wanted to run for office or get anywhere in business, I'd hate to have it against me, so I'd be a chump to say that I think it's a lousy rag!"

Undue Recall of the Prominent   Modern Americans are exposed to so many communications every day and every week that it is hard for them to remember where they all came from, often only a few days later. This helps to explain why it is possible to paste an ad of a prominent product into a newspaper or magazine in which it never appeared and still get a fair number of interviewees who will remember having seen it there the day before. They are not intentionally lying—just remembering the appearance of the ad the week before or even in some entirely different medium.

Exaggeration of Minor Differences   If twenty items are recalled to a person's memory, she can probably tell you, with considerable accuracy, the few she likes best and also those she likes least—if there is any real variation between them. But her comparative rankings of Number 12 versus Number 13 and of Number 11 versus Number 10 are not particularly important. In broadcast listening, very high ratings or very low ratings are doubtless important, but a small rise in percentage in the middle ground based upon a small sample is not earth-shaking and should not cause undue jubilation or alarm.

None of the difficulties listed above are intended to imply that since research, like walking, when carefully examined is found to be an enormously complicated process, therefore research and locomotion are impossible. After all, since the biggest part of public relations practice is understanding and influencing public opinion, it behooves all public relations people who wish to be more than witch doctors and hacks to use all the weapons of social science to make their understanding as exact and scientifically valid as possible. It is only a partial basis for criticism that social science still has a long way to go in this field. Practically all progress in social science, in the modern sense at least, has taken place within the past hundred years, whereas the physical and biological sciences have been busily at work on what may be a less complicated assignment, during the several centuries covered by the lives of Galileo, Copernicus, Newton, Harvey, and Darwin.

The liaison between the social scientist and the working public relations person is not very good, because neither of them really speaks the other's language or shares the other's goals. The primary burden to establish a better connection, of course, lies upon the public relations professionals because public relations people hope and expect to be the practical beneficiaries of the many new ways of understanding what people think and how they are influenced. Public relations workers have good reason to want to know, and sometimes also have the money with which to support research.

Both sides need to have great patience. The working public relations person must try not to become exasperated at the slow, detailed analysis of the psychologist or sociologist of what often seems obvious; and the social scientist must not become upset by the "let's get along with the fight and hang the details" attitude so common among active public relations people. Neither side can afford a holier-than-thou attitude. Enormous progress has been made since the 1920s, but the increase in problems, needs, and knowledge is so great that the difficulties now seem even greater than they were some years ago.

Modern public relations practitioners need to remember that, after all, they are simply another kind of teacher, preacher, editor, or politician and that they share with all these persuaders a common interest in the development of the art or science of communication.

THE RELATIONSHIP BETWEEN RESEARCH AND PUBLIC RELATIONS PLANNING

Even within the limitations of research methods, it is still possible to make some marvelous discoveries. In a survey of the images of some twenty major American corporations, for example, Opinion Research Corporation of Princeton, New Jersey, some years ago compared the standings of two large retail-trade companies and found that figures corroborated impressions.

On "believable advertising" the first company was ranked high by 34 percent of the respondents as compared with 22 percent for the second company; on "pleasant to do business with" by 41 percent as compared with 24 percent; on "tries to keep prices down" by 43 percent versus 24 percent; on "good record for steady work," by 28 percent versus 15 percent; on "excellent employee benefits," by 22 percent versus 7 percent; and on "shares prosperity with employees," by 19 percent versus 5 percent. The needs of the second company, compared with those of the first, are apparent and provide the basis for some sound public relations planning.

Valid research helps to answer the question "What do we want do do?" *How* to do it is the next step.

All effective public relations programs begin with careful planning. Where are we? Where should we like to be? How shall we get there?

Answers must be written out convincingly, clearly, and logically and must be buttressed by facts. Planning cannot be done in a vacuum; public relations persons plan not only to provide a blueprint for their own actions but more importantly, to convince others and to obtain *their* support. By themselves they can do little, because they do not occupy a position of line authority from which to command people farther down the line to do what they wish. Instead they must explain, inspire, and gain cooperation. It is possible to make public relations plans without research, but they usually have a wild-blue-yonder, unconvincing quality.

SOME PUBLIC RELATIONS CASES IN WHICH RESEARCH WAS A DOMINANT FACTOR

The Standard Oil Company of California

Beginning in 1944, the Standard Oil Company of California started the practice of running an opinion-research audit of its public standing every few years. Following a 1955 survey, the company had another survey taken in 1957 which involved 2,170 personal interviews by a research company in San Francisco, and the main results were published in five issues of the company magazine, *The Standard Oiler,* in 1958.

In May, 1958, an article beginning the series was headed "What the Public Really Thinks about Us." After telling how the survey was conducted, it said:

> The results were not heartening. All oil companies and big business seem to be subject to increasing public criticism. Favorable opinion of our company, according to the survey, has shown a decided decline since the previous sampling in 1955. Public relations will use the results of this poll in planning future programs and projects to help correct these impressions. But *you* [employees] can help too. Much of our public's attitude is formed by chats with Standard Oilers, so you can help by becoming familiar with the facts about your company and sharing them with your friends whenever appropriate. . . .

The charts which followed showed that the percentage of the survey respondents who said that they liked the company had dropped from 60 percent in 1955 to 44 percent in 1957; "neutral" had increased from 28 to 43 percent; and "dislike" from 12 to 13 percent.

A breakdown of negative attitudes toward the company showed that (*a*) the number who said that the company was too big and powerful had increased from 33 percent in 1955 to 36 percent in 1957; (*b*) the

What the public really thinks about us

*Personal interviews of a cross-section of Western adult public give
clues to recent changes in attitudes about our Company*

EVERY year or so, our Public Relations Department enlists the services of a public opinion polling organization to find out what the general public thinks of our Company and our industry. The latest survey was conducted throughout the seven Western States at the close of last year. It was based on 2170 personal interviews of a cross-section of the adult public.

The results, in general, were not heartening. All oil companies and big business seem to be subject to increasing public criticism.

Favorable opinion of our Company, according to the survey, has shown a decided decline since the previous sampling in 1955. But the shift has been more toward a neutral position rather than toward actual dislike. It's now a stand-off between those who like us and those who are neutral. The "dislikers" are still a minority.

Many questions were asked in an attempt to find out specifically what bothers people about our Company. The most significant complaints seem to be four: They claim we're (1) too big and powerful, (2) too large to best serve the public, (3) a monopoly, and (4) charging too much for our products.

Public Relations will use the results of this latest poll in planning future programs and projects to help correct these impressions. But *you* can help, too. Much of our public's attitude is formed by chats with Standard Oilers, so you can help by becoming familiar with the facts about your Company and sharing them with your friends wherever appropriate.

Next month, THE OILER will begin a series of articles offering up-to-date facts to refute the main complaints of the public as revealed in this poll.

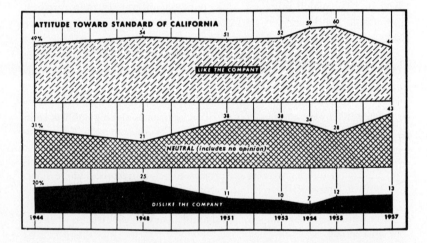

Figure 10–1 A company magazine, *The Standard Oiler,* begins a series of articles reporting to employees the results of research into public opinion of the company.

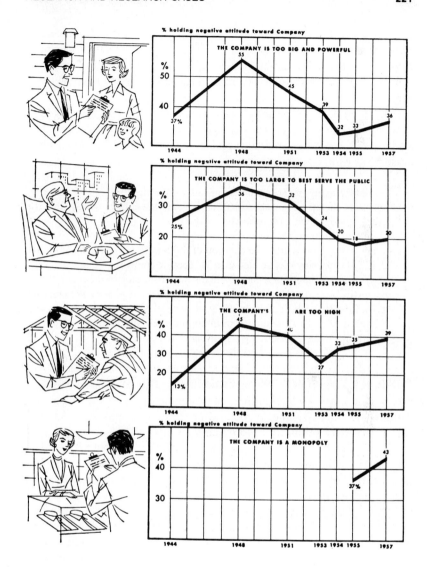

Figure 10–1 (*continued*)

number who said that the company was too large to serve the public most efficiently had grown from 18 to 20 percent; (c) those who felt that prices were too high had increased from 35 to 39 percent; and (d) those who believed that the company was a monopoly had increased from 37 to 43 percent.

In June a two-page article appeared on "Are We Too Big and Powerful?" The story set forth company operating policy in regard to government, customer credits, suppliers, dealers, and other small businesses and wound up by noting:

> No doubt many of those who charge us with being too big and powerful still have the erroneous old belief that we are linked in some way with the other Standard Oil Companies.
>
> This is, of course, incorrect.
>
> In May, 1911, after the decision of the Supreme Court, the old Standard Oil Company was divided into 34 separate companies. Since that date your company has been separate and distinct from each of the other "Standard Oils"—separate in ownership as well as in management. We compete actively with such companies as Standard of New Jersey, Socony Oil, Standard of Indiana, Standard of Ohio and their subsidiaries.
>
> Sure, we're big—but we're not big *and* powerful.

The July issue of the company magazine took up the question "Are Our Prices Too High?" The point was made that Standard's gasoline prices could not be *too* high (above competition) or the company wouldn't sell any gasoline, or too low, or it wouldn't make a profit, and that prices were primarily fixed by competition.

It was further noted that gasoline prices had risen about 65 percent since 1941 (excluding taxes), whereas the price of bread had climbed 123 percent, of coffee, 330 percent; that even automobiles themselves were much more expensive; that gasoline was a minor part of car operational costs; and that gasoline had been much improved over past years. An ingenious photo demonstrated the greater acceleration possible with modern gasoline by showing the difference in time-lapse between a car filled with 1930-type gasoline and the same car filled with a 1958 type.

In August the accusation "Are We Too Large to Best Serve the Public?" was faced, primarily by pictures and by quotations of opinion from six employees ranging from salespeople and chemists to the company president. The strong assertion made by all was that size was necessary for oil exploration, the risks of drilling exploratory wells, large, efficient manufacturing facilities, and on-going research into the field of new products and improvements in existing products.

The final article, in September, tackled the question "Are We Really a Monopoly?" and stressed competition in the oil business. The two photos used as illustrations showed a street lined with filling stations of various companies and a crossroads on the oil-producing desert with signs leading to five competitive leasing areas.

But if Standard of California felt it lacked public affection in the 1950's the roof really fell in during 1973 when gasoline shortages hit the United States because of the Arab oil embargo during the Israeli war. The public blamed the oil companies for the lack of gasoline with which to run its cars.

Standard had not conducted research into the general public attitude toward the company from 1957 when it got a 44 percent favorable, 43 percent neutral and 13 percent unfavorable vote until June of 1973 when its favorable rating was 26 percent, neutral 58 percent and unfavorable 16 percent.

But even this was friendly compared with the public feeling when the impact of oil shortages had really had time to sink in by February of 1974. Attitudes really polarized and the result was a 41 percent favorable rating, 11 percent neutral and 48 percent *unfavorable*. As a result of the crisis, people either felt that Standard was doing about what it could or blamed it bitterly. As one company employee described it, a "generalized hate" became specific.

Company management felt that some actions had to be taken. The first response was a rather low-key television spot series showing oil exploration activities, a tanker being built, and so on. Viewer studies using slightly aided recall of portions of the spots showed about average watching and recognition and some favorable attitude changes. Checks were made of the viewpoint of people who had seen the spots and of those who had not and the viewers became more favorably inclined than the nonviewers. Basically the approach was to assure the public that the oil company was trying to help end the shortage problem.

Despite some success in this effort, public attitude problems continued and shifted ground. As prices rose people became very negative about oil company profits and the government began to urge conservation strongly. This led to two communications campaigns, one of which seemed to work and the other of which didn't. The successful campaign was a radio series in the San Francisco area urging conservation in a lighter vein. There was some suspicion as to why an oil company would urge drivers to use less of their product, but acceptance of the need to conserve gasoline. There was also some laughter associated with Standard Oil for a change. The other campaign, planned for television, was less successful. It consisted of employees telling what they did. One, for example, was a financial analyst for Standard of California who said: "Many of you believe oil companies make 60 cents on every dollar of sales. I'm a financial analyst for Chevron, and last year we made 6 cents on every dollar of sales—not 60 but 6 cents. That might surprise some people."

A research firm tested this approach on about 100 people in advance of its use. Most thought the man was an actor, not an employee, and 30 percent said they didn't believe the message—so for this, and other reasons, the approach was dropped, but the light-hearted radio approach was adapted to television use.

The television spots that resulted were light bits about the formation of oil in ancient times from dinosaurs and other organic sources followed by the conservation message that "we're plumb out of dinosaurs" so when you jump in your car, don't waste gas. Cartoon illustrations were teamed with light music. These spots not only scored higher in attention and in recognition but were also followed by a marked improvement in attitude toward the company.

Perhaps not all of this change for the better could be attributed to the advertisements, although research studies showed that those who did see the spots became more favorable than those who did not. Times were still changing as the immediate shock wore off and specific cause and effect are hard to connect in complicated human attitudes. The important thing was that the survey research showed that the company had a serious public opinion problem, spurred it to try several solutions, and indicated clearly what the best one would be. This avoided a waste of money and also the likely danger that the attempted solution might only aggravate the problem, which sometimes happens. After opinions polarized into strong favorable and unfavorable groups, the only way that the total favorable attitude could be increased was by winning over some of those who were hostile, since there were few neutrals left. This was achieved, so in this case, at least, it paid to advertise to a hostile audience.

The American Bankers Association

The image problem of any one bank is how to stand out within its service area, thus attracting more deposits and making more loans. But in this it is affected by the general public attitude toward *all* banks which influences whether people put their money into banks, or savings and loan associations, or into the stock market, or under the mattress; where they choose to borrow money; and how much government regulation of banks they think there should be and of what sort. These problems are beyond the control of any single bank and this was the reason for the existence of a national television advertising campaign explaining the functions of banks. It was sponsored by The American Bankers Association and all members paid a portion of the cost for this common benefit to improve public attitudes.

The big question for the Association was: What will be most effective and how can the members be shown this?

The answer lay in research. A sample of television viewers were shown very brief excerpts from some of the Bankers Association commercials and were asked to describe the remainder of the spot. When they were able to do so it proved that they had seen and remembered it. Then, about a year later, as many of the same people as possible were reinterviewed after they had had a chance to see additional Bankers commercials and this time there were again questioned about their attitudes towards various aspects of banking. The changes between the groups which had seen and which had not seen the commercials were a measure of the effectiveness of the spots. At the same time the memorability of different spots was revealed as well as the extent to which the whole campaign had been heard at all.

The conclusions reached were that the better commercials performed well in reaching people but that the whole campaign needed more exposure to get the cumulative effect attained when people see several similar spots in a series. Not enough people had heavy exposure and more airing was needed for greatest effectiveness. A comparison of people who had seen the spots was made with those who had not showed more favorable attitudes among the viewers than the nonviewers (except when altered by unfavorable publicity or poor personal experiences). In many cases nonviewers during the year developed certain negative attitudes toward banking while viewers did not. The questions for the members of the Bankers Association thus became not whether the television commercials were effective, but how much of its budget it felt it should spend on them. This, of course, is a management decision.

It might be noted also how close in this instance and the preceding one are the "research" and "evaluation" steps in the R-A-C-E formula —one merges imperceptibly into the other. Research into attitudes suggests solutions which are tried and evaluated.

The Minneapolis United Fund Drive

In the summer of 1959 the people of Minneapolis and the various health and welfare groups which solicit funds from the public in the area were considering the advantages and disadvantages of grouping as many of these solicitation drives as possible into one United Fund effort.

It was decided to find out what the public thought about the subject. A 600-person set of interviews was conducted, based upon a probability-type multistage sample. The questionnaire for the study was designed by a local research corporation with the advice and assistance of a citizens' committee. The sample took into account such things as residence in the city or suburbs, sex, age, family income, and occupation, all of which might be expected to make a difference in response. The main findings were these:

1   In answer to an open-ended question, "How do you feel about these drives to raise money for health and welfare organizations?" 46 percent of the people interviewed in the city of Minneapolis and 64 percent of those in the suburbs volunteered that there were too many drives, although 53 percent in the city and 44 percent in the suburbs also felt that all were for good causes and that the money was needed. About 15 percent suggested that appeals should be combined. The spontaneous suggestion showed evidence that they had been thinking about the subject, since the interviewers had made no comment previously. About 10 percent questioned the wise or proper use of the money—a "wiseacre," defensive reaction which is not uncommon in these discussions. About 5 percent disliked being asked for funds at several places, such as at home, at school, and at work; and an average of about 3 percent felt that such drives should be government-supported. There was a difference in response between men and women; women felt more strongly that there were too many requests, yet also that the money was needed. Those with higher incomes complained more strongly about the numerous requests than did those with lower incomes.

2   In answer to a question about the *way* in which health and welfare organizations raised their money, about 36 percent felt that no other method was possible, but about 10 percent felt that a united appeal would be better.

3   Respondents were then shown a list of funds and were asked if they had been requested to contribute to them, and if they had been asked, where and by whom.

As a check, a nonexistent fund, "The National Pancreas Research Fund," was inserted along with the agencies actually soliciting in the Minneapolis area within the past year, and about 5 percent said that they had given to it also.

Identification of other funds and claims of giving to them, however, were about in proportion to the known activity of these organizations within the area and nationally.

4 Citizens were then asked how much they had given to these various causes. The great majority (usually about 70 percent) said they had given under $25, and almost all were under $5.

5 About 94 percent of those interviewed stated that neither the respondent nor a member of his family had served as a volunteer worker in collecting charity funds during the preceding year; but 88 percent felt that such activity was highly commendable.

6 When asked if there were "more," "about the same," or "a smaller number" of money-raising drives now than formerly, 82 percent of the people in the city and 92 percent in the suburbs felt that there were more, and almost half added unhappy comments. When, at this point, a question about their reaction to a combined drive was broached, 70 percent favored a combined effort. The biggest reason for preferring separate drives was that they enabled givers to select the organizations they favored. Those preferring a combined drive felt that it was more economical and efficient, and that the money went where it was most needed.

A survey such as this provides an answer to those who insist, "But this city is *different*"; encourages those who are in favor of a project and disarms those who oppose it; and points out ideas which should be incorporated into a program, such as the prime point that spoken opposition to the unselectivity and impersonality of a United Fund drive could be counteracted by allowing givers, if they wished, to specify the use of their donations.

Opinion Research Corporation

As indicated in the Standard Oil and American Bankers Association cases earlier in this chapter, individual companies or groups *can* affect public opinion regarding them if they have sufficient resources and make the right approach. However, all organizations and particular groups of organizations are subject to groundswells of public opinion which are so massive that they are beyond immediate change; all are swept along in the same tide and the important thing is to know its strength and direction and how one's own organization fares in relation to others in the same field and others not related. This is the background of immediate problems upon which public relations people should be fully and accurately informed.

Much of this valuable background work is done by general opinion survey research firms for publishing or broadcasting companies and appears as a part of the news because of its general reader interest.

Deeper studies of greater specific interest to business or other groups are often financed on a continuing basis by regular payments to a survey research firm by those needing the information. When several companies combine their efforts in a research field which concerns them all, they gain a number of advantages. Not only is the cost lowered, but, more importantly, each organization sees how it stands in comparison with others in its own and other areas of business. Such a service has been provided for many years, for example, by the "Public Opinion Index for Industry" surveys of Opinion Research Corporation (ORC) of Princeton, New Jersey.

In a speech during the summer of 1977 before the Public Relations Society of America Institute, the Executive Vice President of ORC noted that broad attitude survey research concerned itself with (1) the public's personal concerns, (2) its attitudes toward business in general, (3) overall attitudes toward types of industries, and finally, (4) attitudes toward individual companies.

Personal concerns include individual satisfaction with life, sense of financial well-being, problems apparent to the public, and priorities for action on these problems.

Attitudes toward business in general include feelings about the social obligations of business, confidence in business as compared with other organizations, appraisal of the ethics and morals of business people, the degree of profit made by businesses, and a judgment on how much business contributes to the progress of America. Surveys are frequently broken down to include the attitudes of specific groups such as women, college students, or governmental people when there is a significant difference.

Attitudes toward types of industries would include public familiarity with them and their perceived strengths and weaknesses.

Attitudes toward particular companies would include public familiarity with them and favorable or unfavorable beliefs about them. Further research into particular points can then be done. A company may be little known, for example, because it makes a highly specialized product sold to only a few buyers. Or a company may be well known because it produces a product which millions of people use.

The managers of one company, for example, were much concerned because their organization was the target of severe government action and they felt it would have serious public opinion effects. Surveys showed that it did not have such effects and a massive effort to "rebuild" its reputation would have been costly and perhaps harmful. Another company was foreign-owned and assumed this to be a liability, whereas in fact there was little awareness or concern about it. Another company had a long-established product symbol and wanted to diversify into other lines of manufacturing. Surveys showed that its old product symbol was too limiting to new lines and should be changed.

But beyond such specific company questions is that the nature of our times is increasingly critical. Communications are more varied, faster, and plentiful than ever before. This has served to sensitize people to the real or imagined flaws in the world about them. There is a lot of free-floating anxiety and anger. Things that were once accepted or taken for granted are the subject of complaint and efforts at reform.

An ORC survey of trust and confidence in American institutions, for instance, showed that churches ranked the highest with a 63 percent *high* and 10 percent *low* vote. Banks followed with 60 percent and 5 percent respectively (the unnamed percentage in each case was *medium*). Colleges and universities were 46 percent high and 6 percent low and labor unions 22 percent high and 28 percent low. But large companies scored only 18 percent high and 21 percent low. The stock market, incidentally, brought up the rear with only a 10 percent favorable rating and a 24 percent negative rating.

When asked about ethical and moral practices, 76 percent rated physicians as excellent or good and only 4 percent as poor. College professors rated 60 percent good, news reporters 55 percent good, lawyers 49 percent, and corporate executives 36 percent good and 11 percent poor. This time the rear was brought up by federal government officials who rated 28 percent good and 24 percent poor.

Despite these skeptical attitudes toward business and business leaders, the public still felt that business would be a major contributor to the country's future progress. The survey in 1977 showed that 37 percent felt that business would do the most toward America's progress and this percentage had not changed much in a dozen years when in 1965 33 percent had said the same thing. By comparison only 16 percent looked to government for the greatest aid and 19 percent to labor.

In other words, while the public was increasingly critical of business people, it still believed in the system and felt that it could do more for the future than any other group.

When public *information* about business activities was examined some interesting (but not new) facts emerged. The public has always overestimated corporate profits and the degree of overestimation continues to grow. This is probably caused by reporting of massive "box car" final profit figures in the press without their division being shown or the expenses involved in attaining these earnings. These are so much above the average individual's budget as to cause a "Gee whiz, they must just be wallowing in wealth" reaction and need to be interpreted. Political attacks on profits also have their effect and are always popular. But in 1976 the public surveyed by ORC estimated the after-tax profits of the average manufacturer at 29 cents on each dollar of sales. In fact it was 5.4 cents. The auto companies fared even worse with an imagined profit of 37 cents against a fact of 5.1 cents. Oil companies were thought to be a veritable bonanza with 43 cents profit per dollar of sales whereas the fact was 8.7 per cent.

Naturally, from this misinformation, the public thinks that business profits are too high—so in the 1976 survey, 50 percent of them said so, up from only 26 percent in 1971. This leads 55 percent to conclude that the government should limit profits, up from only 33 percent in 1971.

Examination of studies such as this on public attitudes shows much that is contradictory. People, for example, have the least confidence in the integrity of Federal government officials, yet feel that these same officials should regulate company profits. They distrust the ethics of business people yet look to business more than any other force for the growth of the country.

Such contradictions do not indicate faulty research but rather faulty human logic and behavior. It is possible for the public to entertain conflicting propositions in its mind and this fact indicates that the humorless logician type of mind in the practice of public relations will often have difficulties. One of the values of good opinion research is that it documents such human inconsistencies, giving pause to the dollars-and-cents logical type of thinking which rules much of business and has directed some unfortunate public relations efforts in the past.

Advertising Research Council Survey on the American Economic System

Public ignorance and misinformation about the American economic system has long concerned American business people and from time to time they have felt that broad public communications efforts should be launched to do something about it. Many of these attempts have been intuitive or based upon the opinions of friends in the same upper social classes. Self-interest has often been apparent. Many of the efforts have been failures or have alienated numbers of their audience. It would seem only wise to make a scientific survey research effort to find out what people really do know before attempting to communicate with them, yet this has not always been done.

But the problem remains. With increasingly participatory democracy, which extends to many economic decisions as well as the more traditionally political ones, the public is now being asked to understand terms such as "balance of trade," "energy trade-offs," "transfer payments," "productivity," and "money supply" (or at least the concepts involved in these terms) and to advocate or oppose government positions upon them. If the people are incapable or unwilling to aid in directing their own economic destiny it will pass into the hands of others who are eager to do so. And if the people choose poor economic policies many are injured and the prosperity of the whole nation suffers.

In the mid-1970s, The Advertising Council, composed of representatives of most large advertising agencies and companies in the United States, planned a major communications effort to the American public on the nature and choices of our economic future. But before deciding what to say and how to say it they wisely decided first to find out what people really knew and thought through about 3,000 interviews in late 1974 and early 1975.

These were conducted in 200 locations in the United States using a questionnaire which was almost entirely "open-ended." Interviews took about an hour and a half and care was taken to see that interviewers did not suggest answers by the type of questions they asked.

In building the sample many factors such as sex, age, income, race, community size, geographic location, occupation, education, home ownership, religion, and political activity were taken into account and obtained in a percentage close to the actual U.S. Census breakdown. The sample was large enough that differences between these segments could be meaningfully compared, for example, working women versus nonworking or well-to-do versus poor.

One of the first things that respondents were asked was to describe in their own terms the United States economic system. The answers varied widely, of course, and many times several ideas turned up from the same person. But the outstanding finding was that most people described the economic system in terms of what it did for *them*—the ability to move from one job to another, the opportunity to start a business, personal freedom, or creativity; not in terms such as "free enterprise," "supply and demand" or a "profit system"—although these were mentioned by a considerable number of respondents.

When asked what was good about the system 54 percent mentioned personal freedoms and opportunities, another 12 percent the high standard of living, and only 9 percent such abstract ideas as free enterprise or private enterprise.

Asked what was bad about the system, specific complaints such as inflation (27 percent) or the power of big business (18 percent) or unemployment (8 percent) were most often noted.

When asked what changes should be made, specific, timely complaints again came to the fore with 31 percent urging that inflation be stopped, 20 percent for tax reform, and 19 percent for reforms in big business such as antitrust laws or profit controls. More government regulation was favored by 56 percent although 35 percent felt there was too much at present.

Well-educated people of higher economic status were more inclined to stress personal freedoms and were more able to describe the roles of business, labor, consumer, and investor in the economic system than disadvantaged or younger groups. Yet only about half of the "elite" were able to formulate their understanding of the system very exactly.

There is much more information from such a widespread opinion research study than described above, but the salient point is that most respondents viewed the American economic system in terms of how it affected *them,* primarily in terms of freedom and opportunities and satisfactions rather than in terms of material goods. They did not think of abstractions and many economic terms were unfamiliar to them.

Research such as this would indicate, for example, that an attempt to communicate to the broader American public through abstract economic doctrines or even such high-flown terms as "free enterprise" falls flat or, even worse, because of the prevailing suspicion of big business has a negative effect—"Methinks the lady doeth protest too much," as it were. It would also indicate that an appeal to the grosser instincts of self-indulgence such as living well would reach only a small number who valued the system primarily for this, and might also have negative effects because indulgence is frequently considered sinful.

Such guidance as what *not* to do is valuable, but it does not entirely tell a would-be communicator what *to* do. It points the way and suggests an approach. But the *style* with which this is done is all-important. Great care must be taken, not to be condescending, for instance, because this provokes wrath or repulsion in the receiver. Communicators may be better informed; in fact they will hardly be listened to unless they are. But they must not lecture or demean their receivers in imparting information.

They may have a self-interest; and it is better if they do not try to conceal it.

They may wish to talk a long time; and their listeners may not wish to hear that much. Or they may be brief; and their audience wonders what is left unsaid.

Even the appearance of a communication is part of the message. Should it be light or serious? Through what media should it be conveyed and in what connection and at what times?

Within the framework of good public relations research, there is still plenty of room for the best creative effort and good judgment. Adequate research assures that you probably won't make any terrible mistakes and may start off in the right direction. It doesn't mean that you'll get there.

SUMMARY

Sound research underlies most effective public relations work. Among common research objectives are:

1 Probing basic public attitudes
2 Measuring true opinions
3 Identifying leaders of opinion
4 Reducing costs by concentrating upon valid targets
5 Testing themes and communications media
6 Achieving good timing
7 Ascertaining the strength of opposition
8 Achieving two-way communication
9 Revealing trouble before it happens
10 Providing facts which can be used in public relations programs

Modern opinion-research methods have been largely developed within the past thirty years, and their use has been marked with increasing success but also by some notable failures.

Among the main types of research used by public relations practitioners are (1) simple fact gathering, (2) opinion research, and (3) motivational research.

Knowledge of possible errors in common research is important. Among the more common of these errors are the following:

1 Nonrepresentative listening
2 Undue reliance upon advisory groups
3 Weakness in planning representative panels
4 Field reports
5 Improper samples
6 Biased, untrained, or dishonest interviewers
7 Foggy responses
8 Undue recall of the prominent
9 Exaggeration of the importance of minor differences

Every public relations person needs to know the fundamentals of valid research. But research is a highly developed discipline in itself. When confronted with a major problem in this area, an investigator should usually seek the help of those who are highly trained and who have had wide experience.

ADDITIONAL READINGS

Babbie, Earl F., *The Practice of Social Research.* (Belmont, Calif: Wadsworth Publishing Company, 1975.) [Primarily a look into research methods.]

Meyer, Philip, *Precision Journalism: A Reporter's Introduction To Social Science Methods.* (Bloomington: Indiana University Press, 1973.)

Robinson, Edward J., *Public Relations and Survey Research.* (New York: Appleton, 1969.) [Designed for public relations students and contains examples of research use.]

Chapter 11

Action and Action Cases

The English language is full of sayings to the effect that "actions speak louder than words" or that "what you are speaks so loudly that I can't hear what you say." Their popularity tends to indicate that, as a people, we are by nature somewhat suspicious of rhetoric and are more impressed by deeds. Words alone are often regarded as feeble or downright harmful when the claims they make cannot be justified, and even the best advertising cannot sell a bad product twice to the same customers. For these reasons, public relations practitioners approaching a problem of popular persuasion think primarily not in terms of "What can we *say?*" but in terms of "What can we *do?*" Action is an essential ingredient in successful public relations practice.

Public relations people do not always create the actions to which they seek to direct attention; many times the action is inherent in the very nature of the organization which strives for greater understanding and good will. Planes which fly on time; water that spurts merrily out of the tap, clean and pure; and banks which take good care of your money and pay generous interest for its use, are all engaged in actions typical of the standard operating procedures of good airlines, reliable water companies, and sound banks; but such actions are not news, and organizations can say only a limited number of things about them without seeming to brag about the obvious. Public relations practice goes beyond the worthy performance of everyday duties. Like the public itself, public relations assumes that such efficiency is to be expected and seeks to go an extra mile in demonstrating the value of a service, the characteristics of those who produce it, and its worth in the public interest. Public relations thus operates not only as a spur to the maintenance of already good performance (which is assumed), but also as an incentive to the creation of better products and services.

The number of important actions which can be shown to the public is limited. One cannot do too many things and get attention for all of them; the net effect of too many busy actions is likely to be confusion. The public relations worker finds that the choice of good actions demands even more care than the choice of telling words.

Actions may be inherent in the existing situation; they may arise out of the opportunities created by facilities or events; they may be carefully planned to focus attention upon certain aspects of an organization; they may be created to serve the public welfare; they may be cooperative with other groups; they may be created primarily to serve communication needs; or they may consist largely of organizing people into a common effort, itself an action and a means of communication (creating something in common).

Public relations actions may be either large or small: as large as a national science-talent search or as small as allowing the public to fish in a company lake. The instigators of an action should almost never call attention to its virtues. The onlooker is supposed to draw conclusions (with the aid of proper publicity). The best actions are those which the onlooker hears about indirectly, usually those which meet some need very much in the social interest, and which make it possible for others to achieve *their* goals. Trivial actions should never be proclaimed as important, and the big ones will speak for themselves if well known.

ACTION INHERENT IN AN EXISTING SITUATION

Sometimes the facilities and operations of an organization are set up so well that, with ingenuity and imagination, they may easily be converted into actions which will earn public goodwill and appreciation.

The Indianapolis Water Company

The Indianapolis Water Company had two large reservoirs upon which it permited boating by free special permit. The company initiated a "Fireman Citizen of the Year" award to honor outstanding firefighters, not only for performance in the line of duty, but also for their extracurricular activities in the public good. (The fact that firefighters are great users of water at fires can scarcely go unnoticed!) The company also sponsored a television weather program (related to rain) and such fitting events as television sports coverage of swimming meets.

Figure 11-1 A public relations advertisement of the Indianapolis Water Company stressing the investment and labor needed to supply a large city with water.

The company used a series of water-company newspaper advertisements, several of which were cited by the Bureau of Advertising of
the American Newspaper Publishers Association for their outstanding
quality. A copy theme was, for example, "Water, water everywhere . . .
but—" followed by the fact that "Your Indianapolis Water Company
Has to Inventory It" (or distribute it, or make it safe to use). A motion
picture was developed for use by schools, churches, libraries, and other
groups. Radio broadcasts of high school sports were sponsored along
with billboards, participation in various civic events, and employee activities.

One of the main efforts of the water company was to keep the press
thoroughly informed of all news, good and bad; not only plans to construct new mains or to save the city money by helping to pave a street,
but also news of how long service will be shut off when a pump breaks
down or when a contractor, bulldozing the head off a valve, creates a
small flood in one spot and a complete drought elsewhere.

Community Relations at Rockefeller Center,
New York

The world's largest privately owned business and entertainment area,
Rockefeller Center, supports sixteen skyscrapers built on 15 acres in the
heart of New York City, where 40,000 people work and even more visit
every day. Its reputation came first from its size and from the fact that
when it opened in 1933, the Center was a pioneer in its construction,
concept, and land use. But its further reputation for quality and primacy
has been carefully fostered over the years by a well-planned public
relations program, which has as its objectives: (1) projection of the
Center's corporate personality through newsmaking events, exhibits, and
visitors; (2) communication of the corporate story to all media; (3) close
association with the tenants from whom its income is derived; and (4)
an integrated personnel who contribute heavily to the community program.

The policies which govern the Center's special events and exhibits
are good taste, civic responsibility, appropriateness, and consideration
for both the tenants and the public. Within this context an amazing
variety of newsworthy projects has been possible: ice skating and folk
dances; dog shows and vintage cars; singing and speechmaking; philan-
thropic rallies; international ceremonies; and gatherings to honor
achievements, ideas, and personalities. The setting for these events is the
95- by 125-foot recessed lower plaza which serves as midtown New
York's "village green."

Because of the publicity value of this location, the public relations personnel of the Center, although they say "yes" to many requests for events, have to say "no" to an equal number. Among them have been plans as varied as rigging up a cable car from the observation roof of the seventy story RCA Building to Central Park some eight city blocks away; a request from an opera star to sing from the top of the Center's big annual Christmas tree; and a demonstration of a new parachute by an ex-fire chief, who proposed to jump from the top of a high building and guaranteed to float to the street at the pace of 9 seconds per floor.

Seasonal flowers, shade trees, benches, a skating rink, flags, murals, mosaics, and sculpture, plus tours, are among the attractions for visitors. Regular contact is also kept with the building tenants and with the employees who service the buildings and are recognized by management as its front-line public relations emissaries.

The influences of Rockefeller Center reach far beyond its 15 acres and have been reflected in the refashioning of communities across the United States and overseas. When new buildings are erected in Philadelphia, Pittsburgh, Caracas, Paris, New Delhi, or Sydney, the newspaper clippings are apt to describe each new project as "another Rockefeller Center." The value of consistent, careful public relations planning in connection with the operation of the Center has been incalculable and has added greatly to the net worth of the buildings, far beyond their steel-and-concrete dollar valuation.

Atlas Van Lines, Inc.

A public relations program undertaken by Atlas Van Lines, Inc., some years ago, though on a completely different scale, still shows public relations inherent in the operation of an organization.

Moving day probably comes for Americans more often than for any other highly civilized people on earth. Corporate shifts and opportunities to seek new jobs cause the big vans to be backed up to the doors of houses in almost every neighborhood every few weeks. Adults often have been through upheavals before and may taken them in their stride; but what is merely sadness to them may be an almost catastrophic uprooting to their children, particularly to teen-agers, who may have their deep and often their only roots firmly fixed in the neighborhood.

This problem is peripheral to the physical job of the long-distance, over-the-road movers in bundling furniture from one city to another, but it is inherent in their business and offers an opportunity for useful public relations action in aiding adults to solve the problems of their children in adjusting to a move.

The *action* taken by Atlas Van Lines was to commission the Association for Family Living of Chicago to make a special study for the moving company of the emotional problems of children of families involved in cross-country moves. This study was then distributed to Atlas agents as a sales tool in dealing with customers, furnished the basis of publicity in newspapers and trade publications, and was made into a reprint booklet. A sample of its flavor can be obtained from portions of the general publicity release upon the story:

> Of all the events which can occur in a family—from a new baby to a new job for father—moving day stands out as a time of upheaval. . . . The Association for Family Living, Chicago, pinpoints some of the problems and possible solutions in a special study made for Atlas Van Lines, Inc., Chicago. . . .
>
> "Toddlers and pre-school children demand, more than any other age group, familiarity and predictability in their daily routine," the study stated.
>
> "Between the ages of one and four, a child learns to recognize the physical characteristics of his surroundings and takes comfort in their stability and permanence."
>
> "Any drastic alteration in these surroundings will be accompanied by a correspondingly diminished feeling of security."
>
> Family Living's study detailed the experiences of one typical young family—the Garfields—in moving from one city to another.
>
> The couple had three children—David, six months; Bobby, three years old; and Jane, 11. Like more than 60 percent of all moves today, the Garfields' was necessitated by a job promotion and transfer for the father, Henry.
>
> The new home was too far from the old to permit frequent trips back and forth. However, on one visit that both parents made there, the Garfields traveled on a weekend so that the oldest child, Jane, could accompany them. Henry also took many pictures of the house, both inside and out, which all could consult at any time.
>
> The Garfields decided to include Jane and three-year-old Bobby in as much of the preparation as possible, but without overburdening them with a mass of detail. . . .
>
> It was decided that Jane should be permitted to help select the color scheme for her room and to arrange the furniture as she wished. Mrs. Garfield knew that Bobby did not fully appreciate the fact that he was leaving his old home, so she decided not to change any of the furnishings in his room and to decorate his new bedroom just like the old.
>
> Jane was quite worried about the changes ahead. What would the children be like in the new neighborhood? Would they like her, and and

would she like them? Would she fit in easily at the new school? Would the teachers be as nice as those she was leaving?

Mrs. Garfield took pains to explain to Jane that they had selected a house and neighborhood with these thoughts uppermost. This served to give Jane a measure of reassurance. . . .

The story then went on to tell how actual packing was not done until the last moment to avoid a sense of loss among the children, how three-year-old Bobby went on a visit to friends the day of the moving so that he would not see strange men upsetting his familiar home, and how family understanding and participation in planning could make the day of departure an adventure into a bright future rather than a day of tears.

The story received good play in the press because it was authentic, human, and helpful and dealt with a situation familiar to a great many urban newspaper readers. It was not contrived, but was an action which grew very naturally out of the regular activities of the moving company.

Detroit Diesel Allison

Sometimes if you cannot get the customer to come to you, you must go to the customer. This was the situation faced by Detroit Diesel Allison, a division of General Motors Corporation, in trying to reach an estimated 200,000 to 300,000 independent truckers who buy their own rigs at $40,000 or $50,000 each and who are away from home for long periods driving on the road. Conventional advertising was not geared to hit this moving target, so Detroit Diesel Allison decided to take its story to the truckers where they worked.

This was done by means of a well-planned caravan of five specially built and equipped trucks which made 27 stops at big truck stop stations over a 10,000-mile route from coast to coast in the United States during August, 1974. The crowd-puller was a live on-stage country music show by well-known country music stars that the truckers had heard many times on the radio. There was a "dream truck" for drivers to inspect and in another trailer drivers could push buttons for computerized answers to the best combinations of tractors and trailers for various loads and road conditions as well as for self-testing in safety situations. But the main purpose was served by an exhibit of the company's new engines and new automatic truck transmission with simulated driving devices to try it out.

Advance promotion and publicity for this elaborate and costly program was not left up to chance. A series of truck magazine ads and radio

Figure 11–2 Truckers like country music so that is what Detroit Diesel Allison used to attract their attention to the travelling exhibition at truck stops.

Figure 11–3 This elaborate trailer was part of the show too and offered truckers a chance to use computerized analysis of their equipment needs.

spots on nineteen country-music radio stations heralded its coming. Company publications promoted it and a 12-minute country-music film was used by truck distributors. A 27-minute film was shot during the tour and later used by theaters, television, community groups, and dealers. Local distributors near the stops lined up local newspaper publicity, offered rides to the area, made additional truck displays, set up booths at the shows with free refreshments, and made personal contacts with truckers in their areas. Waitresses at the truck stops wore special buttons, posters were in place in advance, free log books were offered to drivers, and balloons distributed. One news conference was held with the national trucking press in Chicago and others with the entertainment press in New York. Public relations specialists went along with the caravan to assist the local press and broadcasters at each spot with pictures, releases, and help with on-the-spot interviews. A telephone message recorder was installed in the Detroit public relations office to take after-hours calls for information.

After the month-long tour was over, four employee shows were held, the two product exhibits toured dealers for another six months, promotional meetings were held at hundreds of truck dealerships. Truckers were given safety kits and stereo cassettes for their tape decks for getting product demonstrations at their dealers.

The results of a program such as this are not instantaneous because heavy truck engines and transmissions are long-term purchases made only every few years. But thousands of cards distributed during the caravan tour were returned by truckers asking for more information, the caravan played to 25,000 people at its wind-up at the Trucker's Jamboree in Wheeling, West Virginia. Stories and films appeared in scores of magazines and newspapers and many broadcasting stations reaching millions of readers, viewers, and listeners.

The important thing about the *action* of this program was that it was not new. The engines existed as did the transmission. The problem was to do something that would reach and interest the people concerned. The caravan itself was new and created interest in the products which it displayed. Many organizations have similar opportunities.

ACTION CAPITALIZING UPON AN EXISTING FACILITY OR EVENT

Action which makes use of a fortuitous occurence or an historical event reaches a shade farther into the field of public relations actions. It involves the imaginative utilization of something which otherwise would not have been put to work.

Detroitbank Corporation

A number of years ago when the deep foundations of a new downtown skyscraper office building for The Detroit Bank & Trust Company were being dug, the excavators crunched into old timbers and a rusted cannon. It was one corner of Fort Lernoult, build by the British in Detroit in 1778. Earlier excavations for other buildings in the area had hit other portions of the long-abandoned fort.

The public relations staff of the bank saw the opportunity that this discovery offered. The news would not only attract additional attention to the new bank building but would also offer an opportunity to publicize the name of the bank in connection with promotion of the city's history.

Archeologists and historians from Wayne State University in Detroit were called to the scene and determined what portion of the old fort had been uncovered. From these measurements they were able, using old maps, to draw the entire size and location of the original structure. Artifacts such as cannon balls, coins, buttons, and human bones were recovered. The bank aided the Detroit Historical Society in commissioning a Wayne State University professor to write and publish a well-illustrated booklet on Fort Lernoult. This was later simplified into a coloring book distributed to thousands of school children in their classes. Information was continuously supplied to and used by the news media.

When the American bicentennial in 1976 approached, thought was given as to how this event of some years before might fit in. Fort Lernoult had been built by the British in 1778 when the American Revolutionary War was in progress because they feared that the earlier French fort, Fort Pontchartrain, which they occupied, could be overwhelmed if a well-armed force were to occupy a hill to the north of it. The British continued to hold Detroit for more than a dozen years after the war ended but finally surrendered Fort Lernoult to the Americans on July 11, 1796. It was the first place at which the American flag flew over Detroit.

To celebrate this occurence Detroitbank commissioned a skilled museum artist to create an exact-scale model of the original fort as it existed in the eighteenth century on a scale of 20 feet to the inch. Facts obtained in previous historical research were used to make a miniature diorama model including buildings, trees, people, animals, roads, and the river. Standing above it the viewer could see exactly how the old fort looked as if seeing it from a low-flying airplane.

This historical model which took hundreds of hours to construct was first presented to special guests in a civic reception during the evening at the bank's downtown office. It was then placed on public view

Figure 11-4 This highly detailed scale model of Ft. Lernoult and of part of the Detroit riverfront in 1779 was prepared by Detroitbank Corporation to help celebrate the 1976 American Bicentennial.

Figure 11-5 Note the extent of the detail in this tiny horse-drawn wagon held upon a person's fingers. The Detroit Bank & Trust Building now stands upon a portion of the historic site of which the model was made.

for several weeks during normal banking hours in the lobby. Finally it was placed permanently in Detroit's Fort Wayne Military Museum.

Union Pacific Railroad

Centennials offer a great opportunity for action to create news and interest when they are well-known and important. Such was certainly the case in 1969 when the hundredth anniversary of the driving of the golden spike connecting the Atlantic and Pacific coasts of the United States by rail rolled around.

A re-enactment of the event at the scene in Utah was obvious, but because of the remoteness of the desert location only a few hundred could be expected to attend. Some way was needed to bring the story closer to people's own lives and experiences. The Union Pacific Railroad decided to develop a special train to tour towns upon its 9,500-mile system of tracks.

Reproductions of the original locomotives were placed upon flat cars facing each other as they had when they met in 1869. Golden-Spike-

Figure 11–6 This is an original photograph of the meeting on May 10, 1869, of the Union Pacific and Central Pacific locomotives in Utah marking the completion of the first transcontinental railway across the United States. Courtesy Union Pacific Railroad Museum Collection.

Figure 11-7 This is the way the driving of the golden spike was re-enacted in 1969 using similar locomotives at the same location. Courtesy Union Pacific Railroad.

driving ceremonies were repeated at stops using local people and gaining attention from local news media.

Other cars of the train contained exhibits of the old and modern railway. The train travelled more than 16,000 miles in seven months and visited ninety-nine different communities. Almost a million people visited the show and by actual count more than 600,000 toured the displays in the golden spike exposition car. Local reaction and interest was enthusiastic.

Chautauqua Institution

Located on Lake Chautauqua in New York state near Buffalo, this long-established cultural family summer center began in 1874 and by the early 1900s was known throughout the United States. Not only did thousands of people come to its wooded grounds in the summer for a few days or a few weeks to listen to lectures, plays and music, and to engage in lighter studies; the ingredients were also packaged in tent shows which toured the smaller towns of the country and brought cultural attractions for several days at a time by a subscription plan to places which were

Figure 11-8 Because of the remoteness of the desert location where the original track joining took place only a few hundred people could attend, so historic locomotives were placed on flat cars and the re-enactment was repeated in ninety-nine different communities. Courtesy Union Pacific Railroad.

hungry for elevating entertainment. Small summer camps, replicas of the original New York state chautauqua, sprang up all over the country, filling a need for wholesome entertainment and informal education in the arts and sciences. Many noted religious and political leaders as well as actors and teachers went on chautauqua tours.

But with the coming of automobiles, motion pictures, radio, and finally television, the isolation which had rendered small town and rural people so hungry for cultural sustenance disappeared. By the 1930s the travelling tent chautauquas had largely disappeared and most of the fixed summer camps in other states had disappeared. The original Chautauqua Institution in New York state continued but times were obviously changing.

In 1972 the managers of the original New York Chautauqua decided to use the 1974 centennial of its establishment to revitalize the organization and to make it known throughout the nation. Committees were appointed to plan special programs for the summer of 1974 and a

Figure 11–9 The original New York state chautauqua also went on the road in the early 1900s visiting smaller cities all over the United States. Courtesy Chautauqua Institution.

public relations counseling firm was engaged to make it known through-out the country. Some of the steps which they took were: a new history of Chautauqua was written; a noted sculptor designed an official centennial medallion; the U.S. Postal Service issued a commemorative stamp; Chautauqua was designated a National Historic Site; a Centennial Flag was designed; a coloring book for children was prepared; an old-fashioned gay-nineties ice cream pavilion was opened; a Centennial Ball and opening night press reception was planned. All of this, along with modern and historic pictures, was sent to a media list including 1,200 people specially interested in the fields of art, music, and literature. New program books and other summer literature were designed to celebrate the centennial theme.

As a result of such effort at least forty feature articles were published in newspapers and magazines. Many news stories on the events appeared in regional newspapers and on television stations in Buffalo, Cleveland, Erie, and in Pennsylvania. The president of the Chautauqua Institute was interviewed on the NBC Today show. The PBS-TV network pre-

Figure 11-10 The travelling chautauquas disappeared, but the original Chautauqua Institution in the town of that name in upper New York state continued to flourish. This is a part of its centennial celebration which was held in 1974.

sented three one-hour concerts by the Chautauqua Symphony Orchestra and a Buffalo station a similar number. Twenty visiting critics came to the summer series to review plays, operas, and concerts. The *New York Times* carried a story in its travel section.

Chautauqua had been a going institution before the centennial with nearly 10,000 persons in residence during its eight and a-half week summer session, 2,000 students in its summer school and a total attendance of about 300,000. But after the publicity it was an even more going-institution. Attendance increased 13 percent over the previous year, more than 2,500 people contributed over $700,000 and the Institution ended the year in the black—the first time in many years. New ideas, such as off-season educational weekends for Senior Citizens were adopted, and the organization acquired new vigor.

The American Chemical Society

One reason for the success of the American Bicentennial in 1976 was that it attracted the effort of many business, professional, and social groups to cooperate with it. One such organization was the American Chemical Society. Here in many ways the main need was for stimulation of local chapters by passing on ideas for them to engage in their own programs and by providing a national source of publicity.

Among the many projects was the restoration of the famous chemist, Joseph Priestley's laboratory in his home in Northumberland, Pennsylvania. Scientific companies both contributed to the project and publicized it.

Many other professional groups were engaged in similar programs in the national bicentennial year of 1976. Each of them attracted its own following and interest. In total they contributed to a memorable national observance without the necessity of a huge governmental expenditure or the risks of a major world's fair and exhibition, most of which have lost money in recent times or have become subject to disruption or violence.

ACTION TO DISPLAY THE EXISTING CHARACTERISTICS OF A PRODUCT OR AN ORGANIZATION

Johnson Motors

Demonstration is one of the oldest devices of sales. It is feeble and commonplace simply to *assert* in advertising that a boat motor is dependable; it is quite another thing to show that it is so under the toughest conditions. And if this can be done with human interest and news value, so much the better. You could run a motor, for example, for so many hours in a tank full of water and have a perfectly valid test, but this would be of little public interest. The same motor running the same number of hours across a wide ocean would capture the imagination!

One of the main public relations goals of Johnson Motors has been to develop more public confidence in its products. To help attain this goal, Johnson in 1958 co-sponsored the crossing of the Atlantic Ocean by a small boat using two Johnson engines.

A public relations man and a photographer went to Copenhagen, Denmark, to arrange details of the sailing and to disseminate the news. One of the details was to arrange with a steamship line for the small boat to tag along with a large freighter for resupply of fuel and as a "mother ship" in case of trouble.

Several severe storms did cause trouble. Although the small boat was able to ride out the weather, it was obliged to reduce its speed so materially because of the rough seas that it had to be picked up by the freighter, which carried perishable foods and had to maintain its ten-day schedule to New York City.

At first glance the project appeared to have failed, but two things saved it:

1   The small-boat crew insisted on being put back into the ocean with their tiny craft as soon as the weather had calmed sufficiently to enable them to keep up with the freighter. The same loading derrick which had plucked them from the sea launched them back upon it.

2   The company photographer recorded every step of the project, both removal and replacement of the small boat, in still pictures and in colored movies.

Because the boat crew refused to quit and the photographer was alert, what was first thought to be a failure turned out to be a sizable success. The press, including the important boating trade magazines, chose to regard the initiation of the project as highly significant. The achievement of the small boat was a solid foundation of fact. Newspapers and broadcasting stations carried the story. Johnson advertising used it with great reader interest. And a motion picture of the adventure was widely used. The boat itself was widely displayed at boat shows and the project was an undoubted success in demonstrating the reliability of the motors.

In 1968 Johnson repeated the exploit under even more unusual circumstances. A 20-horsepower motor and sail were used to power a 25-foot catamaran that an English-born adventurer took from Waukegan, Illinois, where the motor was manufactured, to Dakar, West Africa, in 106 days. The navigator reported that he used 200 gallons of fuel and used the motor for hundreds of hours without a breakdown or difficulty in starting. He returned across the South Atlantic in 47 days to the Virgin Islands and then up the inland waterway along the east coast of the United States and through the St. Lawrence river and Great Lakes to Waukegan, adding hundreds of hours more use to his engine since it was the only means of propulsion in these inland journeys. This also was well reported.

Demonstrations, of course, need to be relevant and truthful. The press and public are quick to spot triviality or deceit. But demonstrations cannot be surpassed if they are valid.

Miniaturization Awards

Big things always get our attention because we cannot help noticing them, but in recent years many scientific product breakthroughs have been possible by making components extremely small, as in the field of electronics and space-flight equipment.

Several years ago a New England company which manufactured extremely accurate tiny ball bearings (the smallest of which was about the size of the period at the end of this sentence) wanted to be better known in the industrial and scientific worlds and turned to a public relations counseling firm for advice.

The counseling firm saw that a trend toward miniaturization was under way and decided that the best way to help its client was to call attention to that trend and, in passing, to the miniature ball bearings maker's role in it. The manufacturer was small and could not accomplish much alone, but it was a leader in one phase of an important national development.

The counseling firm recommended an annual awards contest for the most distinguished examples of miniaturization in any industrial or scientific field during the year.

A capable judging committee was selected; a sculptor was commissioned to produce an unusual and attractive awards statuette; a descriptive folder was prepared and mailed to manufacturers, leading research institutions, editors of scientific journals and government bureaus; the ball bearing company's magazine featured the contest and its salespeople made a special effort to get entrants on their calls. As a result there were fifty-four entries the first year, many from leading companies.

The winner the first year was a laboratory of the U.S. Army Ordnance Department which had reduced a complicated fuse assembly from the size of a man's hand to fingertip size. (It used no ball bearings at all.) Presentation of the award was made at the Institute of Radio Engineers' annual convention and was followed by good publicity and a touring exhibit. Through this promotion the New England ball bearing manufacturer not only helped in the development of its field but also became better known for its particular part in that field.

Demonstrating Public Response

A number of years ago the author was the promotion manager of a newspaper in a large midwestern city. The advertising salespeople for this newspaper found selling difficult because their newspaper was third in circulation rank among the three daily newspapers in the city at that time. Although its actual circulation was more than 170,000, both of its competitors were larger and spread the word that it had little power to get response in the community. Some tangible demonstration of reader response to the newspaper was necessary because the opposition had more than twice as many salespeople out on the streets selling. Simple assertion of pulling power had been done before and would not be believed.

But a demonstration involved considerable risk, since to get reader response meant public promotion of an event, and failure to attract a big crowd would have provided dramatic confirmation of the rivals' charges. Whatever was attempted had to be both gigantic and successful.

It was decided to risk an outboard motorboat race in a location along the waterfront where thousands of people could easily reach and see it. Making the race possible involved getting in touch with local boat-racing clubs; sponsorship and prizes; promotion to attract contestants; building a temporary harbor and service facilities for the contestants; Coast Guard and police clearance; rescue craft; fire and first-aid provisions both for racers and spectators; drinking water and toilet provisions; food concessions; insurance; judges; a stand and invitations for dignitaries; and many smaller details extending over several months' preparations. Murphy's Law that "if anything can go wrong, it will" demanded foresight to prepare for every possible contingency because there would be no time to correct or to improvise once a major public event began.

Promotion of crowd attendance included every possible device and 60,000 to 100,000 people turned out for the event and stayed most of the afternoon in scorching summer heat. There were a number of heat prostration cases which the first-aid tent took care of. Police handled traffic smoothly. There were no accidents among the racers. The whole event was well publicized and pictured in the sponsoring newspaper and even its rivals were forced to give it brief notice. The morale of sales staff was noticeably improved because now they had something to talk about that was not defensive.

Later, an air show was staged, which attracted an even bigger crowd, creating traffic problems which got completely out of hand in blocking a main four-lane highway. After this final proof that the newspaper had readership in its community, such spectacular demonstrations were dropped in favor of youth, sports, educational, and scientific activities of smaller size but of unquestioned public worth.

Major public events of this sort should probably not be attempted today. There is too much risk in them and policing and public order are much greater problems than they used to be. If they fail to draw a crowd or result in injuries or fighting, they backfire badly, harming instead of helping the sponsor. The public relations person who attempts one puts his or her head on the block. But there could be no arguing with their success at one time.

ACTIONS WHICH SHOW THE CHARACTER
OF AN ORGANIZATION THROUGH
SERVICE IN THE PUBLIC WELFARE

The best public relations actions, of course, are *related* to the nature or background of the organization which supports them, but they may also be *created,* at times, with the specific intent of showing something about the organization's character—or, in a way, to even assist in creating a character for it. They are, in the best sense of the word, "window dressing" because they display some of the science, or technology, or interests of the organization which developed them. Like the windows of a department store, they show the passing spectator a few of the many things inside. No one expects that the windows will exhibit a completely representative sample of the entire contents of the store, but only that they will be characteristic of the store and that the merchandise displayed *is* to be found within. Like good windows, good, creative, public relations actions demand both artistry and imagination along with a sure sense of spectator interests. And programs which purport to be serving the public welfare, but which have an interest beyond the immediate gain of the sponsors and enlist the aid of many others in their success, should really be doing so. People are quick to judge and condemn programs which have no real value except to the promoters. This is one of the reasons why the very term "public relations" has sometimes been used as a criticism. Yet it need not be, since a mixture of motives is not uncommon in individuals trying to help in public causes. Few are entirely disinterested; nor should we ask them to be if good results can be achieved.

The Travelers Insurance Cycle Safety Program

Insurance companies have an obvious interest in safety because if there are fewer accidents, the fewer insurance claims they will have to pay. Since there are many insurance companies, each one of them also has a need to make itself well known and remembered because they all offer similar services and the public tends to patronize those with whom it is most familiar and in whom it has the most confidence.

Many people, of course, share this interest in safety—parents of young children, policemen, doctors, teachers, among others.

These were some of the reasons why Travelers Insurance Company of Hartford, Connecticut, in 1973 thought of a bicycle riding safety program for youngsters. The number of bicycle riders in the country was rising as energy conservation efforts promoted bicycling instead of cars. Accidents involving bicycles were increasing to 100,000 a year. Travelers had had a PEP (Physical Exercise Pays) program for some years stressing swimming, jogging, and sports for better health. Bicycling was a part of that program but young cyclists particularly faced dangers and insured motorists around them also faced the danger of hitting them. There seemed to be a genuine public need. Many places, of course, already had bicycle safety and inspection programs, and Travelers Insurance agents could help these. But many others did not, and a complete program could be offered. The local agent with local contacts would be the key.

Figure 11–11 The Bike Rodeo (first called a "Bicycle Safety Clinic") was sponsored by Travellers Insurance Company to promote bicycle safety. This scene is from a pilot program in a West Hartford, Connecticut, elementary school. Courtesy Jack W. Connell, Photographer.

First, of course, a complete program had to be developed and materials prepared. After a test of a bike safety clinic program in cooperation with the Hartford police department in 1973, a larger pilot program was set up with selected agents in 1974. Then in 1975 the program was launched on a nation-wide basis. It consisted of the following units: a film on bicycle safety entitled "Just Like A Car"; plans on how to conduct a bike rodeo for youngsters to test their skill in riding safely; posters and ads and publicity stories (to be retyped and localized) on the rodeo; guide booklets for volunteers helping with the rodeos; judge, contestant and other badges; certificates for those passing; and reflector dots to go on bicycles that shine in car headlights. These, along with the other material, bore the distinctive red umbrella Travelers emblem.

The heart of the program was the Bike Rodeo. In testing it had been called a "Bicycle Safety Clinic" but it was soon seen that this had no appeal to youngsters. The rodeo consisted of seven events such as riding slowly in a straight line, avoiding obstacles, turning sharply without skidding, and stopping promptly. Young riders were divided into age classes. The course was marked off in chalk or water paint on a school playground, in a park, or even in a blocked-off street.

To do this required the cooperation of local school and political authorities as well as judges and volunteers to stage the event smoothly. The local Travelers Insurance agent who took the lead in setting up the program was responsible for getting this cooperation, for recruiting volunteers (often from a service club such as Kiwanis or Lions), and for providing the local newspapers and broadcasting stations with publicity and information. Without such cooperation the rodeo could not be held. But when it was carried out it served a useful purpose which all could appreciate. For such a program to succeed it must serve a genuine and widely recognized need. So long as the need exists, the help will be welcomed by those who are concerned about the problem for various reasons.

The Plymouth Trouble-shooting Contest

One of the oldest public relations service programs in the United States, which has been going for almost thirty years, serves what is almost a permanent need—and that is to encourage young people to become good automobile mechanics.

The Plymouth trouble-shooting contest is directed at high school students who attend auto mechanic vocational classes. In 1976 students from more than 2,000 schools throughout the country participated. Students are sponsored by local Plymouth automobile dealers and screened through written preliminary contests. At the state finals the winners confront a group of automobiles which have been deliberately "bugged" with a dozen or more malfunctions. Starting at a signal, under the supervision of judges, each contestant's assignment is to get the assigned car going and to drive it a specified distance. The winners receive trophies, awards such as tools, and perhaps scholarships or other prizes. Runners-up receive smaller awards. State winners then go on to a national contest which in 1976 became international as teams from Canada, Mexico, and the United States competed in the United Nations Plaza in New York. In addition, for the past several years there has been a special competition in American prisons, only in this case there is no national face-to-face competition, winners being named from times and scores sent in by the judges from each competing prison.

This program started modestly in 1949 in Los Angeles. It was simple but has served its purpose well. It is a cooperative effort made by the Chrysler Company (which provided know-how and promotional material), dealers within an area (who provide labor, promotion, and prizes), and school officials (whose permission and cooperation is necessary).

From the automobile company's viewpoint the publicity is important, but also important is the contact established between Plymouth dealers and future good mechanics who are always hard to get. As a result of only one contest, for instance, fifty students were hired as mechanics by the dealers.

From the school viewpoint the program helps furnish students in shop courses the motivation and recognition comparable to the stimuli which might have urged them on as members of an athletic team. Representing the high school at a state trouble-shooting contest parallels the importance of being a basketball or football star, and the newspaper and television publicity about winners reflects credit upon the quality of shop courses within a school and is good for teacher morale. In addition, the contest performs a national service in the public welfare; in an age of multiplying mechanical contrivances, good mechanics are always in increasing demand.

The Plymouth trouble-shooting contest is a good example of an action created to serve numerous public relations purposes successfully and which has endured for a long time.

The American Optometric Association

This is a professional organization of almost 20,000 doctors of optometry and students over the United States who examine patients' vision and who prescribe glasses, corrective therapy, and other means of improving

Figure 11-12 The American Optometric Association sponsored a "Joy Of Seeing" art program in the schools. This is the grand prize winner submitted by a 12-year-old North Carolina girl. Courtesy American Optometric Association.

vision. They handle most of the nation's sight problems and are the first to note systemic diseases and other problems which are referred to other medical specialists.

The impetus for their public service program arose from the approach of the 75th anniversary of the founding of their professional association. Since there are so many professional groups, it was felt that a simple commemoration in the form of a medal or meetings or postage stamp would be little noticed or appreciated. An observance was sought that would be interesting and also bring out the importance of the work of the association. The value of good vision to children was the area selected.

The method selected to gain this attention was a drawing contest for children ages six through twelve in which they would show in their own art what the joy of seeing meant to them. It was hoped through the attention directed to their fresh, new work that the importance of good sight to children could be emphasized and that parents and teachers would become more aware of it.

In order to test the program a pilot model was run in the state of Kansas one year before the national program was launched. This not only gave valuable experience but served to encourage optometric associations in other states by a real example of response. The success of the entire program (as is often the case in such national professional associations) rested upon the voluntary response of the state and local associations who had the local contacts and volunteer labor and would donate the money for local judging and prizes. If they accepted the program the national publicity and organization would be of some help, but if they did not, few entries would ever arrive at the national contest for final judging.

State cooperation was good with about 103,000 children submitting drawings nationwide.

The final judging was done in New York City followed by a one-day visit to Washington and a three-day tour of Disney World in Florida in which all finalists participated.

Ford Motor Company of Mexico

Two activities of Ford Motor Company's Mexican organization could well be listed under the "International" public relations chapter later in this book, but since they are excellent examples of successful public relations action programs in the public welfare they are included here instead.

The major program is a company plan to assist Mexican needs for more elementary schools. This is done by actually building primary schools. From 1968 to 1976, for example, Ford of Mexico built 105 primary schools at a cost to the company of several million dollars. These are called "Ford Schools" and the buildings are then maintained by Ford people while the instructional staff is supplied and directed by the Mexican government. Schools are located, after careful consultation with Mexican educational authorities, in villages where the need is great and where funds would not permit the building of a school otherwise. They are modest six-room structures, constructed at a minimum of expense.

Half of the money for their construction is given by Ford of Mexico, one-quarter by the local area Ford dealer, and the other quarter is raised by subscription from local people, so there has to be local support before a school can be built.

The cost of the buildings is not high—somewhat more than $40,000 each—but they are functional and periodic inspections by Ford corporate managers have found them maintained in excellent condition. In 1977 seven new schools were built and plans call for continuing the program into the indefinite future because the aid has generated much goodwill from the Mexican public and authorities.

The other Ford of Mexico program likewise serves an important national need. This is a "Rural Training Program" to aid the government in improving the agricultural productivity of some 55,000 small village farmers in remote areas who are largely illiterate, and who still farm with primitive methods raising corn and beans.

In 1967 the Mexican government Agricultural Department assigned three well-trained agricultural engineers to begin visiting these communities to teach soil and water conservation, and the use of fertilizers, insecticides, and hybrid seeds to improve crops. Ford and its dealers furnished pick-up trucks with gasoline, oil, and maintenance. By 1977 the program had grown to 28 agricultural engineers and their transportation.

In many ways this program resembles the long-established agricultural extension program in the United States which transformed farming in this country. It is, of course, not the only aspect of agricultural knowledge extension in Mexico and the government has an active program reaching larger farmers. The Ford contribution is to make it possible to stretch the pesos, which are always in short supply, so that thousands of farmers who would otherwise be neglected can improve their productivity and lives. Next steps include formation of marketing groups and eventually industrialization of farm products through packaging and small canneries.

Sometimes agricultural improvement has meant a complete change as when a western Mexican mining town where the inhabitants were subsistence-farming corn and beans shifted to avocado orchards and increased their income per acre fifty times. Often the gain is only to improve present practices. But in each case Ford and its people are performing a much needed service in the public welfare.

This is particularly important where a company is operating outside its own nation in a host country because a feeling always exists that foreigners' only interest is to siphon off profits. When a foreign company can be seen contributing to the national welfare as well as making a profit, its public respect is much improved.

The Westinghouse Science Talent Search

This is one of the longest-established public relations programs in America, having been launched in 1942 and having since then awarded $1,-126,000 to 1,440 young scientists, two of whom later achieved Nobel Prizes and two of whom won Field Medals for excellence in mathematics.

Every year 300 finalists are selected of whom forty are chosen as winners at a meeting in Washington, D.C. The program has endured so long because it serves the needs of many parties—the sponsoring corporation, the science teachers of America, and the students who compete. A survey of former winners showed that all had or were attending college and 99 percent had chosen some field of science. Of those who had completed college 70 percent had received Ph.D.'s or become physicians. The prize awards which range from $10,000 for the top winner down to $250 had often been of material assistance in meeting college expenses.

Science Fairs

The Westinghouse science talent search confines itself to high school seniors. Yet many teachers have observed that scientific ability manifests itself at a much earlier age and could well be encouraged among younger children, even in the elementary schools. This observation led to the rise in the 1940s of local "Science Fairs" which eventually became national. These were not competitive with the Westinghouse effort but rather complementary to it.

The first local science fair of which the author knew began in Providence, Rhode Island, in the late 1940s under the sponsorship of the daily newspaper there. It was visited by a St. Louis, Missouri, high school science teacher who, upon his return home, approached one of the newspapers there with the idea that such an event might be developed in St. Louis. Its quick success demonstrated that cooperation between several groups in the public good in which all benefit is the best kind of public relations for all involved.

The partners in the venture soon became:

The newspaper which provided money for publicity mailings and entry forms, advertising, and news space in the newspaper and on the radio, several organizational dinners and administrative aid.

The science teachers of the St. Louis area who joined together to provide volunteers for the promotion of the exhibit, supervised its actual

conduct, and solicited judges, award money, and college scholarships for
the winners. (It would not have been proper for a commercial sponsor such
as the newspaper to have asked for these.)

Washington University in St. Louis which provided the use of its field
house as an exhibit space, janitorial and maintenance help, assistance in the
judging, and general sanction including an opening address by the chancel-
lor of the university, who was himself a noted American scientist.

Various St. Louis companies in scientific or semiscientific field such
as chemicals, electric power, metals, and so forth, who donated prize money
totaling thousands of dollars and who also gave the time of some of their
scientific personnel to assist in judging.

Regional universities and colleges, who contributed scholarships
worth about $20,000 to winners in the fair. These were given only to high
school juniors or seniors and were also based upon grades and other measurements of ability. Lesser awards given to a large number of entrants
consisted of cash and ribbons of merit.

The program was a success from the start, having about 1,300
entries the first year and 3,000 within three years when the size of the
field house required limitation of the number shown. The quality of the
entries ranged from very high for the more advanced students to sometimes amusing efforts by the smaller children, but all were of supreme
importance to those who submitted them and to their teachers and
parents and friends. Attendance was about 20,000 not including the
exhibitors or their teachers.

The most worthwhile part of the program besides unquestioned
public benefit was the close relationship that it established between the
newspaper, the teachers, the colleges, and the industrial concerns in
fostering youthful scientific development in a way which no one of them
could have accomplished alone. Working together in a common effort
established strong bonds.

Providing there is a genuine need to be served, the alert public
relations practitioner might find similar cooperative ventures on a local
basis in other fields such as music, art, or drama. The point is not to
invade an area in which someone is already doing well, but rather to
facilitate goals which would not be achievable otherwise.

COOPERATIVE ACTIONS STIMULATING OTHERS IN WORK FOR THE PUBLIC WELFARE

Public relations actions may take the form primarily of encouraging and
aiding others to help themselves. The participation of the stimulating
organization itself is apparently very modest but actually its expenditure

in salaries and time may be considerable, especially in planning, attending meetings, offering awards and dinners, and picking up the checks for miscellaneous expenses such as printing or publicity writing. The advantage is a complete lack of self-puffery since being the facilitator of something of merit is quite enough in itself.

The "Rochester Idea" of Xerox Corporation

Xerox is one of the largest employers in Rochester, New York, with more than 14,000 employees in that city. It takes an active role in supporting cultural and civic causes in the community and many of its people are involved in these functions.

Nevertheless in the mid-1970s there were some problems. In 1969 Xerox, for good reasons, had moved its small headquarters staff to Stamford, Connecticut, close to New York City. Five years later rumors still persisted that Xerox might move more segments of the company out of Rochester. There was also a feeling that since headquarters had been transferred Xerox might have lost its interest in the future of Rochester. Like all older cities in the Northeast, Rochester had its share of problems —decayed inner areas, racial divisions, citizen apathy in the face of problems that defied easy solution. As a long-established major force in Rochester, many people seemed to expect that the company would aid in the leadership of the community. The question was "How?" since the days of solo, "Do-it-my-way" leadership are long past.

The public relations staff of the company decided that Xerox could serve as a stimulating and collecting agent for ideas for community improvement that Rochester citizens themselves might offer. To do this three cosponsors joined the project; The Rochester Arts Council which has sixty-six member organizations within it representing a wealth of talent and interests; the Rochester chapter of the American Institute of Architects; and the Urbanarium, a privately funded organization dealing with urban problems and operated as a part of the Rochester Institute of Technology.

A project director who had seen a similar plan working in Toronto, Ontario, was appointed and the Xerox manager of public relations in Rochester served as administrator of the effort.

A kick-off luncheon for about one hundred community leaders was held. Xerox committed $13,000 for campaign expenses, the use of its downtown exhibit center, and a 28-foot motor van to visit Rochester groups and neighborhoods to collect ideas for the improvement of the city. The van travelled through the community for about three months,

Figure 11–13 For better community public relations the Xerox Corporation sponsored a "Rochester Idea" program to collect good ideas for improving the company's home town. Part of the effort included this 28-foot van which visited neighborhoods and schools to gather suggestions.

made about one hundred stops and was visited by 2,750 people who had ideas about city improvement. It stopped at such places as schools, shopping centers, churches, suburban community town halls, and senior citizen centers. Publicity in newspapers and on the air accompanied the movements of the van.

About 200 ideas were developed for use in an exhibition in the downtown conference center of Xerox which lasted for six weeks and which was launched with a special opening night for about 150 business, government, and community leaders. More than 40,000 citizens viewed the ideas and there were more than forty features and news stories upon it. A workshop and seminar was organized following the opening of the exhibit at which the idea-presenters and city and county planners discussed the ideas and possible means of implementing them. A publication was developed containing the essence of the ideas so that they would not be forgotten.

Many of the ideas became actuality. For example, city maps and information guides were posted in specially designed kiosks downtown to aid in locating major landmarks, business and governmental buildings; house numbers were included on all new street signs; a public market was reopened; a study was begun on reopening a bridge so that visitors could see a falls in the river; flowers were planted; a television documentary on the problems of handicapped people getting about the city was aired; and efforts were made to get groups to adopt other ideas which had been presented. Not everything was accomplished, of course. Funds and backers were lacking for most projects. But the city at least made some progress in which numerous of its citizens participated and Xerox had had an important part in this common effort. The role of the company had been to aid others in doing what no single organization alone could have accomplished. The effort can be continued over many years since there is no final "success" in a constant endeavor to make a big city a better place in which to live.

"Project Pride" of the National Bank of Detroit

Cities change. Their needs become different and the role of businesses in them alters. The capable public relations person sees such changes and meets them.

In recent years the population of the city of Detroit has become more than half black people. During World War II and thereafter hundreds of thousands of blacks, many from the South, poured into the city to work in the automobile and other factories, taking the only housing they could find in the central part of the city. Aided by freeways which enabled rapid automobile travel, whites left and built new homes in rapidly growing suburbs, outside the political boundaries of the city of Detroit but still within its economic area. Few of the white business or cultural leaders of the city lived in the city itself any longer. Retailers, professional people such as doctors and dentists, small businesses and even factories followed them until property values in the central city declined drastically, public services based on tax income worsened, buildings were abandoned and often destroyed. Only the headquarters of banks and other financial institutions, government offices, and associated services such as insurance or lawyers continued to flourish downtown. The same pattern has taken place in scores of large, older American cities, particularly in the Northeast.

The cause of this revolution was not the blacks who filled up the boundaries of the older central cities as the whites moved out, but rather the arrival of the automobile which enabled the cities to explode outwards while collapsing within. People no longer had to live near where they worked or even near public transportation. The change began in the

1920s, was frozen somewhat during the Depression and World War II, and burst out again in 1945. A change taking a half-century involving the movement of a great portion of the American population to new houses and job locations can not be easily reversed, if at all. Too much money and by now too many roots are invested in the newer suburban communities. Energy problems present unanswered questions since it is not easy to re-establish public transportation when workers go all different directions and distances from their homes.

In the meantime the predominately black population of declining central cities has faced difficult housing and governmental problems such as sanitation and police and fire protection. At first, when national resources seemed unlimited, the solution seemed to be to tear down older apartments and houses and build huge new high-rise box-like apartments and appropriate large sums for social services.

Sometimes this worked, but often it didn't. People cannot be stacked in buildings as if they were bricks unless they were in the habit of living this way and the buildings are well administered. Even money for needed social services has to be given out wisely and honestly. It is often easier to appropriate money than to use it.

Much of the residential property in Detroit, for example, passing into the hands of black families had been considered good housing and had it not been for the automobile revolution would have continued to be inhabited for many years with only slight changes. The streets were shaded by trees, the houses were large and often built of brick, the architectural styles were pleasing, and light and air were adequate. The homes were well-built although on smaller lots and not in the rambling ranch-house suburban style. Because of rental and neglect many of them later ran down, but with paint and upkeep and pride they could give many years of good service.

Whatever solutions were achieved, whatever improvements were to be made in the black community of Detroit, had to be done by the local population. Detroit's experience had been that for a program to work involved equal planning on the parts of blacks and whites in the community, as well as business and government. Blacks must have meaningful participation and there must be tangible results which all can see.

This was the background that the public relations staff of the National Bank of Detroit, the areas's largest, faced in the early 1970s. The result was "Project Pride" a clean-up program covering 55 square blocks populated by 23,000 members of the black community.

The role of the bank was to facilitate and to aid—not to assume public leadership. The objective was to encourage and aid home-owners and renters to clean up trash, repair homes, plant yards, get street lights repaired and to show pride in their neighborhood. A smaller pilot-test area was first set up and local club and church groups cooperated in obtaining citizen help in its clean-up. The bank obtained city government aid in trash collection; supplied money for posters, buttons, leaflets and campaign meetings; aided in getting the Red Cross and others to feed volunteer workers. After the pilot program was a success, media of all sorts were used to inform the people of the success of the test effort, especially radio and television. The participation of the bank was now apparent and a large one-day effort was launched in the whole area. In this effort more than 4,000 local volunteers freed the 55-block area of 500 tons of trash and discards, 150 abandoned cars, and thousands of rats. They were assisted by city sanitation workers who scheduled special pick-ups. Hundreds of pounds of flower and grass seed were given out along with a thousand trash cans. Dozens of street lights were repaired. Owners and landlords painted and repaired their houses.

The success of the program led to its being conducted on a city-wide basis the following year and the national publicity about it resulted in scores of requests from other businesses and cities throughout the nation who wanted to know how it had been done. The public relations value to the National Bank of Detroit is obvious but the effects in stimulating pride and self-help in black communities are more important, if less tangible. There can be little doubt that programs of this sort have important national effects that are beyond the power of governments or more conventional leaders in other fields to match. They must be judged not only on the narrow basis of what they achieve in a given instance but also on the changes they make in people's thinking.

Working Together on Community Parks

As costs increase and taxpayer resistance to expenditures mounts, it is often difficult to get a favorable public vote for local bond issues to improve or develop public parks. Schools also face the same difficulty.

Sometimes the solution lies in community self-help in which various businesses and organizations take on a part of the project and in which some group or organization offers leadership. This may be a business or an association or a governmental unit. Getting people to work together is good and inexpensive public relations.

The author recalls two instances:

A 23-acre abandoned gravel pit whose lake was a hazard to inexperienced young swimmers and a breeder of mosquitoes was given to a suburban town near Syracuse, New York. Two other towns were nearby and the three formed an association to develop the area into a recreation park. A master plan was drawn up first. Nineteen firms in the area loaned heavy equipment for grading, three oil companies donated fuel. The public relations department of a nearby major industry supplied publicity for the plan. Meetings were set up and various local service groups and businesses volunteered for portions of the project which was completed at minimal cash cost.

In another town, Bryan, Ohio, a 40-acre plot near the town which required drainage was given to the city for a park site. Much of the necessary digging and tillage for this was donated by local companies and a few thousand dollars was spent for a master plan drawn up by experts and adopted by the Town Council after extensive discussion and publicity. Then the various town organizations such as the American Legion, Scouts, Rotary Club, schools, and churches each took a particular project—baseball diamonds, bridle trails, picnic grounds, and wood cabins, for example—as their own jobs designated by name. Each wanted to do a respectable job in a prompt fashion. As a result the park grew in an orderly pay-as-you-go fashion without resort to extra taxes or the chance that the whole project might have been turned down by an adverse bond vote.

ACTIONS NEEDED PRIMARILY TO ACHIEVE COMMUNICATION

Frequently something needs to be "done" in order to have something to talk about. This is not only the nature of news but also the nature of human interest because we pay attention to extraordinary happenings rather than to matters which simply go on in a routine fashion, especially if their connection with our own affairs is not very close. Thus it is often up to the public relations person to make something happen which will provide a basis for legitimate news attention and which, ideally, will also be something that touches receivers of communications directly or into which they can project themselves by imagination.

The U.S. Army Corps of Engineers Celebrates Two Bicentennials

For most Americans the work of the United States Army Corps of Engineers is quite remote from their lives. This is to be expected, of course, for the military aspects of their work such as the construction of fortifications with which the ordinary civilian is not likely to come into contact. But the Engineers also have other important peacetime functions, among them maintaining and improving the navigability of rivers and harbors as directed by Congress, including dredging, shoreline stabilization and dams. In the past generation or so they have changed the Missouri River, for example, from a wild, uncertain yellow flood wandering across its flood-plain and navigated only hazardously by a few shallow-draft steamboats to a permanent, controlled, 9-foot depth channel from its mouth above St. Louis as far northwest as Sioux City, Iowa. Great dams regulating the flow of the river have been built in Montana and the Dakotas. Similar navigation programs have been developed throughout the entire Mississippi River system in the central part of the United States. In other regions canals have been constructed or proposed, harbors deepened or marshes drained.

A few years ago this aroused little public controversy. No one (except competing railroads) questioned the value of making America's big rivers suitable for barge transportation, of stabilizing river banks to protect farmland, of building dams to regulate streamflow, or of dredging and deepening harbors. But with the development of environmental movements in recent years, the Corps of Engineers found itself criticized by protectors of wildlife habitats and as a spender of public money on big waterway projects of doubtful value. It was easier to criticize the Engineers which visibly did the work than to nail down a shifting Congress which ordered and authorized them to do the work. As the 1975 bicentennial of the Army Engineers and the 1976 bicentennial of the nation approached, the Corps of Engineers thought of how they could tell the story of their work to the American people so that their side of the controversy would not go unheard.

Simple publicity about current projects was limited in its interest except to people in areas directly affected, although such news of what was being done was desirable and proper. Few people would pay much attention to it or, more importantly, see the role that particular projects played in the major successes of flood control and navigation that had been achieved over the years. It also seemed defensive. Something was needed which could reach people where they lived, which would be interesting in itself and which would show the whole work that the Corps of Engineers had achieved over several decades.

Like the General Motors diesel truck display or the Union Pacific Railroad centennial train covered above, the Engineers had one natural advantage in reaching people if they could use it—they were related to transportation. The interior Mississippi River system and related waterways reached all the way from Sioux City and Tulsa and Houston in the west to Pittsburgh and Knoxville in the east and from New Orleans to Minneapolis.

The result was a floating exhibit of the Corps' history and work which could directly reach hundreds of thousands of people and through local publicity millions more.

A forty-year-old towboat, the "Sergeant Floyd," had done its work on the river and was due to be scrapped. A 100-foot barge built even earlier could be pushed in front of it and an exhibit depicting the work of the Corps of Engineers placed on both vessels. This was prepared and the floating display dedicated in June of 1975 at the St. Louis levee in front of the gateway to the west arch in the national park there. Then in the next eighteen months the "Sergeant Floyd" and its exhibit barge plied the rivers from Minnesota to Alabama and from Oklahoma to Pennsylvania.

The big job was seeing that the news media and the public knew about the exhibit's visits. This meant not only press kits and pictures but also such things as an 8-minute film for advance publicity, sheet music of the Corps' song, "Let Us Try," for school singing groups, special programs involving local people at each stop, posters, leaflets for visitors, and special training of the staff people who would conduct the tour.

This action of taking its story to the people met with a strong response. More than 250,000 people visited the exhibit in the eighteen-

Figure 11-14   The work of the U.S. Army Corps of Engineers on America's rivers includes navigation, flood control, and bank stabilization. To show this complex story in many river towns the towboat "Sergeant Floyd" pushed a barge containing exhibits of the Corps' work. Courtesy U.S. Army Corps of Engineers.

months but, more importantly, its presence resulted in hundreds of news pictures and stories in print and on the air. It was not only local news wherever it came but there were also national press wire and magazine stories as well as picture and film coverage for both external and internal use.

One of the biggest benefits was renewed pride and enthusiam on the part of Corps of Engineer personnel, many of whom saw for the first time the whole scope of the work in which they had been engaged and were able to express and explain better than before.

After the floating exhibition ended, portions of it along with pictures and films were taken to other parts of the country. It was planned to continue this for some time after 1976.

None of this would have been possible without the *action* which made news—the development and tour of the floating exhibit; an action which reached people right where they lived and then was reported on a nation-wide basis. Attempts at communication without some such action would have been much less effective because we live in a sea of communication and only things of some immediate importance are likely to be noted or remembered. It took *doing something* to provide a basis for *talking* about it. The important thing is to find an action which is fitting and proper within the realm of the group which stages it because both the media and the public are quick to deride actions which are far-fetched or too contrived. They are often called "public relations gimmicks" and should be since they are really very poor public relations, doing more harm than good.

The tour of the veteran "Sergeant Floyd" and its exhibit along the rivers which the Corps of Engineers had developed was directly related to understanding the work of the Corps and was a proper presentation of its case.

The National Cotton Council of America

This is not as striking a case as the preceding because its objective is less exciting—namely to get people to buy more cotton cloth. But to cotton farmers who face competition with a host of artificial fibers it is equally important. Again, some form of action is needed, beyond the simple assertion that cotton makes good cloth of an attractive appearance. In some way this needs to be *shown* so that people will pay attention to it.

Beginning in 1939 the solution of The National Cotton Council of America has been an annual "Maid of Cotton" contest in which an attractive young woman from one of the cotton-producing states is chosen to be a promoter of the fabric for one year. Selection is based upon

Figure 11-15 For almost forty years the National Cotton Council has annually selected a "Maid of Cotton" to dramatize the utility of cotton and the beauty of cotton
cloth. This is the 1976 winner modeling a cotton print dress.

beauty, personality, background, and training. The winner then spends
a year as an ambassador for cotton products all over the United States
and in foreign countries to which American cotton products are exported.

One of her jobs is to model attractive cotton dresses and her efforts
have had a considerable effect in elevating cotton cloth in the world of
fashion. She is invited to Washington and has lunch with the President,

Secretary of Agriculture and members of Congressional committees and is featured at a fashion show for Congressional wives. She works with department store style shows and visits cotton fabric mills and design studios.

The action of selecting a young woman annually to represent a product is not unusual, but care in selection and picking someone from a cotton-producing state gives the action legitimacy which would be lacking were this not done. Again, an *action* (the selection of a person) provides a basis for local or specialized publicity of material which otherwise would have to be classified by the media as advertising.

Ford Builds a "Federal" Pinto

"Show me" is really a call for demonstration by action rather than assertion. In 1975 the management of Ford Motor Company wanted to dramatize the effect of Federal safety and emissions standards on the cost and performance of 1978 cars. To do this they lined up four cars, an actual 1971 Pinto, an actual 1975 Pinto, a 1978 "Federal" Pinto which would meet all government requirements, and the type of Pinto that the company wanted to produce in 1978. These latter two, of course, had to be prepared especially for the occasion.

Not surprisingly, the 1978 "Federal" Pinto was a good deal more costly and less fuel efficient than the Ford version for 1978 because of its extra weight and equipment. The company asked if the extra safety and emission control thus gained were worth the extra cost and lowered gasoline milage. The question was a legitimate one and must be answered as a matter of public policy if government controls are to be used at all —as they are being used.

In the broadest sense a demonstration action such as this is a part of the company's public relations program, since it puts the responsibility for the decision upon those who regulate it rather than letting the impression prevail that in some magical way all goals can be achieved at once. Such facts could be stated as the results of engineering studies without demonstration, but few would read, comprehend, or believe them.

ACTION AS SEEN IN ORGANIZATION
FOR PUBLIC RELATIONS PURPOSES

Often the main accomplishment in public relations is to bring together scattered forces and to unite them in one positive program. This "action of organization" is largely internal and consists of the development of: a program upon which most can agree, its vigorous selling, obtaining the active participation of members and others, and then in keeping the program sold. The external program itself may be far less trouble and require far less skill and patience to actuate than the task of persuading the scattered legions all to march together, an achievement which does not show at all to the outside observer.

The task is not always so arduous, of course, but all those who work with trade and professional associations are familiar, through long experience, with the difficulties of persuasion and agreement in voluntary groups in which the role of the public relatiot.s director is that of catalyst rather than director. In large national efforts the amount of work to be done is so great and the local connections so important that the best the public relations director can do is to plan well, get the full backing of the board of directors and then engage in a hectic behind-the-scenes campaign of encouragement, suggestion, and question-answering by mail, telephone, meetings, and personal visits.

Law Day U.S.A.

In 1958 by Presidential proclamation and in 1961 by Joint Resolution of Congress the first of May each year was set aside as a "special day of celebration by the American people in appreciation of their liberties and the reaffirmation of their loyalty to the United States of America." Each year since the President has issued a proclamation and local Law Day proclamations are usually made by governors and mayors.

The sponsorship is that of the American Bar Association which represents more than 200,000 American lawyers and it is estimated that 50,000 separate Law Day programs are held on or near May 1 each year with the attendance of more than 5 million people. There are speeches, sermons, school assemblies, mock trials, courthouse tours, naturalization ceremonies, essay contests, television and radio shows, films, dramatic performances, special exhibits and window displays by banks and other business institutions.

Its purposes are to advance equality and justice under law; encourage citizen support of law observance and law enforcement; and to foster respect for law and understanding of its essential place in the life of every citizen of the United States. In recent years, as the amount of litigation in the courts has increased so greatly with resulting delays in justice and rising legal costs, it has particularly directed public attention at learning what the major problems of the courts are, in becoming involved in local efforts for court reform and modernization, better selection and support of judges, and popular education in how the law works or should work.

Of course the legal profession has a selfish interest in such a program since it both makes lawyers more respected and the practice of law easier. But it happens that the users of the law and the public which pays for the maintenance of the law have a direct interest also.

For example, a Law Day pamphlet points out that your *rights* under law include:

> The right to equal justice in our courts and equal protection of the laws.
> The right to have legal counsel of your choice and prompt trial if accused of crime.
> The right to be free from arbitrary search or arrest.
> The right to choose public officers in free elections.
> The right of free speech, press, and assembly.
> The right to own property.
> The right to equal educational and economic opportunity.
> The right to attend the church of your choice.

But, on the other hand, the *duties* of citizens include:

> The duty to respect, obey and uphold the laws.
> The duty to be informed on issues of government and community affairs.
> The duty to vote in elections.
> The duty to practice and teach the principles of good citizenship in your home.
> The duty to serve on juries and as a witness if called.
> The duty to support agencies of law enforcement.
> The duty to honor the rights of others.
> The duty of allegiance to the Constitution of the United States of America and to work for its betterment and perpetuation.

The American Bar Association is careful to point out that law was not developed for the benefit of lawyers, but rather for the protection of citizens. It is concerned about the rising tide of public criticism, often merited, of judicial procedures. Much of the goal of "Law Day U.S.A." is educational. One news release, for instance, quoted the dean of the Yale University Law School to the effect that the typical courtroom judge does not leisurely saunter in at 10 A.M., take two hours for lunch, and then adjourn at 4 P.M. Instead the true-to-type judge gets to work at 8:30 A.M., takes nearer 30 minutes than 2 hours for lunch, and concludes court around 5 to 5:30 P.M. The rest of the time behind the scenes is spent meeting with lawyers working on cases, often in an attempt to get settlement without a trial, looking up facts and laws that needed to

be known during a trial, and conferring with court-appointed psychia-
trists or probation officers. During the time that a judge is on the bench
he or she must concentrate intensely on what is going on to prevent an
improper ruling which would mean that the case would be overturned
by a higher court on appeal. And in the evening, with so much new law
being made today, a judge must study to keep up with changes.

The key to success in a national program such as this is the participation of local Bar Associations all over the nation. The national Bar
Association public relations staff can provide plans and materials such
as prepared television spots and radio scripts, window displays, speech
outlines, sample mock trial texts, newspaper ad mats, films and award
plaques. It also prepares a substantial manual suggesting programs for
Bar Associations of various sized cities. But the actual work of the
program must be done by committees of the 800 local Bar Associations
spread across the country because they alone have the needed personnel
and personal contacts. They, in turn, can succeed only if they obtain the
cooperation of other local groups such as civic clubs, business people,
political leaders, law enforcement agencies, churches and schools who
share some of the same goals and concerns. Attendance of school children at a trial to see how it works, open house in a courthouse for the
public, a speech by a judge before a local Chamber of Commerce luncheon—all happen only because someone locally talked to people and
arranged for them to happen. Ideas can come from headquarters but the
work must be done locally.

Law Day U.S.A. is also typical of programs which continue because
their need continues. The needs of 1978, for example, are not the same
as the needs of 1958 when the program started. Each year the facts and
the public perception of them changed. But in a democratic society the
problem of citizen understanding and support of the laws is constant. As
long as the program can reach new people (such as the millions of new
voters every year), as long as the problems of the law change, and as long
as some new angle can be given to it, the program remains valid.

The Philadelphia Anti-shoplifting Program

Police and courts are limited in their enforcement of laws to the criminals
they can catch. (And, as implied in the preceding case, to the number
they can handle after apprehension.) Much of the job of crime prevention, especially petty, widespread crime, rests upon public attitudes toward such crime. Shoplifting is an excellent example.

By the mid-1970s theft from stores had become a serious problem
amounting to $6.5 billion in merchandise averaging 2 percent of sales
volume per store. This loss was not only that of the store owners but also

a public loss since it had to be added to the cost of merchandise for store owners to stay in business. Small businesses suffered most severely, more than three times as badly as large retail establishments, and such theft was one reason so many of them failed because they could not afford the losses or the high cost of protection.

About half of the shoplifters were teen-agers who stole after school. About half took only one item but the others seemed to make theft a regular pattern, in many cases to support a drug habit. Of the remaining thieves about 25 percent were housewives, 10 percent college students, and the remainder of various sorts. In one city one out of twelve "customers" was a shoplifter. Most of the theft was in suburban stores and at least three-fourths of the shoplifters had money to buy what they instead stole. It was estimated that the average American family paid a "hidden tax" of $150 a year to shoplifters.

Various explanations were given. Discount department stores suffered most, suggesting that the self-service honor system of checking out was one cause. Some blamed parental neglect of teaching children standards of honesty. Others saw a youthful rebellion against "society." In many instances peer group pressures were cited. Many noted that when parents were not honest and bragged about it, their children could scarcely be expect to be better.

But the practical problem was what to do about it. One-way mirror surveillance, television monitoring, and changes in the laws of most of the states to permit apprehension and search of a suspect before he or she leaves the store were part of the answer. But the biggest part would have to come from making shoplifters (or potential shoplifters), and in many cases their parents, aware that what they were doing was morally wrong, an injury to the public, and likely to be disastrous to themselves. This called for widespread public communication—public relations.

In 1971 Philadelphia merchants, government officials, educators, clergy and others banded together to sponsor the nation's first extensive antishoplifting campaign utilizing extensive public service advertising and other public relations techniques. It was called S.T.E.M., an acronym for Shoplifters Take Everybody's Money, and was designed to create an awareness that shoplifting was a *serious* crime and could hurt the individual even more than the retailer. It was designed by a Philadelphia public relations and advertising agency.

Ads were pretested on high school students before being used to be sure that the message got across and had an effect. Once approved they were used extensively. In the first year, for example, local television stations ran 550 free spots worth $216,000—many of them in prime evening hours. Radio ran 6,700 spots. Newspapers and outdoor advertising ran extensive copy. S.T.E.M. printed 200,000 pamphlets for teenagers and 1,000,000 for adults.

The copy was direct and hard-hitting, stressing the risks of theft. Many ads drove the point home with painful case histories: "Ken swapped a college education for a $6.50 shirt." "Carol just traded a $150-a-week job for a $5 belt." "Meg just traded her engagement ring

The shoplifter saw nobody watching and walked off wearing the jacket he had been trying on.

But somebody was watching.

S.T.E.M. INC.
NO IFS, ANDS OR BUTS, SHOPLIFTING IS STEALING.

Figure 11-16   Philadelphia merchants used public relations to tackle the program of shoplifting by talking directly to potential thieves. This ad appeared in newspapers and also as a poster.

Figure 11-17   This ad in the anti-shoplifting series was more directed at parents to remind them that shoplifting was a serious crime and it was their duty to warn their children against it.

for a $10 blouse." Shoplifting is a criminal offense, the ads stressed, which can kill your chances for a good job, cause a thumbs-down when you want a loan, or hurt your educational opportunities. Sophisticated detection devices such as television watching of store stocks and detective use of walkie-talkie radios were noted. Ads directed to parents stressed the need of teaching children and of knowing what they were doing, especially with money and goods.

The program worked. Surveys showed that people were reading and hearing it and getting the message. Philadelphia retailers reported decreases in store shortages on an average of 20 percent (after ten years of rising losses) following S.T.E.M.'s first year. Further decreases continued to be made in following years although not at the same pace. Other cities adopted the program and in one, Milwaukee, two major department stores reported a reduction of shoplifting losses from 20 to 30 percent after the first year of operation. Arrests were down similarly, especially in some suburban areas.

It would be presumptuous, of course, to say that all of the decline occurred solely because of the public relations campaign against shoplifting since many causes were involved, nor do the originators claim that it did. But it seems certain that the massive S.T.E.M. campaign produced effects which would not have occurred as soon or as greatly otherwise. And the *action* involved not only the preparation of communications material but also the organizing of retailers and other segments of a community into one common effort.

Other Examples of Organization for Public Relations

Associations of all sorts provide the most frequent examples of organization for public relations purposes. In many cases their membership is composed of relatively small manufacturers or other organizations which do not individually have the financial resources to meet the local or national public relations problems which are common to all of them.

One such illustration would be "The American Music Conference" sponsored by makers of musical instruments in the United States. More than thirty years ago they became concerned about a decline in the sale of trumpets, tubas, violins, and other ways of making music. Radio, television, stereo tapes, and records, and more time spent outside of the home were thought to be reasons. The amount manufacturers could afford to spend on conventional advertising, based on their sales volume and profit, was obviously inadequate to change the situation so they turned to a well-known Chicago public relations firm for aid.

This counseling firm engaged in extensive research into Americans musical interests and then launched an extensive program aimed primarily at the encouragement of school music and the formation of musical groups, either amateur or professional. The help of all those interested in these developments was enlisted (knowing, of course, that the sale of musical instruments would inevitably follow).

In many cases, as in professional groups, direct advertising is not only impossible for financial reasons but would also be felt to be in poor taste because it is "special pleading" which is all right for a commercial manufacturer but rather crass for a doctor or a dentist or a lawyer, for example.

Relations with the communications media are also involved. A newspaper would not carry a free advertisement for musical instruments because it would feel that a manufacturer ought to pay for a selling effort which benefits sales. But if a local chamber music society is formed, its activities are legitimate news and would be covered even if this inspired some readers to go out and buy violins or cellos.

Even more, as in "Law Day U.S.A." or in "S.T.E.M.," the direct aid and editorial support of the news media can be enlisted if there is a broad public goal of unquestioned benefit in which many groups participate.

SUMMARY

Classifying public relations actions into distinct categories is not easy because many aspects may be present in each instance, as the reader will doubtless have observed by now. However, it is worthwhile because it sharpens the perception of a practitioner in examining an existing situation.

1 Action may be inherent in an existing situation, in which case it must often be made clear and be communicated.

2 Action may go farther and capitalize upon an existing facility or event which would not always be apparent in the first place.

3 Action may need to be developed to display the existing characteristics of a product or organization.

4 Actions may need to be entirely *created* to demonstrate the character of an organization through its services in the public welfare.

5 Action may take the form of cooperation with others to aid and stimulate them in the public welfare, while the prime mover remains relatively in the background.

6 Action is sometimes needed to provide a basis upon which worthwhile and effective communication can be built.

7 Action sometimes consists primarily of organizing various units into a common effort so that they may together influence public opinion. Organization is itself a form of action.

Creating good actions involves much imagination upon the part of the public relations person. Questions must be answered such as: Will this be interesting to the public? Does it serve a real public need? Will it get sufficient coverage by the communications media to justify the

expense and time? Is it truly representative of the nature of the organization? What will the public judgment be? Can it help other groups attain
their goals, thus attracting enthusiastic cooperation? Will it perhaps
grow over the years or diminish?

Action is one of the things that sets public relations apart from
advertising. The latter is largely "saying" while public relations is frequently more "doing." Action thus relates the public relations function
properly to the top management of an organization which is the only
source from which things can be ordered done. There is nothing more
important because without substantive actions there cannot possibly be
good public relations for long.

A primary motive for organizations engaging in praiseworthy actions may be a way which would not otherwise be possible. Other organizations may also be stimulated to similar actions. Selfish motivation
often leads in time to genuine altruism through habit. In any event, human motivations for good deeds, whether on the part of individuals or
organizations, are seldom unmixed. As long as those having a self-
interest candidly recognize it and do not fool themselves or others about
their mixed motivations, no harm is done and often much good. As
Robert Heilbroner said, "Public relations may be a commercial conscience—but a conscience nevertheless!"

Chapter 12

Communication and Communication Cases

"Letting people know" is the backbone of all effective public relations programs, because no matter how virtuous one's actions may be, they can have little effect until they are widely known. The saying attributed to Emerson, "If a man builds a better mousetrap, the world will beat a path to his door," may have testified truly to the fame of simple well-crafted materials among close neighbors a century ago; nowadays "the world" buys its mousetraps from the manufacturers who are most talked about, without examining too closely the reason for their renown.

In fact, the truly unique function, for which all sorts of organizations are willing to pay in hard cash, is the public relations practitioner's skill in communicating. This, of course, includes writing skill, knowledge of the media of communication and their uses, and acquaintance with the experts in the field. But it also involves far more! It includes the ability to approach readers, listeners, or viewers in such a way as to command their attention to create pictures in their minds, and to obtain their interest and agreement.

This is not easy. People communicate today, as they always have, through words, symbols, and the simple relations of friendship; but they communicate more effectively if they have a thorough knowledge of the *principles* of successful public relations communications as they have been demonstrated time and again. A completely exhaustive list of such principles of effective communication has not yet been made and is not likely soon to be made, for social scientists are continually discovering and refining them.

The cases which follow in this chapter are listed under the heading "communications," not because they illustrate this activity exclusively but because the communicating was exceptionally well accomplished.

Among the principles covered are humanization, suiting the message and the means of communication to the audience, speaking the receiver's language, timeliness, dramatization, two-way communication, reaching your own people first, facing the facts, performing a needed service, stressing positive benefits, repetition, overcoming refusal to pay attention, using leaders of opinion, preconditioning the audience, and keeping all communications in harmony.

There is no magic in any of these principles; most of them have been known for several thousand years, and varying lists could be drawn up at any time. Whole books have been written about all, or parts, of them. But in today's world of overflowing communications the important thing to remember is that while people may be easily bombarded with messages, they will pay little attention to most of them unless the communications are of considerable personal interest; and this usually means that the messages must, in some way, recall and reinforce the experiences or goals of the recipients. Since such experiences are much wider than they used to be, and since the number of communications has multiplied even more, the role of communications expert requires increasing knowledge and discrimination. Mere volume of communication is no longer the sole prerequisite to success. In today's great flow of communications, in fact, only a few of the greatest organizations can hope to beat down indifference by sheer massive assault. Aim is becoming increasingly important.

THE PRINCIPLE OF HUMANIZATION

People find it hard to think in the abstract and usually attempt to give human characteristics to inanimate or even abstract things such as nations, governments, business corporations, and social or religious organizations. We identify a nation with its president, dictator, king, or queen; and the companies which stand out in our minds are those in which a colorful personality—the original Henry Ford or John D.

Rockefeller—has made a mark. This tendency has both its advantages and its dangers: Real people make mistakes, lose their tempers, and often act in foolish ways which may reflect badly upon the organizations which they personify. The ideal human symbol, perhaps, is a fictitious person who is always wise, serene, and pleasant, like General Mills's "Betty Crocker" or General Motor's "Mr. Goodwrench" Everyone knows that these people do not exist, but they still fill a definite purpose in pleasant identification.

The Minneapolis Gas Company

The Problem   Everyone agrees that gas is a clean, convenient fuel. Yet how much personality does a gas company have? We take its service for granted because gas continually arrives, quiet and unseen, in an underground pipe; we notice gas only if it ceases coming and the house gets cold, or if it leaks, smells, or explodes—although the monthly bill gives us a reminder too. But what mental image can a name like "the Minneapolis Gas Company" evoke in the public mind? Probably nothing more than a string of letters in a certain style of type or the remembrance of a big downtown office building. This was the problem of the Minneapolis Gas Company; it had little personality.

The Solution   The answer was a little Indian maiden with a cheerful smile and a bright blue gas flame in her headband in the place where the single feather ought to be. Her name was Minnegasco—a corporation-coined name to be sure, but one with the local flavor of Minneapolis, Minnesota, Minnehaha, and Minnetonka, with which people of the upper Midwest are quite familiar. The little Indian girl wore an ample brown elkskin garment from under which her feet peeped out coyly.

Gas company employees were first introduced to the Indian maiden, learned how and why she was created, and were told what the company hoped to accomplish with her winsome personality. Minnegasco then met the public through a full-page color advertisement in the *Minneapolis Sunday Tribune;* next became acquainted with the company's 12,000 stockholders by arriving in the annual report; and finally visited the homes of 200,000 customers by direct mail, her initial mission being to explain how the unusually cold weather had boosted gas bills.

To make Minnegasco a fellow employee, she was featured at a company party where a Minnegasco button adorned every coat lapel and dress; the name of the employee newspaper was changed from the *Pilot Light* to *Minnegasco News;* brightly colored cardboard Minnegasco cutouts were put on display in all offices; and all new brochures and letter-heads featured her prominently.

Minnegasco helped to humanize the company for customers by becoming a permanent part of a redesigned gas-service bill. She was featured with the company name on cars and trucks, and Minnegasco stickers were placed upon appliances to indicate the date of service calls. Meter readers even stuffed their pockets with Minnegasco buttons and became the favorites of the small fry.

Strengthening the company image in the community took several forms, including a series of advertisements boosting Minnegasco Land as a place in which to live and work. One ad, for example, praised the development of the arts in the upper Midwest, but others hit more closely

Figure 12-1   A newspaper advertisement featuring "Minnegasco," the little Indian maiden developed to give personality to The Minneapolis Gas Company.

at matters in which a gas company would be vitally concerned. A "good schools" ad pointed out that Minnegasco pays the largest single amount of school-supporting personal property tax in twenty-two of the twenty-five communities she serves. An "it's-fun-to-eat-out" ad not only scratched the backs of local restaurants but also noted that the best cooking was done with gas, and another ad proclaimed "The fresh air's fresher because greater Minneapolis goes first class with gas"—a plug for the use of smokeless fuel in homes and factories.

A full-page color ad in the local newspapers offered 300 free 21-inch Minnegasco stuffed rag dolls just for filling in an entry blank with name and address at a local gas-appliance dealer's store, and every customer received a free Minnegasco headband and blue feather.

In another newspaper ad the Indian maiden held a big pencil with which to sign up for a budget plan on gas heating, and in a summer gas air-conditioning ad she appeared as a little figure in every action picture. A press relations ad in *Page One Yearbook,* a local journalistic publication, showed the heads of the three members of the gas company public relations department with feathers in their hair, while Minnegasco herself followed close behind.

Other community-wide efforts included a "Birth of Minnegasco" presentation before business clubs; special folders distributed on Business Education Day to teachers visiting the company; and thousands of memo books, paper plates, buttons, and matchbooks.

Results   Minnegasco's impact was immediate. In a survey made only three weeks after her introduction, 37 percent named her correctly or almost correctly from her picture alone, and 56 percent associated her with the gas company.

Children organized Minnegasco Clubs and wrote in for headbands and feathers; a Minnegasco skit was featured in a Gridiron dinner of the Twin Cities Newspaper Guild; an attractive woman dressed as Minnegasco was a hit at a home-builders show; employees and customers were full of comments and suggestions; and from a gas company as far away as Chihuahua, Mexico, came a request for suggestions in developing a similar program there. The Minnegasco program won first place in the Community Relations classification of the American Gas Association Public Relations Awards.

Discussion   Serious-minded people may consider this attempt to assume a personality foolish, but their scorn is unjustified. Why should a company be known only by a string of letters, spelling a word which means only the name of the city in which the company does business and another word, "gas," which names an immaterial product that the consumer can neither see nor touch?

Sometimes, of course, word names do evoke pictures, such as Lincoln Life Insurance Company, Bell Telephone Company, Hercules Powder Company, Ford Motor Company, or Edison Electricty Company. Each of these names suggests a person, although it is a fair guess that the public has largely forgotten Alexander Graham Bell and substitutes for his name an image of the Liberty Bell. Other names may suggest products or may be simply fanciful, like Carnation or Pet Incorporated.

Often company names come to acquire a certain aura of meaning, although the words themselves are almost unintelligible to many people —the Atchison, Topeka, and Santa Fe Railway, for example, or Pan American Airways. Most companies are named after persons who are quite unknown to the general public; or they are named after the companies' functions, as is the Metropolitan Electric Company; or they present grandiloquent generalities related to their functions, such as Trans-World Airways or Continental Airlines. Many today form an "alphabet soup "such as ITT, TRW, SCM or AMAX. Only through their connotations do these names acquire meaning.

The average citizen today, faced by the vast multiplication of companies and organizations, needs more visual symbols to replace or to amplify words if he or she is to remember and understand names. Some observers also feel that the advent of television has made the public more symbol-minded. Symbols are the oldest form of written language; the crown, the cross, the swastika, the hammer and sickle, the torch, the shell, the snake, and the eagle are all symbols which often speak more clearly than words. Flags are potent symbols. But the best symbol is a human being, who can be responsive. A human symbol can talk to us and we can talk to it; hence the particular virtue of friendly little Minnegasco! A good symbol is often the only thing that can transform an abstract, perhaps somewhat unfriendly, name into a reality and finally into a personality.

THE PRINCIPLE OF SUITING THE MESSAGE AND MEANS OF COMMUNICATION TO THE AUDIENCE

One of the most serious dangers in public relations communication is the illusion of having achieved it when in fact there has been no communication at all—only a one-way outpouring. A mass media approach is generally noticed only by those who agree with it; the rest ignore it. Yet the sender, convinced of the rightness and knowing the wide potential coverage of newspapers, magazines, or broadcasting, assumes that the message has been attended to and has done its work. People see what they want to see and hear what they want to hear, and therefore the act of sending is not equivalent to communication; to assume that it is often results in unpleasant surprises.

The Case of the Unhappy Deer Hunters

The Problem   Every fall in a large midwestern state approximately a half million deer hunters pour into the woods to bring back the venison. About four out of five of them are disappointed (sometimes the proportion is greater than that). What a customer relations problem for the state conservation department, especially since much of the department's annual income comes from deer hunters' license fees!

To make it worse, a great number of these hunters fancy themselves experts, and this delusion is not confined to the city sportsmen who enter the woods once a year; it is probably endemic among the small-town and rural hunters who feel that they know all about deer through their own experience and their forebears life in the wilderness. Very few are willing to blame their own lack of skill for their failure to bring back the antlers.

Actually, the management of a statewide deer herd is extremely complex, and few individuals making random observations within a limited area can know much about it. Literally tens of thousands of wooded or brushy square miles are involved. In each of these square miles a hunter may see only a few deer and may be fortunate to shoot one during the season; yet census-check drives will show that there may be thirty to thirty-five deer in each square-mile area. The total deer herd of the state is more than 600,000, and during a long snowy winter up to 50,000 deer may starve to death from lack of browsing food. Scores of experienced people are needed to estimate deer population by spot checks, to get an idea of how many are shot legally during the season, and to tramp the frozen cedar swamps to see how many deer are starving in the places where they hole up for shelter in the cold winter.

Actually, the limiting factor on deer population, in most instances, is winter food and not hunter pressure; and all the grandfathers' tales about the times when there were deer behind every tree (or no deer at all) are probably true, though the dates and places may be somewhat hazy. Big pine timber stands support only a few deer becase there is nothing growing in the shadow of the dark trees for them to browse on. Obviously, in the days of the first pioneers and the Indians, there were not many deer in the virgin forests; neither were they many hunters. With the clearing of forests, which were replaced with tasty green brush, came a boom in the deer population. Next came fires and unrestricted market slaughter of deer for meat—and a great decimation of the deer herds, which reached their lowest numbers about 1900 to 1910. Following this period, a fire-control program resulted in a great increase in woods food available for deer, and this, together with laws preventing market slaughter, brought about a deer boom.

For some years the state conservationists charged with management of the deer herd felt that the herd has outgrown its food supply. The large number of deer starved every bad winter and the poor condition and small number of fawns of those surviving in the spring was evidence. The state conservation officers felt that if more deer were killed by hunters in the fall, there would be no total diminution of the herd. Laws restricting shooting to bucks were passed in the 1920s, but the Conservation Department had, for the past several years, instituted a limited doe season.

Now for the essence of the state conservation department's public relations problem:

Last fall's deer season was very poor. Only about 60,000 deer were shot compared with about 100,000 in several preceding years. Some hunters and hunting-resort operators made a great outcry. Bills were introduced into the state legislature which would take deer regulations out of the hands of the conservation department and put them under the control of county supervisors—dozens of rules for dozens of counties! The conservation department was composed of employees averaging more than five years' university training and about fifteen years' experience on the job. They felt that they knew their business and that no one else knew it so well. They believed that a bad, rainy opening day of the season last fall was the main reason for the smaller number of deer taken and that a limited doe season should be continued. They were particularly stung by the proposal before the legislature that their carefully planned scientific study be scrapped and control be thrown into the hands of local amateurs. It was a refutation of all they had worked for most of their lives.

What had gone wrong? Why did a significant portion of the deer-hunting public seemingly lack confidence in the ability of their own state conservation game-management department? Had there been a failure to communicate? What should have been done differently? What was the next step?

This is a public relations problem—a persuasive communications problem. Laws cannot solve it; in fact, law right now seems to be in danger of going the other way.

Solutions In the past the state conservation department had relied mainly upon the following ways of telling its story to the public:

The press. The department maintained a steady flow of good releases to daily and weekly newspapers of the state. The articles had been widely printed and, generally speaking, press contacts were favorable. Many editors and outdoor writers were willing to go out of their way to support the knowledge and positions of the conservation department officers, even at the risk, sometimes, of personal unpopularity.

Department publications. The department published a magazine and booklets. They were well written and attractively illustrated with photographs and cartoons and contained all the facts a person would need to be well informed.

Conservation clubs and schools. State conservation officers made numerous appearances before clubs and schools, frequently showing motion pictures or slides of their work.

Other methods of public contact included some radio and television broadcasting, although conservation department members were unhappy about the controversial situations in which they have been placed by some broadcasters who were more interested in "conflict" and a "lively show" than in true reporting. Department scientists are not so articulate on the air sometimes as they would wish to be, and even someone who knows the subject well may suffer when contrasted with an impassioned opponent who may ask more questions than can be answered with absolute certainty.

Discussion The methods just described seemed to be missing the target. Was the method of communication used suitable to those for whom it was intended? Obviously not, or the conservation department would not have been in danger of having its authority stripped from it by the pressure upon the state legislature exercised by disgruntled hunters and resort operators.

The trouble seemed to be that the news stories, booklets, and club and school appearances had been doing a good job of informing and influencing the segment of the public which was *already* well aware of the ability and devotion of the state game-management department. More news stories, more newspaper support, more booklets, and more speeches to schools and conservation clubs would not succeed in communicating with those who had not read a great deal, who had their own minds already firmly set and had ignored printed material, who failed to attend talks, or who took their opinions primarily from a circle of similarly minded friends rather than from what some distant, aloof, scientific expert. A new approach was needed if these people were to be reached.

The key to contact with the opposition may lie in asking two questions: To whom do these people turn as leaders of opinion? How do they arrive at their opinions? It seems probable that they draw their opinions primarily from their circle of friends. Primarily these opposition groups consisted of rather close-knit, small-town hunters. Leaders of opinion in these circles tend to "know from experience" and to distrust or ignore other sources.

If the aid of the key persons could be enlisted, other members in the group might be willing to open their ears to thoughts which run contrary to the presently prevailing norms in their cliques. One solution might be for conservation officers to ask their help in going into the woods in late winter to count deer-starvation kills or to help in checking browse conditions. This would have to be done with care, because one thing which may be causing some local leaders to assert their own knowledge strongly is a feeling of inferiority in the presence of the irritating assurance of the supposedly scientific, highly educated professional game-management staff. Much of the communication with key people in these groups must be managed personally; only then will other media of information and persuasion have a chance to be heard.

Another useful solution might be to set up demonstration areas where game-management methods could be shown in outdoor museums. The conservation department controlled several large sites adjoining main highways. A walk-through or drive-through plan with signs, a small zoo, and rest and picnic facilities could tell the story of deer-herd management in an interesting and convincing way to those who have to be *shown* because they are "from Missouri." If local labor and advice is solicited in arranging these museums further participation will be gained. Promotion of these places and the attendance of large crowds would doubtless be gratifying to local resort owners, and might answer, in part, their question: "What does the state conservation department ever do for us?"

Other efforts to encourage participation and favorable two-way communication along the lines suggested could be arranged. The important thing would be to suit the message and the means of communication to the predisposition of the audience which they had thus far failed to reach.

THE PRINCIPLE OF SPEAKING THE RECEIVER'S LANGUAGE

Even when a communication is directed toward the right people, it may still fail because its words are outside their range of understanding or because they convey meanings to the receivers quite different from those which the writer had in mind. The danger of misunderstanding is not the only cause for concern. The writer may be under the illusion that words which are reasonable and familiar to him have done their work and that he needs to make no further effort. He may be suffering from the "illusion" of communication.

The Case of Gobbledygook[1] Employee Communications[2]

Failure of communication, to a large extent caused by different understanding of words, created widespread interest among public relations people during and after the nationwide steel strike of 1959. Two organizations, Group Attitudes Corporation, a subsidiary of Hill & Knowlton, the public relations firm which was representing the steel companies, and, later and independently, Opinion Research Corporation of Princeton, New Jersey, conducted extensive surveys to discover how well workers understood words commonly used in the negotiations and what their reactions to them were. Their findings are probably still true today.

The Problem   Opinion Research surveys showed that only about 12 percent of the employees reading typical economic messages addressed to them by business really grasped their meaning. Much of this material was written on a high school-graduate or college level, and many of the employees had not progressed far in school; or sometimes their memory of technical terms had faded through disuse.

Words affect our intellects and our feelings. To impart *information,* the writer and the reader (or hearer) should not only know what a word means, but should both have the same meaning in mind. To provoke the *feeling* desired, a writer must use a word that awakens the right emotional overtones or connotations in the mind of the receiver. Neither one of these achievements is easy.

Consider the word "capitalism," for example. Out of hundreds of workers who were carefully interviewed by Opinion Research, only 55 percent claimed that they knew the word, and only 26 percent could describe its meaning. Those who did attempt a definition often came through with quite unfavorable emotional reactions, such as "The weal-

---

[1] A word devised by Congressman Maverick of Texas to describe high-sounding, meaningless government communications.

[2] John W. Hill, formerly chairman of the board, Hill & Knowlton, Inc., in *Public Relations Journal,* August, 1960, and from a January, 1960, study of Opinion Research Corporation of Princeton, N.J.

thiest people take over," "Big business has so much money that they freeze the little fellow out of business," "A dictatorship by the rich."

It is quite obvious that to the exponents of capitalism the word has one meaning and that to many workers it either means little or arouses hostility. How a word acquires unfavorable connotations would be difficult to discover, but we might suspect that while American workingmen unequivocally rejected communism, they had picked up some of the meanings of the word "capitalism" given to it by Karl Marx and his followers. Words can serve equally as instruments of confusion and of enlightenment, and agreement can be achieved only when we are talking about the same things. "Capitalism" is not one of these agreed-upon words, although tests showed that "free enterprise" come closer to being mutually understood. Any words, however, can become hackneyed and acquire unpleasant or different meanings over a period of time, depending upon who uses them and for what purpose.

Solutions   To convey information, writers should be sure that all the words they use will be readily understood correctly by their readers. The Group Attitudes Corporation survey at the time of the steel strike, for example, found that such words as "accrue," "contemplate," and "delete" had little meaning for the readers.

"Accrue" was changed to "pile up or collect."

"Contemplate" became "think about or expect."

"Delete" was translated into "cancel, take out, or remove."

Whole phrases were also found to be confusing or meaningless. "Changes would be sanctioned only if . . ." became "no changes would be allowed unless . . ."

"Jointly chaired" meant "took turns as chairmen."

"Rejects summarily" was another way of saying "turn down flat."

The words and phrases that the Group attitudes survey found to be most frequently misunderstood and their translations are contained in the table below.

Thirty Words and Thirty Phrases[*]

The following are thirty words and thirty phrases found by Group Attitudes Corporation's interviewers to be most frequently misunderstood by steelworkers and a translation of these words and phrases into "steelworker" language.

Thirty words

"accrue"—*pile up; collect*	"delete"—*cancel; take out; remove*
"compute"—*figure*	"designate"—*name; appoint*
"concession"—*giving up (something)*	"deterioration"—*breaking down;*
"contemplate"—*think about; expect*	*wearing away*

Public Relations Journal, August, 1960.

"detriment"—hurt; damage; harm
"economic problem"—a cost problem
"efficiency"—the way it should be
　(e.g. operating a machine the way
　it should be operated)
"embody"—contain; include; hold
"equitable"—fair; just
"excerpt"—section; part
"facilitate"—help along; speed up
"fortuitously"—by chance; accidentally; luckily
"generate"—create; build; produce
"impediment"—barrier; road block

"inadequate"—not enough
"initiate"—begin; start
"increment"—raise; increase
"inevitably"—in the end; finally
"injurious"—damaging; harmful
"jeopardy"—danger
"magnitude"—size
"modify"—change; alter
"objectivity"—fairness
"pursuant"—in agreement with
"perpetuate"—keep alive; continue
"subsequently"—later
"ultimate"—final; end

Thirty phrases

"avoid further inflationary pressures"—avoid the things that make prices go up
"best long-term interests"—better in the long run
"changes would be sanctioned only if . . ."—no changes would be allowed unless
"endeavored to interest Union leaders affirmatively"—tried to get the Union leaders to agree to
"exclusive function"—sole right
"fundamentally the same"—almost exactly the same
"insofar as practicable"—as far as possible
"impartial men"—fair men; men without an axe to grind
"in all sincerity and complete conviction as to the merit in the public interest"—because we sincerely believe it is best for everyone
"jointly chaired"—take turns as chairmen
"meet reasonable requirements of business demands"—do our best to serve our customers
"misrepresented these proposals as devices"—unjustly attacked the proposals as ways
"modify the discipline"—lighten the penalty
"men of outstanding qualifications and objectivity"—fair men of broad experience

"not justified on any basis of equity"—all give and no take; not a fair deal
"protection against arbitrary discharge"—guard against being fired without cause
"representatives of both parties"—men from both the Union and the Company
"retain the sole discretion to decide"—be the one to decide
"reject summarily"—turn down flat
"seek to demonstrate a cooperative attitude"—try to be fair
"share new economic progress"—share in future gains
"substantially in accordance"—almost exactly like
"take precedence"—come first
"take affirmative action"—go along with; move ahead
"to make it consistent with"—to make it agree with
"ultimate solution"—the final answer; the end result
"union studiously vilified the companies"—the Union went out of its way to attack the companies
"unnecessarily restrictive"—too binding; too strict
"wholly inconsistent with their professed desire"—not what they say they want to do
"with the objective of facilitating"—with the idea of helping

Words convey more than information, however. They frequently have strong emotional overtones, and sometimes a word may be familiar and understood, but not liked. In a survey Opinion Research attempted to delve into this aspect of word recognition by asking workers not only whether they were familiar with words and could define them, but also what thoughts occurred to them most readily in connection with them. Often words which might be considered almost synonymous had very different "favorable–unfavorable" ratings.

Management sometimes uses "work stoppage" and "strike" as if they were the same thing; yet to employees a strike is considered largely justified and has little unfavorable connotation, whereas a work stoppage has many unfavorable feelings associated with it because it can also be construed as a wildcat strike or even a lockout. Employees generally regard the term "profits" with favor but prefer "company net income." They may understand profits better but feel that an aura of "excess profits" or "profiteering" clings to the word. Both "investors" in a company and "stockholders" are regarded favorably, but stockholders is the more popular designation because investors are felt to be a distant group, bigger, and less intimately connected with the company. "Layoff" is a very bad word (though most people know what it means), but "reduction in the work force" is a little less unpleasant.

The phrase "hidden wages and salaries" provokes a generally unfavorable reaction, probably because of the possible sinister meaning of "hidden," but "pension, insurance, and hospitalization benefits" scores near the top in favorable response. "Fringe benefits" is well accepted, but "employee benefits" is more popular.

Much of this reaction to a word depends upon how you look at it. To the factory manager the money spent in hiring mill hands is "labor costs," but to the mill hands themselves, it is "money paid in wages and benefits." If the factory manager is writing to the board of directors and to other factory managers, he or she will obviously use one term, if to employees, another.

"Piece rate" is a bad word; "incentive pay" is much better (although less understood).

"Annuity" was understood by only 25 percent of the workers interviewed, but was regarded favorably by those who did know the meaning of the word.

"Compulsory union membership" was only slightly favored, probably because of the word "compulsory," but the phrase "union shop" scored near the top.

"Government ownership of business" was less well regarded than "socialism" (although both are on the unfavorable side of the score), presumably because few workers had a good idea of what socialism is.

And, interestingly enough, the name "corporation" was much more coldly received than "company"—a holdover, perhaps, from the phrase "soulless corporation."

Discussion   Why do so many business people use cold, little under-stood, or unfavorable "businessese" terms when writing to employees and to the general public? Their language fails completely to communi-cate. It is too simple to say that those in business aren't writers. While most of them are indeed not writers (they are accountants, lawyers, and administrators), some of them are good writers, and they have the means to hire good writers (though they may not know a piece of good exposi-tion when they read it). The same accusation of failure in communication can be leveled at scientists, educators, heads of government bureaus, doctors, and generally experts in *any* field.

Probably the main reasons for a person's inability to speak another person's language are selfishness, lack of imagination, and a desire to impress colleagues rather than those at whom the message should be aimed. Good writing is not just a matter of knowing a great many words and stringing them together prettily; it first consists in putting yourself into the other person's shoes and saying, "If I were a steelworker in Youngstown, Ohio, how would I understand and regard this?" or "If I were a homemaker in Des Moines, Iowa, what would my reaction be?" To do this takes a lively and experienced imagination. It is not a job for the boss's offspring just back home from a literary course at the univer-sity. Writers have to want to communicate and be interested in the people they are addressing. And finally writers must forget about the language of their own trade or clan and write for the benefit of others, not their fellows. The erudition that impresses the company president may confuse or anger the outsider. Speaking the receiver's language is the least writers can do in return for the gift of time and attention!

THE PRINCIPLE OF TIMELINESS

Probably the main reason why big recent events constitute news is that most people have a share in them. The events are a part of their common experience. It is no accident that most conversations between strangers begin with the weather, which is current and of universal interest.

Alert public relations people are on the lookout for news—the more current and commonly experienced the better—which will help them to approach their public. Timeliness is frequently the key to attention, and it offers a rare opportunity to communicate, since news that has been built up by the press has a ready-made audience. If everybody is participating in an event and talking about it, related items are certain to be absorbed also.

"News," of course, does not have to be headline news. But it does have to be something that is current and that is widely known. The following examples will illustrate this.

The Transamerica Pyramid

In the early 1970s Transamerica Corporation, a large national conglomerate, erected a new headquarters office building in San Francisco. Had it been box-shaped like the usual downtown office skyscraper there would have been little reaction; approval from those who liked to see more jobs in what otherwise might be a declining central business district and perhaps some protest from those who object to business in general or who dislike change. But this building was different—and it stirred a storm of controversy!

Forty-eight stories tall, it rose in a pyramid mounted on pyramidal crossed girders and was based in a small park planted with redwood trees. Its white spire outline stood out from other conventional buildings, a startling landmark from the bay. It could not be ignored. Critics compared it to a stiletto; admirers praised its innovative design. From the moment the plans for the project were unveiled the problem was not to get attention but to deal with the news that it created.

The first step was to get Planning Commission approval, but after this was granted opponents called television stations for coverage and started picketing demonstrations for the cameras in front of the current Transamerica building in another San Francisco location, giving an on-the-air impression of massive public disapproval. This was answered by counter-publicity while work on the building proceeded. Only when the structure was finished were the ceremonies more than low-key while the viewing public made up its mind about how it liked it. New buildings are like new art; there is an immediate tendency to oppose anything unusual. But after a couple of years the verdict was generally favorable. The building was innovative but with clean lines and pleasing proportions. It was something that San Franciscans talked about to visitors. It seemed unusually safe in a city which always has earthquakes in the back of its mind. To many it became a point of local pride.

Because of such intense news interest, achieving communication was no problem for company public relations people in this instance.

Figure 12–2 The forty-eight-story tall Transamerica pyramid was an architectural novelty in San Francisco and its design presented public relations problems.

Instead, the problem was judicious handling of communication in a controversial hot news situation.

Looked at in another way, the whole decision of the design of the building could be said to be connected to public relations along with other factors. Prior to the building not too many people, even in San Francisco, knew about Transamerica, much less what it did. After the news about the building awareness increased greatly and a rather vague company name became visually identified with a structure. Buildings, architecture, and landscaping are a part of public relations communication just as much as words are and often provide the basis for verbal or pictorial communication. If the exterior of a food company factory, for example, looks dingy, passers-by will conclude that the inside is also, although it might be spotlessly clean. Factories and offices do not have to look commonplace and dull any more than people do. The important thing is for the external appearance to match the character desired, whether it be striking or conventional—and then for the actuality to live up to the image so conveyed. Lack of harmony between appearance and reality, as in a restaurant which looks like a fine French restaurant on the outside but which serves poor-quality frozen dinners on the inside creates lasting public disfavor. So public relations properly includes physical appearances and operating procedures to match those appearances.

Gas Drilling Off Galveston

Gas and oil drilling offshore in the Gulf of Mexico is common and accepted in Texas but a few years ago when geological surveys revealed sizable quantities of gas immediately off the tourist beaches of Galveston, Texas, a special public relations problem was created. The white sandy beaches of Galveston are a big attraction to people in the hot interior of Texas during the long summer. Many people in Galveston depend on such visitors for their incomes. Anything that would injure the attractiveness of the beaches would be unwelcome.

George Mitchell & Associates, Inc., the largest independent producers of natural gas in Texas, proposed to develop this offshore gas field. Mitchell had already drilled more than 1,500 natural gas wells without trouble or disruption to the surrounding environment. Some of these had been on land within the city limits of Galveston. Mr. Mitchell was a native of Galveston and the company had large real estate holdings in Galveston including a resort-home area on one of the beaches. It would scarcely be interested in doing anything which would harm its own investments.

But despite all these favorable facts a complete and open public communications program was needed. It would not be enough just to get the official permissions needed to start work. People needed to know what was planned, what its effects would be and what the time schedule would be. This would require a special effort to inform them since most people do not carefully follow city council meetings or permits from the U.S. Corps of Engineers. These things come out in the news over a period of time in incomplete driblets. The surprised beach business-owner seeing a large sea-going rig offshore some morning might well exclaim in anger, "Why wasn't I told of this?"—when, in fact, the news had been in the papers or on the air for quite a period of time. Mitchell needed to make an extra effort to see that everyone did know and understand what was involved.

Drilling from the large and highly visible platform rigs (see Figure 12–3) would be done only during the tourist off-season between October and May. When a gas well was completed, it would be capped with a small above-water valve stand, painted to be hardly visible from the beach a mile away. Only one well would be drilled at a time and there would be no gas storage at the drilling sites; all gas would be brought ashore by underwater pipeline. There would be the best blowout protection and in case oil was discovered along with gas (a possibility regarded as remote) it would be brought ashore similarly.

Figure 12–3   A gas drilling rig immediately offshore of the Texas resort city of Galveston could be expected to present immediate public relations problems. Courtesy Mitchell Energy.

Figure 12-4 The finished well head after the drilling was completed was almost invisible. A good communications program was needed to assure citizens in advance that this would really be so. Courtesy Mitchell Energy.

The arguments presented in favor of this development were that it would result in considerable tax payments to Galveston and to the state of Texas and that it was greatly in the national interest. It was also pointed out that it presented a minor hazard compared to the parade of large oil tankers constantly going up the Houston ship channel near Galveston.

Support was further presented from university research people and from pipeline companies indicating the need for gas.

Based on complete information, public acceptance was obtained and the drilling proceeded successfully as planned. Without such a determined effort at going the extra mile in providing information there might well have been an uproar. It would not have been enough to have a good case; the case had to be put forth in such a way that everyone concerned had a chance to hear it. Citizens could not have any feeling that they had been ignored or that there was any attempt at secrecy (even if there wasn't any). The public relations person could not depend on the media alone and unaided to disseminate the news but had to take extra steps such as booklets, meetings, and public appearances to see that it was done.

ARCO Looks at the Bicentennial Differently

Nothing could be more "timely" in one way than America's Bicentennial celebration in 1976. Yet, in another way, the Bicentennial presented a public relations challenge because it was certain that thousands of organizations in the United States would try to connect themselves with it in some quite obvious way with greater or less validity. The problem was to find some new and fitting aspect.

The Atlantic Richfield Company, a large American oil company, decided that the way to do it would be to look forward to 2076 instead of back to 1776. To do this they asked the public, through an extensive advertising campaign, what it felt about certain current issues that might affect 2076 and also requested opinions and suggestions. This was not a contest, because no prize money was given. Nor was it an untried idea because the year before Atlantic Richfield had run a similar national advertising campaign seeking public ideas about the future of transportation in this country and had received 70,000 replies. It was a "two-way" communication (discussed more in a later section of this chapter) in which thoughts were sought from readers rather than the usual "I'm telling you" format of most advertising.

The program was successful, generating more than 35,000 replies. More importantly, it undoubtedly had a high degree of reader interest and stood out amid the sea of backward-looking Bicentennial advertising and promotion. Although there was nothing in it specifically selling ARCO, it elevated the stature of the company by showing that ARCO was interested in providing a forum about national problems. In times of real or incipient shortage the character of a vendor becomes of first importance.

Kansas City "Prime Time"

To many Easterners the name "Kansas City" is associated with an image of a rough, uncultivated cow town—a cluster of buildings on a flat prairie —undistinguished by art, architecture or the civilized amenities of life.

A message about the future from Atlantic Richfield Company.

Starting next month we will launch our new advertising campaign to celebrate America's Tricentennial.

That's right, Tricentennial.

Remember about a year ago when we asked for your ideas on Public Transportation? Well, we received more than 70,000 ideas. We found that we had tapped a source of wisdom and invention and plain old common sense that otherwise would have gone to waste.

In the final analysis, our Public Transportation campaign amounted to a whole new form of advertising communication – the public talking to us instead of the other way around.

Now, in our Tricentennial campaign, we want to broaden this consumer dialogue to include not just one subject (like Public Transportation) but all ideas pertinent to America's future. America will change a great deal by the year 2076, and we want you to tell us what you think those changes should be.

Our new campaign is coming soon to newspapers, magazines, and your favorite TV screen. So get ready with your hopes and dreams and visions.

Celebrate America's Tricentennial 100 years early.

Petroleum Products of
AtlanticRichfieldCompany

Figure 12–5 How do you celebrate a bicentennial? Most organizations looked back —but ARCO decided to look ahead. This was a newspaper advertisement.

In fact, Kansas City is quite different and has been for many years. The agricultural business at which America excells is booming, particularly in grain, but Kansas City is no longer a big cattle stockyards center. There are many diversified industries including the first ranked envelope and greeting card manufacturer and second in automobile production. The terrain of the city is not flat but consists of many rocky hills and trees. There are hundreds of millions of dollars worth of new buildings, many architecturally distinguished, hundreds of miles of three-lined bou-

An American Portrait 2076.

Several months ago we started our Tricentennial Program by asking for your thoughts on life in America by the year 2076. Instead of a lot of ideas about space ships and robots of the future most of the more than 50,000 responses we've received have been about people's visions of our future as a nation.

The main point that came through, letter after letter, was that most people believe a lot of the things that made America what it is today will shape our future as well.

An overwhelming number of you – ninety-one percent – told us you want the family to remain our basic social unit.

Sixty-two percent feel the nation will be better off when there is no racial, sexual, or religious discrimination.

Seventy-three percent of you told us you expect a reaffirmation of religion and faith by the time of our Tricentennial.

There is a strong desire – almost two-thirds – for more individual participation in government through better communication.

Nearly three-quarters of you are in favor of a slower paced, more rural life.

What's better than statistics is the feeling that the majority of people believe that life in the future can be better than it is today. But we've always been like that. It's what's been called the American Dream.

You've shown us that the future of America lies not in the land or the technologies we master but in the hearts and minds of the people, our greatest resource.

We didn't intend to do a scientific survey but your responses show significant insight into the problems and opportunities that face our nation. We plan to make those thoughts available in a book reflecting many of the interesting letters we've received.

Please note that all ideas submitted shall become public property without compensation. Tricentennial P.O. Box 2076, Los Angeles, California 90053

Petroleum products of
AtlanticRichfieldCompany

Thank you for helping us celebrate America's Tricentennial 100 years early.

Figure 12–6   After public ideas on the future had been solicited, this ad reported what people had said. A more detailed booklet was also available.

levards, scores of beautiful fountains, colleges and universities, a nationally-famous art gallery, a giant sports complex, and one of America's biggest new airports.

Among the 300 national metropolitan areas Kansas City ranks 25th in family buying income and 26th in number of households. Its metropolitan area is home to about 1,250,000 people and it covers 316 square miles as compared to New York City's 300 or Philadelphia's 130. In this lies a good deal of the secret of its recent success, while other more tightly-bound cities have lost business in their centers and seen their citizens move to suburbs, Kansas City has been able to retain much of this developing area. Another reason has been that Kansas City people, from local business leaders to working men and women have been proud of their city and willing to help its progress by telling their friends, by voting for civic improvements, and by personal aid.

The trouble was that not too many people outside the Kansas City area were aware of these changes. Old reputations of forty or fifty years ago linger forever unless something is done to alter them. This requires public relations. A well-known national public relations counseling firm headquartered in New York City (which also handled the Hallmark Greeting Card account whose headquarters is in Kansas City and whose founder is deeply involved in the development of the city) was hired. The fee was small for such a major effort and included no funds for advertising or press visits to the city.

The program had three objectives: (1) To stimulate Kansas City's economic development through new business, new investment, conventions and tourism; (2) to encourage local business expansion; (3) to further the pride of local residents in the good things about the area. The problem demanding public relations ingenuity was to find things about Kansas City of sufficient news and interest value for newspapers, magazines, and broadcasters to cover—especially when other areas were naturally interested in promoting their own attractions. The problem was so well-met that in 1972, 1973, and 1975 the Carl Byoir public relations firm which handled the account received a Silver Anvil award for the program's excellence from The Public Relations Society of America. Direct results could be seen in the great increase in news material about Kansas City, its favorableness, and in business and convention growth.

This required *timeliness* in capitalizing on interest in Kansas City which was created by other events, for example, an All Star baseball game in the new stadium or the 1974 Mid-Term Democratic Convention. There was also the central theme of interest in how, during a period when many American cities such as New York or Detroit were rapidly falling into serious financial and social difficulties, Kansas City seemed to be avoiding them. But as public relations made the Kansas City facts better known each year, the problem of newsworthy interest became more severe. As the Kansas City story became better known, it also became "old hat."

So when the 1976 National Republican Convention was slated for Kansas City it offered a golden opportunity. Hundreds of reporters would attend and would want to know and write something about the host city. Television would show pictures and make comments all over the nation. National magazines would time articles to coincide with the natural news interest inherent in the convention coverage. No effort could be too great to see that the press was supplied with all the help it needed to report things as they really were—not as someone remembered hearing them from a generation before or as some reporter encountered them walking down the block from a hotel. Not to make an effort would insure inadequate or out-of-date reporting of Kansas City because the press came there to cover the convention and not the city, which was incidental but not unimportant in preconvention coverage or if the news was slow.

Press kits were assembled, press rooms arranged, telephone number folders issued, and personal help was rendered in getting pictures, interviews, transportation, and in a myriad of other ways.

There were more than 400 newspaper and magazine stories and some twenty-five national network television feature stories that ran a total of nearly 80 minutes. An audience of about 260 million persons was reached. From 90 to 95 percent of the coverage of Kansas City was favorable and much of it strongly so. About 75 percent made use of the preconvention information that had been supplied. (Kansas City people were informed of all of this.)

In many ways this public relations campaign has now done its work. Its impressions, unless changed by new facts, will be as lasting as the old impressions were until they were changed. The product to be sold, Kansas City, was excellent but it took professional public relations effort to alter the picture and it would have been accomplished much more slowly, if at all, without it.

THE PRINCIPLE OF IMAGINATION IN DRAMATIZING COMMUNICATIONS

Stunts have somewhat fallen out of favor among many conservative public relations people in recent years. The excesses of their fraudulent use among Hollywood and theatrical promoters, a certain country-fair flavor, and the fact that victimized editors were frequently roasted by their readers contributed to the decline. But since so much good communication is still nonverbal, worthwhile dramatizations that are honest and in good taste often manage to make a lasting impression and to say things that words alone cannot so well convey.

The Case of the Paper Swimsuit

One such imaginative approach was put on by a major chemical manufacturing company a few years ago. The company had invented a chemical which would retard the wetting of paper so that it would not lose its strength and break easily. The product had many important potential uses, such as in making shopping bags which would not burst and other protective packaging; but simply to tell about it was very dull. The solution was a *demonstration.*

A press conference was set up at the Waldorf-Astoria Hotel in New York City. The main feature, besides the usual press kits of releases, fact sheets, pictures, and statements by company officers, was a large and very wet bath shower spraying into a temporary pool in the middle of the room. At the proper moment, a beautiful women arrived, dressed in a paper bathing suit, and skipped into the shower. Needless to say, nothing happened to the bathing suit. Thanks to the new chemical, it *was* water-resistant.

Other paper objects were also dunked, but the paper bathing suit made the biggest impression and the best pictures.

THE PRINCIPLE OF TWO-WAY COMMUNICATION

In today's complex society, where people are more talked *at* than ever before, the opportunities to talk back are not very numerous. Yet two-way communication is the essence of communication itself. How is it to be achieved in large organizations where the natural flow of communications always seems to be downward and never upward? If it is not achieved, what are the psychological consequences of its neglect?

Failure to achieve two-way communication, or at least to make recipients feel that they *can* answer, results in some serious problems. One is the resentment people feel when they are always talked at and have no opportunity to direct their own destiny, a rock upon which the paternalism of many industries (and of parents and governments too) has foundered. Companies have sometimes done everything for their employees in lowcost housing, recreation programs, benefits, and retirements only to be shocked by ingratitude. They should not have expected that goodwill could be bought with good works. People prefer that which they have made themselves. "A poor . . . thing, sir, but mine own," says Touchstone in Shakespeare's *As You Like It,* in a somewhat similar reaction.

Another cause of resentment arising from one-way communication is a feeling of helplessness. "I am so little and alone and the Great Father is so big and powerful!" No one likes to be afraid or subordinate, and in today's world fear and loneliness are common feelings. This is one of the reasons why workers value a union, which gives them a feeling of equality. It is said that the steel-company magnate, Judge Gary, used to say that there was no need of a union, that his office door was always open to any employee who wished to discuss a problem. But most of us realize the inequality of the positions of the two men on opposite sides of the desk.

Continued lack of two-way communication has another serious aspect for would-be communicators: It results in the inability of recipients to hear! Unless they have a chance to take part in some way in the communications process, they soon turn a deaf ear to sources which for them are no longer interesting. There are many other more rewarding things to attend to. Those who wish to be heard, then, must also be listeners and must show that they are listening.

Two-way communication, upward as well as downward, is a necessity to companies that wish their employees and communities to hear them, to politicians who desire real support, to school administrators who seek public understanding and votes, and to governments that wish to influence other people abroad. It is a problem of particular importance today because of the size of almost all organizations and the one-way nature of communication in the omnipresent newspapers, magazines, television programs, and films, always pouring out but never stopping for an instant to listen to whatever thoughts their output may have stirred up. Only genuine two-way communication can overcome latent feelings of resentment, helplessness, and boredom, and can win genuine gratitude for those who are willing to engage in it.

Revitalizing a Suggestion Program

Suggestion boxes, which are fairly widespread through American industry, offer a formal, limited beginning at two-way communication. Employees often use them for voicing gripes or for submitting bright ideas which they hope will result in financial gain or improvement of status; but since they *are* available and anonymous, suggestion boxes do indicate that management has an ear.

Twenty-seven suggestions submitted per one hundred employees would be a good average in any one year in an industrial plant. When Owens-Corning Fiberglas Corporation of Toledo, Ohio, noted that its box activity was far below this level, it decided to open up this disused channel of communication.

Ten key principles were applied to the system:

> Secure energetic support of top management.
> Set up awards large enough to furnish adequate incentives.

> Make it easy for employees to make suggestions.
> Open the system to all types of employees.
> Process and act upon all entries promptly.
> Make sure that each employee knows that each suggestion has received full and careful consideration and why it has been turned down or accepted.
> Pay only for constructive ideas.
> Adopt all those paid for.
> Give public recognition to all winners.
> Use every possible means to encourage participation in the program.

A suggestion-award committee was set up, and suggestions were processed quickly and thoroughly. A manual was prepared to guide the committee and other administrators who might be called in, and the maximum award for suggestions was raised from $1,500 to $2,500.

The name "Ideas for Progress" was applied to the new program, which was promoted among employees by an extensive cartoon-type, in-plant program including booklets, posters, letterheads, memo pads, pay-envelope stuffers, and employee publications.

The suggestion blank itself was redesigned with spaces to fill in labeled "This is the present condition," "I suggest," and "This is what will happen." The bottom part of the blank, perforated and serially numbered to match the upper portion, was to be torn off by the employee to serve as a receipt. The numbers were intended to preserve anonymity. Boxes were repainted and located in important traffic spots in the plant near promotional posters.

At the start of the program employees received a letter from the president at their homes which described the Ideas for Progress plan and stressed not only the awards, but also the importance to the company and thus to the employee's job of steadily increasing efficiency of operation.

In the first six months of the new system, the suggestion rate increased 50 percent above what it had been and rose 32 percent above the national average. Awards were approximately $20,000, and savings were estimated at $100,000.

While a suggestion program has limited objectives, it also has strong intangible values in establishing that management is listening and is interested.

Harnessing the Power of Small-group Discussion

Real two-way communication which overcomes the curse of bigness and impersonality must go deeper than casual talk. E. I. du Pont de Nemours

& Company decided seriously to explore employee opinion on a nation-
wide basis in the middle 1950s. Its program was a classic in careful
planning.

The Problems   It is a very large company, operating all over the
United States with thousands of employees in many plants, ranging from
scientific workers to sweepers. It was one thing to tell supervisors and
employees that costs were rising, competition for sales was intense, and
the premium on high and rising productivity was never greater; it was
quite another thing to get employees to adopt the problem as their own
individual responsibility; to visualize their own role in solving it; to
originate ideas for improving performance within their sphere of action;
and to accept ideas for change introduced from outside of their own
operational group. Chain-of-command orders may impart information,
but they cannot create cooperation, imagination, and a genuine desire to
be of help.

It is widely recognized that small-group discussions within operating areas provide one of the best ways of give-and-take two-way communication; yet such discussions have their dangers, since, unless well
planned, they may be a wandering waste of time. Dominant leaders may
offend participants, and ignorant or uninterested leaders may disgust
them. "Getting to know you better" sometimes results in less respect and
interest rather than more. Even to maintain effective small-group discussions in a large multiplant company requires the training of many adroit
discussion leaders, almost every one of them converted out of present
middle and lower management. How was this to be done?

The Solutions   It was decided to hold discussions within certain
departments, for example, sales, engineering, plant management, research, and plant-personnel management. The objectives of the discussion training were to be to save time in meetings, bring out more ideas,
solve on-the-job problems, build a sense of participation, improve decision making, and build acceptance for management policy. A headquarters institute was set up in which 160 employees were given a forty-hour
training program in discussion. Classes were limited to groups of eight.
These employees then returned to plants and other company locations
and gave a fifteen-hour similar training program in discussion-leading
techniques to more than 4,000 du Pont managers and supervisors.

The main points stressed in the training were careful preparation for
meetings, stated objectives, stimulation of full participation, keeping a
neutral role for leadership, staying on the subject, and getting partici-

pants to put ideas in writing as a means of forcing concrete thinking. Through focusing on these objectives, meetings moved to results in a pleasant atmosphere, and people got to know, respect, and like one another better. The main problems remaining were for leaders to stay neutral, since the nature of supervisors who lead discussion is to be dominant, and to stimulate participation by members of the group who, either through caution or shyness or indifference, took little part. Some problems, of course, cannot be solved by such discussions. Certain personal situations demand a private approach; and certain matters of broader company policy should be recognized as being beyond the group's proper authority. In initiating this program, the company had no intention of abdicating its responsibility to run the organization, nor did employees expect it to do so.

The benefits were many. The executive in charge of one of two plants in which a pilot plan of the program was first tested said:

> We don't want people just to take orders. We want them to have a part in many job decisions. We have a lot of operators who are doing more than just working with their hands. They are intelligent people who are closest to the job. They see these problems first and often come up with the best answers.

Other Means of Two-way Communication

Surveys of public opinion (employee, stockholder, or community, for example) are in themselves a two-way communication device. The surveyor not only learns what is thought but also gives the thinkers a chance to express themselves in telling. Reports on the results and action, if any, are usually welcomed by participants.

Letters to the editor of company publications, to which careful, considerate answers are given, are another form of response. The writers are listened to, and others with the same thoughts who might have written felt that they, too, have been answered. The editor must be prepared to respond to all sorts of questions, not just to the nice ones!

Mass meetings are a less effective form of two-way communication, because when a group gets beyond the small-discussion size of eight or ten, the opportunity for questions is limited by the patience of the mass, and only the more courageous or less wise are likely to talk much. Nevertheless, when carefully and democratically run, mass meetings are better than straight published pronouncements. Planted questions may be necessary to bring out points and to get the ball rolling.

Tours with well-trained guides, committee participation in planning and executing events, and employee representation of the company in civic activities outside the walls are other ways of achieving two-way communication.

There are many good ways of handing down orders and information (bulletins, newspapers and magazines, public-address systems, large mass meetings, radio, and television, to mention only a few), but it still remains difficult, costly, and time-consuming to devise comparable ways of achieving *upward* communication. Yet effort expended upon it will be well worthwhile because of its profound effect in producing receptive attitudes and willingness to listen.

THE PRINCIPLE OF REACHING YOUR OWN PEOPLE FIRST

The front line of communication frequently consists of your own employees or the members of your organization. Not only do they constitute a significant public in themselves, but they also engage in effective word-of-mouth communication with other publics, and their actions frequently speak even louder than words. The old saying that "a man is known by the company he keeps" is reversible into "a company is known by the employees it keeps."

Moreover, employees should feel that they enjoy a special communications relationship with their employer. The relation of friendship cannot, of course, be fully achieved in the bigness of modern organizations, but an approach can be made and will be appreciated.

Information   Every employee is regarded by friends as an expert on the company. Patients in a hospital often confuse the orderlies with the head surgeon; the employee who handles a minute portion of a chemical process is supposed to be informed upon the most abstruse details of modern chemical manufacturing; and the one who refuels the airplanes may be regarded by friends as an expert in aviation. This confusion is particularly noticeable in the large cities, where many of us now live and where private life and professional activity are so often separated.

Under these circumstances, most people are ashamed to plead ignorance of their jobs when their friends question them, and it is only kindness to provide them with enough facts about the huge process in which they are engaged to enable them to discuss their work with enthusiasm and accuracy. Nature abhors a vacuum, even an informational vacuum. If correct information is not provided, misinformation will flow in to take its place.

The data given need not be elaborate; sometimes they can be very simple. A large grocery company had 1,400 supermarkets in twenty states with 40,000 full-time and 20,000 part-time employees. Its annual report for employees one year consisted of a 2½- by 4-inch wallet card with a capsule history of the company and description of its size on one side and a division of its sales dollar on the other side. Another annual report was in the form of a grocery tape 1½- by 7 inches in eight pages telling the story of the previous year's sales.

Many companies distribute full annual reports to employees just as they do to stockholders, while others carry information of this and other matters in employee newspapers and magazines. Whatever the method, the objective is the same: to help employees to present a better image of their company to the public. The informed employee is likely to be a better public relations representative than the one who has to confess ignorance and that no one has ever bothered to tell him or her.

The worst situation of all, of course, develops when outside people learn of company developments through the public press before employees have yet had a chance to be informed, and then ask them questions to which they must confess ignorance. This really results in a loss of face!

The World's Biggest Company Picnic

Communication with employee publics is not entirely verbal; actions often give the basis for communication. In 1975 R. J. Reynolds Industries, Inc., of Winston-Salem, North Carolina, decided to hold a picnic for hometown employees, their families, and company retirees. Before it was over the day-long event hosted 50,000 persons.

The logistics of an event like this (seven tons of barbecued pork, 50,200 pieces of corn-on-the-cob, 100,000 ice cream bars, or 10,000 gallons of soft drinks, for example) or the arrangements for entertainment including country music stars, auto racing, and an amusement park with twenty different rides for children are a big job in themselves and took an eleven-member committee to administer. The event filled a fairgrounds and an adjacent university stadium. Every contingency such as rain, accidents, or fires had to be considered and provided for in advance, even if the precautions turned out to never be needed. There is no excuse for lack of foresight.

Everything went smoothly but the value of the event lay in its communication as much as in the good time enjoyed by participants.

Figure 12–7 Probably the world's biggest company picnic was held by R. J. Reynolds Industries in Winston-Salem, North Carolina, in 1975. About 50,000 people attended the fairgrounds event.

Sharing a common activity gave all employees something in common to talk about. The picnic was also the talk of the city and its area. Because of its size the picnic was news elsewhere in the nation and was covered on press wires and by broadcasters. Special arrangements were made for reporters to visit the party.

Gulf Oil's "Crisisport"

Multiplant companies and other organizations with many offices face a particular communications problem—whether to try to centralize all news and crisis handling in some high office at headquarters or whether to allow local plant managers to deal with the press at the local level. Carried to the extreme neither practice is entirely satisfactory. If all press questions must be referred to a distant headquarters for answers, local reporters and broadcasters miss deadlines, fail to get the company's side of the story, often report one-sidedly simply because of the pressure of time. Moreover, they lose their respect for local company officials because, obviously, they lack the authority to say anything important without an OK. But if local managers are allowed complete freedom to meet the press they may say what they don't mean, look incapable, and say things which are not in keeping with overall company policy.

Large organizations frequently vacillate in handling this problem. Often by omission of definite orders local managers acquire considerable freedom, especially in dealing with press inquiries on noncritical matters. Then some day a distant plant manager says something to a national news medium like the *Wall Street Journal* that causes headquarters in New York or Pittsburgh or Los Angeles to hit the roof and issue an edict that henceforth *all* statements must be cleared through the president or at least a central public relations office.

The trouble with such rigid centralization in times of fast-breaking news stories is that it usually just doesn't work. It is too slow and lowers the stature of local plant managers in the eyes of the press too greatly. But if local plant managers are to be given more freedom and responsibility, they need more training and information. To do this was the decision of The Gulf Oil Company in the early 1970s.

Gulf's public relations department took a year to devise a training program which would have the right degree of realism. It was apparent that one could not just lecture mature, responsible managers with a "do this" and "do not do that" approach and expect any real learning or participation. Gulf sought the advice of its public relations agency, Burson-Marsteller, which had already designed similar training programs for other U.S. firms.

The result was a one-day role-playing series of seminars in which fifty managers were divided into smaller groups and then confronted simulated public relations problems. One group, for example, got a newspaper (an actual printed dummy) in which the lead headline was about the firing of a Gulf employee because he had "threatened" to disclose plans for a new oil terminal the company was planning to build. Another mock newspaper headlined the sudden emergence of a committee to oppose offshore oil drilling near a refinery town. The managers were given extensive facts about the situation and asked to come up with their solutions which were presented to the whole group. In each instance the facts included that the local manager had been absent or unavailable for comment to the press. The same program was followed in Spanish for some of Gulf's Latin American facilities.

At the noon luncheon, more trouble erupted. Featured speakers turned out to be actors who took Gulf over the coals for misdeeds in consumer relations or race relations. There was a city council meeting on an anti-pollution issue and a simulated refinery fire.

The confrontations were tough. Some people lost their heads or their tempers. Television interviews were sprung on participating managers without warning and reporters fired unfriendly questions. But out of

Figure 12–8   An actor hired to represent a black activist confronts Gulf Oil Company local managers at one of the "Crisisport" sessions designed to show how to handle difficult public relations problems.

it all came not only a willingness to learn but an anxiousness to do so and much of the public relations responsibility was returned to the local plant level where it belonged. Distant "spokesmen" by their very nature lack credibility with the local press or audiences but local managers are known. Headquarters clearances now are required only when the facts are company-wide and beyond the knowledge of the individual plant manager. If clearances are needed, they can be obtained speedily to meet news deadlines rather than going through committees and legal staffs for days until they are very minor news indeed.

An organization which gives additional public relations responsibility to its local heads must be ready to accept mistakes from time to time, just as local managers might make mistakes in areas such as finance or processing in which they have been given considerable freedom. Managers' reputations now rise and fall with their public relations wisdom as well as with their performance in these other fields. Since they have probably not been taught this in the past, it is a responsibility of their organization to aid them toward better handling of these situations. It cannot properly hold them to account otherwise. With the increasing importance of public relations in management generally, such training will doubtless become more common in academic business courses in the future.

Because of the special problems of oil spills from tankers and in marine unloading terminals that followed the great increase in sea transportation of oil in the middle 1970s, Gulf originated a similar program for key ship officers and refinery personnel. This was called "Bad Day at Bunker Point" and involved not only what to do in case of a major spill but also how to handle the public information needed. "No comment" was ruled out at the beginning as a solution.

The idea evidently spread. In July of 1977 the chairman of another big oil company, California Standard, told a meeting of broadcasters that the U.S. oil industry was a glaring example of the failure to communicate and that about 200 California Standard executives had recently gone to a school to learn how to be interviewed by reporters.

"I told my people I don't want any more 'No comments' given to the media," he said. He said he realized they might stick their feet in their mouths occasionally, but told them they wouldn't be chewed out for making a comment.

"No one in our company has been criticized because they said the wrong thing. They are criticized if they say 'No comment.' "

THE PRINCIPLE OF FACING THE FACTS

Uncompromising honesty in facing an unpleasant situation is usually the best procedure if communication is to be established. The American public and its news media respect forthrightness and courage. Straight talk builds a reputation for reliability, which gains attention and promotes belief in the communicator who is known to practice it.

The San Francisco Bay Oil Spill

It was a foggy night long before dawn on January 16, 1971. The *Arizona Standard* tanker inbound crashed into the *Oregon Standard* outbound, rupturing its hull and loosing 840,000 gallons of fuel oil into the harbor. No lives were lost and the two ships drifted to anchorage just inside the Golden Gate Bridge.

A worse place for an oil tanker collision could scarcely have been found. Thousands of people could see the spreading oil slick from their homes or as they went to work. San Franciscans are fiercely proud of their bay which had been celebrated in songs, pictures, and stories ever since the days of Brett Harte, Mark Twain, and Jack London. The ecology movement was just getting into full swing and the city had hundreds of enthusiasts. Standard Oil of California which owned the tankers was headquartered in San Francisco. The city swarmed with news media.

Immediately after the collision about 2 A.M. two sets of company activities immediately went into effect.

Telephones started ringing beside the beds of top Standard Oil operating personnel. Each immediately called five others by a prearranged plan. Within an hour a military-like campaign, mobilizing several hundred different pieces of cleanup equipment, hundreds of company workers and thousands of volunteer workers was under way. It had been planned a long time before and on a scale large enough to cope with an oil spill one-fifth larger than actually occurred. It would take three weeks to accomplish and cost a great deal of money.

At the same time a parallel activity was taking place in the company's public relations department. Immediately after the accident the phone beside the bed of the company's press relations head began ringing as newspapers and broadcasters sought to establish the facts. By 7:30 A.M. the downtown news office of the company was open and by midmorning the deluge of media phone calls had caused a near-breakdown in communication between the San Francisco company news office and its own reporters calling in from the scene of the accident and from a refinery where operating personnel working to contain and remove the oil spill were headquartered. Special telephone line arrangements were made and then twice a day public relations staffers started issuing a miniature newspaper of their own telling what was going on from the different cleanup fronts. These were delivered by hand and by a business teletype wire reaching the newsrooms of more than thirty northern California newspapers. This avoided the jam of giving the same facts by phone to scores of news people as they called in.

Radio stations wanted live voice tapes to broadcast. Television asked for live experts to appear on newscasts and talk shows. To provide a qualified company employee for each of these broadcasts for several days was out of the question because most of them were actively engaged in the cleanup so several boat trip press conferences were offered in which Standard hired a boat to go to the scene and a knowledgeable company operating official accompanied it to give information, answer questions, and be interviewed for print or broadcasting. Then came panel television shows in which Standard officials fought through hostile questions.

With all this there was a barrage of phone calls from the general public and special inquiries from boaters and beach operators. There was a predictable rush by nature lovers to rescue and scrub birds which had ingested oil and company public relations handled this, too, since the more general clean-up occupied all other efforts. This was, by and large, unsuccessful since most of the birds died from eating oil or from the shock of being handled and scrubbed.

The main public relations object of the company was to let people know what was being done and to convince them that Standard would do its best to clean up the mess promptly.

It would not be enough just to do the job—it had to be known. The lessons that Standard public relations people drew from their experience included these:

Be pessimistic—prepare for the worst. Be sure that your company has disaster plans in detail ahead of time.

In advance of an emergency select and train operating people who have ability to communicate effectively at press conferences and before television cameras. Let them have authority to speak as the need arises. Public relations personnel cannot always be there nor will the press always be satisfied with talking to them. They'll want higher-ups.

Get acquainted with the people who will be in charge *before* a disaster happens. It's necessary for you to know each other beforehand.

Have an emergency plan for public relations people also—where to get them, how to get more help if needed. See that the press knows how to get them too. Assign staff coverage jobs.

Plan how to communicate when telephone lines jam. Citizens-band radios might be useful.

Keep in close touch always with your top management so you know what they're doing and what they may have said to the public.

The rewards can be considerable. Within a month after the crash, San Francisco newspapers were noting that Standard had done a good job of cleaning up and that a lot of the hysterical accusations which almost said that the company had staged the wreck for profit were silly. One religious publication pointed out that if we insisted on using oil for car fuel and for making electricity to run our televisions and washing machines we could expect some mishaps in its handling. A local daily pointed out that the tanker accident in which no human lives had been lost but about 3,000 birds died had gotten reams of publicity but a big highway accident in the fog about the same time in which six people were killed, twenty badly injured, and twenty-five cars and trucks destroyed had scarcely been noticed and asked what our sense of news values was. Letters of appreciation for the cleanup job were received.

None of this could have happened unless news of the cleanup effort had been made widely available without attempt at concealment or delay.

Fire Blanks Out 173,000 New York Telephones

A telephone is something that you don't miss until you don't have it. Then if you're expecting a call from your husband as to when he'll be home to dinner, or a call from a woman friend, or if you're running a business which depends on phone calls for orders or information—you're blank!

That's what happened in a 300-block section of lower Manhattan in February of 1975. As many telephones as there are in the state of Vermont stopped working for eighteen days. This was less than 6 percent of New York City's phone service, but still it was the equivalent to the loss of all telephone service in a city of 250,000 people. It didn't affect the rest of the city unless you wanted to call in or out of that area, but within the silent zone messages had to go in person or by letter only.

The cause was a fire in an eleven-story regional switching center building. It apparently started in a short circuit in a basement vault and never flared into a big blaze but ate its way stubbornly along lines of cable insulation hidden in conduits up through the entire tall building. It was hot, intense, smoky and very difficult to get at. Sixty pieces of equipment and 700 firemen took 16 hours to put it out and the black smoke could be seen all over the metropolitan area. In a public utility interruption such as this, operating restoration efforts and public relations work very closely.

Even while the fire was going on phone calls in the rest of the city which would normally go through the burning center were rerouted so that most service was halted only briefly. Then vans containing extra pay phones were moved in large numbers to streets just outside the area served by the lost exchange. Store fronts near the burning building were

Figure 12–9   Fire blazed for 16 hours in New York Telephone's Second Avenue building decommissioning 173,000 lower Manhattan phones. Mechanical repairs were an operating problem but providing emergency telephone service and public information were a public relations problem. Courtesy Tri-County Photo Service, Inc.

rented to provide information to residents. Limited switchboard service was provided for hospitals, police precincts, a public power company, and two large department stores. But it would be two or three weeks before service could be restored to most customers.

Calls went out for aid all over the Bell systems in the United States. Soon some 3,900 telephone company workers, many from other parts of the country, were working around the clock to repair the damage. Equipment was flown and trucked in from all over the country.

But since days and weeks are a long time to be without phone service, communicating this activity to the public was of equal importance. The press needed complete information at once.

Residents of the affected area could call free to a special number from the pay phones ringing the region and get a constantly updated recording of the situation in either English or Spanish. Announcements were run on eleven radio stations telling about this service. Special advertisements appeared telling about temporary service aids available and what to do in case of emergencies. 36,000 special flyers were distributed. These were in English, Spanish, Chinese, and Yiddish and also contained maps showing location of emergency coin phones. Posters were also used.

A few days after the fire, a service was set up by which people outside the affected area wishing to reach someone in it could call a special number (requiring one hundred operators to handle) and leave their name and number to be called along with the name and number of the business or professional person who was asked to call them. Then messengers from a city youth job project were hired to deliver these requests. About 80 percent of them got through. (The service was not extended to private individuals because of the impossibility of getting enough messengers.)

Telephone company volunteers helped get groceries and medicines and carried messages out for persons in the area who were blind, sick, or otherwise disabled.

All of this and more was constantly reported by the press which was given tours of the rebuilding while Bell people were constantly available for information and interviews. Coverage was extensive but friendly. When service was restored to the affected area banners were placed on the rehabilitated building celebrating the completion of the repair work and ads were run thanking customers for their patience.

In this program AT&T, the parent company of the Bell Telephone companies all over the United States, had a message: The quick restoration of service was made possible by the large national resources which the local New York company could call on both in expert personnel and equipment. It was the same message that has been featured in previous natural disasters such as hurricanes. The natural conclusion would be that the Bell companies were better able to give service as a united organization than they would be if split up into smaller companies as some have advocated.

Figure 12-10 When the job was done it was properly celebrated and publicized so that everyone would be aware of it. Customers were also thanked for their patience during the three-week blackout. Courtesy Tri-County Photo Service, Inc.

The Black Hills Flood

The Black Hills, rising to an elevation of more than 7,500 feet in western South Dakota, are a well-known tourist attraction. Borglum's huge sculptures of four American presidents adorn one of the granite peaks in the pine-forested mountains. A great gold rush occurred there in the late nineteenth century with accompanying wild west stories. A noted

Passion Play depicting the last week in the life of Jesus is held in a Black Hills town every year. More than 2.5 million tourists visit the Black Hills every year and tourism constitutes the second largest source of income for South Dakota—next to agriculture and ranching.

On June 9, 1972, just as the summer tourist season was beginning, it started to rain in the mountain canyons of a portion of the Black Hills immediately above Rapid City, a city of 43,000 people and the largest in the area. Because of unusual weather conditions which might happen once in a hundred years 14 inches of water poured down in a small area and the resulting flood swept into Rapid City at the base of the hills drowning 238 people, leaving 5,000 homeless, sweeping away roads and buildings. Immediately the news flashed over the nation and tourist cancellations poured in and thousands more doubtless made up their minds that there was no point in visiting the Black Hills that summer. On top of the loss of lives and perhaps $100 million dollars in property damage, the area would now suffer a great loss in its $300 million an-

Figure 12-11 A sudden flash flood in a portion of the Black Hills of South Dakota was bad enough in the damage it did. But a more serious loss of tourist business threatened the whole area, when in fact the destruction had been confined to a small area. Courtesy *Rapid City Journal*.

nual tourist business which was the chief source of income in the Black Hills. Everyone in the nation knew about the flood disaster but only South Dakotans appreciated the full extent of the coming tourist disaster.

Flood losses were largely within an area a half mile wide and five miles long in and near Rapid City. Other damage in the Hills (which cover an area bigger than Delaware and Rhode Island combined) was small. A few roads were closed, but good alternate roads existed to reach main attractions. Even in Rapid City itself out of 2,630 rooms available for tourists only 200 were destroyed. Most places in the Hills had received only moderate rains and were actually brighter and greener than usual, with full lakes and flowing fishing streams.

The public relations problem was *how* to get this information to prospective visitors as rapidly as possible. The chief burden fell upon public agencies and business associations since the usual tourist services are small and local. It was a state-wide concern since rumors had areas hit which were many miles away.

One of the first to tackle the problem was the Communications Division of the State Highway Department. Swift action included contacting all national news wire services and telephoning every major media news editor in the United States.

In an emergency such as this more help was needed so a national public relations firm headquartered in New York was hired to assist.

All nationwide travel agencies were contacted with the facts. Over 250 radio and television public service announcements by the governor of South Dakota were mailed to major national broadcast stations and a good percentage of them were used.

Within three days a press conference was set up in which the state governor and mayor of Rapid City made a plea that vacationers not cancel their plans to visit the Black Hills. There was no attempt to minimize the damage but rather to state the facts and ask for aid in the form of planned travel and not gifts.

Nearly 2,000 copies of a press release from the Highways Department giving facts on roads and attractions were mailed. The tourist and highway departments of neighboring states such as Wyoming and Montana which also profit from Black Hills business were urged to join the effort and did. Over 150,000 copies of a hurriedly prepared color folder, "The Black Hills Today . . . After the June 9th Flood" were distributed throughout the country. Statements were solicited from the U.S. Secretary of the Interior, Secretary of Agriculture and South Dakota's two U.S. senators because their names also made news.

Phase two of the highway department's flood effort dealt with the more long-range objectives. Influential news and travel editors were invited to the Black Hills to see for themselves. Many of them did so and their stories reached more than 80 million readers and viewers. When an area has been in the news (even bad news) there is such keen public interest that an invitation such as this will get a good response when in normal times it would not, so bad news offers a public relations opportunity as well as a problem.

More teams of South Dakotans were organized to travel to the state's major tourist market areas for radio, television, and newspaper interviews. This reached perhaps 48 million people.

Major national publications such as the *New York Times* were contacted with feature suggestions on South Dakota. Interest generated by the upcoming candidacy of South Dakota Senator George McGovern for the U.S. presidency helped in this.

A paid radio spot and outdoor advertising program was started. A tour package of the Black Hills was developed with a nationally advertised rent-a-car company.

Families touring the Black Hills were photographed and (with permission) their pictures and quotes were sent back to their hometown newspapers (largely in smaller places).

South Dakota residents were urged to invite a friend to visit the state by sending in names to the Highway Department which then sent a packet of tourist literature. Owners of hotels, restaurants and other tourist services were given "thanks" buttons to wear while at work—the purpose being to thank tourists who did come to South Dakota that year, usually in conversation following questions about the purpose of the button. A second round of market tours was planned in which the governor and the Rapid City mayor would visit five tourist market cities to thank people for their aid in coming to see the Black Hills in 1972.

As a result of this effort the feared tourist disaster did not happen. Indicators such as vehicle counts on state highways indicated an increase of about 5 percent in travel over the year before the flood and by the end of summer most tourist attractions in South Dakota were reporting nearly normal business.

Even more important was the effect on the future. The American Society of Travel Writers scheduled its next years convention in South Dakota. Press interest in the state continued strong. By quick, adequate public relations not only was a secondary loss by the flash flood avoided but the area emerged stronger than before.

THE PRINCIPLE OF COMMUNICATION BY
PERFORMING A NEEDED PUBLIC SERVICE

As noted earlier, elements of "action" frequently occur in communications programs and this is true of the following cases—cited because their main element of approach was *communication* which gained attention by being obviously in the public interest. The fact that it also served its originators is incidental.

The American Academy of Pediatrics

There are about 20,000 doctors of medicine in the United States who specialize in the care of children. Their national professional association is the American Academy of Pediatrics (AAP). The Academy has a small communications and public information budget, in 1974 about $200,000, and most of this is spent on internal communications and membership programs.

But there are still huge health problems among America's millions of children that doctors see all of the time in their practice but which they as individuals are powerless to solve. Among these are preventive programs such as disease immunization, nutrition, and child safety. Much of the time pediatricians deal with the sad results of failure in these programs as they attempt to save the lives or health of small children who are already ill, malnourished, or injured. "If only parents and others could be persuaded to take preventive action in time," thousands of doctors have often said to themselves. There is no question as to the public need. But a tiny budget could do little to reach the millions of parents and others in the United States who are responsible for the health and safety of children. Others must be enlisted in the effort.

In 1974 the need resulted in a nationwide health education television program entitled "An Ounce of Prevention." The 15 minute program could be expanded to a half-hour by local stations using interviews of comment from local pediatricians. The following year it was extended to a full half-hour broadcast. The series provided information on poisons, ear infections, tooth decay, nutrition, and immunizations. Money for the production was provided by a grant from the Kellogg Company of Battle Creek, Michigan.

Other separate television programs were then developed with AAP aid by stations in individual areas such as one in Boston on child nutrition or a one-hour special on being a father shown on PBS stations throughout the nation.

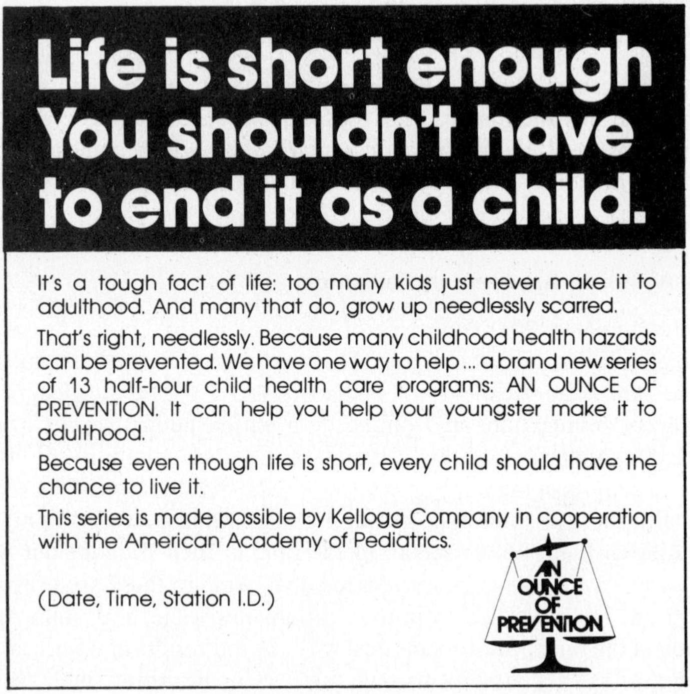

Life is short enough You shouldn't have to end it as a child.

It's a tough fact of life: too many kids just never make it to adulthood. And many that do, grow up needlessly scarred.

That's right, needlessly. Because many childhood health hazards can be prevented. We have one way to help ... a brand new series of 13 half-hour child health care programs: AN OUNCE OF PREVENTION. It can help you help your youngster make it to adulthood.

Because even though life is short, every child should have the chance to live it.

This series is made possible by Kellogg Company in cooperation with the American Academy of Pediatrics.

(Date, Time, Station I.D.)

AN OUNCE OF PREVENTION

Figure 12–12 The American Academy of Pediatrics developed a television film series on child health. This newspaper ad was to be used by local stations to promote watching it.

The message was also conveyed in short public service spots on subjects such as polio immunization (which had declined alarmingly) and hyperkinesis accident prevention. These were paid for by drug manufacturers and others in the health field. They contained no commercial identification of any sort and were widely used without charge by television stations performing their public service function.

Then an Immunization Action Month program was set up in cooperation with the U.S. Center for Disease Control. Its goal was to increase the proportion of children immunized against polio, measles, mumps, rubella, diphtheria, tetanus, and pertusis. This was done through widespread publicity of all sorts funded again through manufacturers in the health fields without public identification or credit. The national effort consisted of newspaper and magazine coverage as well as broadcasting, all of a public service nature and without space or air cost. The local effort tied in with this often included interviews and statements by local doctors and health and school authorities to the same effect. Facing a huge problem, the common interest of doctors, public health officials, and manufacturers of products used in health maintenance was linked to provide a communications approach large enough to have some effect upon the situation.

As the Director of Communications and Public Information of the AAP said:

"Budgetary and staffing restrictions should not prohibit the initiation and development of solid public information programs when cooperative partnerships can be established with industry, other associations, and the government to achieve mutually beneficial objectives."

The New Milwaukee Art Center

Increasing the use, and hence the support, of cultural activities is the key to their growth and even survival in these times of increasing costs. Symphonies, opera companies, and art galleries can no longer thrive on the largesse of a few wealthy patrons, important as they may be to their development. Public relations is needed to arouse widespread interest.

This was the situation in Milwaukee in 1975 when for the first time the city acquired adequate exhibit space in the form of a new $7 million addition to its smaller art gallery which would enable easy public viewing of many works which had previously been in storage.

The city had had an Art Institute since 1916 which had been enlarged several times but the great breakthrough came in 1970 when a wealthy Milwaukee woman offered her private collection of art, then valued at $11 million, to the Art Center and further added $1 million in seed money to start a subscription toward the cost of a new building to house it and other works. In four years the additional money was raised and the new building constructed—something that a city better known for breweries, baseball, and industry could well be proud of.

The need now was to make thousands of new people in Milwaukee proud of it also, to get them to visit it, take part in its activities, and to support its future development. Many Milwaukeeans regarded the art gallery as a place where the elite met to be photographed and reflected in the newspapers. A research survey showed that the Art Center was little known or thought about by most Milwaukee people. The new building dedication in September of 1975 offered a news handle opportunity to try to change this.

The theme developed was *THE WORLD OF ART FOR EVERYONE* in the *new* Milwaukee Art Center.

An artist was commissioned to develop a four-color cartoon layout depicting fun and people participating in art enjoyment at the new Center. This was used on posters, letters, brochures, calendars and in stuffers which the public utilities sent out free with their bills. Portions of it were used on buttons.

Early in 1975 forty top executives and reporters attended a news conference telling about the Center's plans, problems, and goals. Numerous stories and broadcasts followed.

When the date of the public opening and dedication approached in the fall, a two-week long opening program was announced in which different events and aspects of art were featured. Guest stars visited the city for interviews and there was widespread publicity.

To do all this required the knowledge and manpower of a local Milwaukee public relations firm which was hired for the occasion. Cultural institutions frequently have their own public relations people who can handle day-by-day events but they cannot staff for such special events as this.

Figure 12–13 The new Milwaukee Art Center needed to be well known and well used by the public in order to perform its function and to prosper. This Scottish band was a part of the opening ceremonies.

Coverage of the dedication by the local news media, as might be expected, was widespread and friendly since they had been aware of the program and supported it from the beginning. But the real accolade arrived a few days later when a writer for the *Chicago Daily News* said:

> Historically, the Chicago art world has not regarded Milwaukee as a part of its larger field of attention. That is a euphemism for indifference, and if the attitude reflects a certain lack of intellectual curiosity down here, it also attests to a traditionally quiescent scene up there.
>
> The second half of that equation, however, has just changed, abruptly and markedly. Any Chicago buff who has not seen the Milwaukee Art Center since last week had better refrain from talking about it as if he knew what is going on there.
>
> It is a virtually new place—and, all in all, a vastly better one. From now on any Chicago neglect of it is this city's loss, not Milwaukee's. . . ."

The story then went on to describe at length the development and attractions of the new center.

Approval from nearby, overwhelming Chicago, was gratifying but the most important results of local publicity were seen in changes like these:

> Attendance more than doubled in the Art Center's theater.
>
> One hundred Art Center group tours were booked in the three months following the opening as compared to only 400 in the preceding *six years.*
>
> Public attendance increased 300 percent in the same period and 500 individuals and families opened subscribing memberships. Art Center classes filled or overflowed.

Continued efforts will be needed as new people come onto the scene and earlier impressions fade. But momentum is easier to maintain after a great step forward has been well capitalized upon.

Preserving Historic Annapolis

Vigorous public communication over a long period of time is necessary to preserve the historic character of an area which is urbanizing and changing. In many instances the effort was not even made and decades ago expanding cities tore down and covered over their historic areas—areas which have, in many instances, since decayed and been reduced to slums and parking lots. Only a few isolated historical buildings remain. In other cases more isolated rural towns have decayed until little remained and their restoration, while authentic and well worthwhile as in

Williamsburg, Virginia, has been largely new building. In even more instances largely brand new "old towns," artificially aged, have been created on new or vacant sites, often kitsch and fraudulent with mixed styles and a high degree of commercialism. All kinds of mixtures of the preceding also exist; the public is not very discerning about which is which unless told. It would probably make no difference except that false *visual* history is just as untruthful as false *written* history and can cause those learning from it to be quite mistaken in their understanding of the past and, by extension, of the present and future. That is what honest history is all about.

Figure 12–14 Preservation and redevelopment of historic areas requires public relations for support and understanding. This is in Corhnill Street in Annapolis, Maryland, which has had a famous historical site preservation program. Courtesy Division of Tourist Development, Maryland Dept. of Economic & Community Development.

The little city of Annapolis, Maryland's capital, escaped most of these problems until the 1950s because, while the town was important, it was also small and grew slowly. Shortly after the American Revolution, although the site of the Continental Congress in 1783–1784, Annapolis had only 2,000 people. Even in 1910, while places like nearby Washington, Baltimore, and Philadelphia had grown to be great cities, it had only 8,600 people but by 1960 Annapolis rose to a population of 23,000 and was growing up rapidly. It was close to big cities, on a beautiful site on Chesapeake Bay and highly attractive to boaters, weekenders, tourists, and even full-time residents. Real estate prices (and taxes) rose and local property owners had started selling declining historic buildings which had quietly served many purposes for a couple of hundred years for high prices to be torn down and replaced with hamburger stands, motels, marinas, and office buildings. Unless somebody did something, old Annapolis would soon disappear forever.

Something was done. In 1952, 240 concerned citizens met to form Historic Annapolis, Inc., and to protest city council zoning procedures that threatened to rip away all protection for Annapolis's historic buildings. Then in 1957 the group raised $25,000 to move a home, built in 1722, by Charles Carroll, author of the Maryland Bill of Rights, to the campus of nearby St. Johns College where it could be preserved. Other steps, both legal and financial, followed. Organizations such as this usually have little money and frequently encounter opposition from those who do—or who see a chance to make some quickly. By necessity they communicate through meetings, talks, mimeograph and cheaply printed newsletters, publicity releases and group persuasion. Within twenty years, the Annapolis group was quite successful in its original objectives of preserving the historic heart of the city largely unchanged and enlisted the aid of many members of state government and of the U.S. Naval Academy which adjoins the city.

But new problems continued to arise. Publicity relating the historic preservation created a tourist boom. The fact that historic preservation was good business largely melted the opposition to it within Annapolis itself, but the success of tourism outpaced the city's ability to handle it. More widespread city planning began to be an apparent need also. Local residents began to complain about crowds and parking. It was hard to get the historic preservation movement started; now communication burgeoned so that the problem was how to direct its success. The problem of saving the core of Annapolis did not end but to a large extent succeeded only to be followed by a larger concern.

Not every older area in the United States could do what Annapolis has done. Some cities have nothing to preserve or are so remote from large centers of population as to make it difficult to attract many visitors. But when such authentic success does occur it is based upon persistent communications by dedicated people to an increasingly responsive general public.

THE PRINCIPLE OF STRESSING POSITIVE BENEFITS

Public relations may often be concerned with somewhat philosophical subjects such as economic systems, types of government, the public welfare and education; but such subject matter does not mean that its psychological approach to communications must become high-flown or vague. In most successful public relations efforts, as in most successful advertising, higher appeals to abstract noble sentiments are either avoided or at once backed up with direct answers to the receiver's unspoken query of "What's in it for me?" Such recognition of self-interest should not be shocking because, properly used, it may be more honest and more constructive than other emotional or intellectual appeals.

The Chicago Area Regional Transportation Authority

In 1974 the Illinois legislature passed a bill establishing a Chicago area transportation authority—and then tacked on a provision that it would have to be approved by the voters of the area at a primary election coming up in only sixty-eight days!

There were three million eligible voters in the area. The enabling law on which they were expected to vote "yes" or "no" covered fifty legal-sized pages. The law would set up an organization covering six counties in northeastern Illinois for the purpose of coordinating and establishing systems of public transportation including rail and bus for local travel. It would be supported by fares, by a gasoline and public parking lot tax, by a portion of the state gasoline and automobile registration taxes, and to a minor extent by funds from Chicago or Cook County governments. It could borrow money to be repaid from these sources of income. Its goal was to improve and extend the quality of public transportation in all of the Chicago and suburban areas.

Voters outside the city of Chicago often feared it was to the city's advantage rather than their's; those inside saw it the other way. The taxing powers stirred up fear also. The news media tended to view it as a partisan rather than an economic issue. The long debates in the legislature had solidified viewpoints over the years. A big problem was simply getting its supporters to vote because, although there were three million people eligible to vote in the primary elections on which this proposition was tacked, many of these (including supporters of the transit authority) were not strong political partisans and usually did not turn out for party primaries.

The first problem faced by the public relations counseling firm hired by the protransit committee on the spur of the moment was simply to inform the people of the issue. Ten staff members went to work with the press staging twenty-six news conferences in the region. It was not so important whether news media were for or against the proposal, but rather that they covered it. Aided by more than 150 news releases, feature stories, suggested editorials, endorsement statements, and photo features as well as complete background press kits, they did. More than 200 speaking engagements arranged by a RTA speakers bureau gathered additonal coverage. Buttons, brochures, and posters were also used widely.

The second problem was to get RTA supporters to the polls on election day. (Many a good publicity program has failed because it forgot to garner the votes that it had created.) This took endorsement by local political and civic people.

But the second question in the Q and A brochure issued by RTA supporters was: "What's in it for me?" (The first was, what's RTA?). The answers were:

> If you ride public transportation now, RTA will stabilize your fares, make sure that existing service continues and provide new and more convenient service. If you drive, the RTA will lure enough other drivers off the road to reduce traffic congestion and leave enough gas to go around. For people who do not now use public transportation there will be attractive new services . . . between outlying areas. . . . public transportation is essential to a healthy economy . . . in short RTA means jobs.

In the referendum sixty-eight days after the campaign began there were 1.3 million votes—one-third more than in any previous referendum tied in with a primary campaign. Creation of the RTA was approved by a margin of only 13,000 votes, a small number, but decisive. Without a professional public relations program, quickly mounted and full of information appealing to the public's interests, the result would probably have been disastrously negative.

THE PRINCIPLE OF REPETITION

A common failing in public relations efforts is to quit before the battle has been won. Many a good idea has been abandoned before it could take root because its weary sponsors grew tired of it before a distant, busy public even realized that it existed. What looks like a great outflow of press releases, institutional advertising, booklets, speeches, and films as it leaves an organization, often looks like a few scattered spots amid a sea of other messages every day in the consciousness of recipients—if it makes even this much impression.

There is evidence also that the mere fact of repetition creates a tendency toward belief, because if a thing is heard often enough it gradually becomes accepted as a part of one's mental equipment.

With repetition, of course, a reasonable degree of variety in the basic idea benefits those observant people who may happen to become annoyed with identical repetition. This is particularly true of television spots which are often played over and over because of their high initial production costs and because viewing studies show that up to a certain point they continue to gain total audience attention.

This is undoubtedly true and in the case of commercial product advertising may do no harm. In selling ideas, though, as in public relations, there may be more danger of resentment and it would seem worthwhile to present the same tune upon different instruments, as it were, to avoid boring or insulting the intelligence of your audience.

THE PRINCIPLE OF OVERCOMING REFUSAL
TO PAY ATTENTION

One of the most baffling problems facing a public relations person arises when an audience resolutely refuses to pay attention to attempts at communication or even becomes irritated with them. There can be several reasons.

Sometimes your public perceives no personal ground of concern with the communication. Sometimes the message goes so much against the value system of the public and their social group that it is repulsive. And sometimes the communication may be so threatening that they prefer to ignore it entirely.

A classic case of unconcern occurred a number of years ago in Cincinnati, Ohio, when a tremendous campaign was put on to popularize the idea of the United Nations. A heavy barrage of newspaper stories, radio and television programs, posters, films, and speakers apparently brought no increase in the public awareness of the United Nations or its functions. Surveys after the campaign corroborated this impression. Evidently Cincinnatians simply saw little in the United Nations that seemed relevant to their lives; almost any amount of propaganda in favor it would have been ignored. Simply increasing the amount of promotion would have availed little and might even have served as a irritant, resulting in a negative reaction. A solution might have been to have connected the United Nations in some more direct way with the daily living concerns of the audience.

Mental avoidance of messages because of their unpleasant nature often seems to occur in safety propaganda. Here the tendency seems to be not to understand the message or not to consider it applicable to oneself. The "other fellow" may be a bad driver, but "not I." Under these circumstances scolding is useless, because the receiver feels that the scolding is properly aimed at someone else. Perhaps an appeal to pride or to intelligence would be more effective than an accusation.

Psychological studies have frequently shown that when persons are confronted with a great threat they tend to ignore it or minimize it because it seems too much to cope with. On the other hand, lesser threats can be overcome, so the messages containing them are heeded rather than tuned out.

A good example was the public reaction to the great effort mounted by the United States government in the 1960s to encourage civilian defense against atomic weapons; the magnitude of such a deadly threat caused people to close their ears to it and go about other things.

One of the heads of the U.S. Office of Civil and Defense Mobilization, speaking to a group of public relations people, said:

> ... Civil Defense as a consumer item has almost everything against it. The very concept involves the unpleasant admission that we are vulnerable to attack and destruction almost beyong imagining. ...
>
> But we in civil defense have no choice. *Our* product was created by the nuclear age in which we live. And for the sake of the nation we have got to sell it. ... public disinterest and even hostility to civil defense are just as natural and just as predictable today as the very same reactions were a hundred times before in the course of history under similar circumstances.
>
> There is nothing new about it. The plain truth is that people don't want to be told unpleasant things. That is why people walk away from us when we talk about the possibility of an attack that will involve their homes, their families, their lives. ... If we persist in our efforts to warn people, some of them get mad. The rest take refuge in defeatism. ...

The speaker then went on to propose that civil defense be presented as program which would make America strong, enabling us to have freedom from fear and pressure as a nation, not as a form of personal protection which might not work anyway.

But in a few years American interest in civil defense seemed to die down to almost nothing. Capable observers were divided in their estimates of the situation, some agreeing "What's the use?" or "Let's not look and it may go away" reactions had taken over, others perhaps thankful from a practical point of view that people did not face the problem logically because to have done so might have led to panic or war, but the problem remained.

In dealing with issues like this, public relations people undertake a major responsibility. They cannot always know whether what they are doing will be successful or even if it is the right thing to do. They can, however, understand the psychology of people and respect it.

THE PRINCIPLE OF CONCENTRATING UPON OPINION LEADERS

Faced with insufficient funds to communicate with everybody, public relations workers either aim at specific target publics which are the most important to their goals or resort to the idea of trying to influence leaders of opinion, who, it is thought, will then influence others by their positions or by their writing or speaking.

There can be no question of aiming at specific target publics when the goal is limited; some examples follow. But although the idea of using opinion "leaders" to reach more general publics seems sound enough also, in modern times it faces some questions:

Who *are* leaders of opinion? In the relatively simple society of the early 1900s they might have been the town banker, the leading merchants, the editor, the clergy, and perhaps the teachers. But do people now really take their opinions from these local mentors (if they ever did)? If not, then to whom do they look? Are today's leaders of thought perhaps remote people—television personalities, popular writers, newspaper columnists, or perhaps national political leaders? Or does the public make up its mind in small family or social groups which are not readily distinguishable from the individuals who compose them? Does opinion actually trickle down from leaders to the mass of the public?

Despite the difficulty of identifying today's leaders of opinion and ascertaining their true influence, it is still sound public relations strategy to cultivate the understanding and support of many of them. They are worthwhile in themselves, but even more importantly, they often control the *gateways* of communication. People who speak, write, teach, or preach come into contact with the public regularly and what they say will be heard, whether they advocate it or not.

In addition, these persons and others of respected rank often serve as *validators* of reports as well as means of transmission. "It ran in the *Journal*" or "Professor Jones said so, and she's an expert in physics."

Although it is common practice for public relations practitioners to aim their first efforts in a campaign at opinion leaders before trying to reach more general publics for courtesy and amplification, there are not many examples in today's increasingly democratic society of public relations efforts directed solely at general opinion leaders, but instances of aiming at opinion leaders in specific groups are quite common.

Kaiser Aluminum and Chemical Corporation Investor Relations

For several years in the early 1970s the profitability of Kaiser Aluminum and all other aluminum producers was severely depressed by a worldwide excess of metal capacity and low demand. Financial community opinion leaders became severely disenchanted not only with the current profit picture but also with future expectations in the aluminum industry.

Then demand rose greatly and shortages began to appear all around the world. Prices and profitability increased markedly. In addition, Kaiser had eliminated unprofitable divisions and strengthened profitable ones so that its aluminum division pretax profits almost doubled and earnings per common share of stock increased greatly.

The need was to spread this news rapidly among those who might buy stock in Kaiser, who might recommend the buying of stock, or who might be instrumental in lending it money for development. The method was to reach opinion leaders in these fields as rapidly as possible.

Chief officers of the company made special presentations to institutional investors' groups and financial analysts' meetings. The press was invited to these meetings, same-day press release summaries issued, and speech reprints were mailed to key press and financial analysts.

Interviews were set up with the company president and chief financial officers on financial results and the company and industry outlook with writers for publications such as the *Economist* of London or the *Wall Street Journal* of New York.

An advertising campaign briefing the same facts appeared in financial newspapers and magazines in the United States and abroad.

The company annual report and quarterly reports featured the developments and these were widely mailed not only to shareholders but also to financial opinion leaders.

At the end of the first year's effort a one-day press seminar attended by twenty-five trade press and financial writers and editors was held to discuss the prospects of the aluminum industry.

This was not an unusual program. Many companies have acted similarly. But it was timely and effective. The news would have spread anyway, but less rapidly and completely than if opinion leaders in the financial area had not been fully informed first.

Coca Cola Protects Its Trademark

How much of the value of a firm such as Coca Cola is to be found in its right to the exclusive use of the registered names "Coca Cola" and "Coke"? Obviously many millions of dollars, because if anybody could produce a similar product and sell it under these names the buying public would be confused. The millions that the company has spent in advertising and selling its product would be dissipated and others who had invested little or nothing would gain from the popularity that it had laboriously built up over many years. An established trademark is often the largest asset of a company, especially in a competitive consumer goods field.

But how could such a trademark be lost? Is it not registered with the United States government? If someone else tried to use it, would there not be a suit and if the Coca Cola Company could show that its mark had been used without its permission would there not be a cease and desist court order and an award of damages?

The answer is "yes"—with a general exception that leads to a Coca Cola Company public relations problem with a certain group of opinion leaders. (A problem which all other companies, such as du Pont or Minnesota Mining and Manufacturing Company, also holding valuable registered trademarks share.)

If a trademark has become so widely use that it is synonymous with the generic name of that type of product in public usage, and especially if the originator has let it become so without a defense, it can pass into the public domain of the language and anyone making a similar or identical product may call it by that name, since this is general public usage. For example, if all cameras over a period of years came to be called "Kodaks" and the Eastman Company did nothing to correct the misuse, the names in time would become synonymous. Then anyone producing a camera could sell it as a "Kodak" since the meaning of the terms was generally recognized to be the same.

This has actually happened in many instances. A registered trademark can be "lost" if a company permits habitual use of its brand name by the public as a general term. For example, "Thermos" was once a valid trademark owned by the Thermos Division of King-Seeley Company, but it was habitually used by the public as a generic term for every "vacuum-insulated" bottle so eventually the courts ruled that "thermos" (with a small "t") had become a synonym for any vacuum-insulated bottle, and other companies were permitted to market thermos bottles.

Many other trade-marks have been similarly lost, among them shredded wheat, aspirin, corn flakes, milk of magnesia and cellophane.

A company defends its trade mark by noting with a small circled "R" under it that it is registered, by capitalizing the word or words so registered whenever used, by being especially careful to do this in its own communications such as advertisements or house magazines—and by constantly trying to correct others who use the trademark in a general sense. The Coca Cola Company, for example, will always object when it sees or hears the name of its product being used as a description of all similar soft drinks. This is for the court record if it should ever come to that, but since most misusers that the company becomes aware of are writers and editors, a notoriously touchy group of opinion leaders, this defense also presents a public relations problem.

When a newspaper clipping with "Coke" used with a small "c" comes to the Coca Cola offices a polite letter goes to the editor asking him or her not to do it again and explaining why. Most editors know why but may still be irritated and in any case will resolve not to give the product any free plugs in the future (Coca Cola doesn't want them without a capital "C".) The same applies to broadcasters where, because the words are spoken, not written, the use of the specific trade-mark for the generic product lies in its context of meaning.

To overcome these feelings and to further defend its trade-mark, the Coca Cola Company runs advertisements in trade papers usually read by writers and broadcasters.

In addition, to keep on good terms with writers and broadcasters, the company takes booths and distributes free Coke at conventions and engages in other goodwill activities. If an editor really gets angry about a "correction" letter, a company vice-president has been known to hop on a plane in Atlanta and fly out to west Texas or wherever to further explain the company's position. Frequently brochures explaining the need for trademark protection and how it can be done are sent to the news media, since staffs change all of the time and a new group of writers is always arriving.

No one can accuse the Coca Cola Company of not defending its ground. The problem is how to do it constantly and with tact.

"Coca-Cola" and "Coke"
Trade-mark®   Trade-mark®
Our trade-marks have endured stock market crashes, world wars, the nuclear age, and would be imitators.

But can they endure the typewriter?

Ahh, that's the key to our survival! For the typewriter, has many means of destroying us.

For example, there's the hideous torture of being lower cased to death.

Or the painful demise of strangulation through pluralization.

Or, worse yet, the agony of being stretched on the rack of the possessive.

These are the nightmares which keep our lawyers awake and trembling at night. They're strong, courageous men, who will go beyond the call of duty to protect our trade-marks. But alas, even a trade-mark lawyer has his breaking point.

So please. Watch your typewriter. All you need remember is our simple trade-mark rule: **"Always capitalized, never pluralized, never possessive."**

The Coca-Cola Company

Figure 12–15 Protecting trade-marks is also a public relations problem. This Coca-Cola ad was used in magazines which go to newspaper writers and editors.

The Forest Industries Council

Unlike oil or minerals, trees are one of the few renewable natural resources that America has. Forests not only provide building lumber, but also paper, resins, and the base for chemicals. In the future they may provide an increasingly important source of energy in alcohol liquid fuels. They are an old way of converting solar energy into practical energy.

In the past generation, also, forest management has changed greatly. Tree farming has replaced random cutting. The South has become an important source as poor crop lands have been replaced with trees that mature within a few years. Faster-growing trees have been developed and large areas that are otherwise agriculturaly nonproductive can be planted in trees and harvested year after year without diminution of supply.

The public relations problem is that much of the public doesn't know this or how it is done. Most of America's largely urban population only sees trees in parks where they are carefully preserved rather than being cropped. People are raised on an early conservation belief that nothing should be disturbed including dead timber and diseased trees. The idea that forests should be planted and harvested just as wheat or corn is somewhat repulsive and "unnatural" to some. People are concerned about the fate of the birds, bears, and deer in managed forests. They have the mistaken notion that America's forests are being depleted and that greedy industry is responsible. They do not understand the process of recycling paper and think that it is largely to "save" trees.

There are, of course, occasional legitimate reasons for conflict such as the preservation of public parklands or streams and these need to be fought out on a case by case basis. But there remains a general informational need about the role of forests in modern America.

In the early 1970s the Forest Industries Council addressed itself to this job. The communications effort was directed initially at opinion leaders such as journalists, government officials, educators, and professional people; in addition to forest users such as hunters or hikers, industry employees, stockholders, and wood product users such as builders or printers.

Means used included advertising in special interest publications for these groups, booklets, films, television news features, forest and mill tours, film strips, and teaching materials. Some of the larger forest products companies, such as Weyerhaeuser, had excellent public advertising which had been used for many years.

THE PRINCIPLE OF PRECONDITIONING AN AUDIENCE TO A VIEWPOINT

The most effective public relations communication often takes place not *after* issues have been joined, but *before*. When a discussion reaches the stage of controversy, the participants are apt to shut their minds to additional information unless it happens to agree with their own convictions. Then it is usually too late for any amount of communication to influence them; in fact, an overdose may have a strong negative effect.

Sides have been chosen and positions publicly taken from which it is not easy to back down. Friendships and social group approvals back up the rigidity.

Good public relations communication well in advance, however, may provide the framework upon which decisions are later reached. Thus the ability to foresee coming issues and directions of thought becomes of extreme value and is another reason why the expert public relations practitioner should be something more than a wordsmith; just as in politics the distinction is between the opportunist and the statesman. This is why the would-be public relations expert needs a broad general understanding of human beings and our times as well as the specific means of communication. The problem is *what* to say and *when* to say it as well as *how* to say it.

THE PRINCIPLE OF HARMONY OF ALL COMMUNICATIONS

In today's busy communications world, filled with multitudes of symbols and words, an organization cannot afford to give a scattering appearance of itself, either visually or in thought, if it is to be noted and remembered. Because we see only at a glance, graphics or a few words need to be reinforced whenever we come across them. An organization must assume a clear name-style and graphic appearance and then see that it is used widely throughout its communication of all sorts. In this way one impression aids another.

Hawaiian Air

For some years this busy inter-island airline had painted its planes in unimaginative stripes and its other identifications similarly nonrepresentative of Hawaii. Then the company hired a well-known San Francisco design firm to create something that would be attractive and typify the glamor of the islands that it serves.

The result was a striking, warm-colored head of a native girl against a flowing hibiscus flower. The name of the company, "Hawaiian Air," was changed to a stylized block of capitals reminiscent of early Hawaiian native architecture. As shown in the illustrations, this design was used on the planes themselves, on ticket folders, drinking cups, stationery, and even on the flight attendants' uniform buttons. It was, of course, used in advertising and in the many other media in which the company came into contact with the public.

Since all airlines fly the same sort of planes and perform similar transportation services, the problem is how to give airlines a personality

Figure 12–16 An organization must have a good visual image to be remembered and it should be used throughout the organization. First, Hawaiian Air redid its planes.

Figure 12–17 Then the same visual device was used in ticket folders and pocket calendars. Courtesy Jeanne Riesman, Staff Photographer, Walter Landor Associates.

Figure 12–18   Even in drinking cups . . . .

Figure 12–19   . . . And, of course, on stationery . . . .

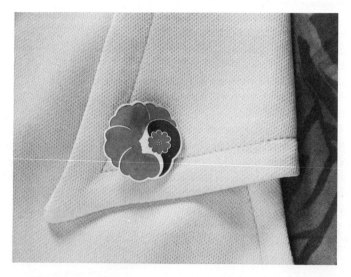

Figure 12–20   . . . And even on the pins that flight attendants wore on their coat lapels.

which will be easily remembered. A striking design and its consistent use throughout all company communications, visual or written, is the first step.

Sherwin-Williams Changes

The Sherwin-Williams Company started in Cleveland, Ohio, more than a hundred years ago when two men of those names began producing and selling ingredients from which customers could make their own paints, as was customary in those days. Because they sold everything necessary to make many colors in 1870 they decided to adopt a chameleon as their company trade-mark. This little lizard, it will be recalled, has the ability to alter its color to match the object upon which it happens to be sitting at the time.

But after a number of years Sherwin-Williams began selling ready-mixed paints in various colors, so in 1905 it adopted a new trademark that was so well promoted that it became among the ten best recognized in the world. It consisted of an inverted paint can with the initials "SWP" on it pouring paint over the globe with the words "cover the earth" on the gooey paint dripping over the globe. It was a graphic idea and easily remembered.

In the 1970s, however it became increasingly apparent that a new insignia was needed. The company had expanded into areas such as adhesives and chemicals. Surveys showed that most people thought of Sherwin-Williams only in terms of paint and that, for whatever reasons, it was better known among older people than younger. The nonpaint operations of Sherwin-Williams felt themselves orphans and were increasingly driven to explain or to assume their own identity. A well advertised and accepted trademark was becoming a liability to company expansion and diversification.

Changing a corporate identification should never be done lightly. Too much of the worth of the concern is tied up in its well-known name. There is the great danger that the old familiarity may be lost and the new title not well recognized—a disastrous situation. So the Sherwin-Williams changeover took several years. First came research into the images of the old trade-mark; then pretesting of a proposed new design. When

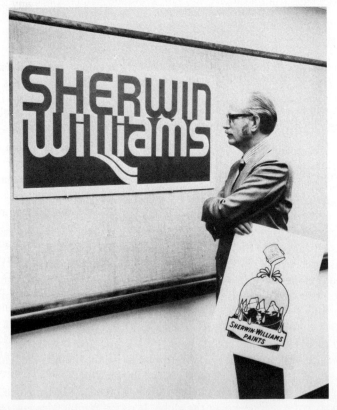

Figure 12–21 Sherwin-Williams Co. had a good insignia as long as it was primarily a paint company, but diversification into other lines demanded something not so restrictive. The president of the company looks at the new corporate symbol.

this proved satisfactory a department had to be created to see that all of the new material needed, such as signs, letterheads, store identifications, and advertising, would be ready at the right times. Then all employees had to be informed of the change, reasons for it, and the timetable.

The whole effort took more than two years from the time the project was started until the time it reached the retail markets and more time would be needed for the followup. Substantial advertising accompanied the change. Everything from labels to truck signs had to be altered at as nearly the same time as possible so that old insignia and the new one would not be conflicting any more than was necessary.

The new trademark was not particularly startling, as can be seen from the illustration. But it was clean and forceful and preserved the century-old company name and made it easy to extend it to many kinds of products other than paint.

Prudential Insurance Company

Over the past decades there has been a steady trend toward visual simplification of trademarks. In an earlier Victorian day, flourishes and complexity were thought to indicate reliability and "class." But as visual competition increased in magazines and newspapers and, especially, in television, simpler, more forceful designs stood out better and were remembered longer. The rise of self-service supermarkets in which customers walked by rows of shelves and hundreds of products all striving to be seen was another reason. Nowhere is this better illustrated than in the insignia of the Prudential Life Insurance Company of America.

As shown in Figure 12–22, around 1896 the company had a rather detailed engraved trademark with descriptive material on it as well as the slogan: "The Prudential Has the Strength of Gibraltar." Then about 1945, the ribbons and selling material along with the clouds were removed but the slogan was retained. This lasted for twenty-five years but someone must have been getting increasingly concerned about the military impregnability of the famous British fortress. After all, the empire had declined, the Spaniards were increasingly noisy about getting the rock back (which the British had taken from them in 1732), and this was an atomic age. So in 1970 the slogan was dropped and the rock alone retained. In 1976 this was farther stylized, almost in the manner of a wood-cut, and the bold, underlined name "Prudential" was added. (By this time the company was in many fields of insurance.)

With all these changes went the necessity of harmonizing all company communications with the changing insignia.

Figure 12–22   Trade-marks evolve. In 1896 the Prudential Insurance Company symbol was quite elaborate. By 1976 it had been simplified to that shown at the bottom.

SUMMARY

Fifteen principles of effective communication:

1   Humanize-identify in terms of people if possible.
2   Suit the message and means of communication to the audience.
3   Speak the receiver's language.
4   Be timely.
5   Dramatize communications.

  6 Use two-way communication.
  7 Reach your own people first.
  8 Face the facts—even when it is hard to do so.
  9 Perform a needed public service.
10 Stress positive benefits.
11 Repeat if necessary.
12 Overcome refusal to pay attention.
13 Concentrate upon leaders of opinion.
14 Precondition the audience to your viewpoint.
15 Keep all communications in harmony.

Look at communications from the receiver's viewpoint. Public relations persons who put out a large number of news releases and stories, hold conferences, make motion pictures, and engage in many activities may seem to themselves and to those near them to be creating quite a bit of communications material. The receiver gets only scattered bits now and then unless he or she is connected with the organization in some way. The material sent out may be both plentiful and of absorbing interest to the producers, but how does it look to the receivers?

Sometimes effective communication is achieved by the happy coincidence of accidental common interests; successful authors and editors who happen to publish at the right time feel that the gods have been propitious. But public relations workers, having more fixed objectives, cannot rely upon such fortunate circumstances and instead must use imagination to seek out areas in common with those to whom they want to speak.

Chapter 13

Evaluation and Evaluation Cases

Ascertaining the results of a public relations effort is, for a number of reasons, the most neglected branch of the art. Such evaluation is difficult because it deals with that most difficult of things to measure—changes in human opinion. As Burns W. Roper, a partner in the nationally famous Elmo Roper and Associates research firm, once said:

> Measuring public relations effectiveness is only slightly easier than measuring a gaseous body with a rubber band. Unless a person is in some way personally connected with a company, he is not very much concerned about the company. When a message is beamed at him about this company, he doesn't stop everything and pay strict attention. Thousands of messages are beamed at him from other companies, the government, his wife, his boss, his kids, his friends, and many of these messages come much closer to the mainstream of his life. How can you measure the effect of a particular flyspeck in this person's life?

Because it is difficult, evaluation of the results of public relations is also expensive, and once an organization feels that a public relations effort is reasonably successful, it is usually disinclined to spend a lot of money to estimate the degree of its success. Besides, public relations people live in a constant press of work and new challenges. The natural tendency of the business is to say, "What can we do next?" rather than to examine past results.

Many variables are involved. In the natural sciences, controlled conditions for an experiment can usually be relatively easily established; but human thought takes place in a constantly changing environment in which not all the factors may be known. It is often extremely hard to say that "this" caused "that," and yet some such connection of cause and effect must be a goal of public relations activity evaluation.

Empirical evidence of change frequently seems quite adequate, and it may really be so, for practical purposes. Scientific studies of opinion change are of the most value if done periodically, in order to keep a continuous record of change, and they are even better when norms are available for comparison. An absolute figure, such as "Ten percent of the people said they believed this," may not tell much. Is that good or bad? If it was 20 percent or only 5 percent last year, and if the norm of other similar companies is 15 percent this year, then the figures give us something to go on.

But with all these problems, the future of public relations, of many a public relations person, and to some extent of the social sciences themselves, depends upon an increasing ability to evaluate the results of communications in affecting the opinions and attitudes of recipients; and difficulty is no excuse for giving up.

If a simple, 100 percent effective way of evaluating changes in attitude or opinion is not within public relations workers' grasp, nevertheless they should make certain attempts.

The first is personal. At least annually they should evaluate the success of the work in order to measure their progress and to set new goals. If they find this study hard, then perhaps the difficulty itself is an indication that they need better evaluative procedures.

Next they should employ various empirical and scientific methods of research. It may be hard to get the money to carry on this work. Perhaps funds should not be spent on evaluation that could be spent on action or communication; on the other hand, perhaps nothing is more important. The choice depends upon the internal circumstances of an organization.

In any case public relations persons should be humble. *If* people think better of their organization than they did before, perhaps their efforts, out of a great many other stimuli, had something to do with the change. *If* they think worse, perhaps other factors overcame their best efforts. (No one can tell for sure how much worse it might have been with no efforts). And once in a while they may have to mutter to themselves in a moment of truth, "That set of boners really hurt"; because occasionally, though not often, public relations efforts do harm instead of good.

AN ANNUAL AUDIT OF PUBLIC RELATIONS EFFECTIVENESS

Just as a business measures material progress in its annual report, so a public relations management may profitably engage in stock taking at least once a year. What are employee attitudes now as compared with those noted a year ago? Did our activities have anything to do with their change? How about community relations? Press relations? Consumer relations and relations with schools and colleges? Stockholders? Government? Dealers and suppliers? Others?

Sitting down to supply the answers not only forces public relations to account for time and money spent; it also makes it face its problems anew, ask what has changed, and consider what the course should be from here on. Evaluation inevitably creates plans; and public relations *must* be in the forward-looking vanguard of any organization.

Planning and looking to the future are not things that alert public relations people do in their spare time; these functions are almost their main reason for being. Such plans and forecasts may not always be accepted, but if they are not in the forefront of thinking, with ideas well buttressed by facts showing what has been accomplished and what is still needed, they are failing their function as the public eyes and ears of the organization. In the full circle of public relations activity, evaluation inevitably becomes the research which leads to the next steps of action and communication (unless it is a one-time program which will never be repeated).

EMPIRICAL EVALUATION METHODS

The whole business of asking "How successful were we?" in a field so hard to measure as the effect of persuasion upon public opinion is fraught with peril. No other investigation brings with it a greater tendency toward self-delusion, wishful thinking, and the vanity of being overimpressed by what friends say or of thinking that because much was issued, much resulted.

Several types of empirical evalution are constantly in evidence:

Faith   If we issue sound statements and if they are read to any great extent, we tell ourselves that they must have some good result. We can check readership fairly easily if we go about it in an orderly fashion, but we cannot assume that the desired results followed. Probably they did; usually such an empirical assumption is valid, but we cannot rest entirely upon it. For example, people who know more about something do not always like it better.

Random Evidence   Column inches of publicity, mail returns, comments, field reports, requests for participation—all are valuable in showing that something is happening, but they do not tell exactly *what* is happening inside people's minds, and they may reflect intensity rather than breadth.

Associated Effects   Suppose that employee turnover diminishes after the installation of a good employee communications program. Should the public relations person rush right in and claim credit? Probably not; cautiously, if at all. Too many other factors may have been at work—worsened jobhunting conditions, better wages, increasing age of the work force, for example. The communications program may well have had a part in stabilizing employment, but other factors may have helped even more. Some year an even better program might be overwhelmed by a combination of unfavorable factors. What would one say then? *Post hoc, ergo propter hoc* logic cuts both ways.

An association of effects may appear in many fields. Suppose that management seeks an increase in the number of stockholder proxies returned and that after a better stockholder information program is instituted, the number of proxies returned increases. The cause-and-effect relationship is probable, but not certain. Or suppose that a series of company meetings is held, that they are well promoted, and that attendance is good. Did public relations promotion do the trick? Or could people have attended for other reasons? Suppose that a company magazine has a good response to a reader contest. Surely the enthusiasm is evidence of the quality of the magazine! True, but it may also be evidence of the trust and attachment of employees—an attitude which has been built up by enlightened management, good supervision, and benefits over many years. Suppose that the good public relations of a company seems greatly to enhance the effectiveness of its advertising (as it frequently does); again many factors may be at work. The public relations chief will be not only truthful but also politically prudent if modest; many other workers have had a hand in this success.

Opinion Conferences   One empirical method of measuring results is to get special groups together and to encourage them to let you have their candid views—groups such as the press, educators, and clergy. If they're convinced you really want frankness and if they are not afraid of retaliation or of hurting your feelings, such informal soundings may be highly worthwhile.

Insurance   One thing we shall never know in most public relations practice, because of the many factors involved, is the answer to "What would have happened if we hadn't used this program?" Any theory is bound to be speculative. The probable answer is "Nothing much—except that things would have been a little bit worse . . . and the year after that they would have been still worse . . . and in future years yet worse." The business of making human impressions is both slow and continuous. The sins of the parents are visited upon the children down to the third and fourth generation, and youngsters in school today are still damning corporations because of errors in the Teddy Roosevelt era. Only the very wise who expect to be in business a long time look far ahead.

SCIENTIFIC EVALUATION METHODS

Empirical methods are not all bad if their limitations are considered; neither are scientific procedures.

It is often fairly easy to measure the receipt of a message; it is much harder to measure the resulting response and attitude changes. One way is to poll comparative groups, one of which has been exposed to a program and the other has not. But if such a method is used, it is best that the test group not know that it is being used as a test group; otherwise its interest in the subject will be alerted to an abnormal degree and will make its reaction unrepresentative. The reaction of a test group is open to suspicion, because in simple before-and-after measurements with the same people the first exposure may blur the second attempt.

Depth interviews, semantic differentials, and other fairly complex psychological tests on selected comparable groups may often yield good results, but at great cost in arriving at a conclusion that often seems

almost self-evident from an empirical viewpoint. Most corporate managements are not enthusiastic about spending too much money in after-
the-fact-evaluation. They would rather use it as an underpinning to some
new venture.

Select Your Own Methods—But Evaluate

In thinking about public relations, no one ever forgets the phrase known
as *communications,* and today almost everyone is familiar with the need
for *action. Research* as a basis for action and communication is becoming quite commonplace too, but examples of careful *evaluation* are still
rare.

Evaluation is the new frontier of public relations, and the practitioners who can present valid evaluation of their work are certain to get a
reputation as pioneers and to prosper accordingly in their own wisdom
and professional standing. There is a keen hunger for evaluation, and it
is in the area of development of human relations that it is most promising
and important.

THE CASE OF THE TELEPHONE COMPANIES

Of all the business in the United States, the various operating Bell
Telephone Companies of AT&T and some other telephone companies
such as General Telephone and Electronics, undoubtedly do the best job
of keeping their hand upon the public pulse. They not only *think;* they
know what the public feels about more than a score of aspects of telephone service, all the time and for many years back. Because of this
knowledge, they keep little trends from becoming big troubles, and they
avoid major mistakes. Almost every step of telephone activity is constantly analyzed.

If this care seems excessively meticulous, consider what is at stake.
Basically the telephone company has only one thing to sell—service.
Telephone service is of necessity a monopoly, but not necessarily a
profitable monopoly or in private hands. If service were to decline seriously, if public regard for its efficiency and good citizenship were to
diminish, it could always be nationalized. Private-enterprise telephone
service exists on sufferance, good will, and the public conviction that it
administers a monopoly of telephone conversation at least as well as, and
probably better than, a government body could.

In 1959 the president of Illinois Bell Telephone Company, said:

> The Bell System, together with the rest of the telephone industry, has a
> reputation for being progressive, efficient and useful to our economy—

which reflects both our imaginative technology and traditionally superior service. Our communications system is looked upon as an outstanding business achievement representing the best of free enterprise in America. This is our heritage. It represents the work of many telephone people over more than three-quarters of a century of industrial growth in America. This was largely an era of individualism in business with *material values* playing a significant part in the philosophy of industrial management.

Today we are operating in a new kind of business climate. More and more, people are measuring business character to the extent to which it respects *human values*. People in this sense include representatives in government, educators, the press, the clergy, our customers—in fact much of our population. . . .

It's timely, therefore, that we appraise our concepts of management . . . to see how well we reflect this new order of things in our decision making. . . . The overall quality of our service, as we measure it, is better now than it has ever been. But in spite of this we are often criticized for the manner in which we deliver it. We are sometimes referred to as a cold, impersonal monopoly that has a rule for everything. And why is this? It may be because we do things in ways that cause people to think we are not sufficiently considerate of human values. . . .

The information about public attitudes to which the president referred came, in large part, from a constant series of evaluations, some of which are detailed below.

AT&T Continuing Customer Attitude Surveys

Almost every year since 1946 some form of customer attitude survey has been conducted by AT&T in addition to numerous one-time studies by various Bell System operating units throughout the country. In this way it has been possible to keep track of customer attitude trends, both for *research* into what may be needed and for *evaluation* of public relations programs in effect, as well as the effect of changing operating procedures by the telephone companies and changes in the general public-attitude climate.

This concern began a long time before 1946. In December, 1883, Theodore N. Vail, then General Manager of the American Bell Telephone Company in Boston, Massachusetts, wrote a letter to managers asking the following three questions:

Is the telephone service as it is now being furnished, satisfactory to the public?
. . . are the relations between the public and the companies improving?

Where there has been a conflict between the Local Exchange and the public, what has been the cause of the difficulties and what has been the result?

The "Service Attitude Measurement" surveys which began in 1946 consisted of mailed questionnaires. Although they provided useful guidance there was increasing concern that they were not entirely accurate. About 45 percent of those receiving surveys did not respond. What was the attitude of this group? There was no assurance that the respondents were the ones who had the experiences reported. It took a long time for the questionnaires to be returned and they did not reflect changes over a precisely measured period. Bad experiences of a long time ago were related as if they were recent and many people wrote so much that it could not easily be tabulated.

Beginning in 1971 the customer opinion interviewing was shifted to the telephone, with careful safeguards to see that the subject was willing to be interviewed in this way and was the person most familiar with the situation regarding the use of the telephone. Proper sampling procedures and adequate numbers continued to be observed.

The interviews were designed to take as little of the customer's time as possible and those responding were asked how they liked the telephone method, to which a high percentage responded approvingly.

This method not only cost less; it was also timely and better able to take advantage of detailed computer analysis. Special questions could be added in particular areas where different situations existed.

The fundamental objective of these continuous telephone surveys was to provide managers in the various regions with a useful outside perspective on the quality of service that they were rendering. The companies might have their own standards of accuracy, speed and cost, but were these the same as the public standards? What were the public expectations of their telephone service? How were they changing? And how did the companies measure up to these expectations?

In earlier surveys the focus had been on setting national company norms to which all regional managers had access and by which they might measure themselves. Now the emphasis was shifted to keeping close, constant track of what telephone users in each region expected and how the service of each regional Bell company was fulfilling those expectations. In some regions, for example, expectations for speed in service were higher than in others for historic and social reasons. The important thing in these areas was to continue to meet these expectations and the fact that someone elsewhere had more relaxed criteria was not the main point. Cost expectations might vary similarly.

Because they knew how they stood and how they were progressing, local managers and other employees could develop a sense of proprietory responsibility as they saw how their actions and policies affected their customers.

Trends were a main point. If, for example, the attitude toward some aspect of service grew increasingly unfavorable, what was the reason? Customer comments might provide an answer, but often the customer was dissatisfied and not able to point to a corrective action needed to affect improvement. (After all, the *user* was not in the telephone business!). It was up to management to find out and to act.

To do this they could be aided, upon request, by increasing the size of the sample to get more information on particular pockets of discontent, by adding special questions to the regular survey, by cross-related breakdown of the results which was easily provided by computer, and by special regional studies if needed.

Managers are often puzzled by fluctuating results in such surveys. They were informed that slight variations of a few percentage points each month up and down might not be significant; the important thing was the trend over several months or longer. They were also given a table to show the normal variations that might be expected in survey results depending on sample size. For example, in a survey of 200 people, if 95 percent of them were reported as saying something or other a variation of 3 percent one way or the other would not be significant.

This continuous monitoring of customer perception of telephone service served as a check upon corporate policy decisions, a guide to allocating resources, a guide to internal practices, and a basis for informed discussion with consumer groups and regulatory bodies.

In addition to this general continuous survey special questionnaires on customer reaction are constantly used in special cases such as telephone installation or repair and operator services to probe response to recent specific contacts.

A More Specific Problem

The customer is not always right in dealing with public utilities. There are those who don't pay their bills, steal telephones or electric service, or take advantage of free services at considerable cost to other customers since all costs are figured into the general rate base. But in dealing with dishonest or thoughtless customers, public utilities have to exercise great care since, except in cases of outright theft, customers can always gain sympathy by representing themselves as the oppressed victims of a rich monopoly. It is a well-known fact of public relations and of political life that accusations far outrun reasonable answers.

A certain percentage of those who dislike all business or bureaucracy is always ready to turn out and if they are numerous enough or loud enough they may gain political clout with regulatory agencies and legislatures.

One example of customer abuse of a free telephone company service occured in connection with calls made to the operator at no cost for information about the telephone number of other users of telephone service. Almost all of the time these numbers were in the regular telephone directories issued to every customer but the information callers simply didn't want to bother to look them up. Only a small percentage of the public did this, but those who did were habitual. According to one company study it cost 11 cents in operator time alone for each directory assistance inquiry. Since there were thousands of calls, the total expense that had to be charged to other customers bills was considerable.

There were legitimate occasions for directory assistance, of course. Some people could not see well enough to read the phone book listings, others could not pick it up. Sometimes people called from pay phones or motel rooms where directories were not available or wanted to call areas for which they did not have directories. But by far the great bulk of the calls to operators for telephone number information was unnecessary. Getting their numbers down, however, represented a delicate public relations problem.

In the early 1970s it was decided to try a test in Fresno, California, to see if advertising could get customers to cooperate in reducing the number of directory information assistance calls. A pair of television spots were prepared by the telephone company's advertising agency. They featured the message that such calls cost all the users in the Fresno area $40 million dollars a year. Pretesting of the two spots showed that the message came through clearly and caused almost no negative reaction. Radio spots, newspaper ads, and bill inserts were then prepared using the same message and the campaign was launched for eight weeks.

To evaluate its effects a survey of a sample of Fresno customers' use of directory assistance calls and their attitudes toward the service was made a month before the ad campaign began and then repeated in the month after the ad campaign ended. At the same time a count was made of the number of calls for directory assistance actually coming into the telephone company during the period.

After the campaign the volume of assistance calls actually dropped for the next several months by about 10 percent below what it was estimated it would have been otherwise. The ad campaign cost about $14,000 but the five-month cost savings from it were $44,000 in operator wages and benefits.

Of equal interest were the facts revealed by the surveys. Three out of four heavy users of directory assistance recalled the test advertising when interviewed after the ad campaign. The most frequently mentioned place seen was on television. Respondents recalled the message of "looking up the numbers for yourself" and also that "forty million dollars was the cost of providing the directory assistance service." Most felt that the advertising was believable and there was little negative reaction to the ads. Four out of ten heavy users of directory assistance who had seen or heard the ads said they used the telephone directory more often than they did before seeing the ads.

After the advertising 38 percent of the general public said that directory assistance service "costs a lot" for the company to provide as compared to 26 percent who said this before the eight-week advertising campaign. In the same post ad survey 60 percent said they would look up local numbers in the directory as compared with 48 percent before. This shift occurred almost entirely among those who had seen or heard the advertising.

As a check it was noted that in areas other than Fresno where no advertising had been used directory assistance use during the test period increased about 7 percent whereas in Fresno, it declined almost 10 percent.

The advertising had great effect among the heavy users. The average call reduction among those who had been exposed to the advertising was 6 percent but among other heavy users who had not seen or heard the ads the reduction was only 1 percent. Business heavy-user calls declined almost twice as much as residential users—perhaps because business people could see the sense of saving money more.

Not surprisingly, the number of people in the post-ad survey thinking that a charge for excessive directory assistance calls would be reasonable was greater among the general population than among heavy users —36 percent versus 24 percent.

A great deal more useful information was gained from the "before and after" surveys than can be detailed here because they pin-pointed the sources of the problem and suggested what could be done about it. Demographic portions of the surveys showed the age, sex, occupation, and other facts about heavy users—facts which would serve to suggest the most effective advertising approaches and media. Both the survey evaluation and the empirical results showed that the messages worked.

Gaining Acceptance for a New Policy

The Bell system in Fresno used advertising to gain public cooperation in not over-using a service which had been free for a long time. The public relations staff of General Telephone and Electronics Company of Florida, headquartered at Tampa, in 1975 faced what was, in some ways, a more difficult problem because it involved gaining public acceptance, within a limited time, of an action that had already been taken.

GTE of Florida serves 800,000 customers. About 15 percent of them made 80 percent of all directory assistance calls. GTE asked the state public service commission for permission to charge 15 cents a call for all such inquiries beyond six a month. Calls from hospitals, motels, hotels, and from the handicapped would be exempted. The public service commission approved the plan on August 29 to go into effect on October 10, decided to reconsider on September 15, and then took final action approving the charges only on October 6—just a few days before the charging started. Even then permission was finally granted only under the condition that the commission would review the change in charges after a six months trial. This meant that customers had to be informed almost instantly. Their understanding and approval had to be obtained in a very short time so that the plan could be continued.

The job was made harder because all of this vacillating attracted considerable press and consumer attention, much of it of an unfriendly nature. Increases in costs by utilities of any sort are never popular because of their monopoly situation and because the public sees no alternative. The problem was to show that those who over-used the directory assistance service actually did so at the expense of other rate payers. (Although the situation is not comparable, the public attitude problem is somewhat akin to that in the Philadelphia shoplifting campaign given earlier in this book. In each case the defense is made that a rich corporation can afford loss and the answer is that all other customers wind up paying for the losses.)

The objectives of the rapidly developed GTE public relations program under these conditions were: (1) To inform customers of the effective date of the directory assistance charging. (2) Inform customers of the details of the directory assistance charge, including exemptions. (3) Reduce the number of directory assistance calls. (4) To create customer understanding that charging for excessive directory assistance calls would affect only a small minority of customers directly, while indirectly benefiting the majority of customers through reduced operating expenses.

With literally only a few days in which to work before the new charges began, an advertising agency was retained to assist the company public relations staff and a variety of paid and nonpaid communications tools was quickly developed to meet the need. These included telephone bill inserts, a letter and enclosed folder explaining the charges mailed to 2,200 community leaders, a circular delivered to new customers with their telephone directories when telephone service was installed, specially imprinted billing envelopes, advertising in newspapers and on television, news releases, and appearances on radio talk shows.

The newspaper advertising was designed primarily to communicate the details of the directory assistance charging procedure, to answer specific customer questions, and to encourage a reduction in directory assistance calls. The theme was that it costs $5 million a year to provide such service and that with the new 15 cents per call charge beyond six inquiries per month 95 percent of the customers would not be affected.

The 30-second television spots reinforced this message but did not attempt to go into detail for which the broadcast media are not well suited. One of them, for example, pictured the man shown in the newspaper ad talking to an operator and making a long string of directory assistance requests. The voice-over then said "That's why we're now charging fifteen cents for directory assistance calls. But if you're like 95 percent of our customers, you won't pay *anything extra*—because there's no charge for the first six calls each billing period." The camera then focused on the telephone directory itself and the audio concluded: "For better telephone service . . . it pays to go by the book."

News releases were used to give details of the plan and to report its progress. The reasons for the charge and the fact that it had been successfully used in other states were noted.

The bill insert, the "Sun-dial," was used to explain the exemptions from the charges such as who was "handicapped" and how such persons should apply for relief from being billed for their charges. The cover showed a directory assistance operator at work.

A later issue of the "Sun-dial" consisted of a list-sheet upon which frequently called numbers outside the subscriber's own directory area could be written down and kept.

The introductory advertisements were ready only eight days after the first meeting with the advertising agency which prepared them and ran just a week before the new charges went into effect. The original-

When he plays the numbers game he adds $5,000,000 to your telephone bill.

Starting October 10ᵗʰ we're going to do something about it.

Telephone Directory Assistance has been an important service for our customers. But some people and businesses have been taking advantage of it by making hundreds of such calls a month. And most of these calls are for listings that are readily available in the telephone directory.

All of this costs us – and eventually you – more than five million dollars a year. That's a lot of money. Money that could go into providing you with better telephone service.

The new 15¢ charge for Directory Assistance calls

Starting Friday, October 10th, we will begin charging 15¢ for calls to Directory Assistance in the "813" area. *Your first six calls per billing period will not be charged.*

Business customers will be allowed six calls for each main station or PABX trunk. CENTREX customers will be allowed six calls for each eight main CENTREX telephones.

95% of you will pay nothing extra

Almost all of our customers make less than half a dozen Directory Assistance calls a month, including requests for new listings. The new service charge will not affect their bills at all. But we can only maintain this service by charging heavy users for their calls.

These are the exceptions and exemptions

Directory Assistance calls placed from coin telephones or from hospital or hotel and motel rooms will be exempt from charges. And we won't charge customers with visual or physical handicaps who are unable to use the phone book. If you think you qualify, just call your local Business Office and ask for an exemption form.

A good tip: Write the number down

When you obtain a telephone number from Directory Assistance, write it down for future use. Then you won't have to call Directory Assistance again for the same number. In the long run, by helping us, you'll be helping yourself.

GTE
GENERAL TELEPHONE

For better telephone service, it pays to go by the book.

Figure 13–1   Newspaper ads were used by GTE of Florida to gain public acceptance of a directory assistance information charge. This is a much reduced copy of a full page newspaper ad. Television and radio were also used.

Sundial is published by the Public Affairs Department of General Telephone Company of Florida, P.O. Box 110, Tampa, Fla. 33601.

On the cover... Directory assistance operators are presently handling fewer customer requests for phone numbers because of General Telephone's charging plan that became effective October 10. Already, the average daily volume of local directory assistance calls has declined by more than 60 per cent from previous months, with some 500,000 fewer calls being placed each week.

Phone Mart

General Telephone is getting into the "store" business in December with the opening of the company's first Phone Mart store in a retail environment—at the University Square Mall in Tampa.

Phone Mart is a new approach to servicing and distributing residential phones. Customers will literally shop for the phones of their choice at the Phone Mart store, take them home and plug them into pre-wired phone jacks for virtually immediate service.

Future plans call for Phone Marts to be located in other areas served by the company. Customers will be informed of these Phone Mart store openings as they occur.

Greetings by phone

Sending Christmas cards to friends and relatives is traditional. But have you considered the expense? The cost of the card, postage, and your time may be on the average between 25¢ and 50¢. Why don't you call your greetings by phone instead? It may be less expensive. For example, a call you dial yourself to San Francisco after 11 p.m. costs only 22¢ for the first minute, and from Tampa to Miami even less, excluding tax. Time yourself. You'll be surprised how much Christmas cheer you can spread in one minute. So, maybe it's about time you started a new tradition, one that will save you money.

Christmas calling hints

When you place your calls at Christmas -

time, try to do it **before** Christmas Day—traditionally the busiest day of the year for your telephone company. Last year, more than 830,000 long distance calls were placed by General Telephone customers on Christmas Day...a record for the total number of calls placed in a single day.

There are a few ways in which you can assist us in getting your calls through with minimum delay:

- If possible, exchange your holiday greetings before Christmas Day.
- If you must call on Christmas Day, place your calls early.
- Use Direct Distance Dialing (DDD) when possible. Such calls usually go through faster and cost less, too.
- If a call does not go through, wait a reasonable length of time before trying again.

Merry Christmas

That's our wish to you...an enjoyable and safe holiday. Please remember that General Telephone's business offices will be closed on Thursday, December 25, but will reopen the next day.

Who's handicapped?

On October 10, General Telephone Company began charging for calls to directory assistance. The first six calls each month are free; additional calls are billed at the rate of 15 cents each.

Charges do not apply when calls are placed from coin telephones, guest rooms of hotels or motels and patient rooms of hospitals. Also, customers who are certified as being visually handicapped and customers with certain physical handicaps—that would preclude their use of the printed directory—are exempt from charges.

Application forms for those desiring to apply for certification are available from General Telephone business offices.

In reviewing applications, General of Florida uses the following definitions as cited in the Federal Register, June 30, 1970:

- Legally blind—those whose visual acuity is 20/200 or less in the better

eye with correcting glasses, or whose widest diameter of visual field subtends an angular distance no greater than 20 degrees.

- Visually handicapped—those whose visual disability with correction and regardless of optical measurement with respect to "legal blindness" are certified as unable to read normal printed material. (For telephone company exemption, this includes identity of telephone book size characters.)

- Physically handicapped—those who are certified by competent authority as unable to read or use ordinary printed materials as a result of physical limitations. (This also includes identity of telephone book size characters.) Examples of physical disability cited are: loss of hands, or use or control of hands; constant severe tremor, spasticity or paralysis; uncorrectable double or triple vision; incapacitating confinement in an iron lung; severely debilitating conditions such as found in advanced Parkinson's Disease, cancer, and the aftermath of stroke.

GTE
GENERAL TELEPHONE
"An Equal Opportunity Employer"

12/75

Figure 13–2 The "Sun-Dial" is a customer letter going out with bills. The cover shows an operator looking up numbers and the inside explains the costs.

campaign was planned to run for thirteen weeks and then to be continued at a reduced scale as necessary.

But along with the communications program an immediate research and evaluation program was equally necessary to show how the message was getting over and to measure its success. This was needed not only because the telephone company itself wanted to know, but also because it would be important to show to the state public service commission when the six-month trial period was over as evidence for the continuation of the cost-saving program and for its possible extension state-wide.

An independent professional research firm was hired and conducted a telephone questionnaire among a scientifically selected random sample of GTE customers in the area just as the communications program began and before the charges went into effect. This would provide a base measurement for a similar survey some weeks later. Its preliminary results were ready within a week.

They showed that 87 percent of the customers knew there would be a directory assistance charge made soon (doubtless from news of the public service commission hearing that had been going on for a long time) but that 85 percent did not know when it would take effect. Only 59 percent identified the reason as a cost reduction program and only 22 percent reacted favorably to the idea.

The second similar survey was made nine weeks later, after the communications program had been in effect for that length of time. It showed that the percentage of favorable opinion about the charge had risen to 54 percent from 22 earlier. In the second survey 75 percent knew that a number of directory assistance calls were free and 64 percent correctly named six as the number.

In the first survey 59 percent felt that GTE was charging for local directory assistance to reduce costs but in the second survey this figure had risen to 71.5 percent. But there remained a constant hard-core of 11.5 percent who felt that the charge was to increase profits and to rip-off the customer (similar to the Standard Oil Company of California figures cited in Chapter 10). Eighty-six percent of those surveyed in the second questionnaire had no specific misunderstandings about the program.

The important empirical evaluation of both the installation of the charge and of its accompanying communications program was a dramatic 75 percent reduction in directory assistance calls from about 1,000,000 a week to about 250,000 a week. This change began about the first of September before the charges actually started on October 10, and continued after that date before tending to level off. This drop was reported in press releases and in large newspaper advertisements headlined "It's Working—Directory Assistance Calls are now down by more than half a million a week. Here's why that's good news for you." A trend chart was included along with the copy noting that "97 percent of you paid nothing extra for Directory Assistance calls."

Public utilities live in a highly political climate since their profits are to a large extent determined by what public rate-setting bodies will allow

IT'S WORKING!

Directory Assistance calls are down by more than half a million a week. Here's why that's good news for you.

Recently we announced a 15¢ charge for excess Directory Assistance calls in the 813 area.

Since then there has been a dramatic drop in unnecessary Directory Assistance calls.

That's good news for all of us because Directory Assistance calls — most of them for numbers readily available in the telephone directory — have been adding millions of dollars a year to your phone bill. Millions of dollars that could be used to provide you with better telephone service.

97% of you paid nothing extra for Directory Assistance calls.

Since October 10th more than 97 per cent of our customers made six or less Directory Assistance calls, including calls for numbers not in the directory, or numbers in other cities in the 813 area.

As long as you keep helping us reduce unnecessary Directory Assistance calls, you'll be helping yourself.

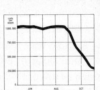

GTE
GENERAL TELEPHONE
For better telephone service, it pays to go by the book.

Figure 13-3 Reporting on a program not only tells people what they want to know but also gains continued cooperation.

them to earn and these regulators are sensitive to public opinion. The managers of enlightened public utilities have long been aware of this situation and have given their public relations staffs commensurate responsibilities.

It seems likely, though, that in recent years more fields of business such as oil and automobiles have in some sense acquired the aspects of public utilities and should consider their public relations problems similarly. As businesses increase in size and their products become a necessity this tends to become the case. The problem becomes not only production or sales but also public understanding and acceptance. In some cases this may be the most important.

Evaluating the Effects of a Special Public Relations Activity

In 1976 Southwestern Bell Telephone Company conducted a survey to try to determine the difference in attitudes toward the telephone company by college administrators and teachers who had participated in company-sponsored College-Business Seminars that year and the preceding year; college people who had not; and a comparison with the general public.

College-Business Seminars are meetings held by telephone company officials with selected faculty and administrators of local colleges and universities. The seminars offer both groups a chance to exchange ideas about company policies, practices, and services. Main topics discussed had included earnings, regulation, competition, and employment opportunities for college graduates.

The mailed survey used in seeking opinions from the college people who had attended the Seminars and those who had not was the same as that used in getting opinions from the general public and had been in use for some time. Thus a comparison was possible with public attitudes and college attitudes and of those college people who had met and discussed these matters with telephone people and those who had not. Trends in general public attitudes were also available because the questionnaire had been used with the general public for some time but similar trend information was not available for the college groups since the seminar programs had not been held for several years.

The questionnaires were mailed to college people in August and September. Despite this poor time when many are absent or engaged in getting school started, the company got about a 60 percent return, which is excellent and much higher than the 47.5 percent return of general public questionnaires the same year. The sample included 253 college people who had never attended a seminar and 93 who had. The rate of return from both groups was almost the same. As in all mail questionnaires the opinions of the nonrespondents in all groups remained unknown so the greatest value lies not in absolute figures but in comparisons and trends.

College people as a group, both those exposed to Seminars and those not exposed, showed many significant differences from the general public; and those college people who had met with telephone company officials personally often had different attitudes from their colleagues who had not done so. For example: When asked how they would rate the quality of the telephone service they were getting, 26 percent of the general public said *excellent* compared with 40 percent of the college faculty or administrators who had attended seminars and 33 percent of the collegians who had not attended seminars. The general public 26 percent "excellent" rating had dropped almost 8 points in the preceding year, which doubtless had given the managment of Southwestern Bell cause for concern.

In response to a question about the telephone company being concerned about the problems of the individual customer 22 percent of the general public rated it as "excellent." (Here, again, the general public rating from the previous year was down by 8 percent.) This was also the response among college people who had not attended seminars. But those who had attended seminars scored it at almost 35 percent. Personal contact in the Seminars seems to have made the difference.

As to whether telephone company employees knew their jobs, 22 percent of the general public said "excellently" compared to 33 percent of the seminar attendees and 24 percent of the nonattendees. On "treating customers with courtesy" the general public ranking was 27 percent "excellent," 35 percent among seminar attendees, and 26 percent among nonseminar attendees. On rating telephone employees on their interest in community affairs 10 percent of the public said "excellent," compared to 25 percent of the seminar attendees, and 15 percent of the nonattendees. So, again, personal contact with telephone employees seems to have made a difference.

On the nonpersonal basis college people were often more critical than the general public. When asked if there was anything about their telephone service that was in any way unsatisfactory 39 percent of the public said "yes," compared to 47 percent of those who had participated in the college seminars, and 56 percent of the college people who had not participated in seminars. The biggest single cause of complaint among all was rates and regulations which was complained about by 28 percent of the public (up a whopping 17 percent from the previous year and a good reflection of soaring inflation costs in 1975), 63 percent of the seminar participants, and 50 percent of the nonparticipants. Personnel troubles ranked second but here the collegiate groups were somewhat less critical than the public.

On "Do you feel that you get your money's worth out of telephone service?" 48 percent of the public felt they usually did compared to 60 percent of the seminar participants, and 52 percent of the nonparticipants. On the other hand, both of the college groups were less satisfied with long distance costs than the general public, perhaps because they used such services more often. Seminar participants felt much more strongly than either other group that costs of extra telephone equipment such as extension phones were unreasonable, perhaps because they had added such extras more often.

About three-fifths of all groups rated telephone company efficiency as high, although seminar participants scored it about seven points better than the others. And on the company being interested in its employees they ranked it about ten points better.

The responses on the desirability of competition in the telephone business were interesting. A total of 48 percent of the general public felt that if the telephone company had more competition the quality of its service would be much or somewhat better. Among former college seminar participants the figure was 44 percent and among nonparticipants 60 percent. This, of course, was a somewhat hypothetical question since public utilities are by their nature regulated monopolies.

Former seminar attendees generally felt more than others that the telephone company was an excellent place to work and hired employees without discrimination on race, sex, or religion.

As to sources of information about the telephone company, word of mouth, telephone people they knew, and leaflets with the phone bill ranked first among college respondents in the nonmass media with television and newspapers coming next. Among the general public the leaflets and television ranked first. All groups (about two-thirds in each case) felt it was an advantage for the local telephone company to be a part of the national Bell System. About 10 percent of the public, 13 percent of the seminar attendees, and 21 percent of the nonattendees said their opinion or large companies was largely "unfavorable."

Reporting of the details of such research could be carried on to infinity, and there is a danger of reading too much into one instance. Continuation over a period of time with different random samples and by different methods would be needed to establish complete validity. But it offers guidance not only to public response to operating procedures and insight into the general opinion "climate" surrounding an organization, but also shows how this may be affected by public relations informational activities.

SUMMARY

Evaluation of the effects of actions and communications remains in most instances the wilderness of American public relations, but it is also the wilderness of the social sciences in general. While evaluation is not an exact science, some businesses and other organizations are doing much to advance its standing and usefulness.

Three steps in evaluation are recommended for public relations practitioners:

1 At least an annual audit to review accomplishments, shortcomings, and goals. This should concern itself primarily not with effort expended, lest inches of clippings or numbers of mailings substitute for results, but rather with evidences of reception and response.

2 The use of empirical methods to check response.

3 The use of more scientific methods of opinion research as explained in Chapter 10. If a more thorough study is desirable, an outside research organization can be employed, and will bring to the work the considerable advantages of objectivity and experience.

The amount of money to be spent upon evaluation depends upon several factors, including the scope of the effort being evaluated, its duration, novelty, and importance to the organization. Internal considerations, for example, the need of support for public relations staffs and the need to present concrete evidence of the worth of their somewhat intangible work, are also important. In some organizations such as utilities, which are generally quite conscious of the importance of their public relations, matters of cost need not occupy more than a minor part of the public relations staff's total time; in others, such as trade associations, they may be a major consideration.

Chapter 14

Worldwide Public Relations Developments

It is commonplace, but nevertheless, true, to say that we live in a period of rapid change. The past few decades have seen the fall of empires, two world wars and several smaller ones, a major depression, the development of automobiles and airplanes, atomic power, intercontinental missiles, interplanetary navigation, a world population explosion, and the realization of shortages in some important natural resources.

At the same time a less-noticed "communications revolution" which began in the 1920s has been racing at an ever-accelerating pace and is perhaps more important than the more spectacular manifestations of human inventiveness and confusion because it brings new ideas to people's minds—and how people think today determines, for good or ill, how they act tomorrow. In a shrinking globe this is sure to have effects upon all of us.

The big change began with radio in the 1920s; this change was accelerated by fast air transport enabling business travelers, government officials, mail, and printed matter to go all over the globe in a few days; was spurred further by great movements of troops and of civilians during World Wars I and II; and is now in a world television phase which is just having its effects. More changes are certain.

One effect of this rapid development of communications has been a "revolution of rising expectations"—observable in many countries.

Consider a farming village in India in 1914 for example. (Or a similar village in other parts of Asia, Africa, or Latin America.) The inhabitants lived and thought much as they had at the time of the Mogul emperors hundreds of years before, or even at the time of Alexander the Great, over two thousand years ago. There were no roads or automobiles. The nearest railroad was miles away and few of the inhabitants had ever seen a train, much less traveled on one. No one went anywhere; no one visited the village; few were able to read and there was little to read anyway. Life was hard and uncertain, but had it not always been that way? Wasn't such the common and necessary lot of all mankind?

But with the communications revolution the genie came out of the bottle! The day the first little radio receiver appeared in the village or the first automobile chugged in from somewhere; the day when some people learned to read and received newspapers, pamphlets, and books, the whole outlook of the village began to change, never to be the same again. People were exposed to a host of new ideas and information which had never been available to them before.

This is a particularly serious problem because it is much easier to bring about a communications revolution which gives people new ideas than it is to satisfy the hopes that these new ideas may generate. To put a simple radio into a village, to ship in some pamphlets and train a few people to read and debate, is a much simpler task than to develop new farming methods, develop new mineral or other natural resources, build factories and establish modern transportation and distribution systems, or to alter conflicting claims and beliefs built upon hundreds of years of experience and prejudice. Such development inevitably takes both time and capital. Communications revolutions inevitably outrun the changes in physical conditions which they set up a longing for, and often, because of rising population, political disorganization, or graft, conditions may actually get worse while the population ardently hopes for improvement!

Even if there were not conflicting governmental and economic ideologies in the world such as various brands of communism, dictatorships, and democracies, it seems likely that we would now be in a period of turmoil and discontent because of the communication revolution, if for no other cause. With such conflicts and the ill will engendered, it becomes doubly difficult to help production catch up with expectations. Nor is this problem confined to the more newly developing nations; it manifests itself in group and even in generational struggles in societies which have been exposed to an abundance of communications for much longer, as in the United States and in Europe.

Another effect of the communications revolution has been to make possible much larger economic business units than before—both within nations and operating internationally. It is easy for managers to travel by air within a few hours to any place in the world or to send duplicated information similarly. Telephone service enables immediate conversations and other means of instant communication are developing. International freight shipments have been speeded and the rise of international banking makes for a world business community. Advertising and public relations have played an important role in these developments also.

Before the practice of public relations can develop within a country, though, there are at least three conditions needed:

1 The rise of industry and a reasonable standard of living, popular education, and literacy. Without these there is nothing for public relations people to communicate about.

2 The availability of mass communications media such as newspapers, magazines, radio, direct mail, and television. Without these there is no way to reach people on a large scale.

3 Freedom to communicate. There is little private public relations practiced in a police state because the government monopolizes all information and persuasion. If public opinion is to count for anything, people must be free to speak their minds to each other.

Generally speaking, the more democratic a country is and the larger it is, the more important the practice of public relations in it will become. Democracy presupposes many persuasions; size makes specialization and skill in delivering them necessary.

Whenever these conditions prevail, the development of private public relations practice is ready to begin. As a public relations man in Holland once observed, "The seeds are always there. It just takes the right combination of weather to cause them to sprout." With a communications revolution underway in the world, the weather has been increasingly right in many places for the past few decades and international public relations has grown accordingly.

THE PUBLIC RELATIONS OF INTERNATIONAL BUSINESS

When an American company sells goods abroad, or establishes a subsidiary company on foreign soil, or when foreign manufacturers such as Swiss watchmakers or Belgian lacemakers or British woolen manufacturers or Japanese automobile or television producers desire to promote their wares in the United States, a host of new public relations problems come into play. As world trade has increased, especially with the lowering of tariff barriers and with the rise of organizations such as the European Common Market, new scope and dimensions have been given to the public relations of international business. Questions are not only economic, such as those arising from the different price of goods, but also political, social, and cultural as different values and ways of thinking meet.

When an American firm, for example, exports its capital to buy a European factory, or when a German or British company buys a concern in the United States, it is sensible to establish as good public relations as possible within the country where the new plant is located. Indeed, much of the impetus for the development of public relations after World War II in Western Europe came from the example of American firms there, especially in the operations concerning oil, aviation, and automobiles. Those who set out to do business in any foreign country face several problems that they might not encounter at home.

Foreigners are automatically suspect. People fear that foreigners may get too much power within their country; local employers may complain that the wage rates offered by foreign-owned firms are too high and that they lure local workers away from domestic firms. There is always the ultimate danger that popular clamor may be organized to lead to government seizure and nationalization of outside-owned plants, sometimes with little compensation. It is no longer readily possible any place on the globe to call in the United States Marines to set things right if such confiscation does take place. Exporting capital without also trying to export some understanding of its value seems foolish.

Good public relations are essential abroad even in the normal course of doing business. There are often natural patriotic preferences for home-produced goods over foreign-owned brands and in a country with a difficult balance of payments problem, these are certain to be encouraged by the government. Local competitors will also take advantage of them. No two countries or regions are alike. Each is complex with its own background and the wisest course for a business abroad is to heed certain good counsels:

   1   Hire good local public relations people if possible. Without years of experience, for example, few Americans can know all the things about a foreign situation that they ought to know, and in any case they are at a disadvantage in public relations compared with native-born communicators simply because they *are* foreigners. Americans show their origin in speech, looks, and ways of thinking. Finding a good local public relations representative abroad is not always easy; in some less-developed countries they may not even exist. An American firm may have to train a foreign public relations person itself, or it may be able to use an established foreign public relations firm or an American public relations firm with connections or personnel abroad. An American business seeking a good foreign public relations person will have to do a great deal of hunting and checking because in many places public relations is even more of an elusive intangible than it is here. There are quacks, front men, frauds, influence peddlers, disloyal or dishonest people in any field, and in the little-developed public relations profession in some countries they are particularly hard to sort out.

   2   Don't expect public relations in Brazil, Italy, Japan, or any other country to be just like public relations in the United States. Not only are there differences in industrial development, but there are also vast differences in social and cultural customs, in the communications media, in the characteristics of opinion leaders, and in the basic patterns of thought and influences upon thought. Some public relations ideas which work well in the United States *may* work well in another country; but, on the other hand, they may fail or even do harm. Before you take action in public relations abroad ask questions and listen attentively. Don't try to tell a foreign public relations employee to do something without getting his or her viewpoint. Another land may have a different sense of the value of time; different ways of measuring money and position; and may very often have an ingrained suspicion of motives. A classic illustration concerns an American oil company which found it could not give away free university scholarships in a Latin American country until it tacked on a requirement that the recipients had to agree to work for the company for a period of years after graduation. The suspicious inhabitants could see through this requirement and accept it; but doing good deeds for the sake of general goodwill was so unfamiliar a concept that no one could believe that it did not conceal some insidious plot such as brainwashing. In the United States a similar no-strings offer would have been accepted without question.

   3   If you hire a good foreign public relations person, spend some time with him or her. He may know his local field, but he doesn't know *you.* Loyalty, interest, and enthusiasm are qualities which cannot be bought—only won. Only personal contact and friendship can engender them, and this is particularly true in many foreign countries where people insist upon liking their employers as well as accepting their pay.

Large American companies doing business abroad usually make it a point not only to visit their foreign public relations employees, but also to bring them to this country to meet executives, to see processes, and to know the company as a group of people rather than just as a name and a balance sheet.

EXAMPLES OF TWO-WAY INTERNATIONAL PUBLIC RELATIONS

The Luxembourg Bank Branch Opening

Celebrating the opening of a new overseas branch at the site of the branch itself is a common enough public relations practice, whether done in the United States or Europe, but celebrating a European branch office opening at headquarters in the United States and then reflecting the events back to the European location as a form of two-way communication is somewhat unusual. This was done in 1973 when Northwestern National Bank of Minneapolis staged a Luxembourg Fair in its downtown Minne-

Figure 14-1 A reverse-twist was given to an old theme when Northwestern National Bank of Minneapolis opened a branch in Luxembourg in 1973—the celebration was held primarily in Minneapolis instead of in Luxembourg. In the background is the Moselle Brass Band flown over for the occasion.

Figure 14-2 A benefit to Luxembourg was the opportunity to promote American tourism by way of Icelandic Airlines which flies there. This gained goodwill back in Luxembourg.

apolis headquarters to celebrate the opening of its new branch bank in the Grand Duchy of Luxembourg in Europe.

Attractions in Minneapolis included gifts of roses for those attending, exhibits and pictures of Luxembourg, a brass band composed of players flown in from various Luxembourg towns, and a motion picture by Icelandic airlines which flies from the United States to Luxembourg. The Luxembourg ambassador to the United States, the editor of a Luxembourg magazine, and a representative from the country's tourist office in New York were present for the week.

Attention was called to Luxembourger migration to the United States, especially to Minnesota in the 1850s, and to how American soldiers liberated Luxembourg in the closing days of World War II. More than 5,000 Americans are buried in the U.S. Military Cemetery there, including General Patton.

Local Minneapolis news coverage was good and 100,000 people saw the fair. In addition, the U.S. event was covered in newspapers and magazines in *Luxembourg* including news from the local band members who attended. The bank's efforts to aid tourism and business in Luxembourg and to promote the country's beauty and history were appreciated because with only 340,000 people and an area smaller than Rhode Island,

Luxembourg does not get a great deal of coverage in the American press and does not have the money to spend on extensive promotion.

In this way a plus value was added to what otherwise could have been a nice but routine promotion of another foreign branch bank in a small country which is already a busy financial center.

Low Key Public Service Abroad

Xerox Corporation entered the Latin American market in 1964, relatively late, but its copier technology soon became widely available in the area. The Latin American public, however, still knew little about Xerox as an organization so the company sought a way to express its willingness to aid the social and economic progress of the nations in which it did business.

Since it deals in the quick duplication of writing, Xerox is by nature concerned with education, and education is a big problem in many of the countries in which the company was operating. There were 34 million children in Latin America in the 3 to 7 years age-group and in many places older children as well as adults were illiterate.

Xerox decided to contribute by encouraging one of the newer media in the communications revolution, television. It made a one million dollar grant to the Children's Television Workshop in New York to produce and distribute throughout Latin America Spanish and Portuguese language versions of "Sesame Street." The grant did not cover local telecasting and was meant only to make the series possible to those who wanted to use it. The Xerox "commercial" consisted of a 10-second acknowledgement of the grant seen only at the start and at the end of each broadcast.

To make the public further aware of Xerox support of the series, advertisements in newspapers and magazines and on the air as well as publicity and posters were used to make the availability of the series known and to promote viewing. Telecasting began late in 1972 in Puerto Rico and since then has been aired in more than fifteen countries and often repeated several times.

(See also the discussion of the Ford Motor Company school building program in Mexico in Chapter 11, which is similarly service-oriented in its approach.)

Extending the Influence of a World Scout Jamboree

Many types of organizations such as churches, service clubs, educational and health groups, service organizations such as the Red Cross, professional organizations such as those among doctors, editors, or scientists, and cultural groups in music or art have long been active in membership in many countries. World communications changes making it easier to correspond and travel have increased their effectiveness. In many ways these informal nongovernmental groups are the precursors of more formal semigovernmental units such as the European Common Market or even the United Nations. Physicians or artists or business people in one country see that they have needs and interests in common and such contacts lay the groundwork for international organizations.

A good illustration is shown by the 1975 program of the World Scout organization, headquartered in Geneva, Switzerland, to extend the influence of its World Scout Jamboree held in Norway that year. Only about 15,000 of the 15,000,000 Scouts in the world could attend the Jamboree, but through an extensive public relations program two to three million others all over the world were able to share in their experiences.

Scouting began in England in 1907. Today there are Scout organizations in 109 member countries. Each national organization is autonomous and its membership in the International World Scout organization at Geneva is voluntary. The bureau can make suggestions, but it cannot "give orders" to any national Scout organization.

Every four years Scouts hold a World Jamboree which is attended by thousands of delegates sent by their member country organizations. One Jamboree was held in the United States in 1967, another in Japan in 1971, and another in Norway in 1975. Realizing that 99.9 percent of the Scouts in the world could not attend this Scandinavian Jamboree, World Scout headquarters in Geneva thought about ways in which those who had to stay at home could, at least to some extent, take part in the interest and learning of the distant event. The result was a "Join-In Jamboree" public relations program.

The 1975 World Jamboree was sponsored by the five Nordic nations of Iceland, Norway, Denmark, Sweden, and Finland. A Viking theme was appropriate for the event. A booklet full of ideas for local participation in the event was published and sent to Scout groups all over the world. In it the five Nordic nations were described and some of their more famous people mentioned. Under Denmark, for instance, Hans Christian Andersen was named and the suggestion made that Scout groups could dramatize some of his famous stories. For Norway, Thor Heyerdahl, who drifted the Kon-Tiki raft across the Pacific Ocean, was listed and a raft building project was proposed. In Sweden, Carl Linnaeus was named and a study of botanical classifications suggested.

Then came a description of coming events at the meeting in Norway (called NORDJAMB) and suggestions on how Scout troops all over the world could share these experiences with others. They included exchanges of slides, tapes, magazines, games, stamps, tourist literature, handcrafts and amateur broadcasts. Contacts could be arranged through an office in international headquarters.

The Viking theme was then developed by a description of these historic people and ways were described in which Viking costumes and jewelry could be made. There were suggestions on how to make Viking food and camps, the use of old runic letters and reproduction of Viking dragon long-ships.

Other promotional efforts included idea-exchange articles in regular Scouting publications, a special Jamboree logotype for badges and T-shirts, regional Scout conferences, a 48-hour "Jamboree-on-the-air" linking 6,000 Scout amateur radio stations worldwide, and special information kits for Scout editors.

After several months the results of this work began to appear. *Scouting* magazine in Britain published a full page of Join-in-Jamboree ideas in six monthly editions. *Canadian Leader* presented four-page lift-outs for three months. Brazil published a seven-installment JIJ Handbook. Upper Volta and Ivory Coast in Africa who sent 7 and 14 Scouts respectively to the Jamboree in Norway held a joint JIJ camp which reached more than 220 Scouts who had to stay at home. South Korea sent 42 Scouts to "Nordjam" but multiplied their experience at 127 District Camporees reaching 41,739 Scouts.

In various ways millions of Scouts from all over the world participated to some extent in the World Jamboree and regarded its activities with more interest. When the program ended the world headquarters public relations office asked national member organizations for their suggestions and also asked if they would like to participate similarly in connection with the 1979 World Jamboree to be held in Iran. "Intensively" said 57 percent and "some" said 43 percent. None said "not much."

This internal Join-in-Jamboree public relations program was in addition to the normal extensive news media coverage of NORDJAMB itself and much enhanced its effectiveness. It is similar to the continuous internal public relations programs of many international voluntary organizations which reach across national boundaries without much thought of nationality or too much concern for the details of political or economic systems. They exist, of course, only where freedom of information and movement are permitted. Governments that insist upon a monopoly of communications for the purpose of controlling the thoughts of their own

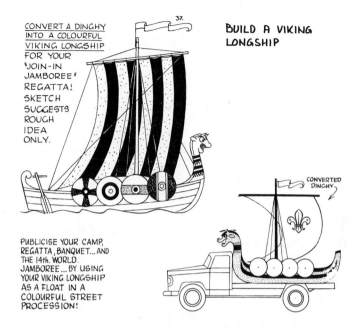

CONVERT A DINGHY INTO A COLOURFUL VIKING LONGSHIP FOR YOUR "JOIN-IN JAMBOREE" REGATTA! SKETCH SUGGESTS ROUGH IDEA ONLY.

BUILD A VIKING LONGSHIP

CONVERTED DINGHY

PUBLICISE YOUR CAMP, REGATTA, BANQUET... AND THE 14th. WORLD. JAMBOREE ... BY USING YOUR VIKING LONGSHIP AS A FLOAT IN A COLOURFUL STREET PROCESSION!

ADAPT IT TO THE VIKING THEME

There are many Cub and Scout games that can be adapted to the Viking theme. You can create atmosphere in many other ways - such as naming a prominent tree in camp the Igdrasil Tree, and holding council meetings under it in legendary Norse style. Camp signals can be given on a Gjaller-Horn - blown kudu-horn style by someone appointed as Heimdal the Watchman.

USE THE NORDIC LEGENDS

These fascinating stories are the myths of the old Norsemen, called by them The Eddas. They've been retold in modern times. See if your local Library can provide you with a book such as "Norse Legends — Retold From The Eddas — By Rosa Hobhouse." They're all short stories — ideal for tales around your Viking campfire. Or, use them as a basis for a sketch or play.

Figure 14–3 Only a small percentage of world Scouts could attend the World Scout Jamboree held in Norway in 1975 so a program was planned to enable more to take part even if they could not be there. This is a page from a booklet suggesting ways in which Scout troops in various countries could use the Viking theme.

people usually do not allow communications competition. It is one of the tests of the commitment to freedom of a government as to whether or not it will freely allow its own citizens to take an active part in such international organizations without hindrance or penalty.

With the communications advances of the past decades it becomes increasingly easy to establish international contacts and increasingly hard to bar them.

Explaining Multi-national Operations at Home

Caterpillar Tractor Company is headquartered in the small midwestern American city of Peoria, Illinois, but it operates in fifteen countries over the world, a change developing between 1950 and 1976.

Internal communications to employees, family members and friends are important to such international companies because work is the rather tenuous link which binds all employees together. As a part of this program Caterpillar Tractor Company issues a distinguished company magazine called "Caterpillar World" which is published four times a year in English, French, and Portuguese.

Articles frequently discuss Caterpillar's production, sales competition, and progress on a worldwide basis so that all employees may be

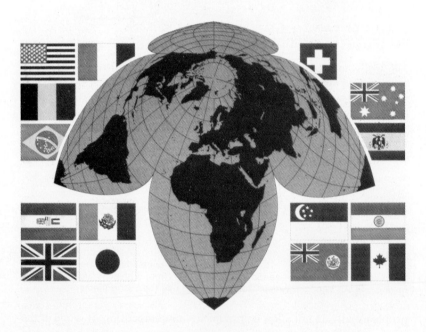

Caterpillar **World**

1976 SPECIAL MULTINATIONAL COMPANY ISSUE

Figure 14-4 Caterpillar Tractor Company is headquartered in Peoria, Illinois, but has plants and business world-wide. This is the cover of a special issue of the company magazine which goes not only to American employees but to all others explaining the international development of the company and the reasons for it.

equally informed. One of the four 1976 issues was entirely devoted to Caterpillar's international development in the preceding twenty-six years.

In it, for example, the business reasons for Caterpillar expansion overseas were plainly set forth; the methods and chronology were described in detail; growth in investment, employees, sales, taxes, and earnings was listed year by year; economic political climate was discussed; technology, employees, suppliers, and dealers were covered. Anyone reading the thirty-two well-illustrated and graphed pages would obtain as good an idea as anyone could of the nature and operations of Caterpillar Tractor Company worldwide.

Many companies engage in similar information programs for employees internationally and do it well. It can be readily seen, however, that the work and thought required is substantial and that the standards of excellence should be high.

STATUS OF PRIVATE DEVELOPMENT OF PUBLIC RELATIONS IN VARIOUS COUNTRIES

The United States is acknowledged to be the leader in the world in the development of private public relations practice, but the conditions of educational, industrial, and communications media development, coupled with democratic freedom to speak which made the rise possible here, exist in other nations also, so the practice of public relations has grown in many other places in recent decades.

Western Europe, of course, is an area where these conditions largely prevail so it would be expected that public relations growth would occur there, which has been the case.

Leading western European countries have professional public relations associations and practitioners are often people of high ability with an exact understanding of the nature of their work and a serious concern about ethical practices.

Most of the development of professional public relations in Western Europe dates back to about 1946, the end of World War II. The example of American military forces at that time, and of many American firms later, lent powerful impetus to public relations ideas which would probably have come anyway with the booming business of the 1950s. Since circumstances were different, however, there were many factors to be overcome: a tradition of secrecy in industry; long-established class and sectional frictions leading to popular suspicion of all communications; government controls; the weakness (or in some cases the purchasability)

of the communications media; a strong lingering distrust of all information dating back to experience with dictatorships, censorship and propaganda in World War II; and an almost complete lack of university-level
education in public relations, journalism, advertising or related fields of
communication. Not all of these applied to any one country, of course,
and they varied from nation to nation, so some examination of each is
in order.

Great Britain

This is the most highly developed country in public relations and has
many similarities to the United States. The size and stature of its professional organization of public relations people provides a measure of the
progress of the country, The British Institute of Public Relations was
founded in 1948, grew to 770 members by 1955, to 1,400 in 1962 and
by 1976 had approximately 2,600 members. (By comparison The Public
Relations Society of America which was founded in 1946 now has about
7,000 members. The population of Great Britain is about 55 million and
that of the United States about 210 million so in relation to total population Britain is actually more developed.)

In 1958 the British Institute of Public Relations issued the first
guidebook to public relations in Great Britain. The Institute is active in
meetings and conferences and sponsors educational courses. A system of
examinations administered by an outside agency has been devised and
membership in the Institute is available to (1) mature people who have
had five years comprehensive public relations experience and are acceptable to the Institute; or (2) to those of slightly lesser age (26 years) who
have had two years public relations experience and who have received
a diploma in public relations following courses and examinations at one
of several study centers in Britain.

As has been the case in the United States, many British public
relations people come from newspaper or broadcasting backgrounds.
The press is probably the single greatest means of communication, although exhibits, tours, films, and booklets are more extensively used in
Great Britain than here. The compact nature of the country tends to
center activities in London which is by far the largest city as well as the
seat of government, whereas in the United States activity is more
diffused. Inexpensive, quick, rail transportation also contributes to centralization. But because of the importance of local governments, community relations programs are as common as they are here.

Government public relations work was developed earlier than industrial public relations in Britain, going back to about 1912 when Prime
Minister Lloyd George hired a group of speakers to go about the country

explaining the new National Insurance Act. Government information activity in World Wars I and II expanded the field which is now centered in the unusual Central Office of Information in London. Industrial and other commercial or associational public relations efforts began later and are still developing.

Like many things British, public relations in the United Kingdom is usually conducted in a quieter key than in the United States. It tends to be more informative and personal as might be expected in an older, smaller, more compact nation, but in spite of its avoidance of noise it is usually thoroughly modern and effective. The use of a common language in the two nations encourages an interchange of public relations thought between Britain and the United States. At the same time, the location of Britain near the continent of Europe and its close trade relations as a member of the Common Market countries often enable British public relations people to serve as a link between American concerns and those in Europe.

West Germany

Public relations has developed rapidly in this country in the past ten years. The long period of rebuilding after war damage, preoccupation with the partition of the country, soul-searching about World War II, and concern about former acceptance of Nazi propaganda misinformation, and a deep authoritarian habit in both government and industry delayed the development of public relations in West Germany. It was not until 1958 that the Deutsche Public Relations Gesellschaft, centered in the Rhine industrial area, was formed. From about eighty members it has now grown to about 800 and it is estimated that the total number of public relations practitioners in the country grew from about 2,500 in 1966 to perhaps 6,000 in 1976. Several good books on public relations have been published in German and the subject is now taught at several leading German universities as well as in continuing education courses and in courses and seminars on the nonuniversity level.

Today public relations practice is found in nearly every sector of public life including the federal and state governments and the cities, political parties, industries, trade and professional associations, cultural affairs, religious groups, nonprofit organizations such as welfare associations, and clubs such as Lions or Rotary. It was estimated that 600 to 800 million dollars was being spent in Western Germany on public relations activities by 1976.

West Germany has become the leading European industrial nation and the largest producer in the Common Market bloc with strong worldwide exports. At the same time, there are contacts with eastern European countries within the Soviet sphere of influence. As the nation has overcome its production problems, groups within it have become more active and vocal and it can be expected that the importance of democratic persuasion methods as exemplified in public relations efforts will continue to increase.

Italy

An association of professional public relations people was established in Italy in 1954 and after some changes between various associations emerged as The Italian Public Relations Federation in Milan in 1970. The Federation now has about 550 members, 138 of whom are counselors or agency owners, 362 of whom are public relations officers in private or public organizations, and 30 of whom are university lecturers or scholars. The Federation has drawn up an agency and consulting services handbook and has obtained official government recognition of public relations as a profession. It has also organized several national meetings on public relations and communication and represents Italy in the European Public Relations Federation.

The practice of public relations within a country, of necessity, reflects the history and circumstances of that country. Italy, for example, has a much more centralized government than that of the United States, Britain, or Western Germany. Many more decisions relating to schools, labor relations, or policing, for instance, are made in the capital at Rome rather than in local communities. Thus the practice of community relations in public relations is not as common in Italy as it is in the nations mentioned above.

At the same time, there is a great contrast between the development and wealth of northern Italy and the region south of Naples and in Sicily, so this poses internal public relations problems. Italy has a large Communist party vote (whereas the United States, Britain, and West Germany have very little) so there is much more public relations concern there with the economic future. Italy also is a country whose national independence dates back only to 1870. Before that it was a disunited nation ruled in the north by the Austrians, in the south by local Bourbon kings, and the center by the Church and elsewhere by a number of local nobles or republics such as Venice. From the late 1920s until 1945, Italy was under the control of Mussolini's dictatorial Fascist party which permitted very little freedom of expression. So many of the aspects of national unity and freedom which are somewhat taken for granted in Britain or in the United States are present problems, or nearly so, in Italy. Italy also has no oil or coal as the basis for modern industry.

Because of these problems, public relations in Italy often concerns itself with basic citizen and government, or citizen and industry relationships. But Italy has made great progress since World War II. There is keen interest in the public relations field which should continue to grow as far as it can be financially supported.

France

Public relations development in France has been slower than might have been expected in a major industrialized country with a strong democratic tradition. In a report at the Seventh World Public Relations Congress in Boston in 1976, Claude Chapeau, a French public relations man, noted that a tradition of secrecy existed on the part of French industry because of the fear of government intervention, that shareholding was far less widespread than in the United States, and that the government did not require disclosure of corporate information to shareholders and hence to the public. He also noted that the nation was deeply divided into progovernment-ownership and antigovernment-ownership political parties and that it was very difficult for the two groups to talk to each other. In addition the press, lacking economic strength and independence, often sells news space or ties the use of news stories in with the purchase of advertising space. This practice makes it hard for public relations people to get proper news releases run (if some other organization has already bought the newspaper) and has made the better informed public suspicious of the truth of reports in many newspapers and magazines. French newspapers tend to represent parties and beliefs rather than serving as impartial carriers of the news. Radio and television are controlled by the government and hence not generally available as media except under special circumstances of supervision.

Yet despite these handicaps, a small number of gifted, hard-working public relations people turn in an excellent performance. In the years following World War II, a number of firms, led by the international oil companies, established public relations departments and in 1952 ten practitioners from these firms organized a club, "La Maison de Verre," to promote the understanding of public relations. The name means "the glass house" and came from an observation which the French philosopher Comte made more than a hundred years ago that a business enterprise ought to be open "like a glass house" to enlighten public opinion. By 1969 a course in public relations was added to the Sorbonne University curriculum and by that time a number of major companies and governmental departments had developed public relations departments.

The future of public relations in France seems to depend more upon its future political and economic organization than any other factor. So long as deep class, ideological, and economic antagonisms exist, the credibility level of public utterances is low and it is hard to engage in effective public presentation of a case. The audience is more inclined to say "Who says it?" than to consider the merits of the argument. Faced with such incredulity, those who have information are more inclined to hide it for their own purposes than to issue it. There are good historic reasons for this: much of French industry was rightly accused of collaboration with the conquering German armies from 1941 to 1945. Beginning with the revolution of 1789 the country has been split into extremely liberal and conservative blocs and alternated between Napoleonic and Bourbon monarchies until 1870. War losses in World Wars I and II were terrible.

But this is not true of France alone; many nations share similar problems. And public relations only flourishes well in situations where there is a high degree of trust in the integrity of fellow citizens, a willingness to hear their side of the case, and an anxiousness on their part to state it. Such a condition does not come about easily. It takes a long time to establish it and such fellowship throughout a nation is constantly being eroded by many hates, discontents, and dishonesties. Having it is no basis for complacency because constant effort is needed to maintain it. This, perhaps, is sufficient justification for national holidays such as July 4, Memorial Day, or Thanksgiving, and for nation-wide observances such as the American 1976 Bicentennial. Despite the constant cynics and wiseacres who elevate themselves in their own estimation by being superior to such events that move most of their fellows, these "public relations" events perform a vital function in the national consensus which enables citizens to debate with each other reasonably and peacefully.

The Low Countries

Before 1952 the idea of public relations was generally unknown in Belgium, but in the latter part of that year a number of practitioners formed the Centre Belge des Relations Publiques which today has an active program and about 240 members.

In Holland, the Nederlands Genootschap voor Public Relations was formed in 1954 and now has about 300 members.

Located in a highly industrial area at the main sea entry into Europe, Belgian and Dutch public relations practitioners often have worldwide connections and serve as a bridge between Britain whose public relations practices theirs much resemble, and the Continent. Many of the practitioners have university connections and higher education in the field has developed. The seat of the headquarters of the European Economic Community (Common Market) is at Brussels, Belgium, and that city, along with Geneva, Zurich, or London often serves as a headquarters for organizations which are active in several European countries. Amsterdam, also, because of its central location and available talent, is a major distribution point for corporations wishing to disseminate information throughout Europe, Africa, and the Middle East.

Switzerland

This small country of only about 5 million people has three official languages—German, French, and Italian. In smaller populations public relations does not tend to emerge as a specialized function so often as in larger groups where formalized communications programs are more necessary. Meetings, exhibits, tours, and booklets are relatively more important, but Switzerland also serves as world headquarters for many organizations which practice public relations on a global basis.

Other European Nations

Professional public relations groups are also to be found in Denmark, Finland, Greece, Ireland, Norway, Portugal, Spain, and Sweden. All of these, except Spain, are relatively small nations and development there has only been underway for a few years.

Other Countries

Associations of public relations people exist in many other parts of the world. Some of them such as in Canada, Australia, or New Zealand, are similar to their British or American counterparts except in size. Other nations, while fairly large, such as India or Brazil, reflect the conditions of the nations of which they are a part. Japan, a major industrialized nation, has a developing public relations practice. Many Latin American countries including Argentina, Chile, Columbia, Venezuela, Ecuador, Paraguay, Uruguay, Mexico, Peru, and Panama list associations of public relations people as do the Republic of China, (Taiwan) Singapore, Indonesia, Iran, Israel, Hong Kong, Lebanon, Malaysia, and the Philippines in Asia; and Ghana, Kenya, Nigeria, Rhodesia, South Africa, Egypt, and Tanzania in Africa.

Practices naturally vary greatly, those in Canada, for example, being equivalent to those in the United States; but in less developed countries public relations may be largely handshaking, political influence, and partying. It must be realized, however, that articulate and powerful publics are limited in less-industrialized, less-literate countries without a long tradition of popular participation in government and in business. Hence the attempt to reach a smaller number of leaders may serve for the present as a substitute for widespread *public* relations. The danger is that as leaders change, national publics may come to think that such attempts at the communication of ideas are confined to leaders only. As the general dissemination of ideas continues to grow among publics with the progress of communication methods, this may leave public relations efforts which are directed only at rulers dangling in the air, lacking a base of broader popular understanding. Each situation presents a different problem and requires real statesmanship and knowledge for successful long-term international public relations success.

INTERNATIONAL PROFESSIONAL ACTIVITIES

The International Public Relations Association, a worldwide group of public relations practitioners, doing business outside the borders of their member nations as well as within, was founded in 1955 and is headquartered in London. Nearly 500 members in forty-seven countries comprise an international network of sources of professional competence, experience, and aid which can be tapped by all its members. Regular meetings are held and publications issued. In 1977, IPRA began publication of *IPRA Review,* which appears twice a year and contains articles of special use to international public relations practitioners.

In 1961 IPRA adopted an international code of conduct for public relations; in 1964 IPRA was recognized by the United Nations; in 1974 it sponsored a seminar in Athens on the environmental problems of the Mediterranean Sea; and in 1975 sponsored the first All-African Public Relations Conference at Nairobi.

A world Congress of Public Relations is sponsored by IPRA every third year. The first in Brussels in 1958 was followed by Venice, Montreal, Rio de Janeiro, Tel Aviv, Geneva and Boston in 1976, which was attended by 1,500 practitioners. World Congresses are organized and cosponsored by the national public relations organizations in the countries where they meet. The 1979 Congress is scheduled for London.

In addition to the IPRA there is also a Centre Europeen des Relations Publiques formed in 1959 and headquartered at Brussels. This regional group consists of members from thirteen nations and is a federation of professional associations.

In 1961 The International Conference on University Education for Public Relations was established at the University of Louvain, Belgium, and has been busy aiding the development of public relations education.

Some Problems of International
Public Relations Practice

Problems of national loyalty and of differing standards in business or communications ethics appear in the public relations activities of organizations which are active on a global scale.

The first can be illustrated when a conflict arises between the economic or political interest of a client in one country and public relations activity in another. The promotion of tourism in another country is usually considered an innocent and normal activity, yet in case of strained relations between two nations might lead to accusations of national disloyalty against a public relations firm which practiced it for another nation. Promotion of the sale of goods from another country may be criticized by the local manufacturers hurt by such competition and at the extreme felt to be un-American or un-British, or whatever the case may be. The representation of ideas and national viewpoints such as those of the Arabs or the Israelis or the South Africans is even more delicate and conditions may change rendering a previously "respectable" representation unpopular, as happened to a well known American public relations man in the 1930s with the rise of Nazi Germany. A public relations firm in the United States must think about such possibilities when approached by a foreign client—and, of course, the reverse is true when a foreign person is approached by an American client. But as contacts grow, such divided loyalties become increasingly common.

The problem of varying ethical standards in different countries only moved into the forefront of public consciousness in the United States in the late 1970s and presented a great difficulty for many companies doing large businesses overseas. It was triggered by the requirement of the U.S. Securities Exchange Commission that "improper" payments for influence or favor abroad be disclosed to the shareholders of the companies making them—and hence to the world. This does not in any way prevent expenditure on all public relations activities abroad as we understand them here. But in many other nations, especially those ruled by dictators or small ruling classes, it has long been common for powerful political figures to receive substantial "gifts" from foreign companies buying or selling there. Sometimes this is a shakedown to avoid hinderance. Sometimes it is asked for; other times it may be offered when unnecessary.

Often it has seemed necessary to pay someone well to even get a hearing—usually a relative or friend of a ruler. These contact persons may call themselves "public relations" people and are so reported in the press. In case of government contracts whether for weapons or industrial development, great payoffs have been made.

American companies abroad often followed these practices for many years along with their European or Japanese counterparts without anyone thinking much about it. In many ways it might be considered more the problem of the host country to prevent graft on the part of their own elected or appointed officials than that of the firms who were either asked to give or who freely offered payments. After all, the citizens of the country supporting the grafter were the losers in inflated costs and poor quality. They should clean their own house—but often they do not have the power or the inclination to do this. Keeping rulers honest is always difficult, even in well-developed nations with a free press and powerful democratic tradition.

The problem with giving bribes (beyond accepting them) is that dishonest practices tend to spread back home as a way of life too. Buying influence abroad leads to buying influence here also. And in addition, as the SEC pointed out, investors in a company have a right to know how large sums of their money are being used.

The issue is not settled because business and government standards over the world are not uniform. American public concern is proper. Things should be sold on their own merits and not because of kickbacks. Corruption one place leads to another. A public office is a public trust. But can practices abroad that are long established be suddenly stopped —especially if competition is keen and if the people of a host country have little control of their own officials?

This becomes a real public relations problem within the United States for companies operating internationally, as so many do. It encourages the American dislike and fear of *all* business no matter where practiced. Yet in a time when it is increasingly necessary to sell American products abroad to pay for the oil and other raw material we import, how high can standards be abroad? In earlier times this was not much of a question, but it is today.

GOVERNMENT PUBLIC RELATIONS PROPAGANDA

The rise of rapid, profuse world communications systems could have been expected to affect the governments of national states, both in the impact of outside messages upon their own citizens and in the efforts of nations to reach out and influence the thinking of other people in the world for trade, tourism, ideological, or military purposes. Governments became big communicators.

This became apparent in World War I (1914–1918) when each side in this global conflict strained to get the last ounce of effort from its own people and to blunt or distort whatever contrary messages they might receive from the opposition. Words and ideas were conceived of as weapons and often rather crudely used. Censorship was used to keep discouraging news away from home receivers and elaborate falsehoods were concocted to mislead the enemy and to prevent local citizens from being discouraged.

When the war ended the losers felt duped by the endless flow of misleading encouragement they had received during the war when in fact conditions were steadily worsening. The credibility of their governments was completely destroyed along with the credibility of almost any government. Revolutions ensued.

Even the victors were disillusioned when the "facts" they had believed turned out to be half-truths or exaggerations. Many educated people resolved to believe almost nothing that they heard in the future. It was at this point that propaganda received a bad connotation that still clings to it; although originally the word simply meant to spread an idea. Many intelligent people thought that future conflicts could be avoided if only the nature of propaganda was better understood and exposed.

They reckoned, however, without considering some factors. The global communications revolution speeded up in the 1920s and 1930s with the coming of radio, better motion pictures, and airplanes to distribute people and printed matter rapidly. More people could be more easily reached with more information. Change was in the air and new ideologies were quick to take advantage of it, among them Communism and Fascism.

Also there was (and is) the problem of open versus closed societies. In the democratic system citizens are free to present their own views and to listen to the views of others, whether native or foreign. In a totalitarian system, whether of the right or left, the information that citizens might receive is carefully screened and what might be said is limited. Both groups, of course, feel free to try to spread their viewpoints abroad, but the democratic system cannot handicap its people's listening whereas the totalitarian system can by mail censorship, limitation of travel, jamming of broadcasts, and punishment for listening to or reading forbidden material.

World War II (1939–1945) threw the global communications struggle into high gear again on the part of all governments engaged because the stakes were survival. Methods were perhaps more subtle, particularly in democracies, because of World War I propaganda memories. In the United States, after Pearl Harbor, there was little need to whip up enthusiasm for the war, but the effort was even more vigorous and sophisticated.

The end of the war did not mean the end of communications influence struggles because a great many new nations soon appeared as old empires disintegrated and were wooed by various ideologies and interests and the shrinking globe forced people and thoughts into uncomfortably closer proximity. A global battle of words and agitation and influence continued and there was no escape from taking part in it if a nation or its ideas wished to have any part in the outcome.

This worldwide struggle of words is not just the sideshow to the main event which centers in military weapons or economic might. These are important, no doubt, but the spread of nuclear weapons and the decline of financial power by single centers may mean that *persuasion* is the main weapon.

In 1954, after the hydrogen bomb had demonstrated its awesome capacity to wipe out all life over hundreds of square miles, Sir Winston Churchill remarked that since wars could now destroy the leaders of all nations and their prized possessions, he expected "elaborate and cautious cross-cultural persuasion" to take the place of warfare as an instrument of national policy. It was no longer safe or profitable for great powers to use military might to force other people to do what they wanted them to do. And as the secret of the atom continues to spread, hostile action becomes increasingly unsafe (although that does not mean that atomic war may not happen somewhere, sometime). In such a stalemate of military terror, nations attempt to spread their influence and ideas by persuasion and other methods that fall short of total ruin for all concerned.

So for more than two decades past there has been an increase in the global communications efforts of various governments including the United States, the Soviet Union, and Great Britain.

The U.S. International Communication Agency

The present International Communication Agency of the United States was established in 1953 as the United States Information Agency, an arm of the executive branch of the United States government. Its director and deputy director are appointed by the President with the advice and consent of the Senate. Historically it grew out of World War II international information programs which were absorbed by the Department of State at the end of hostilities. Its budget in 1978 was $269 million and in August of 1977 it had 8,370 employees. About half were Americans and the other half were non-Americans hired locally in foreign countries. Of the American employees about a thousand were overseas and three thousand in the United States, principally in Washington, D.C. The biggest single unit of the USIA was the radio broadcasting service known as the Voice of America which had almost three thousand employees, a budget of $62 million a year and broadcast in 36 languages.

Early in 1978 the USIA was renamed *The United States International Communication Agency.* Its functions remained much the same but it was shifted to direct operation under the Secretary of State with its director reporting to both the Secretary and to the President. At the same time the Bureau of Educational and Cultural Affairs in the State Department was shifted into the new USICA bringing in about 255 additional personnel. The change was made to provide for closer coordination with State Department policy. The word "information" was dropped from the name because of its limited scope and different meanings in other parts of the world.

At this point it should be observed that the United States probably does not have the largest international information organization in the world. In broadcasts, for example, the Voice of America engages in 789 hours per week of direct broadcasts, the Soviet Union 1,969 hours, the People's Republic of China in 1,406 hours, the Arab Republic of Egypt in 1,093 hours, the Federal Republic of Germany in 767 hours, the Republic of China in 754 hours, and Great Britain in 714 hours. True budgetary and personnel figures for other countries are hard to obtain and often show only part of the effort since other costs and personnel are buried in varied departments or concealed.

The reason for considering the USICA first and in some detail is that it is American and that we have complete information upon it.

The USICA communicates by the following methods:

Personal Contact   USICA officers serving abroad provide a person-to-person link with local opinion leaders and promote contact between American and local experts through lectures, seminars, symposia, and other means of direct contact. Most of the USICA's work, other than the Voice of America, is directed at specific audiences and groups since the means does not exist in many cases to reach mass audiences. One of these groups, of course, might be the press of a foreign country which in turn would reach larger audiences in its own way.

Radio   The VOA has 113 transmitters here and abroad with a total power of 23 million watts. In addition VOA and field-produced USICA radio programs are often broadcast by local radio stations in other countries.

VOA has a long-established policy of broadcasting objective, comprehensive news reports giving a balanced view of American society. This was confirmed by Congress in 1976 when it wrote into law that:

1 VOA will serve as a consistently reliable and authoritative source of news. VOA news will be accurate, objective, and comprehensive.

2 VOA will represent America, not any single segment of American society, and will therefore present a balanced and comprehensive projection of significant American thought and institutions.

Figure 14–5 Voice of America broadcasts overseas from famous American locations. Here the hosts of a VOA breakfast show interview two guides in front of Independence Hall in Philadelphia during the 1976 Bicentennial.

3 VOA will present the policies of the United States clearly and effectively, and will also present responsible discussion and opinion on these policies.

This, of course, is not any easy mandate for anyone to live up to and would be a splendid platform for any news medium. Opinions on whether the VOA achieves these goals in specific instances may well vary according to the biases and enthusiasms of the one making the judgment, but the basic point is clear; The VOA is to "tell it as it is" and not to temper the wind to make America (much less any particular party or executive) look good abroad. It is somewhat like the story of Oliver Cromwell of England who told his portrait painter in the 1600s that he wanted to be painted just as he was, "warts and all."

There are many temptations to stray from this course, and many well-intentioned pressures to do so, but the trust of listeners cannot be gained in a moment and can be lost forever by falsehood or significant ommission. American and British overseas news broadcasts have generally adhered to a high standard of accuracy and completeness, even when it hurts, and have been correspondingly trusted.

One other aspect of the laws establishing the USICA should be noted here, and that is that they specifically prohibit the USICA from directing any of its communication efforts to this country. This, of course, is to prevent the establishment of an official government means of swaying American public opinion at home. It has had the unintended by-product of rendering most Americans rather ignorant of USICA activities since unless they seek out USICA annual reports or come into contact with USICA employees or hear about the USICA in news of congressional discussions (usually critical since that is the nature of news), they do not come into contact with the agency's work and cannot judge it.

Films and Television   The USICA produces about 200 videotape programs a year for use by local leaders, the press and universities abroad, and makes available to its posts overseas copies of many U.S. network news programs. The agency also makes about seventy-five films a year and acquires over 300 films and television programs on American life for post nontheatrical and television use. Foreign television stations are supplied with news clips of U.S. events and foreign television news teams are assisted in obtaining material for their use.

Press   Policy statements and interpretive material are radio-teletyped to 126 overseas posts in five regional transmissions of from

8,000 to 10,000 words five days a week. Features, photos, and reprints from U.S. newspapers and magazines are regularly mailed to USICA posts abroad for use by local news media and for information to those requesting it.

Publications USICA publishes *America Illustrated,* a monthly magazine in Russian with several hundred thousand copies distributed in Russia (for which a similar number of copies of a Russian magazine in English are permitted to be distributed in America).

Horizons USA is a bimonthly in English, Spanish, and twelve other languages; *Topic* in English and French is published eight times a year for sub-Sahara Africa; *Al Majal* eight times a year in Arabic for Near East and North African countries; *Dialogue,* an intellectual quarterly in eight languages including Polish, Romanian, and Russian; *Economic Impact,* a quarterly in English and Spanish; and *Problems of Communism,* bimonthly in English. In addition numerous local magazines, pamphlets, and posters are published by USICA locally for use in over a hundred countries.

Exhibitions An average of ten exhibitions a year are produced for trade fairs and other international events, often being exposed to a half-million people at a single event.

Libraries and Books The USICA maintains or supports libraries in 253 information centers, reading rooms, and binational centers in more than ninety-five countries. USICA also assists American and foreign publishers in the distribution of about 5 million books a year, especially trade and textbooks, and develops promotional campaigns to aid the sale of American books overseas.

American Studies and Language The USICA serves as a link between American and foreign universities, academic associations, and scholars. It sponsors direct English teaching in hundreds of binational centers, its own information centers, and posts attracting more than 350,000 persons a year.

Cultural and Educational Exchange USICA administers abroad the Cultural and Educational Exchange program, formerly part of the Department of State.

In addition to the above, USICA engages in considerable opinion research to determine the effectiveness of its efforts and to find out what directions it should take in reaching people.

Figure 14–6   Books and libraries are an important part of United States International Communication Agency activities overseas. Here, in New Delhi, India, Indrani Rahman, noted dancer, and other Indians examine books in an American Bicentennial exhibit. Courtesy Photo Lab, USIS (India). Photo by R. N. Khanna.

The one thing USICA cannot do, however, is to make American foreign policy or change the nature of the news from the United States that it has to report. Many of the criticisms of the USICA are really criticisms of the actions and nature of this nation.

America has not known what it wants of the world and has frequently wanted the unobtainable. After World War II many people imagined that an American position of pre-eminence was natural and permanent and that American economic and political systems could be exported *in toto* all over the globe to countries which lacked unity, literacy, capital, and a tradition of democratic constraint. We relied too much on gifts and power and were too easily offended when not liked. Our communications were often addressed to high ideals rather than to others' immediate desperate needs. We engaged (and still do) in one-way conversations in which we told everyone else how good we were without listening to or appreciating their virtues and problems—when anyone in personal life knows that to be a good communicator you also have to be a good listener. Every one of our mistakes and failures was immediately noted and proclaimed by the opposition, whoever it might be at the time.

What America really wants is probably much more modest: an orderly, reasonably friendly world, open to trade and to travel and to the spread of ideas, pluralistic with many nations and cultures flourishing without being bound into menacing military or economic power blocs. This goal will be hard to attain and is a major task for all humanity; but it represents an ideal which most peoples who value their own cultures and independence can accept unless forced to do otherwise. Independence and the freedom of the individual and nation are as powerful forces today as they were in 1776.

Britain's Central Office of Information

This organization likewise arose after World War II, but differs in many ways from the United States International Communication Agency. It is worthwhile examining, however, because complete facts upon it are readily available and because it represents a new and effective approach to the needs of a government in communicating to its own people and abroad.

At the close of World War I in 1918, the efficient British government propaganda machine that had operated so successfully during the war was dismantled and except for some specific trade and Commonwealth efforts abroad and necessary departmental communications at home, no general plan was followed. At the end of World War II in 1945, it was realized that the global communications revolution had so changed the world that some form of government communication would be necessary and it was decided to set up a permanent corps of experts in communication who could assist the government in its communications both at home and abroad. This was known as the Central Office of Information and in 1975 had a total staff of about 1,300 headquartered in London.

The COI operates somewhat like an "in-house" public relations and advertising agency, with its accounts being the various departments of the British government. As a pamphlet recently issued by the COI explains it:

> Each government department has its own information staff. As well as advising ministers and officials on the department's public relations, the staff have two main functions: to provide news, information, and facilities for press, radio and television, and to arrange paid-for [advertising] campaigns using some or all of the media—advertising, publications, films, television, radio, photographs, and exhibitions. In the former task they are helped by the COI's News Distribution Service and regional organization; and in the latter, the COI's services are very extensively employed. Infor-

mation campaigns are needed to publicize and explain the effects of new laws and administrative measures; to make the public aware of their rights and duties under social legislation, and to encourage the proper use of the services available; to assist recruitment to the armed forces or other public services; and to improve health and safety. The responsible department briefs the COI, which then either produces appropriate material internally or supervises its production by commercial agencies.

An illustration will help make this more clear.

Suppose, for example, that the British navy wants a recruiting film made. After they have decided what they want and how much they can afford to spend on it, they will take the idea to the film-making people in the COI who will then take on the job of getting a commercial film-maker to do the job, keep contact between the client (the navy) and the film-maker to see that the client gets what is desired, and after much meeting of minds and final approval, the film will be delivered to the navy which then pays for it and takes responsibility for it. If a newspaper advertising recruiting campaign was desired, a commercial advertising agency would be contacted. If a booklet was sought the COI staff of writers and artists would probably do the work themselves.

There are several advantages to a system such as this:

1 It avoids expensive duplication of communications experts in many departments of government, sometimes short of work or making work simply because they are there.

2 It offers to each department the services of people who are expert craftsmen in their particular area of communications. Since the need of help varies from time to time, teams can be assembled for emergency or complicated jobs. These people become widely acquainted with the communications needs of many branches of government and also with the advertising, film, writing, and other commercial people who can help them. They also can look forward to a lifetime career in their own organization where their main business is communications.

3 Most valuable, probably, is that the COI does not bear the ultimate responsibility for *policy* decisions. In the case of the navy recruiting film, referred to earlier, the decision to make the film in the first place and its general content was the responsibility of the British navy which also approved and paid for it. If months later some member of Parliament disliked a portion of it and complained, the complaint goes back to those who ordered, approved, and paid for the film and not to its makers so long as they followed orders. The COI is like the Queen in that it "can advise, warn, and consent" but the final decision is up to the various departments of government who bear the final responsibility.

The COI is divided into two main departments, home and overseas. In the home department there is an advertising division, a photographic division, a publications and design services division, an exhibitions division, and a regional division that maintains offices in various cities in the British Isles. In the overseas department there is a films and television division, an overseas press and radio division, a reference division, and a tours and distribution division. Finance and accounts and research are handled by divisions which serve both home and overseas departments.

The British approach to the needs of governmental communications is quite different from the American, fostered, no doubt, by a smaller country and the need for greater economy. In the United States each department such as Agriculture or Defense maintains its own communications staffs including in most cases technicians. In Britain this is centralized with the responsibility for initiation, approval, and payment remaining with the departments of government.

There is no direct parallel, either, between the USICA and the COI. In Britain overseas information policy is planned by the Foreign and Commonwealth Office and the Department of Trade and implemented by FCO diplomatic missions overseas whose members belong to the diplomatic service. The COI provides them with material for local dissemination in the press, films, exhibitions, factual reference documents, booklets and magazines, posters and photos, and commercially-published newspapers and periodicals. The COI also shows officially-sponsored overseas visitors around Britain and encourages the sale overseas of British periodicals. The COI has no staff permanently stationed abroad but its members sometimes make overseas visits to carry out individual assignments.

The other main arms of the British overseas information services are the British Council and the external services of the British Broadcasting Corporation (BBC) which corresponds somewhat to the Voice of America and follows similar policies of complete news. Neither of these is COI directed.

Because of these differences, a direct financial comparison between the COI and the USICA is meaningless but it is interesting to note that in 1974–1975 financial year the COI spent about $40 million and another $2 million in services was supplied by the government printing office for a total direct expense of around $42 to $43 million. About three-quarters of this amount is spent on the COI home publicity divisions.

An interesting example of COI work some years ago was its aid in helping convert the nation from pounds, shillings, and pence to a decimal system of currency dividing the pound into one hundred pence. This required extensive advertising, films, television, publicity, and other educational means and was rather smoothly accomplished considering that the previous monetary units were centuries old. A similar program is under way for the metric system of measurement of distances, areas, and volumes which will also be faced by the United States.

In general it can be said that British governmental communications efforts are factual, quiet, and well produced. Despite the disappearance of the Empire following World War II, Britain retains considerable world influence and is a major financial and communications center.

World Communications of Other Countries

It would take a book to describe the international communications efforts of all of the countries in the world and the research for it would be very difficult since the figures are not published or even revealed in most instances.

Some idea of its huge scope, however, can be gained from the outside evidence. We know, for example, that the USSR is on the air more than twice as many hours as the USICA and that Egypt pours out more radio air time than the USICA. The volume of printed matter from many nations is also large and there are an endless number of cultural exchanges, fairs, and meetings. The United States is not alone or even necessarily a leader in this deluge of words! The world is in a state of transition in which we can swim but not direct. The important thing is to be wise and consistent and to keep in mind that other people select what they want and not what we want. We make progress primarily upon things which we *both* want.

Some changes have occurred since 1945. Our inclination for many years was to see all forms of Communism as monolithic and essentially the same and to communicate against all of them similarly. Time has shown great divergences. We have also been humbled by our own national problems and failures which we have not tried to conceal—indeed in many cases we somewhat exaggerate them because it is the nature of domestic news to play up problems rather than things that work well. This is quickly reflected abroad. But in the nature of our society we cannot engage in the other extreme of concealment or falsehood.

SUMMARY

In the past half-century a world communications revolution has taken place which has greatly increased the hopes and fears of people everywhere. This has resulted in the stimulation of the private practice of public relations where possible and in worldwide governmental public relations efforts. The process is still underway and its eventual results are not yet apparent.

ADDITIONAL READINGS

The following articles appeared in the February, 1973, issue of *The Public Relations Journal* published by the Public Relations Society of America in New York City:

Everett, James A., *The Netherlands*
Golding, Peter S., *Australia*
Hudson, Sam, *Norway and Sweden*
Leaf, Robert F., *England*
Mouchley, Harriett, *Israel*
Munekata, Kesaji, *Japan*

Additional articles and books of interest are:

Bauer, Frank, "Some Unorthodox Views On Public Relations In France." *Public Relations Quarterly,* Winter, 1974.

Bernays, Edward L., and Burnett Hershey, *The Case For Reappraisal of U.S. Overseas Information Policies and Programs.* (New York: Praeger, 1970.)

Hartogh, Jules M., "Public Relations In A Changing Europe." *Public Relations Journal,* March, 1974.

Hill & Knowlton International, *Handbook on International Public Relations.* 2 vols., (New York: Praeger, 1967.)

Jefkins, Frank W., *Public Relations in World Marketing.* (London: Crosby Lockwood, 1966.)

Kean, Geoffrey, *The Public Relations Man Abroad.* (New York: Praeger, 1968.)

Schramm, Wilbur, *Mass Media and National Development.* (Palo Alto, Calif: Stanford University Press, 1964.)

Chapter 15

Positions and Preparation

The common service department [public relations], a British government
public relations chief said several years ago, "must never forget that, like
the public relations officers of any organization, it is a servant and not the
master. It has been said that the Queen of England has three functions: to
advise her ministers, to warn them, and to encourage them. In the same way
[the public relations head] can advise, warn, or encourage his clients . . . but
finally he must *do* what they want and *not do* what they do not want,
because they are taking the policy responsibility and will receive most of
the blame . . . if anything goes wrong. . . .

This accurate description of the nature of a staff service function
outlines the circumstances under which public relations leadership
within an organization usually works.

ORGANIZATIONAL RANK OF PUBLIC RELATIONS

The public relations director of a company or other organization is almost always a staff functionary, usually responsible to the highest, or the next to the highest, line officer—ordinarily the president, vice-president, or general manager. He or she is in a similar position to the legal counsel, a financial adviser, or others whose expert services are offered to anyone in the company where most needed and able to do the most good. Unlike line officers, who usually have an immediate superior and numbers of inferiors in a chain of command, the staff public relations people are really responsible to numbers of superiors (or at least peers) for whom they directly or indirectly do public relations work, and they have relatively few subordinates except the usually small numbers on their own staff, such as assistants, specialists, and clerical workers.

It is a mistake to place the public relations director under a sales manager, community relations manager, or some other functionary having only a limited area of responsibility, because the public relations director will then consider this area his or her main field of responsibility and neglect others. Very few organizations do this. A public relations director working for a sales manager, for example, would rightly see the main responsibility as getting product-publicity which would enhance sales. There is nothing wrong with this and if this is all that a company is interested in it would perhaps be logical. But in these days few organizations would be content to operate with so limited a view.

The public relations head is an intermediary dealing in ideas, who engages in informal communication both downward and upward. Some public relations ideas may perhaps come from immediate superiors, the vice-presidents, for example, or the general manager. The problem is to analyze such ideas, to agree or disagree, to work them into operating form, and then to gain the cooperation and goodwill of others in the organization whose approval and aid are needed if the ideas are to be carried out. The public relations head's ultimate trump card, seldom openly acknowledged and almost never played, is support from, and access to, higher power. But if this special access to power is invoked too much, though his position may be respected it may also be feared and disliked because, unlike the line people of production or of sales, he or she touches all departments and knows something about everybody. The work of public relations practitioners circulates through the entire organization and crisscrosses boundaries of authority. Their relationship to the top power may range from truly right-hand to purportedly right-hand, or may simply rest insecurely upon the high, but detached, spot they occupy on the organizational chart.

For public relations people, understanding where they fit into the organization is highly important and sometimes confusing. Where does personnel work end and public relations work begin? Where does the financial vice-president's responsibility end and the public relations manager's begin? What responsibility for sales promotional publicity should be assumed by the sales manager and how much by the public relations director? No two organizations will be exactly identical in their pattern, but it should be clear to have a good understanding and to avoid confusion, irritation, and missed opportunities. Making final decisions as to exact responsibilities belongs, eventually, to top management which oversees all of these functions and many more. But most of the responsibilities can be worked out by the public relations manager and the heads of these other departments in personal conversation. Top management shouldn't have to spend too much of its time adjudicating jurisdictional disputes and will appreciate not having to do so.

In arriving at these understandings a few principles may be helpful:

The public relations department is supposed to be, above all, expert in communication. Thus, for example, it would probably actually write and issue an employee publication. But wage policies, retirement programs, or the length of coffee breaks are operating matters which are the responsibility of the personnel department. The public relations director might have suggestions in connection with such company policies but only the personnel manager or his or her superiors have the power of decision. Or in financial matters, a decision on how to raise new working capital is clearly not in the realm of the public relations director although one would probably handle press relations connected with it.

Those who are most concerned with a function and who are most narrowly affected by its success will tend to keep it in their hands. For example, publicity about a new product is of great concern to the sales department, so it will want a lot of it and will seek to influence its content. As a mediator between the company and the outside press, the public relations director will try to satisfy the sales department need without lowering the press esteem of the newsworthiness of releases from the company. If the public relations director yields too much, the sales department may be happy, but with subsequent injury to the company's standing with the outside press. If he or she is too unbending the sales department may start writing its own publicity on new products, ask its advertising agency to do so, or hire an outside public relations firm for that purpose. If this is harmful to the overall interests of the company, the public relations director may have to ask top management to decide the issue. But it should not come to this if it can be avoided.

This need for accommodation and understanding is one of the main reasons why public relations should be a top staff function on a par with operating departments such as sales or production. Many public relations ideas affect other departments; many actions of other departments affect the public relations standing of an organization. All of the people involved need to be aware of the effects of their policies and actions on an organization-wide basis. Public relations cannot function well if it is ignorant of what is going on in its own company. It needs not only to be aware of decisions but also to have a voice in them.

The relationship between an outside public relations counseling firm and the on-staff public relations people of an organization deserves a word here. Outside public relations firms are hired by organizations for a number of reasons: (1) because the organization is too small to employ a full-time public relations staff of its own, yet needs help; (2) to assist in overloads such as a sudden disaster crisis; (3) to add special expertise such as in financial public relations, distant press contacts, or special media use; (4) to bring a broader view of public relations to the in-house staff through wider experience involving varied clients over a long period of time.

Except in the first instance cited, outside public relations counseling firms usually cost more than an in-house staff but they do bring special help when needed. Because they are outside they can be more objective than inside-staff public relations people who become team members. But for the same reason they often fail to understand the problems and goals of those who work for an organization day-by-day. There may be friction between inside and outside public relations people because each sees a threat in the other.

Many larger companies employ outside outside public relations firms to help with specific projects or media needs. When such a firm is invited in to "audit" the effectiveness of existing public relations work, there needs to be a good understanding all around or there will be a great deal of uneasiness.

Many public relations plans originate within the active imagination of a good public relations person, who then faces the problem of selling them, perhaps first to top management, which will support them, perhaps first to special-interest areas of management, which will carry them to the top for final authorization. Public relations ideas may also originate down the line. If they are good, they can be carried to the top for approval, with proper credit to the source and perhaps with revisions; but if they are poor, they can be acknowledged with an explanation and thanks, but without action. (There is always the possibility that the originator will then take the ideas directly to headquarters—and, even worse, that headquarters may think them wonderful.)

Unlike the good soldier of the line ranks, who simply obeys superiors, works well, and is a good officer to inferiors, the public relations staff people send their ideas coursing through the veins of the entire organization in a manner both exhilarating and dangerous, their work rendered doubly interesting by its constant traffic with intangibles. Production heads can point to the volume, low cost, and high quality of their output as evidence of good work; the sales department can count its figures; and another fellow staff member, the company attorney, can lean for authority upon a ponderous knowledge of what one can or cannot do while staying safely within the law. But although effective public relations, like the air itself, exists, it is often as difficult to measure as air, and the uninitiated find the measurements equally unsubstantial and unconvincing.

In addition, good public relations people must be able to convey upward or sidewise communications as effectively as downward communications. They should know what people in the lower ranks think or what influential publics outside the organization feel, and be able to carry the information to the top. To do this, they must often be away from their desks and plant, spending their time at apparently useless meetings or talking idly, both of which occupations are natural irritants to cost-and-duty-conscious line officers. The public relations gadfly lives in several worlds; connections are mysterious; and output is difficult to assess.

PERSONAL QUALITIES

It is not surprising, then, that several traps are connected with the lively and interesting post of public relations director of an organization.

Gossiping   It is hard to be a many-voiced communicator without carrying tales from contact to contact—a cardinal sin, of course, except to the head person to whom reports are due. The chief who supports you is entitled to know, and presumably he is a person of honor in whom it is safe to confide. With others, however, a reputation for being an "old wife" quickly gets around and ruins all trust and friendship.

Butterflyism   The affliction of "butterflyism" is akin to a similar occupational disease of sales people—an enthusiasm for motion, sensation, and sheer busyness as a substitute for thought. In a salesperson hectic activity may look like work, but in a public relations person it is usually fatal, because it prevents the careful research and thought which are so fundamental to effective communication programs. Its only real merit, in fact, is that it impresses observers who do not know the subject very well.

Megalomania   Production or other line administrators are frequently accounted important because of the *number* of persons they have working for them. Public relations departments on the other hand are and usually should be small. Keeping down the number of workers is sound common sense, because a large department invites trimming. Peak loads can usually be handled by borrowing help or by hiring temporary outsiders.

Officiousness   The wide range within which public relations heads circulate gives them a broad acquaintance with the whole organization. If they are intelligent, they will see things that might be improved, and unless they are careful they will forget their boundaries and imagine that they, rather than the president or the board of directors, are running the company. It is very unlikely that they could do a better job than their superiors do, and if their vanity is discovered it will not be appreciated. To comprehend a function is far easier than to carry it out skillfully, and there is always danger that a flash of comprehension may blind one to the virtues of hard work, patience, and wisdom which are the real secrets of much successful administration.

These are some of the main traps. But what qualities of character are needed to avoid them and also to achieve success in the practice of public relations?

Integrity   Integrity means a quality of moral courage which will enable public relations people to point out a danger when it would be more diplomatic to keep silent; to vote "no" in good spirit and with good reasons and yet, if overruled, to accept a higher verdict; and to see things as they really are, despite their or other people's desires to have them different.

Integrity follows a hard road, and those who are merely cantankerous or self-assertive should not think that they are showing integrity by throwing their weight around upon many small issues. Professional "no" people are almost as absurd in their way as professional "yes" people, but there are times when, after careful investigation and mature thought, a person feels that one should oppose a plan for which top management pushes hard or, even worse, feels impelled to advocate a program which is certain to meet with management hostility.

It must be recognized, however, that some employers prefer servants who always say "yes." If agreement is what they want, that is what they are paying for, and sometimes, if employers have sufficient ability, they may even succeed with "yes" men. It should not be forgotten that in the final decisions, the head of the organization makes the rules, orders them carried out, and takes the responsibility. At this point, line and staff people alike have no choice except to support or to resign.

But with all of these qualifying cautions, we must still maintain that integrity of mind and character is the only thing in a public relations person which can inspire an organization's confidence and give him or her any proper claim to leadership.

Personal Communicative Ability   Because public relations work is intangible, it may require a great deal of explaining within its own organization. One public relations head said wearily, "I spend half my time explaining to people what I'm doing, and the other half doing it!" Line production heads can often be the strong, silent type, because their work speaks for itself. Public relations people, however, must talk, write, and promote their work constantly, because usually it does not speak for itself. They *must* practice at home what they preach abroad or else be misunderstood.

Personal communicative ability means much more than readiness to make a good speech or to write a good letter. It springs from a sincere interest in people and pleasure in their presence and is not to be confused with the outgoing of the so-called extrovert personality which sometimes takes pleasure only in its own presence and which desires to dominate every situation, to the distress of others who would like some recognition. Sometimes public relations workers are expected to occupy the limelight; more often they prepare the stage for others to be seen and heard. But they constantly need to keep their associates aware of what they are doing and thinking, to make their colleagues' goals their own goals, to respond to their enthusiasms, and to have the capacity to inspire enthusiasm in them for their objectives. This cannot be done by an individual who simply does not like people and prefers to deal with things instead of humanity; such an individual belongs in the laboratory or in the accounting office.

Real friendliness is unforced, although it can be cultivated. Often people may seem unfriendly because they are too self-conscious, a feeling often traceable to physical or social inferiority suffered in youth. A public relations person also needs empathy to place himself in other persons' shoes quickly and to see things in the light in which they see them. The chief hindrance to quick empathy, or understanding of others, is egocentrism. One who is too busy seeing the world from his or her own viewpoint cannot appreciate the viewpoints of others and as a rule cannot get along with them. The phrase "to know all is to understand all" may well be extended by adding the additional words "and to like better."

Emotional Stability   There is no denying that the chief problem of people is people; and since the public relations person works with people all the time, he has his full quota of emotional strains. He or she operates often as a intermediary between those who are easily angered, slow, bullheaded, or irresponsible; and at times he may need every ounce of emotional stability that he can summon to avoid falling into absurd behavior himself. How is this steadiness to be achieved?

The cultivation of several qualities and the avoidance of others are important. *Egocentrism* is a hindrance to emotional stability because it prevents separating issues from personalities."Love me, love my ideas!" A realistic, well-proportioned sense of one's personal worth and shortcomings is not easily achieved, and it is often taught only by age and experience, by hard knocks and success. "Let no man think more highly of himself than he ought," said St. Paul.

A *broad intellectual background* helps an individual to place herself in the long perspectives of history and science. Travel and varied experiences are also an aid. A *sense of humor* is the priceless possession of a person who does not take either herself, or other people, too seriously.

And finally an adequate *personal religious philosophy* is a great aid to emotional stability. Different people arrive at an understanding of life by different roads, but all who maturely approach the riddle of human existence must eventually start thinking of ultimate meanings. The facts of life and death alone force the consideration of religion upon everyone.

Intelligence   Public relations is not a life for the slow-witted. Besides a pleasing personality and a sound outlook, public relations practice demands mental quickness, creative thought, and sound judgment.

Some of these qualities are acquired through study and experience, but an intelligent person has also an inherent basic capacity. It is not entirely to one's credit or discredit either to be blessed with, or to fall short of excellence in natural ability. Intelligent people generally know that they are intelligent, but the egos of slow people sometimes make them think that they, too, are quick-witted.

Measuring intelligence is as yet an inexact process; but those whose tests indicate a consistently low level will find it wiser to go into some other field than public relations.

Studiousness   More public relations money is wasted through doing the wrong things or failing to do the right things than through any other cause. The usual reason for the mistakes is lack of study of the situation in advance. An uninformed bright person is often no more capable than a stupid person and sometimes much more erratic.

Studiousness arises from sheer intellectual curiosity and from reasoned determination to master the facts of a situation. It is a habit which may be the most valuable by-product of an education, if indeed it should not be the main product.

Many failures in public relations spring from lack of understanding of the organization for which the public relations person is working and from ignorance of communications processes or target audiences; yet details of the history, organization, personalities, and processes of almost any institution are usually easily available to those who would like to know them before presuming to advise. Public relations depends upon facts as a basis for action, just as good journalism rests upon facts for significant communication.

Health   There are no particular occupational hazards in the practice of public relations, such as the alleged Madison Avenue ulcers or presidential coronaries, but the creative and emotional demands of the work, its long and uncertain hours, and the occasional hazards of banquet tables, cocktail parties, and travel circuits make a stable, if not a rugged, physical constitution desirable. Since for most public relations people their work is also their hobby in the conventional sense, outdoor sports are to be recommended. In a survey of the avocations of du Pont public relations people, swimming ranked first in popularity, with golf, tennis, and fishing following in that order. The forty surveyed were also great readers; they liked music and news on the radio, and they watched sports and news on television.

Work Abilities   After asking "What sort of person is she or he?" the prospective employer of a public relations person also wants to know "What can he or she do?" As seen earlier in this book, the scope of activities within public relations is so broad that the problem is to draw out of this multitude of abilities the absolute fundamentals upon which almost everyone is agreed. Surprisingly enough, they are rather few.

Writing ability is usually named as the most important ability in public relations by employers, other practitioners, and teachers. By "writing ability" is generally meant the power to express oneself in clear English prose suitable to the presentation of a good news story, a feature article, a speech, or a plan for a new public relations program.

Writing ability, of course, depends upon general intelligence and education; no one can possibly write better than he thinks. It is also the result of much reading, of practice in writing and rewriting, as well as of the critical study of good writing in many fields. Writing demands sufficient confidence on the part of the writer to feel that he has something worth saying and that he can say it, and sufficient humility to realize that he must make an effort to interest others and must be willing to repolish or even recast a piece of writing entirely in order to make it clearer and more coherent.

Many good writers (commercial writers, that is, such as journalists, advertising writers, or public relations writers) go through three stages:

First comes what might be termed "the high school sophomore stage," which is, perhaps, but one step above illiteracy. It is a state of simple unhappiness and fear of facing a great number of words. At this stage the assignment to write a 2,000-word essay seems like a prison sentence, and most individuals never progress beyond it.

Second comes an intoxication with words. Suddenly self-expression becomes delightful; often carried along on a tide of freely flowing language, a person would rather write than eat. If such writing happens to coincide with the interests of readers, well and good; if not, it makes no difference; she will write anyway, even if she has no audience but herself. Many one-book fiction writers, including some of the best-sellers, belong in this category. Writing is simply a form of self-expression.

Finally comes acceptance of the discipline of writing for a purpose. The question is not "Will I like it?" but rather "Will the recipients like and understand it?" Such discipline develops a high standard of literary crafting, unwillingness to be satisfied with anything but the best words or phrases, and a versatility which manifests itself in efforts as varied as business letters, addresses of welcome, and advertisements stating company positions in a labor dispute. A disciplined writer is like a big eight-cylinder car with a great reserve of power, running smoothly in any gear. Such writing is hard but rewarding, both in personal satisfaction and in material gains.

Experience in related fields can hardly be considered an "ability"; yet from the employer's viewpoint such experience ranks second in importance.

Historically, the field most nearly related to public relations has been journalism, and today a large number of America's public relations people still come from newspaper staffs, where their work has not only developed writing ability, but has also facilitated wide contacts and has assisted in developing many of the qualities of character previously mentioned in this chapter.

Such fields of communication as broadcasting, selling, advertising, teaching, and preaching can also be drawn upon for practitioners of public relations. The process of passing from one field to another will be discussed more completely in the section on "Education," which follows.

Speaking ability is also often mentioned by employers. Some public relations people are semiprofessional speakers; all have to have the ability to speak adequately, clearly, and convincingly before various groups.

EDUCATION FOR PUBLIC RELATIONS

Occupying a staff advisory position fairly high up the executive scale, the public relations person is hired not only for personal qualities, skills, and experience, but also for wisdom. As a counselor, he or she must have the background to inspire confidence in his counsels. How is wisdom to be gained?

Academic Education   Everyone agrees that a college diploma is almost essential for entering public relations today, and the necessity is increasing. A survey of pre-1935 public relations practitioners, for example, showed that 35 percent were college graduates; by 1953 the figure had risen to 57 percent; a 1960 Michigan survey found that 81 percent of the public relations people in that state had college degrees and noted that "all recent employees have"; and a 1968 survey revealed that 83 percent of those replying were degree holders.

On the general nature of college education needed, almost everyone agrees that a high percentage of liberal arts studies such as economics, psychology, sociology, history, languages, literature, and writing is desirable. In addition, courses in journalism and other forms of communications study—broadcasting, advertising, and related subjects—are thought to contribute valuable material and ideas. A recent humorous adding up of all the "good" subjects totaled, for the ideal, approximately *eight* years in college. Actually, the four-year A.B. degree is most common, although an increasing number of graduate-degree programs are being instituted.

The development of public relations courses in colleges and universities has gone on steadily in the past few years. Almost none existed in 1946, but by 1956 a Public Relations Society of America (PRSA) survey showed about 137 institutions offering courses in public relations and by 1970 the number had grown to about 300. A 1975 survey sponsored by PRSA among 320 colleges and universities known to be offering courses in public relations received a 45 percent return.

This survey showed that public relations courses were usually taught in Journalism/Mass Communications departments (63.5 percent) or in Communications departments (14.0) or in Business (10.4). Slightly more than 7 percent were in "public relations departments" and slightly more than 2 percent in Education. Most students taking public relations courses (61.8 percent) came from Journalism-Communication departments and about 25 percent from Business schools. About 30 percent of the institutions reporting offered an undergraduate sequence of public relations courses and about 12 percent a graduate sequence. Fourteen percent offered an undergraduate major and six percent a graduate major.

At this point it should be noted that all accredited schools of Journalism in the United States require that their students devote at least three-quarters of their four years to a broad liberal arts program and only the remainder of their time to the specific study of journalistic writing, public relations, advertising, and similar subjects. A person who wants to train for public relations does not have to make a choice between a liberal arts curriculum or a communications curriculum but instead makes a blend of the two. The 1975 PRSA study referred to earlier, found, for example, that out of 124 credit hours in a typical public relations curriculum only six would be devoted exclusively to public relations with perhaps thirty-five spent on journalism-communication, sixty in the social sciences and humanities, and nine in business. At the graduate level (M.A.) about one-third of the required thirty credits would be in public relations, often largely accounted for by the thesis.

Business people sometimes feel that their public relations people need more business management background and the student who expects to work in public relations for a business corporation might do well to take at least the basic courses in finance, administration, and labor relations, among others. Usually there is ample elective time in a curriculum to do this.

In addition to course work, institutions offering instruction in public relations usually try to establish strong practical connections with the working field of public relations. Almost three-fourths assisted in getting internships for students, about the same number encouraged PRSA or its student branch, PRSSA, participation, and about 60 percent used public relations campaigns as a method of teaching. Speakers from the working field were used in classes in 98 percent of the cases, often frequently during the year, most of them coming from corporations.

Enrollments increased between 1970 and 1975. In the first year for example, 62 percent of the institutions reporting said they had fewer than 25 students in public relations courses; by 1975 this had diminished to 33 percent and the largest single grouping in the latter year was one hundred or more students enrolled in public relations courses. Graduate enrollment showed a similar gain.

The same increasing complexity of the world's political, economic, scientific, and international organization that created the need for public relations has also created the need for a good education to precede the successful practice of public relations. The unlearned cannot expect to interpret to the learned.

Public Relations Teachers   In 1970 only 28 percent of public relations teachers were full-time as compared with 37 percent in 1975. In addition to an increase in full-time teachers there was also an increase in part-time teachers—largely public relations practitioners. Nearly half of the full-time teachers reported ten or more years public relations experience and most of them had taken their college degrees in Journalism, Communications, or in English and Literature. About 60 percent reported Master's degrees and about 39 percent Doctoral degrees.

The "Ideal" Public Relations Academic Education   In 1975 a commission composed of members of The Public Relations Society of America and The Association for Education in Journalism issued a group of recommendations for the public relations curriculum. Among them were:

English: ... at least two years and preferably more, ... writing is indisputably the basic tool. ...

The social sciences: No PR major should be allowed to graduate without meeting a minimal requirement for certain introductory courses in the social sciences. These may include psychology, sociology, economics, history and political science. ...

The humanities: ... A sprinkling of courses in literature, drama, the fine arts and music is eminently desirable.

The natural sciences: One or two introductory courses in biology, physics, and geology are desirable. ...

Foreign language or area studies: ... knowledge of at least one foreign language. ...

Statistics: ... an introductory course in statistical methodology. ...

Organizational structure and behavior: ... the chief PR staff person should be a member of management. ... [It is] important ... to have an understanding of the managerial structure and function of institutions. ...

Theory and process of communication

Writing for the mass media: ... print and electronic. ...

Copy editing: ... emphasis upon correct grammar, style, reader interest, readability, and clarity.

Graphics of communication

Also recommended if time afforded were advertising, media law and ethics, feature writing, survey research, and communication media analysis. No wonder at least a year of graduate study is suggested for the person who really intends to become a public relations professional rather than just obtain a passing acquaintance with the field!

Education by experience Because public relations departments are usually small, there is less opportunity for on-the-job training in this field than in many others. Training an additional person in a department of only four or five people takes a high percentage of the available time of the working staff. A small department usually needs a newcomer who can pull his or her weight quickly; hired for a record of past performance and good judgment. This is different from the news staffs of most newspapers which are large and in which, amid the rows of desks, there is room to work in an untrained person more easily. Like the young doctor, the young public relations worker's most valuable possession is the confidence of his or her patients, and this has to be deserved and not remain very long just a potential which may be realized sometime in the future.

For these reasons, to which might be added the lack of available college training in public relations in the recent past, the entry into public relations is frequently *by way of other occupations.* Sometimes this oblique approach through related disciplines is accidental but often it is largely planned by those who have their own career goals. Experience in related fields such as journalism, broadcasting, advertising, or government adds to the attractiveness of a public relations candidate. Historically a great many public relations people came out of newspaper work and many still do, although the scope of public relations has widened and the transition is not as easy as it used to be. Others come from broadcasting, advertising, teaching, and even selling. Often this approach is necessary while trying to obtain public relations work; in any case the time need not be considered wasted although it is likely that public relations loses some good workers who get into these other fields, do well, and stay.

Employers also show a tendency to ask for other experience in advertising for public relations people. In a random sampling of thirty job ads for public relations people from the *Wall Street Journal, Public Relations Journal* and a large west coast newspaper, fifteen asked for previous public relations experience, five asked for media experience and seven for experience in the particular field of work for which a public relations person was sought such as banking or electronics. Six specified a journalism degree, two a public relations degree, two an English degree, and two a "college" degree.

Of the thirty jobs advertised twelve were in industry, six in government, five in banks, three in financial public relations, two in public relations counseling firms, and one each in a hospital, an airline, and a trade association.

The most common skill requested was in news relations (seventeen mentions), writing skill followed with ten mentions, then internal communications with eight, and speech writing and advertising came next with five each.

Moving from other fields into public relations sometimes has its problems even though some of the skills may be similar. The journalist, for example, has a different outlook, being trained in objectivity rather than advocacy and frequently being inclined to feel that his job has been done when the facts are gotten out whereas the public relations person is more like the trial lawyer whose intent is persuasion. So not every good journalist automatically makes a good public relations person— anymore than a convincing attorney would necessarily make a good judge.

Confusion may follow if a former news person is either ignorant of the principles of persuasion or opposed to persuasion itself. But if the role is clearly understood, it can be rewarding. Writing in the *Quill,* the national magazine of Sigma Delta Chi, a journalism fraternity, a young journalism school graduate some years ago put it well:

> I found that for those who love to write there are other professions which ... still adhere to the high principles taught in journalism schools. Why advertising or public relations? I found that many companies do not deal with as many half-truths as I had thought. Their objective is merely to present a true picture of their company and its product to the public. Secondly, in so doing they encourage creative writing and thinking, and are willing to pay good salaries to achieve it....

CHARACTERISTICS OF DIFFERENT PUBLIC
RELATIONS FIELDS

Although the practice of public relations in a unity, work for different institutions tends to run somewhat in patterns. A good public relations person or counseling firm can serve one or another, but there *is* a background for each different type of activity to be mastered.

Some of the most stable public relations employment is to be found among the *utility companies.* As service organizations resting solely upon public acceptance, the telephone and electric companies were pioneers in realizing the need for good public relations for their independent and profitable existence. Their public relations activities are characterized by long-range planning, foresight, great attention to the quality of their employees and their service, and frequently by a "political" cast in their thinking, since they are so dependent upon public regulatory bodies. Utilities tend to have fairly large public relations departments, to select their people carefully, and to promote their staffs from within. The electric and gas utilities, particularly, have much more serious problems now than they did before the energy crisis in the early 1970s forced up costs to customers rapidly. Their public relations work must be more far-sighted and careful.

Industries employ the largest number of public relations people, but the size of their departments and their work varies greatly. In small plants in small cities, the chief emphasis may be upon employee and community contacts, and perhaps upon product promotion or shareholder relationships. The public relations director of a small industry is likely to be a solo performer. In large or multiplant industries, more specialization within larger departments occurs. Wages vary also: A 1977 PRSA booklet on careers in public relations noted that the director of public relations in a small to medium-size company might earn $15,-000 to $20,000 a year while in a larger corporation the range would be from $20,000 to $40,000. Salaries from $25,000 to $50,000 are earned by a number of seasoned public relations executives who more often than not carry the title of vice-president and enjoy commensurate fringe benefits. New York and Chicago personnel tend to be the highest paid.

There are about 11,000 *associations* in the United States. In all of them, both internal and external public relations fulfills an important function, whether the title of the association indicates the fact or not. The larger ones, especially those in which promotion or political influence is a major purpose, often have clearly defined public relations directors and quite large, well-paid staffs.

Welfare groups such as United Funds or the health and youth agencies all depend upon extensive public relations and employ many public relations people. Here the maximum pay may be in the $15,000 to $20,000 range which is below that of comparable industrial situations. The greatest satisfactions in this kind of work, however, come from the opportunity to do good and to advance causes in which the public relations worker can take a genuine personal enthusiasm.

Hospital and medical public relations has become a distinct field in recent years.

Labor unions, like the businesses which employ their members, recognize the importance of public relations in building support for their positions and programs. The AFL-CIO, many of its affiliated unions and major independent unions operate news bureaus, sponsor radio and television programs, offer films and educational programs to schools and civic groups, organize speakers' bureaus, and publish a variety of newspapers and booklets. Public relations people who start in the labor movement tend to remain with it throughout their careers.

Education is now employing an increasing number of public relations people, because the need for their services has grown rapidly as both city school systems and higher education have faced increasing financial, social and student problems. However, educational public relations work is still sometimes intentionally disguised, and to further this camouflage, its practitioners may be drawn from teaching or administrative ranks and are sometimes on part-time assignment. The fear apparently is of criticism if public money is seen to be spent for public information programs. Virtue, aided by the press, is supposed to present itself unaided. Only the stronger school systems and the more independent colleges and universities bring in outside public relations personnel to any extent where the director of "information" or "publicity" is often an assistant to the president. Educational public relations thus tends to suffer from inbreeding and from talking to itself. It would benefit from more interchange with the outside world. If the public had a less suspicious attitude toward educational public relations, the work could be more open and effectively accomplished. Fortunately, the many problems of modern education are of necessity bringing this about and the days of part-time, "closet" public relations programs are disappearing.

Government public relations, in general, shares the same problem with the added difficulty of political conflict. It is hard to explain the work of a mayor or a member of Congress or a governor without also contributing to his or her electoral prospects—a fact which the political opposition is quick to take notice. Most government organizations prefer to call themselves "information bureaus" or some variant and the strictly promotional is avoided. This is true of the military organizations also. A large percentage of government public relations people are former newsmen or women and achieve a good deal of security through civil service or military rank. The risky decisions and the larger salaries go to elected or politically appointed officials without tenure.

Public relations *firms* or *counselors* are located in large metropolitan centers. New York and Chicago together account for nearly half of the 1,500 firms in the nation. They range in size from several employing more than a hundred people to the great majority with fewer than a dozen workers. Some specialize in financial or investor relations, media placement, governmental relations, consumer marketing programs, and other areas. A few are parts of advertising agencies; others also serve as advertising agencies.

Independent public relations counseling is (or should be) the capstone of a public relations career. Having had various clients and possessing wide knowledge and long experience, the counselor is hired to advise, to perform specific tasks, to develop or monitor a corporate or other public relations department, and sometimes, in a period of emergency, to handle a program beyond the capacity of the in-house staff. Some small companies also hire public relations firms to do all their public relations work for them because their volume of business does not justify full-time staffing.

A comparison of outside public relations counselors with inside public relations staffs shows advantages on both sides. The outside counselor should have wider experience, a detached viewpoint, a greater knowledge of the media and other facilities. On the other hand knowledge of the client may be superficial, he may arouse internal discontent and be too bold in his actions. An outsider has the courage and freedom of enterprise but not the caution engendered by having to live with mistakes. The insider knows the organization better, costs less, has better lines of internal support—but may say "yes" too often and lose his objectivity. A combination of both is often used by large institutions.

Since the counselor's work demands experience it is usually not a place for beginners except in a subordinate capacity. Nor it is necessarily suited to older hands. Job tenure and benefits may sometimes be less; but those who chafe at the routines of a larger organization, yet enjoy new challenges and the creative ferment that often characterizes a counseling firm may find themselves happier in its environment. And the head or chief partners of a large, successful counseling firm may do as well or better financially than their fully-hired counterparts in industry.

WOMEN IN PUBLIC RELATIONS

The number of women in public relations has been increasing and the top level of their positions has been increasing also. The trend can be expected to continue since there is nothing in public relations work that cannot be done equally well by both sexes. A contributing factor, too, has been the growing number of women on newspaper staffs from which a great many public relations people have come. And more women executives in companies, welfare organizations, and associations with which public relations people work also make the role of the woman public relations person much more natural and easily accepted. Numbers of women have risen to leading positions in public relations counseling firms, associations, and businesses. It would be untrue, however, to say that the opportunities for women in the business world are as yet identical to those of men, since so many of those directing the business world are still men and some of them still feel more confidence in male advice and aid. This problem, though, is not particular to the public relations field which offers women better opportunities than many others. Good writing, planning, and research are not sex-related and these are the fundamentals of good public relations. Women may be expected to continue to make good progress in the public relations field as they have in the past dozen years.

PUBLIC RELATIONS SOCIETY OF AMERICA ACCREDITATION

One big factor leading to the advance of public relations education and professionalism in the United States in the past few years has been the accreditation program adopted by PRSA in 1963 and taking effect in 1965.

PRSA is the national professional association of public relations people. It has about 7,000 members of which about two-fifths have now become accredited. About two-thirds of these achieved accreditation by examination and the remainder were brought in by application at the time accreditation was adopted. Since 1968, accreditation (by examination) has been a requirement for active membership status in PRSA which also requires five years working experience at an executive level and recommendations.

The number of people working in public relations in the United States has been variously estimated from 60,000 to 100,000 so PRSA membership does not encompass the whole by any means. But it is important because most public relations leaders have become members of PRSA and now all who become active members undergo the accrediting examination. This day-long examination requires knowledge of the background of public relations, of publics and public opinion, of various aspects of practice, of communications, and of ethics, laws, and regulations affecting public relations. It not only measures retained knowledge but also involves problem-solving cases and is graded by a firm not connected to the Society.

Accreditation by examination is not unusually difficult but it sets a basic standard and requires study and thought. It becomes more meaningful as more public relations practitioners achieve it and as more and more employers and those who hire public relations counseling firms consider accreditation an asset in a public relations worker. This is happening and in some cases large companies have required that all of their upper-level public relations staff take the PRSA accreditation examination. The initials "APR" after a public relations person's name are constantly becoming more meaningful.

Interestingly enough, accreditation examinations began with the British Institute of Public Relations before they did in the United States. This was probably due to the fact that there was no college or university level public relations or even much similar education in Britain at the time, so the Institute had to set up its own courses for new entrants into the field and for those already working who needed to improve their knowledge. A course of study naturally involves examinations to see if it has been mastered. Certification that the examinations had been passed followed. The British examination is very similar to the American.

There has been discussion of "licensing" public relations practitioners which would mean that those who did not meet certain standards would be prevented by law from calling themselves public relations practitioners or, at the extreme, even prevented from practicing. The parallel between the bar in which lawyers are not permitted to plead before a court until they have passed a bar examination is pointed out. Licensing, however, may be contrary to the First Amendment of the Constitution of the United States which guarantees freedom of speech and petition to every citizen and presumably should be extented to also include the right of a citizen to hire someone to assist him in making such a plea. If the standards of licensing were low it would become a joke and if they were severe it could become a tool by which public opposition could be stifled from effective free speech, so the idea of governmentally controlled licensing has not made much progress.

Voluntary accreditation, of course, will never be a cure-all. It does not assure a brilliant public relations practitioner. But it does assure the employer or client of a certain basic competence and sincerity. It will become more important and those going into the professional practice of public relations would do well to plan on attaining it.

HOW TO GET A JOB IN PUBLIC RELATIONS

As noted earlier, getting started in a specialized staff function such as public relations is not as easy as in some more generalized jobs, whether just out of college or even in moving from another line of related work. Good advice is contained in the 1977 "Careers In Public Relations" guide issued by the Public Relations Society of America:

> No job is harder than finding a job, particularly your first. This is true in any field and certainly so of public relations. Success requires planning, preparation, energy, and enthusiasm—all in large quantities.
>
> Research the field [of public relations] in which you have the greatest interest. Not only should you use library resources, but also find people who work in these fields and particularly those engaged in public relations activities. Sometimes a journalist can also provide useful insights. The knowledge you acquire from all these sources will confirm your interest in the field and will be evidence of your alertness and maturity.
>
> You will need a written resumé of your background. This should contain a convincing, but not lengthy, account of yourself, particularly as it might bear on your potential usefulness in a job. It should include name, address, telephone number, age, possibly a statement of job objectives, your education and work experience including part-time work while in college, reported chronologically or in terms of types of skills demonstrated or the work accomplished.
>
> You should be attentive to the impression your resumé makes by its layout and the way you express yourself. Check and recheck your resumé, particularly for typographical errors. Duplicated processing is acceptable and you will probably find it useful to have your resumé run-off in quantity.
>
> You may learn about possible job openings in advance of contacting employers, or you may conduct a personal mail campaign, sending your resumé with a covering letter to organizations where there is some possibility of staff needs. Personal contacts are perhaps the best source for job leads, and personal referrals are the most advantageous. Placement agencies, associations, firms which service other organizations and "Help Wanted" advertisements are also sources of information about specific openings.
>
> Business directories may be consulted when making direct canvass by letter and resumé. Especially useful for this purpose are *O'Dwyer's Directory of Public Relations Firms,* J. R. O'Dwyer Co., Inc., New York; *PR Blue Book* (4th ed.), PR Publishing Co., Meriden, New Hampshire; and *Standard & Poor's Register of Corporations, Directors and Executives,* Standard & Poor's Corporation, New York.

When possible you should address by name the person immediately responsible for the department in which you might be employed. It is often effective to follow up your letter by telephone to attempt to arrange an interview, even if the position is not immediately available.

It is important to prepare for interviews by attempting to learn as much as possible about the organization beforehand. For major business corporations, financial information may be available from their shareholder relations or corporate secretary office.

Showing samples of your work can prove helpful, but bear in mind that they should represent your best efforts. Quality is more impressive than quantity.

Be ready to take the initiative in describing your qualifications and what you believe you can accomplish on the job, if the interviewer does not choose to lead the discussion. Also be aware of the fact that the quality of your questions about the company and the position can be as impressive and revealing of your potential as your background, particularly if your experience is limited.

Every candidate for a public relations position must keep in mind that the ratio of persons hired for any particular opening is small compared with the number interviewed. Rejection is no cause to suppose that you will not qualify elsewhere. Consider your job hunt as a learning experience. Through perseverance you can win the opportunity to begin your public relations career. . . .

Comments which might be added to the above are that public relations jobs cluster in bigger metropolitan areas where corporate, governmental, association, education, and welfare organization headquarters are likely to be located. "Help Wanted" advertising for public relations jobs is most likely to be found in the major newspapers of these areas. Many good public relations openings, however, are not advertised in the daily press because it results in a flood of poorly qualified applicants who must be sorted out. Some ads, also, are "come-ons" in which the real intent is sales work and in which the term "public relations" is used to attract applicants. If not apparent from the ads themselves, the difference in meaning soon becomes apparent upon contacting the source. Specification of the qualifications needed will usually provide the clue.

A good source of ads on a national basis is in the trade papers of particular occupations such as *Editor & Publisher* for the newspaper field, *Advertising Age, Public Relations Journal,* broadcasting magazines, educational journals, and others.

Since public relations jobs do not occur every day it will pay to know public relations people in your area—and to be known by them. Keeping in contact with the local PRSA chapter is a good idea.

It is always easier to get a job when you have one, and more comfortable, so related employment or part-time or volunteer public relations work should not be scorned. Do a good job on it while hoping for something better, however, because a future employer will probably check on present references and because a lesser or different job in an organization might lead to something in itself. Give value for money received.

Because public relations is an independent type of work, those who enter it take considerable responsibility for their own careers and plan ahead to improve themselves instead of waiting for someone else to tell them what to do.

Chapter 16

Right and Wrong in Professional Public Relations

Persuasive communication is a very ancient art. In modern times it has many forms of expression. Public relations persuasion is only one member of a large, diverse family that includes fields ranging all the way from politics and law to teaching, selling, editing, and the religious ministry. In all these occupations communicators try to persuade.

A political speaker tries to gain support for a cause or to get elected to public office; a lawyer tries to convince a jury of a client's innocence; a teacher is enthusiastic about his subject and would like to make his students enthusiastic also; a salesperson tries to get others to buy; an editor urges viewpoints in his editorials; and a minister of religion is "persuaded of her beliefs" and feels it her duty to convert others also.

PERSUASION IS HONORABLE

There is nothing wrong with persuasion. We may be skeptical or even amused as we watch the enthusiasm of persuaders now and then, but we

432

do not regard them as dishonorable citizens. We do not question the fact that persuaders are engaged in a recognized activity. Instead, we ask, "What means do they use to persuade?" and "For what purpose do they persuade?"

It is perfectly natural that people living together should try to persuade each other. Humans work in groups, and they form their voluntary groups largely by means of the communication of ideas. The power of speech distinguishes man from the beasts.

There are, of course, other ways of getting people to work together. *Power* simply says, "Do this or you will suffer," and *Purchase* promises rewards in money, goods, leisure, or honors. In actual situations power and purchase are often intermingled with persuasion.

Persuasion is the method used along with others in democratic societies. The very nature of democracy involves the opportunity to try to persuade people by reason or emotion (or both) and then to abide by their group decisions. By means of the influence of communication, society changes, progressing steadily and peacefully, without recourse to the brutalities of raw power or the corruption of generous feelings so often associated with widespread purchase. Persuasive communications are therefore privileged in a democracy. A citizen is free to change other's opinions, if he can, because only in this way can society adapt itself to new times and needs. If freedom of persuasion were to cease, democracy would also cease because people could then no longer be exposed to the newly discovered facts and different viewpoints which would help them to make up their minds.

Moreover, in a democracy *all* communication shares this freedom to persuade. The editor is privileged to urge her views upon her readers. They do not have to read, or believe, or even buy her publication. The lawyer is privileged to urge the merits of his client's case before a jury to the best of his ability. The political office seeker may speak to those who can hear him and will listen. The advertising writer may sell her wares, and the public relations person present the facts and arguments which are at his disposal.

A PRIVILEGE AND A RESPONSIBILITY

Privilege cannot be separated from responsibility; the freedom to speak, write, broadcast, and print means power and therefore must be subject to ethical standards. Some responsiblity for communications can be enforced by law, principally by the laws of libel. If a person is falsely accused of a crime, he may sue and recover damages. Those who falsely present material leading to a criminal act, such as marching upon the state capitol and burning it down, may find themselves charged with criminal libel, an offense against the peace and security of the state. But the larger part of a citizen's true responsibility in the exercise of persuasion cannot be determined by law because it rests on the moral sense of the persuader. Responsibility cannot be written out and hedged about in advance, nor can tribunals sit upon it without seriously undermining the necessary democratic right of freedom of speech. A person's liberty to speak is what makes the ethical problems of every persuader so important and interesting.

Right now there is a great deal of public unease about persuasion, and many people would like to believe that it does not exist, or else they wish that it would go away. They would like to think that in some way they simply receive into their minds all the facts of a case and then operate only as reasonable thinking machines to arrive at true conclusions; yet no one who considers the matter carefully can really believe that anyone is so unbiased. We know that we receive our ideas and information from many sources and that we have firm beliefs about many things of which we really have little knowledge. This covert suspicion of our own integrity bothers us, and we sometimes react by wishing that some all-wise source could decide things for us, or by desiring to silence the contending persuaders so that we shall have to listen only to the "right" one, or by dreaming that, like hermits, we need not consider contentions at all.

These reactions are not new. Over two thousand years ago in ancient Athens, the great teacher Socrates sought to warn his students about listening to the speeches of the Sophists, persuaders who were hired to appear at public meetings and elsewhere to urge various causes, or who taught others how to do so. The Sophists made their livings and great reputations by being effective in oratory, skilled in debate, and strong in their appeals to emotion. Socrates warned his students of the devious tricks of the Sophists, pointed out that they got paid for their performances and that therefore a listener might expect them to be more interested in winning an argument than in finding ultimate truth. All those who do business in the world of affairs, Socrates said, work for personal gain, and their own interests influence their opinions.

But Socrates did *not* say that the Sophists should be silenced so that the perplexing problem of deciding which one was right could be eliminated, nor did he suggest that his students should cease to listen to them or retire from the world. Instead, he urged his students to sharpen their critical faculties so that they would be able to recognize faulty reasoning and specious arguments wherever they found them. His counsel was not to seek refuge but to seek wisdom.

Perhaps some of the unease about persuasion among many people in the world today arises from the very factors which have entered into the development of public relations itself—huge mass communications which reach large groups of people primarily living in large urban centers; our own rootlessness and tendency to move about; changes in jobs, society, government, and world conditions; and a very rapid expansion in the number of matters of debate upon which we need to be persuaded. There are so many important issues—all the way from Communism and race relations to education and energy—upon which we are expected to have intelligent opinions, and so many people are so busy urging their viewpoints upon us! No wonder receivers are at times confused!

THE RISE OF "PROFESSIONALISM"

Not too many years ago there were only a few professions in the world —the law, medicine, the ministry, teaching, and the military. Now there are scores and more appearing every decade. Why? What has happened? The reason is not far to seek: It is because of the increasing complexity in our lives which makes us dependent upon the skilled aid of others who know more than we do about certain areas.

Unless you were an expert in medicine, you would not think of being your own doctor. If you had not studied law, you would not think of defending your company in a damage suit. And unless you really knew accounting and tax regulations you would not dream of preparing a complicated income tax return. You do not know how to plan a building, engineer a bridge, run a large public school system, develop a complicated chemical formula, or direct a naval engagement because all of these are "professions" which require a considerable amount of study and background which the busy person in other fields has not had time to acquire.

A "professional" then is someone who professes (claims) to know a great deal about a certain subject. The worst criticism that we can give a "professor" is that he or she is ignorant of the subject upon which he claims superior knowledge.

We are all more dependent upon professionals today than ever because there are so many complicated things in which we have no experience that affect our lives. We are obliged to pay others for their advice and are forced to trust their knowledge and disinterest. Usually this advice is about intangibles which we are not capable of judging ourselves. A profession is more than a skilled craft or a specialty because it requires longer to learn and because the purchaser is less capable of judging its merits.

Some of the things which indicate the emergence of a profession are:

1 *Self-consciousness* Professionals realize who they are and what they are doing. They have a common bond leading to professional organizations for the mutual development of their field.

2 *Defined area of competence* A "professor" is one who claims to know much about a specific subject and is not a jack-of-all-trades. A physician does not claim to be a lawyer, nor a certified public accountant to be an architect any more than any other layman would and their opinions in such other areas are worth no more or less than anyone else's would be—although people are sometimes confused by this.

3 *An organized body of knowledge of consequence* Anything that can be completely learned in six weeks of home study will scarcely qualify as a profession because the customer can judge its merits almost as well as the practitioner. An organized body of knowledge results from a written literature of principles and cases, from an educational process in which those who know more assist those who know less, and often from a period of appreciceship such as that found in medicine, law, or teaching.

4 *Measuring the competence of entrants* Related to an organized body of knowledge is some way of assuring that those who claim to know a profession have mastered it. This may be done by educational achievement, voluntary certification based upon examination, or by regulation and licensing by law. Such a measure of competence is for the benefit of the consumers of the professional's services.

5 *Continuing education* Few professions today stand still for long, especially in fields such as medicine or finance or law. Practitioners must meet and exchange information through published journals and in other ways. Sharing information is a characteristic of professions and hidden methods and trade secrets are considered unprofessional.

6 *Aiding the education of competent replacements* The public welfare is not only served but also the interests of present professionals by preventing the future entry of untrained people who would short-change customers and injure the reputation of the whole profession.

7 *Independence* A professional person's tools are in her head rather than in some equipment, or in being a part of a larger organization, although these may be important too. A doctor is sought for what he knows about curing disease and his diagnostic tests or clinical connections are means to that end. Professionals may work for a salary as in a hospital, corporation, or school—but if the circumstances are favorable the profession can be practiced independent of any supporting organization.

8   *Ethics*   It is apparent that some sort of an ethical framework is necessary in the practice of a profession. We do not think much of professionals who are unaware or uncaring about ethics because we depend on them too much. The freedom of clients to choose their professional advisors and of professional persons to accept or to reject clients establishes a special relationship between them.

9   *Obligations to clients*   A professional person must work loyally for the best interests of his client and not accept recompense from other hidden sources or serve competing interests secretly.

She is obligated to put forth her best efforts regardless of the size of her fee.

He cannot curry favor by being a "yes person"— saying what his client wants to hear even if he knows that it is wrong. Even a professional who is wholly employed such as corporate lawyer or a company doctor has this obligation. A corporation attorney, for example, might believe that a legal case given to him as part of his employment is false and harmful to the public welfare. His course is to advise against it and if pressured, his only recourse is to resign, admittedly a hard decision.

Free communication between professional people and their clients is necessary for competent advice so it cannot be disclosed without the client's consent. The law recognizes this confidential relationship, for instance, between a lawyer and her client and a court cannot force a lawyer to disclose what her client has said. (If it could, clients would not dare to disclose their affairs to their attorneys who then could not present an adequate case.) The clergy is likewise protected by law but the physician not as much so and the journalist hardly at all—so the records are full of journalists sent to jail for contempt of court because they would not disclose their sources of published information. In all cases it is the duty of a professional person not to gossip about clients' affairs and to be discreet at all times.

The professional should not prejudge his client's case but at all times do his best.

10   *Obligations to others in the field*   Professionals are judged not only as individuals but also as members of their profession and their fortunes rise and fall accordingly. "Every man is a debtor to his profession," Bacon said. Obligations to other professionals include not stealing another's clients by derogatory statements, exaggerated claims, often not advertising at all in the conventional sense, and often avoidance of fee structures contingent upon promised results. In many professional matters (as contrasted to building a brick wall or plastering a ceiling, for example) success cannot be guaranteed because there are too many other factors prevalent. A doctor cannot guarantee that an operation will be a success, she can only advise and do her best. Her fee should rest upon that and not upon the outcome because otherwise the field will be invaded by quacks who promise good outcomes of which they cannot really be sure. Unfortunately this is not true in all professions and in law, particularly, the custom of large fees contingent upon success in winning damage suits clogs the courts and increases public costs.

A professional is ready to share knowledge with others in his field and to encourage the support of selection or professionals in areas where it is important—for example of qualified engineers for highway posts, lawyers for judges, or doctors for health commissioners.

A professional person's fee includes the cost of his education and often for simply being available when needed, such as a lawyer's retainer fee. Direct expenses are added to this. A professional person often imparts knowledge to clients and they then know how to continue the service on their own by copying his actions. He thus may have "first time only" clients and is justified in charging for giving away his knowledge permanently, as it were.

Finally, professional people have a responsibility to their fellows in self-policing of their ranks. If they do not discourage or bar lazy, incompetent, or fraudulent members, public confidence will fall, and all will be injured. Eventually public law may take a hand if the injury is sufficiently severe.

11 *Obligation to society* Professions exist because they serve a public need. There are lawyers, for example, because the public system of justice requires people to present the cases of contending parties. Without a lawful society there would be no lawyers. Teachers exist to impart knowledge. Without a need to know there would be no teachers. Journalists or public relations people exist to convey information or to engage in persuasion—and without freedom of communication there would be no journalists or public relations people. At the very minimum a profession should not be harmful to the public welfare and indeed should serve its needs. In its own interest and that of society, a profession should see that the people know the purposes that it serves and the qualifications of its members.

In turn the public has a right to expect public service and spirit from professionals beyond that of other people. They must give their time and energy beyond immediate gain. They should not quit work when the whistle blows, free from all cares. The rewards and status of a profession involve public obligations related to such special knowledge as well as the common obligations of all citizenship.

Many professions are "suicidal" in that their goals, if achieved, would eliminate the need of the occupation. Dentists, for example, urge better dental care, yet dentists would be little needed if everyone had perfect, enduring teeth. If there were no crimes or disputes there would be little work for lawyers. If the public always enjoyed excellent health the need for doctors would be lessened. Yet good dentists continue to promote better dental health, lawyers fight crime, and doctors urge preventive health care. In practice, however, so great are human needs that no sooner is one problem solved than another arises.

ETHICAL CODES OF THE HIRED PROFESSIONAL

The relationship of a professional's obligations to society is not an abstraction and the examination of the codes of some hired professionsals shows this clearly.

The Soldier

At first glance, professional soldiers, lawyers, journalists, and public relations people may not seem to have much in common; yet they all try to influence (or sometimes force) other people to do things, albeit by different means.

Hired free-lance soldiers disappeared from the scene years ago, the last important ones in American memory being the German Hessians whom the British hired to help coerce the rebelling American colonists into submission in 1776. Soldiers today may be paid, but they usually work for a national state, such as France or the United States, of which they are usually citizens, and in whose army they serve. But until comparatively recent times many soldiers were hired, and they had various codes of conduct.

Probably the most fundamental thing about the conduct of a hired soldier, from his employer's point of view at least, was that he should stay hired at the wages agreed upon in advance. Employers naturally take a dim view of vacillating conduct, such as that of the Swiss mercenaries of the Duke of Milan in the late Middle Ages, who met a better offer from the King of France, just before the battle was to begin, and changed sides at once. The Duke spent the last eight years of his life in a cage in Paris, the victim of his foreign, paid troops. Loyalty to one's employer was the most fundamental and lowest level of the code of the professional soldier, even if it was, at times, rather uncertain.

Beyond loyalty, the next question in the code of the professional soldier might be "How does he fight?" This was of particular interest to the professional soldiers themselves, who after all were of the same brotherhood and were more interested in drawing their wages, taking it easy, and plundering than in killing each other. The little armies of *condottieri* who fought for Italian city-states and principalities during the Renaissance were more interested in winning than in slaying, and evolved elaborate codes of fighting which allowed a battle to go on all day with very few casualties. As in a gigantic chess game, the victory came when one side worked the soldiers of the other side into a corner, where by the rules they were allowed to surrender and thus live to fight another day—or perhaps even to join the opposition.

But all these mercenary arrangements disappeared at the time of the French Revolution, when the determined citizen-soldier appeared upon the scene. Now the question was not "How does he fight?" but only "For whom does he fight?" The Marseillaise-singing hordes of revolutionary France knew: They fought for France and liberty!

The Lawyer

The lawyer, according to the Anglo-Saxon concept, is also a hired persuader in the argument between the state or a person who has suffered a wrong and someone who is asserted to have done the wrong. It is a contest, and the lawyer operates within the framework of a court in which facts and viewpoints from both sides are presented to the end that justice may be achieved through the decision of the judge and jury.

When a lawyer takes a case, he may do so knowing that his client is innocent, partly guilty, or entirely guilty of the offense with which he is charged. He takes the case in the belief that all persons have certain rights which must be represented and protected. The lawyer's code calls for loyalty to his client in giving his upmost persuasive efforts in his behalf. If he believes that his client is half guilty, he will not give only half a plea. Half-persuasion would mean that he is judging his client, which is a function left to the court, in the knowledge that lawyers on both sides will present their cases as well as they can. Nor is the lawyer required to volunteer the *whole* truth about his client. He cannot lie, but he is not required to bring forth matters which would argue against his client.

In his presentation the lawyer is guided by the rules of the court, which constitute the framework of a contest whose end is a decision between two contending points of view—a decision which takes into account their relationship to the law. The lawyer, whether for the defense or for the prosecution, works as part of a court procedure whose goal is justice and the public welfare, and his freedom of persuasion is permitted, within limits, to this end. The system, admittedly, is not perfect: A capable lawyer with a weak case can sometimes overcome a poor lawyer with a good case. But it is not easy to find a better system without perhaps entrusting too much power to fallible human beings.

The Journalist

Consider also the code of the journalist. In a daily newspaper of any size, for example, he presents a view of the world. Yet his view can never be entirely objective because by selecting what to run and how big to play it, he is presenting an estimate of what he, or someone else, considers important. Moreover, he frequently finds himself presenting persuasions which are also in themselves facts, as when he reports arguments made in political speeches or in labor issues. In addition, most newspapers have their own editorial points of view, which they urge upon readers as the right way to see facts. The journalist is not as a rule a propagandist hired by someone else, but his communications are at least partly persuasion as well as information, entertainment, and self-expression; and his code must answer the question of "why" he or she persuades, as it does in the famous Journalist's Creed written by Dean Walter Williams, founder of the University of Missouri School of Journalism, in 1908:

> I believe that the public journal is a public trust; that all connected with it are, to the full measure of their responsibilities, trustees for the public. . . .

Here the touchstone is not loyalty to an employer or the nature and tone of the presentation, but instead the primacy of the public good.

THE PUBLIC RELATIONS PERSON'S CODE

What should be the code of one who is engaged in public relations?

Since he or she is a hired persuader, loyalty to the employer is fundamental. This requirement is covered in three of the fourteen articles of The Public Relations Society of America's 1977 Code of Professional Standards for the Practice of Public Relations (see the complete PRSA Code at the end of this chapter).

4   A member shall not represent conflicting or competing interests without the express consent of those involved, given after a full disclosure of the facts; nor place himself or herself in a position where the member's interest is or may be in conflict with a duty to a client, or others, without a full disclosure of such interests to all involved.

5   A member shall safeguard the confidences of both present and former clients or employers and shall not accept retainers or employment which may involve the disclosure or use of these confidences to the disadvantage or prejudice of such clients or employers.

12   A member, in performing services for a client or employer, shall not accept fees, commissions or any other valuable consideration from anyone other than the client or employer in connection with those services without the express consent of the client or employer given after a full disclosure of the facts.

Three other points refer to the conduct of public relations people toward each other:

10 A member shall not intentionally injure the professional reputation or practice of another practitioner. . . .

11 A member called as a witness in a proceeding for the enforcement of this code shall be bound to appear unless excused for sufficient reason by the Judicial Panel.

13 A member shall not guarantee the achievement of specified results beyond the member's direct control.

Six other points refer to the responsibility of public relations practitioners to act in a manner which is consistent with the public interest:

2 A member shall conduct his or her professional life in accord with the public interest.

3 A member shall adhere to truth and accuracy and to generally accepted standards of good taste.

6 A member shall not engage in any practice which tends to corrupt the integrity of channels of communication or the processes of government.

7 A member shall not intentionally communicate false or misleading information and is obligated to use care to avoid communication of false or misleading information.

8 A member shall be prepared to identify publicly the name of the client or employer on whose behalf any public communication is made.

9 A member shall not make use of any individual or organization purporting to serve or represent an announced case, or purporting to be independent or unbiased, but actually serving an undisclosed or private interest of a member, client, or employer.

The American Code is similar to that of The British Institute of Public Relations but the 1976 British Code has some interesting additional articles. Among them are:

9 A member shall not negotiate or agree to terms with a prospective employer or client on the basis of payment contingent upon specific future public relations achievement.

In the United States an earlier prohibition of contingency fees in the PRSA Code had to be modified because of the insistence of The Federal Trade Commission that it was in restraint of trade.

In the author's opinion the practice of public relations and that of law would both be benefited by the removal of contingency fees since in a profession the client hires the best efforts and skill of the professional and the stature of the professional should determine the fee rather than an uncertain outcome affected by the opposition, changes in surroundings, and shifting facts.

Another clause of the British Code:

11 A member shall not, with intent to further his interests (or those of his client or employer), offer or give any reward to a person holding public office if such action is inconsistent with the public interest.

And another:

12 A member who employs a member of Parliament, of either house, whether in a consultative or executive capacity, shall disclose this fact, and also the object of the employment, to the Director of The Institute, who shall enter it in a register kept for this purpose. . . . A member of the Institute who is himself a member of Parliament shall be responsible . . . for disclosing any such information as may relate to himself. . . . The register shall be open to public inspection. . . .

In many ways the practice of public relations can be compared to that of law in its ethical responsibilities with one major exception: The lawyer argues in a courtroom setting with the rules of procedure and of evidence and a prescribed opposition, whereas the public relations person does not face immediate rulings on what may be admitted to debate or not and often faces no immediate opposing case. Hence the responsibility of the public relations person is in many ways greater.

The power of modern communication in America is so great that while some can abuse it some of the time, it cannot be *generally* abused without demands arising that freedom of communication be limited because of fears of "poisoning the wellsprings of public opinion." Without self-regulation other regulation may ensue, perhaps disastrous for freedom itself. Codes set minimum standards to which the wise and honest can adhere, but the real achievement of high ethical practices in persuasive communication depends mainly upon the personal qualities and dedication to the public good of those who practice persuasion—and of those who hire them to do so.

PROBLEMS OF "REAL LIFE" PRACTICE

It is not always easy to be honest and public-spirited, because the rewards of being otherwise often seem tempting. David Finn, president of Ruder & Finn, New York, one of the nation's largest public relations firms, discussed this subject in an article in the *Harvard Business Review* some years ago. In it he asked:

> How honest a picture of its products should a company present to the public?
>
> What part should the artificial "build-up" play in public relations?
>
> How far should a company go in exploiting its contacts with influential people?
>
> Is a company obligated to be truthful about labor, pricing, and other touchy problems?
>
> What role, if any, should ulterior motives play in framing public relations policies?

(Most of these questions could also be asked of an individual in his personal relations with other people.) To be specific upon these points, Finn gave a number of simple examples of cases which illustrated the temptations, conflicts, and agonizing appraisals that can develop.

> Company A decided to build an image of one of its major products as being purer than its competitors. This was actually so. However, advertising claims of purity had been used and abused so heavily in the past by other companies that it decided to undertake a public relations program to get the story across. Accordingly a complicated scheme was invented involving the development of an "independent" research report that was to provide the basis for newspaper and magazine articles.
>
> The trouble was that the research was engineered; in fact it was not even to be paid for unless the publicity appeared in print. To ensure the success of the project, the man who arranged all this had some editors on his payroll as consultants for the research, thus almost guaranteeing eventual publication. It was a neat scheme—effective for the company and profitable for researcher, editor and middleman.
>
> The question was: Is this a responsible method of communicating the image of purity to the public?

Arguments in favor of the action maintained that the product was pure, that the public was not being deceived thereby, that no one was being bribed, and that the research was done by qualified scientists. Against the scheme was the argument that the research was not truly "independent" as represented, and that, because of their special payments, the editors were not free from bias.

After much consideration the idea was dropped. The risk was too great. Exposure would have not only ruined this particular program, but also severely damaged the reputation of the company that engaged in it.

The plan was somewhat dishonest as well as dangerous. Instead, research on a truly independent basis was recommended; it would probably be just as effective. In this case, ethical considerations and practical fears coincided.

Finn prefaced his next example with a question.

To what extent should a company build up its growth on deserved recognition and earned prestige, and eschew the fanfare of artificially stimulated applause?

The accusation that public relations involves an artificial build-up is one of the most serious ever leveled at it. . . .

Company B was seeking special recognition for a new variation of a standard product. To highlight the innovation, a new package had been created. The design was particularly striking, and the suggestion was made that somehow a design award should be arranged. Publicizing this award would help impress both salesmen and customers with the company's concern for high quality and, by association, would bring recognition to the new product's features.

The question was: Should public relations exploit only means of gaining recognition which would be above influence and partisanship?

The design was of high quality and could earn an award on its own merits. However, in order that it might be known by the judges, the package would have to be widely publicized; for instance, samples would have to be sent to experts for examination.

What is an "artificial" build-up? Do not many good things lie neglected because no one tries to make their virtues known? Is it perhaps not true that silence or letting publicity drift with the winds of chance may play down meritorious subjects as surely as undue promotion may build up poor ones? And in today's world of mass communications and few face-to-face contacts, at what point does a build-up using the mass media necessarily become "artificial"? These were some of the questions that lay behind the case of company B. Eventually it was decided that publicizing and sending out samples of the package in the hope that it would win an award were not at all wrong when no undue influence was exerted upon those who chose to make an award.

Influence peddling is another matter, observed Finn, who cited the case of company C:

Company C was extremely anxious to gain attention at an annual trade show. One way to accomplish this was through the local newspaper in the city where the show was being held. The competition for publicity in that newspaper was fierce, with every manufacturer at the trade show vying for it.

A public relations representative of Company C knew a photographer on the newspaper and spoke to him about the problem. The photographer developed a cute idea for a specially contrived photograph which might succeed in getting the company mentioned in the newspaper. He said he would set up and take the photograph for a small fee, with the understanding that if the picture was published in the paper, he would get considerably more money.

The question was: Should the company exploit this special "in" with the newspaper to solve an important problem?

The conclusion was that it should not, because the payment to the photographer contingent upon publication amounted to a bribe; it was an action taken behind the editor's back; and the company could not defend it if questioned about it later. "Honesty is the best policy" may sound more like expediency than the highest level of ethics, but the aphorism voices a practical, working philosophy.

Public relations activities are closely bound to the honesty of the business practices of a company or organization as a whole. There is not much use in trying to gloss over or whitewash basically bad practices. When something is wrong, public relations questions are frequently the first to bring it to light because in the practice of publicity the actions of the company must be examined in the pitiless light of "what will other people think?"

Company D sold its high-quality product to a few scattered discount houses but claimed it did not sell to any. This was common enough policy. But if the truth were told, the company's regular customers would be very angry. And yet the few discount houses it did sell to brought in a great deal of business.

The question was: Was dissimulation a justified business practice?

The practice could be defended on the basis that *generally* the company did not sell to discount houses, but this subterfuge led to an untruth when company salespeople were talking to regular customers or when the company was stating its position publicly. It was decided that the sales to discount houses should be dropped. The practice could not always be hidden from the trade; questions would have to be met with lies; and the whole marketing position of the firm would be jeopardized. The test might be: "Never do anything you would not want to see published in tomorrow morning's newspaper."

The Pennsylvania Truckers versus Railroads Case

Most ethical questions in public relations are questions of personal and organization morals rather than of law, because the relatively simple laws of libel do not extend very far into the areas of freedom of speech and its ethics. But in recent times, in two important instances, courts and proposed legislation have begun to codify ethics into law. One was the 1957 decision by Judge Clary of the United States District Court of the Eastern District of Pennsylvania in the suit brought by the Pennsylvania Truckers against the Eastern Railroad Presidents' Conference. The other was legislation proposed in the Eighty-fourth United States Congress (1956) following hearings before the Special Committee, headed by Senator McClellan, to investigate political activities, lobbying, and campaign contributions.

In the Pennsylvania Truckers versus Eastern Railroads case the railroads and their public relations firm were charged by the truckers with having entered into a conspiracy to destroy the business of the truckers by unethical means.

The suit was brought under the Sherman and Clayton Antitrust Acts, alleging that the railroads were seeking to gain a monopoly of long-distance freight hauling in Pennsylvania by creating public and legislative ill will against trucking to the point where truck-hauling activities were likely to be so severely limited by law as to be no longer competitive.

Methods of injury complained of by the truckers included half-truths, the use of third-party organizations to propagandize with their sources of support carefully concealed, and hidden-source feeding of partly true news and feature stories to newspapers and magazines.

For example, in New Jersey an organization known as "New Jersey Automobile Owners, Inc.," which was supported by the railroads, sent out speakers before civic clubs attacking trucking, and when its support was questioned, completely denied all railroad connections. Mats of photographs were distributed free to smaller newspapers from a railroad-supported "Central States News View Company" in Chicago. Along with sex and sports pictures, the company frequently offered photos of road or bridge damage caused by trucks. In a campaign engineered by the public relations firm, magazine articles exposing the damage supposedly done to highways by trucks were sent by free-lance writers to leading American national magazines. There were many other instances, all handled by the public relations firm, but all paid for and approved by the railroads.

In awarding damages against the railroads, Judge Clary made several points.

1 The case was considered because it came within the purview of antitrust legislation in that an attempt was made to injure a competitor so as to create a monopoly.

2 There was no objection to positive public relations which sought to obtain benefits by building up an organization's own merits or by informing the public or legislative bodies of facts and views upon a situation.

3 The use of persuasive techniques to injure a competitor was questionable, especially if done by means of half-truths, hidden third-party fronts, and concealment of origins of material from editors and others. If a public relations firm engaged in this sort of activity, it could not escape responsibility by pleading the orders of its employer.

Judge Clary assessed 20 percent of the cost of a large fine against the public relations firm and stipulated that the railroads could not reimburse it.

In February of 1961 the United States Supreme Court reversed the award of $852,074 against the railroads made by Judge Clary and upheld by an appeals court. Justice Hugo Black, writing the opinion, said that a campaign aimed at public and political opinion, no matter how nasty, did not come within the realm of the antitrust acts. "Such deception," he said, "reprehensible as it is, has nothing to do with the Sherman Antitrust Act."

This does not mean, of course, that responsible persons think that the tactics used in the truckers-railroad case were good or that they did not do considerable harm by the abuse of public confidence. Probably the suit by the truckers served its main purpose of exposing the opposition, and Judge Clary's opinion, although not upheld in regard to the Sherman Act, is also a landmark which will be well worth watching.

Oil and Gas Lobby Hearings

The hearings before the Special Committee of the United States Senate in 1956 investigating political activities, lobbying, and campaign contributions in connection with the oil and gas lobby investigation also brought forth a number of interesting points.

The word "lobbying" has acquired a sinister connotation because of its occasional connection with corruption and bribery; yet an individual or an organization does nothing wrong in presenting a case before legislators. The citizen has a constitutional right of petition. Those who fail to plead their causes as well as they can before legislators and legislative bodies have only themselves to thank if their negligence results in the passage of adverse or unjust laws.

To enable the members of Congress to know better who is speaking for whom, however, Congress has enacted laws requiring the registration of lobbyists and identification of their clients. In recent years, also, some congressmen have become concerned about "indirect lobbying," or attempts to influence their legislative attitudes without direct contact. The pressure may be exerted by political campaign contributions from those who hope that their support will be repaid in favors, or by building a fire in a congressman's own home constituency. At one time an oil company paid for hundreds of telegrams to be sent to a certain congressman protesting a bill which would have affected the oil company adversely. Many wires were sent without the knowledge or approval of the persons whose names were signed. The action was clearly unethical and illegal.

But writing a law to prevent indirect lobbying in general is another matter. Consider campaign contributions, for example: In these days of expensive mass communications by means of newspapers, radio, television, and billboards which reach millions of voters, large sums of money are needed to finance any important political campaign. How can this amassing of funds be prevented? If corporations and unions are forbidden to give money can a private citizen, no matter how wealthy, be barred from buying an advertisement to express his or her views? It does not seem likely. At what point does freedom of speech end, if end it does?

In deciding upon the rights of "building a fire" under congressmen in their home areas, the decision is equally difficult. False telegrams are obviously unethical. But what about company representatives going about stimulating letters to the congressman, giving speeches, or seeking newspaper editorials in support of their views? Should they or anyone else be prevented from such actions? The area of freedom of speech is soon invaded. Do members of Congress have a right to try to protect themselves from these "spurs to prick the sides of their intent"? Or do they just have to use their own judgment upon the motives and sources of petitions?

These questions have not been decided, and in our democracy it is doubtful whether they ever will be fully answered. Their consideration brings to light some of the ethical questions in public relations practice.

OTHER SPECIFIC PROBLEMS

The whole area of freedom and ethics in persuasion has developed many unsettled aspects in recent years.

For example in many states the public service commissions which regulate the rates charged by utilities such as gas or electricity will not allow the cost of advertising urging the merits of private ownership of utilities to be charged as an ordinary business expense on the books of the utility although advertising urging the conservation of fuel can be so charged. This effectively makes such private ownership advertising more expensive to the company since the funds for it have to come out of profits *after* all business expenses such as wages, coal, and other operating costs have been met. The rationale of public service commissions in doing this is that since the utility is a chartered monopoly it has no right to force its customers to contribute to advertising its good public image and thus encourage its continuance. The effect, however, is to disarm the utility from presenting its case while not handicapping its opponents such as rate-protest and environmental groups which get easy publicity and do not depend on advertising for communication.

The "fairness doctrine" of the Federal Communications Commission requires in general that when a broadcasting station (which is regulated and licensed by the FCC) airs a "controversial" advertising program or spot that it be prepared to give equal time (free if need be) to the opposing side. The net effect of this has been to make stations timid about carrying controversial matter. Some of the oil companies, for example, have had spots promoting their search for offshore oil. This has led to demands from environmental groups that they be given equal time to oppose such drilling. But stations are not in a position to judge the merit or the truthfulness of such material on either side and to handle it accordingly. So a natural reaction is to carry neither side, thus depriving persuaders of a means of reaching the people and people of hearing what they have to say.

Fortunately this same rule does not apply to the printed press, although there are some who would like to have it do so. Newspapers and magazines are free to accept or to reject advertising with a few exceptions. Newspapers of general circulation usually carry all sorts of paid persuasions as a public obligation so long as they are not libelous and are in good taste, but special interest magazines such as those published by religious groups or social causes may be more restrictive. You would not think of placing an argument for liquor in a prohibitionist magazine, for example.

As mentioned earlier, the Securities and Exchange Commission requirement that American companies doing business overseas disclose to their shareholders (and hence to the general public) any "questionable payments" to obtain business has also exposed an ethical problem—how much can standards of business morality differ abroad and how can American firms still remain effective in their selling? Such disclosure, of course, is also required in domestic activities.

THE RISE OF ORGANIZED INTEREST GROUPS

One of the phenomena of the past twenty years has been the rise of powerful organized interest groups in the United States for all sorts of causes—consumers, environmentalist, the elderly and ethnic in addition to previously existing groups such as farmers, business, labor, and religious. Because of the nature of news which features the unusual or controversial many of these have learned to exploit the media easily and get great public attention, often much more than their numbers warrant. This has been particularly true of television news which is limited in the number of items that it can carry, is hungry for the visual, presents everything as of somewhat equal importance because of its sequential nature, and has an air of great immediacy and truthfulness. It is also a very powerful news medium.

It is not hard for any group to attack something or other and get wide publicity for its views. It is also a well-known fact of news and political life that answers seldom catch-up with accusations. The defense is always late, seems self-serving, and is not very exciting to those who enjoy believing the worst, especially if the person or institution being attacked is large and well-established. The defense, also, is usually unable to go over to the attack itself because its target is so small or so righteous that to do so would simply aid its publicity. This becomes a difficult public relations situation.

This is not to say that all special interest group promotion is of this sort, but some of it is because of the common feeling among people who are very excited about some cause that their goal is so important that almost any means is justified in achieving it. At the extreme this may take the form of terrorism. At a lower level it may manifest itself in riots, demonstrations, boycotts and unsupported accusations. There is an element of trying to coerce the general public rather than attempting to persuade it. It is an assault rather than an argument.

This raises the age-old ethical question: Does a good end justify a bad means of achieving it? And in a democracy we must say "no" because democracy is a *way* of life, not an end. It is the way we live together and keep in harmony to achieve the best ends of which we are capable. Our choice of goals and our means of reaching them change from time to time as we learn more and as our surrounding circumstances change. But in living together in a democratic society *truth* remains truth. "Poisoning the wellsprings of public opinion" is not justifiable. Appeals to hate or fear or blind emotionalism are not as good as those to reason and goodwill. And a degree of modesty in being sure of the wisdom of our goals is always fitting because history is littered with good people who turned out to be wrong.

In other words, the ethical requirements of a public relations person for a good cause should be just as high as those of any other public relations practitioner. This does not mean that the procedures need be identical, because these are determined by resources, reputation and other factors. But the standards of honesty, fairness and intelligent persuasion should be as high for one cause as another. Volunteer public relations is subject to the same standards as hired. A noble goal is no excuse for ignoble means.

WHY ETHICS?

There are a number of very practical reasons:

1 Unethical practice invites the imposition of laws which themselves may be injurious and restrictive. At the extreme, for example, if bribery and corruption of Congress became rampant a law might be passed preventing most causes from attempting to influence their members of Congress—which would be a denial of the right of petition. Or if falsehoods were prevalent in public relations advertising someone might propose a law requiring all statements to be approved in advance by some government board—censorship and a denial of free speech.

Ethical practice makes such complaints rare so it preserves our liberties and makes the heavy hand of law necessary.

2 Unethical practice destroys the trust which is necessary to a democratic way of life. If you know that you cannot trust what you read or see or hear, there is no way to come to an intelligent conclusion on important current issues.

We can know little from our own personal knowledge, so it is necessary that we can trust the honesty and good faith of others. This does not mean that we must agree with them. Often we learn the most from those with whom we disagree. We need to hear various viewpoints and to know who is speaking.

3 A profession cannot advance unless it is both competent and ethical. Otherwise people who employ it cannot be sure that they are getting what they paid for and the general public cannot be sure that its practice is to their interests.

SUMMARY

Rules of the Game and Personal Honor

As long as people have interests to achieve or things to sell, they will urge them upon buyers. Persuasive communications exist for all sorts of ends —to get Congress to enact a bill which its unselfish sponsors sincerely believe will lead to world peace; to achieve safety on the highways; to prohibit the sale of alcoholic beverages; to raise minimum wages; to establish free universal medical care; to sell life insurance, automobiles, education, or concrete. Each group believes that its goals are legitimate and good.

Here another ethical problem confronts persuasion. A good end cannot be held to justify a bad means. To use a fantastic example, the hope of enacting a world peace bill would not justify bribery, lies, and deception to obtain its passage (although some of its sponsors might feel that it did). Public relations, like democracy itself, is a *way* of achieving agreement through understanding and persuasion. The way is just as important as the ends sought at any particular moment by fallible human beings; and indeed it may be more important, because democracy lives by the road it travels.

Lies, half-truths, concealed support, personal attacks, false appeals to unworthy emotions, smears upon personal or group integrity are all *bad* means—bad, because their employment destroys the confidence between men, which is the basis of our freedom. Their use is selfish and irresponsible and injures the public welfare, which sustains our very form of government. They have within them seeds of hatred, internal warfare, and suppression.

The power of free communication is great, and with great power goes great responsibility. Public relations people must not only persuade fairly, but they must also guide themselves by what they feel is best for the public welfare as any honest, intelligent, well-informed person may see it.

The Integrity of Us All

We cannot say that, like a stream, public relations practice can rise no higher than its source; occasionally it does. Many public relations people have a keener sense than their employers have of right and wrong and of what conduces to the public welfare; but it is hard to rise much above e, because this is where the money and orders come from. ttions people can advise, warn, and encourage—but then they ually either do as requested or resign the account or their job. ...s is a hard choice which, happily, not many people have to face often. Fortunate indeed is the public relations practitioner who can be in whole-hearted agreement with her cause all the time!

Public relations persuasion is a weapon in modern society. Even when used loyally and fairly, its effects will still depend upon the purposes of those who yield it and upon the morals of the businessmen, public officials, educators, churchmen, and others who hire those skilled in persuasive communication in order to help argue their cases before the bar of public opinion.

But, in another way, public relations is a guardian of the social conscience. Light is always better than darkness, and public relations activities focus light upon organizations. The organization that claims to be good assumes obligations to live up to its claims or to suffer double outcries if it fails. There is no doubt that social consciousness in the United States today is much higher than it was a generation or two ago, and public relations is both an effect and cause of this improvement. Organizations are better and extol their own virtues; they wish to be better thought of, and therefore make claims which they have to live up to. Public sensitivity toward failures of performance to match claims is at a high peak. A commercial conscience, perhaps—but public relations is still a conscience about which cynicism is a luxury, because light should be encouraged rather than extinguished.

ADDITIONAL READINGS

Periodicals

Because there are constant new developments, a great many articles on ethics and professionalism in public relations and in related areas such as journalism and advertising have been published in periodicals such as *Public Relations Journal, Public Relations Quarterly,* the *Quill* of Sigma Delta Chi, *Editor & Publisher, Columbia Journalism Review,* and others. A listing of those particularly referring to public relations can be found in *The Public Relations Bibliography* referred to in an earlier chapter.

Books

Johannsen, Richard, ed., *Ethics and Persuasion.* (New York: Random House, 1967.)

Rivers, William L., and Wilbur Schramm, *Responsibility in Mass Communication.* Rev. ed., (New York: Harper & Row, 1968.)

CHAPTER APPENDIX

PUBLIC RELATIONS SOCIETY OF AMERICA

Code of Professional Standards for the Practice of Public Relations

Adopted and Effective April 29, 1977

(This Code, adopted by the PRSA Assembly, replaces a similar Code of Professional Standards for the Practice of Public Relations previously in force since 1954 and strengthened by revisions in 1959)

Declaration of Principles

Members of the Public Relations Society of America base their professional principles on the fundamental value and dignity of the individual, holding that the free exercise of human rights, especially freedom of speech, freedom of assembly and freedom of the press, is essential to the practice of public relations.

In serving the interests of clients and employers, we dedicate ourselves to the goals of better communication, understanding and cooperation among the diverse individuals, groups and institutions of society.

We pledge:

To conduct ourselves professionally, with truth, accuracy, fairness and responsibility to the public;

To improve our individual competence and advance the knowledge and proficiency of the profession through continuing research and education;

And to adhere to the articles of the Code of Professional Standards for the Practice of Public Relations as adopted by the governing Assembly of the Society.

Articles of the Code

These articles have been adopted by the Public Relations Society of America to promote and maintain high standards of public service and ethical conduct among its members.

1 A member shall deal fairly with clients or employers, past and present, with fellow practitioners and the general public.

2 A member shall conduct his or her professional life in accord with the public interest.

3 A member shall adhere to truth and accuracy and to generally accepted standards of good taste.

4 A member shall not represent conflicting or competing interests without the express consent of those involved, given after a full disclosure of the facts; nor place himself or herself in a position where the member's interest is or may be in conflict with a duty to a client, or others, without a full disclosure of such interests to all involved.

5 A member shall safeguard the confidences of both present and former clients or employers and shall not accept retainers or employment which may involve the disclosure or use of these confidences to the disadvantage or prejudice of such clients or employers.

6 A member shall not engage in any practice which tends to corrupt the integrity of channels of communication or the processes of government.

7 A member shall not intentionally communicate false or misleading information and is obligated to use care to avoid communication of false or misleading information.

8 A member shall be prepared to identify publicly the name of the client or employer on whose behalf any public communication is made.

9 A member shall not make use of any individual or organization purporting to serve or represent an announced case, or purporting to be independent or unbiased, but actually serving an undisclosed special or private interest of a member, client or employer.

10 A member shall not intentionally injure the professional reputation or practice of another practitioner.

However, if a member has evidence that another member has been guilty or unethical, illegal or unfair practices, including those in violation of this Code, the member shall present the information promptly to the proper authorities of the Society for action in accordance with the procedure set forth in Article XIII of the Bylaws.

11 A member called as a witness in a proceeding for the enforcement of this Code shall be bound to appear, unless excused for sufficient reason by the Judicial Panel.

12 A member, in performing services for a client or employer, shall not accept fees, commissions or any other valuable consideration from anyone other than the client or employer in connection with those services without the express consent of the client or employer, given after a full disclosure of the facts.

13 A member shall not guarantee the achievement of specified results beyond the member's direct control.

14 A member shall, as soon as possible, sever relations with any organization or individual if such relationship requires conduct contrary to the articles of this Code.

Chapter 17

The Future of
Public Relations

"Public relations," or the activity of planned, persuasive communication
in behalf of widely assorted causes (by whatever name it may be called),
is certain to continue to expand rapidly in the years ahead.

Immediate economic conditions may bring ups and downs in its use,
and feelings within particular areas may swing from favorable to unfavorable regard, but all the conditions which called public relations into
being earlier in this century not only are continuing but are being constantly intensified. Populations are greater, communications are more
widespread, and issues in dispute have increased in number. The only
way that the growth in the practice of public relations could be halted
would be by the disruption of a major war, a steady decline in the
conditions of economic life to a subsistence level, or the imposition of the
dead hand of state control in the form of censorship or a state monopoly
of communications such as exists within the Iron Curtain countries or
existed in Nazi Germany or Fascist Italy.

Otherwise, as the size of the units of human organization continues to expand, as the interactions of groups of people become more important to all, and as the communications media multiply, change is ever-present, creating a need for the services of interpreters and a market for advocates of these new viewpoints. Since the constant alterations in modern ways of life are sparked by a worldwide revolution in scientific technology, it is not likely that changes will soon cease or that anybody in this world will ever again return to a primitive mental Garden of Eden. Too many people have tasted of the apple of the tree of knowledge, and there are no more Shangri-Las concealed behind unscaled mountains. No unexplored areas are left on the physical face of the globe, and few isolated mental areas exist undisturbed anywhere. To be sure, barriers to the transmission of ideas are forcefully maintained in some places; but even such Chinese Walls against thought are being constantly undermined all the time both from without and from within. Ideas are—and should be—hard to confine.

Public relations is but another manifestation of the new day in communication of thought in which this small planet begins its period of turmoil in drawing up a grand new design for a workable world order and in reaching for the stars. Like the times in which we live, the practice of public relations is still confused, its needs perforce rushing ahead of its knowledge. Some tasks have been accomplished, and others have hardly been begun.

TASKS LARGELY ACCOMPLISHED

Consciousness of Identity   In order that a discipline may progress, its practitioners must know who they are, what role they play in society, and what they seek. In the past several decades, men and women in American public relations have become increasingly conscious of their common identity and community of interest. They know who they are and more and more tend to agree upon what they do. They have formed themselves into organizations, exchanged ideas, encouraged each other (even in the midst of sharp competition), improved their knowledge, and raised their standards. Sometimes they have been almost embarrassingly vocal about their newly acquired self-knowledge; often they have claimed too much; but since it is their business to be vocal, all this talk has had great value in working out identity and has been beneficial when it has not degenerated into self-delusion or self-worship. Public relations is much more important in the plans of almost all organizations than it was twenty or thirty years ago.

The real question is whether public relations people will be equally important. This depends upon their ability as expert communicators, their foresight in seeing what needs to be communicated, and the willingness of employers to entrust them with heavier responsibility.

Literature   Since public relations people are in the business of communication, they have written many books and articles about their work. Some aspects of public relations have been discussed over and over again to the point of satiety, while others have been barely or not at all touched. Public relations is dividing into specialized fields of knowledge such as financial public relations, environmental or consumer. All are complicated and almost occupations in themselves.

In a foreword to the 1974 edition of the PRSA Bibliography for 1964–1972, Scott Cutlip noted that among the 4,000 articles and books on public relations listed for those years there were no up-to-date books to guide public relations practice in public schools, higher education, social welfare, hospitals, labor unions and municipal and state government. This is a common condition in fields which are changing rapidly and in which magazine articles result rather than more expensive and longer-lasting books.

By any standards, however, public relations literature is profuse. The four bibliographies issued under the sponsorship of PRSA since 1957 contain more than 12,000 titles of books and magazine articles upon all aspects of public relations from "advertising" and "aerospace" to "writing" and "youth" in more than a hundred classifications. While complete works may not be available in every field, no one with access to a good library needing ideas or advice need go unfulfilled.

Public Awareness   Although many people misunderstand the nature and purpose of public relations, almost all educated people in the United States are aware of its existence, whether they like it or not. This was not so fifty years ago.

TASKS UNDERWAY

Broader Employer Understanding   A great many thousands of employers of all sorts, from businessmen to school boards, have in the past few years realized the need of skilled communication and have supported at least some of the essentials of good public relations practice. That they have been willing to put out enough money to enter the field is a tribute to their alertness and education.

The problem now is not so much that of getting employers to use public relations as of creating a better understanding of its true potential and its limitations. Too many businesses, for example, still fail at the vital point of customer relations; too many still expect a flood of last-minute communications to do a speedy job of righting situations in which the intended audience has already decided and stopped listening; too many fail to realize that if an organization has become famous through publicity, the public will expect much more of it than of an obscure group or business.

Education and habits of thought can best be given, usually, to future executives while they are still in colleges or in training programs. Widely distributed articles, talks, books and films are also helpful, but broader understanding of public relations principles remains a major need for employers—and for all leaders in a democratic society.

Greater Cooperation with the Social Sciences. Neither scholars nor public relations people of affairs yet know as much as they should about the reactions of human beings to situations and communications. Although by its very nature public relations is concerned with social psychology, it has been deficient in the support of research in this area and in the use of what has been done. The social scientist often does not speak to the practical world and the public relations practitioner cannot understand the social scientist and does not have time to delve into his findings. The same problem exists in fields such as medicine or physics, of course.

Much has been accomplished in universities and in private organizations supplied with funds from business and government resources, but the big break-throughs in understanding human response still seem to be ahead. Perhaps they are dependent upon the development of new measuring devices to detect human responses. Today we remain still largely ignorant about how people obtain the ideas they have and why they select some ideas in preference to others; yet there is no more important subject to be studied. One reason for the problem may be that human responses are in a constantly changing environment, so that in order to predict them it is necessary not only to know how people think but also to be constantly aware of the surrounding conditions. Such inability to control or even understand the environment makes the predictive power of applied social sciences much below that of the physical sciences.

Education for Public Relations Hundreds of American universities and colleges teach one or more courses labeled "public relations," and many offer sequences of courses leading to an undergraduate major, or even a degree, usually undergraduate, but occasionally a Master of Arts. As the idea of public relations has widened from the concept of a set of skills such as those in newswriting or broadcasting, to these skills plus a broad understanding of people, of organizations, and of the changing world, the scope of public relations education has also grown. Today the increasing tendency is to make it possible for those who expect to go into its practice to specialize in the subject at the graduate level, and to offer a number of "principles" courses for the many students in other major fields of interest. Students of business or political science, for example, may want to know at least something about public relations for use in their own areas.

Better education will lead to better users and practitioners of public relations, but there are still many problems to be solved in adequate public relations education. Provision of systematized case material for teachers, better education of teachers, greater cooperation between practitioners and teachers in student enlightenment, and more opportunities for students to obtain practical experience at a decision-making level are among the most needed developments.

Better International Contacts As public relations develops in many nations of the world, a great need arises for closer fellowship between the practitioners in many places. The stimulation and encouragement obtained by studying similar problems under highly varying conditions are extremely valuable. In addition, the shared interests of public relations people of various nations are a strong force for international cooperation, because public relations people of all nations realize that their work may be developed only under conditions of peace and freedom.

World Congresses of public relations are held every three years, the first having been in Brussels in 1958 and the latest in Boston in 1976. Well-to-do public relations people and those belonging to international corporations or government representatives are able to travel much and to meet their counterparts elsewhere, but much could still be done in organizing student and educator exchanges, foreign internships, worldwide publications, special conferences, and other well-planned contacts.

The Development of Ethical Practices The problems of "right and wrong" in public relations, which were discussed in a preceding chapter, are not peculiar to this activity alone; they reflect the moral standards of those who employ advocates and of society as a whole. Nevertheless, the moral problems of public relations are pushed into prominence because the activity makes claims for products or projects, and public relations people are forced to be the keepers, not only of their own consciences, but also of the consciences of the organizations for which they work.

The fact that many public relations people struggle and suffer with their own moral problems as advocates, and also with the problems of their clients, is all to the good. There should be much more wrestling with conscience! If public relations people do not speak for the public in the inner councils of their employers, who else will? (The idea of a corporation chaplain has not been tried so far as it is known.) If no one speaks for the public, if the consciences of those in power do not prompt them to such consideration, then the public will surely find its own defenders elsewhere. A good public relations practitioner should have a tender conscience—and those who hire him should be willing to listen even if not agreeing.

TASKS STILL CHALLENGING

Professional Development   Since public relations offers a service which buyers find hard to evaluate, the establishment of high professional standards for its practitioners becomes of great importance to the development of the activity. Professional standing involves the adoption of basic standards of education, some form of certification testifying to the competence and trustworthiness of the practitioners, and continuing education to keep up with changes. The attainment of these standards constitutes the strength of the professions of both law and medicine. Because of its intangible nature and relative newness, public relation has a much longer road to travel. Probably the goal of state licensing is neither possible nor desirable because its potential conflict with freedom of speech.

The alternative to licensing is voluntary certification administered by a professional organization rather than by the government and requiring meaningful experience and study. Similar examples in the United States might be the emergence of Certified Public Accountants (CPA) or Chartered Life Underwriters (CLU).

The first steps in this field were made by the British Institute of Public Relations a number of years ago with the development or a comprehensive examination and a period of experience as a requirement for membership in the organization.

In 1963 the Public Relations Society of America developed a similar accreditation program which is now required of all new members of PRSA who are then entitled to place the initials APR after their names. Like the initials CPA or MD or PhD after a name, this indicates at least a certain degree of education and intent on the part of the practitioner. It will become more meaningful as entrance standards are raised, greater continuing education developed, and loss of accreditation becomes a more serious possibility and penalty.

Broader Public Understanding of Public Relations The practice of public relations rests upon the right of freedom of speech which is given to all citizens—including journalists, authors, advertisers and broadcasters. This right exists, not for the benefit of the speakers, but in order that those who hear or read may have access to varying views. Yet many people are unaware that freedom of speech is for the benefit of the hearers as well as the speakers. The public is uneasy about possible manipulation of its views and the hidden sources its ideas, and the wild claims of some communications experts have fostered this fear. As a result there is always danger of popular support for censorship or intimidation. Snide remarks about public relations as the equivalent of "falsehood" do not help.

The more the nature of public relations is understood and its practice is accepted as an inevitable corollary to the democratic freedom of speech and listening, the better it will be for society all over the world. More needs to be done to assist public understanding of the rightful role of public relations practice within a democracy.

Clarification of Public Relations's Role in Government The practice of public relations within a democratic government may be a means of informing citizens and of obtaining their cooperation with government. The noisy feuds between Congress and the executive, badgering investigations and heckling need to be replaced with more sober consideration of the uses of government public relations to obtain citizen cooperation in such matters as defense, conservation of natural resources and the development of our national economy. The idea that the successful conduct of a large democratic government in changing times does not need some form of public relations aid is increasingly absurd at a time when the margin for error is diminished and international closeness makes the cohesiveness of the American people and their speed of intelligent reaction more important than ever before. Public relations within various branches of government should be recognized for what it is rather than disguised or excused. The public must be aware of its sources and able to judge. If a nation is to be governed by its people, then the people must be informed or they will not be able to govern.

The Development of Public Relations in America's World Role

The greatest task of public relations has been discussed in detail before but it cannot be over-emphasized. The explanation of America's position in the world is the biggest communications problem this nation has ever faced. A generation or more ago, the world's image of the United States and what we hope for was unimportant; today it seems vital. Skilled as Americans seem in the arts of communication at home, they still flounder if their efforts to influence onlookers abroad.

Our national record needs to be better, not because of vanity or a simple desire to be liked, but because freedom and open discussion are the only basis upon which a workable, lasting world order can be hammered out. Anything founded upon agreements between governments which do not have the consent or support of their own well-informed people is built upon sand. And there can be no mistake; such an order must be created soon. People cannot remain on this small planet, much less explore the stars, unless they "forsake their foolish ways" that earth may be one.

Studied deprivation of access to information or planned deceit are truly crimes against humanity and there can be little place for them in the world's future. Freedom of speech and hearing should be open to all. In such an emerging new world, public relations as the planned advocacy of causes before the bar of public opinion has a unique responsibility. How well it fulfills it depends in large part on the courage, energy, wisdom and honor of the men and women who work in this exciting new field.

Appendix A

Some Additional Examples of Public Relations in Action

1. A BIG BANK SHOWS THAT IT IS SENSITIVE TO HUMAN INTEREST

Hanover Bank (now Manufacturers Hanover Trust Company) at 70 Broadway in New York seized upon an opportunity for news action some years ago with enterprise and imagination that became a public relations classic case.

On December 6, 1955, the Hanover Bank, as coexecutor of the estate of the late William Woodward, Jr., a well-known horse fancier, announced that on December 15 the nation's top race horse, Nashua, and sixty-one of his stablemates would be sold through sealed bids. This was important sports news and got top play in many dailies.

On December 15, Nashua was sold for $1,251,200, and his stablemates brought an additional $615,000. Again, sports editors gave the news top billing.

On December 16, shortly before noon, the Public Relations Department of the Hanover Bank was notified by the Personal Trust Division that the following letter, accompanied by a color sketch of Nashua, had been received:

Dear Sirs:

    I read in the paper today that you are going to sell Nashua and his friends. If you have a horse that no one will buy, I would like to. You can send him or her out to the following address: 22 Rutledge Rd., Valhalla, N.Y.

    The horse will have a good home, 1½ acres of woods and fields and loveing care. I would like a horse that would grow old with me. My sealed bid is $24.03, but maybe by the time you have opened the bids I have earened some more money, I can pay a little higher.

> Sincerely yours,
> (SIGNED) Karen Ann McGuire

P.S. My place is called Bramble Hill.

The Personal Trust Division could not classify this letter as a firm bid. Therefore it was treated as a communication and was not processed with the legal bids that were submitted.

The bank's public relations director saw in this letter an opportunity to show to the public that bankers are human and to associate the Hanover Bank with a heart-warming project that would, through the happiness of a child, give the public vicarious pleasure. Action had to be rapid and most steps were consummated with seventy-two hours after the letter first came to his attention. Here is what was done:

This first press conference was only the beginning. Media representatives were kept informed of Karen's progress in selecting a horse. Before the actual presentation was made, about a week later, the horse had to be bought and equipped with saddle, bridle, halter, and blanket; felt lettering was affixed to the blanket, one side reading, "Karen Ann McGuire" and the other "Hanover's Wishing Star"; a veterinarian was engaged to examine the horse and to issue a certificate of health; and an even larger number of media representatives were invited to the second conference than had come to the first. An additional complication was the fact that the conference actually began forty-five minutes ahead of scheduled time because all the participants got there early! The first press conference had been held at Hanover's midtown branch bank because of its greater convenience for both the press and the McGuires; the second was held at the riding stables in Greenwich, Connecticut, where the horse had been housed until presentation. The bank's president, who made a thirty-two-word presentation talk, passed the bridle to Karen, and remained out of the scene while press, magazine, and TV photographers took pictures for nearly two hours. The bank's own photographer was on the scene and took additional photos, which were later sent to banking trade magazines with a story which told, from the bank's viewpoint, something of the public relations thinking behind the event.

Figure A–1   Quick action, imagination, and friendliness were evident when the Hanover Bank of New York City presented a horse to a little girl who had written a letter in response to a news story about the sale of an estate.

The coverage of this story by the press was extremely heavy, including front-page pictures in the biggest American newspapers of both the East and the Midwest as well as editorial mention.

The outstanding characteristics of the action (which received a wellmerited American Public Relations Association award) were the quick recognition of opportunity by the bank's public relations head, the speed with which it was handled while it was hot news, and the thoroughness with which every detail was covered—all essentials in good public relations actions.

2.   CHANGING A 100-YEAR-OLD COMPANY IMAGE

What do you do when, over many years, the public image of a major company has become blurred and generally unfavorable? The long-range public image of the Kohler Company in 1972 was that of a paternalistic, antiunion, very private corporation making plumbing fixtures in a small town in Wisconsin.

Part of it was true. Corporate headquarters were located in a small town named Kohler in Wisconsin. The town had been established and built by the company. The company had been engaged in the longest major strike in American history, from 1954 to 1962. Its stock was closely held—most of it in the hands of one family for three generations. And it did make bathroom fixtures, excellent ones.

But only part of the picture was true. The town of Kohler was not the dreary "company town" that many imagined. It was beautifully planned with attractive homes of all levels of cost mixed together and had been a pioneer in American well-planned communities. Its people owned their own homes, ran their own affairs, and not all of them worked for Kohler. The company had been engaged in a long strike but now recognized unions and had a good record of employment and wages. It made plumbing fixtures but it also made gasoline motors and electronic equipment. It *was* largely owned by Kohler family members but they had done a good job of running it, had brought in capable outsiders, and were intensely concerned with its future.

The problem was to find an occasion to tell the American public about all this and the vehicle taken to do so was the 100th anniversary of the Kohler Company which occurred in 1973. It was hoped not only to balance the unfavorable news picture but also to call attention to new product lines and to build understanding among employees, dealers, communities, financial sources, and other publics which would provide a fresh start for a successful second century. A major Chicago-based public relations firm was employed to design and help implement a program.

The first step was to find a name and an insignia for the event. This was: "Bold Craftsmen Since 1873." Then followed a large booklet, a motion picture, a Centennial Tour Program inviting the public to visit the town and the plant, new products, construction of a display house in the town to show company products, a major national invitational ceramics exhibition, news releases and features, area newspaper advertising on the centennial, distributor meetings, special issues of the employee newspaper, employee picnics, and, finally, a pink champagne birthday party reception for employees and a centennial gift for all employees.

There is nothing unusual about centennial nor was there about the elements of the program. What *was* unusual was the thoroughness with which they were done and their response. It was estimated that 90 million Americans were exposed to messages about Kohler that year.

Print and electronic media coverage was estimated at about $2 million if it had been purchased—which it could not have been. More than 30,000 people received copies of the color history magazine, 25,000 saw the centennial motion picture, 23,000 attended the ceramics exhibition, and 100,000 readers received the local area special newspaper advertising tabloid. The Centennial picnics for employees were attended by 20,000 and the birthday parties by 9,000 employees and their spouses.

The program received a Public Relations Society of American "Silver Anvil" Award. More importantly, it used an opportunity which comes but once in every one hundred years to create a fresh start in the public mind for an

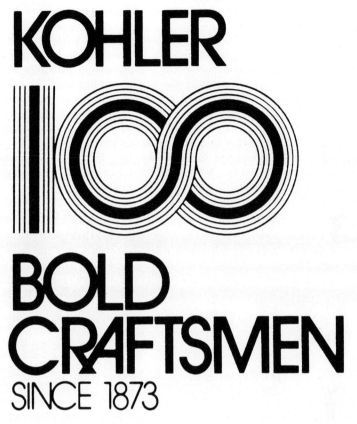

Figure A–2   The first step in the Kohler Company's celebration of its 100th birthday was to design an insignia incorporating the theme of the event. This was used on all literature and advertising.

organization which had considerable success in the previous century but a doubtful public image.

3. TRYING TO GET MORE UNDERSTANDING OF THE OPERATING PROBLEMS OF A COMMUTER RAILROAD

Public utility companies (and especially commuter railroads) have special public relations problems. So long as they do everything well, everyone takes it for granted. But when service fails for any reason, complaints are bitter and most of it gets taken out on the employees, whose morale and will to better service falls accordingly. Of course, there *is* no substitute for good service. That is what a public utility is given a monopoly franchise for. But the complexity of providing good service is not always appreciated—so a better user and public insight into it can be helpful.

A famous public relations program for this purpose was developed a number of years ago for The Long Island Railroad. Its principles would be applicable in any similar situation, whether the utility was privately or publically owned.

As the world's largest commuter line, moving one-fifth of all the railroad passengers in the United States, the Long Island Rail Road was America's biggest passenger carrier, and its public relations problems were correspondingly demanding. With hundreds of weekday trains running only a few seconds apart at the peak of morning and evening traffic, the slightest delay makes 40,000 to 60,000 people late to work or to dinner. In the early 1950s the railroad was in bankruptcy, equipment was run down, and no fare increases had been permitted for several years. Eventually the financial situation was remedied, but a legacy of public ill will remained along with the natural difficulties of a service in which success is taken for granted and occasional lapses are the cause for bitter complaint.

Under these circumstances, a vigorous public relations effort was needed to improve the morale of employees, increase business, and prevent constant public friction. A major information program was entered into; but something additional was needed, and after about a year, the line's public relations director had an inspiration.

What better way could be devised to make a rider familiar with a railroad's problems than to make him an honorary engineer for a day?

In the words of Long Island Rail Road's public relations director:

> Much of the criticism pouring down upon us was a result of the misconceptions most people have of how a commuter railroad operates. . . . We were convinced that all the speeches and press releases in the world couldn't correct this situation. The answer, we decided, was to find some way of giving a cross section of our passengers a behind-the-scenes look at what makes a railroad tick—or what, on occasions, makes it fail to tick—and depend upon them to pass this insight on to fellow commuters. We were pretty sure that both our operation and our employees would stand up well under such a spotlight of first-hand inspection.
>
>   . . . we had a notion that . . . our passengers who hadn't completely outgrown boyhood dreams of being locomotive engineers . . . would see and learn if they were given an opportunity to ride up front with the engineer. . . . So we decided to extend a blanket invitation to all of our regular commuters to be an engineer for-a-day on their way to work some morning.
>
>   Although in our fondest dreams (or our most fearsome nightmares) we never expected the 2,000-odd acceptances we ended up with, we knew from the start that this was something which might take quite a bit of doing. . . . If the program was to be successful we must have the whole-hearted support of the whole railroad, not just the blood, sweat and tears of the two-man public relations department. . . . We moved slowly and

cautiously. The idea (never before tried elsewhere) was thoroughly chewed over at a couple of President's staff meetings and suggestions were encouraged from all departments. From an original it's-strictly-impossible reaction, there evolved not only a feeling that the thing might be made to work, but also a genuine enthusiasm. . . . Then, and not until then, were we ready to shove off.

Invitations to be an engineer-for-a-day were sent to ticket agents (they included a return self-addressed business reply card) . . . and simultaneously a press release announcing the program was distributed to all media.

There was no time to sit back and wonder whether or not the thing would catch on. The response was instantaneous. Within a few hours after the first invitation had been passed out . . . the cards began pouring in. The cards were carefully filed in order of receipt, and each would-be Casey Jones received a letter from the railroad president and a little booklet about the line.

Two weeks after the first invitations were distributed our first guest engineer climbed into the cab . . . selected by lot from the 37 reply cards received in the first mail after the program was announced. . . .

Organizing the program took extreme care. To avoid distracting the working engineer, an officer or supervisor of the railroad met each guest at his station, escorted him to the cab, rode with him, and answered all his questions. Fifty-eight persons volunteered for this job. They phoned personally to four people a week. Hosts, such as lawyers or accountants, who were not familiar with actual operating details of the line, were provided with a five-page briefing sheet.

In commenting on the results of the program, the Long Island Rail Road public relations head said:

One of the many surprises of the program was the unexpectedly large number of letters from those taking the cab rides. More than half wrote in to say "thanks"—there wasn't a single criticism.

These letters, with a penciled "thank you" note from the president were sent to the host and the train crews involved. . . .

Any publicity we might get from the program was secondary in our decision to undertake it. The emphasis was on the person-to-person contact that would be possible. Even so, the volume of publicity many times exceeded anything else we'd ever attempted.

Every daily in New York City and on Long Island, for example, carried full and favorable stories on the initial announcement. The story was also featured on virtually every radio and television station . . . in the metropolitan area and in approximately a hundred weekly newspapers on Long Island . . . also widely used over the country.

We had our fingers crossed the morning of the first ride. Engineer-for-a-day No. 1 had been picked by lot and we had no way of knowing how he would handle himself with the 20-odd reporters, photographers and radio and television people who were waiting at the end of the line in Long Island City. The results couldn't have been better if we had hand-picked him and coached him for a week in advance.

. . . the continuing publicity was very gratifying. Weekly newspapers, for example, carried stories and pictures in virtually every issue of local residents who had been engineers-for-a-day during the preceding week, and more than a score of employee publications . . . carried similar stories on their own people—from presidents down through secretaries and stock-room clerks—who made the trip.

An important by-product . . . was strengthening the morale and pride in the railroad on the part of employees. Capsule comments from letters were carried in each issue of our biweekly publication.

. . . although it took six months . . . and hundreds of man-hours of time by officers and supervisors . . . we're still convinced, almost five years later, that this was by all odds the most successful public relations program the Long Island Railroad has ever undertaken. . . .

4. HELPING HIGH SCHOOL JOURNALISTS IN THEIR WORK

A daily newspaper in a competitive situation in a large American city a number of years ago decided that it would be good promotion to establish closer relations with high school newspaper staffs, many of whom might be future readers or even employees. One of the ways chosen to do this was a "Teen Press Club." It worked like this:

Once each month the newspaper arranged for two representatives from each high school newspaper staff that wanted to take part to spend an hour interviewing some national celebrity who happened to be in the city. Selection of the representatives was made by high school journalism teachers from among the best reporters on their staffs and was frequently changed from one interview to another. Photographers were also welcomed.

Since the newspaper knew in advance of famous political people, musicians, entertainers, scientists, and politicians who would be in town, arranging the interviews was easy and almost always the celebrities welcomed the extra publicity. The newspaper's public relations director acted as coordinator at the "press conferences," opened and closed the sessions and clarified questions if necessary. Meetings were held in varied locations convenient both to the persons being interviewed and to the high school students. A scientist might be at a local university, for example; a politician at city hall; or an actor on the stage of a theater or in a hotel meeting room.

If the interviews were used in a high school newspaper teachers were encouraged to send them in and a small award was made for the one the newspaper's news staff considered the best. Occasionally very good interviews were printed in the columns of the big city daily itself with a brief description of the author.

5. CELEBRATING THE 175TH BIRTHDAY OF THE OLDEST U.S. NAVY WARSHIP

In 1972 the famed old wooden frigate, the USA Constitution, was 175 years old. Since 1934 she has been moored at a special berth in the Boston Naval Shipyard. Each year about 700,000 visitors tour the ship which is now maintained as a naval historical museum.

Every year The Constitution is towed out into the harbor, turned around and then moored again facing the opposite direction. This is done to equalize the effects of weather on her wooden masts and spars. In recent years "going to sea" on the Constitution on this annual cruise had become a sought-after privilege.

In 1972 it was decided by the Navy to invite specially chosen teen-age boys and girls from every state and Puerto Rico to take part in this brief cruise on the ancient warship along with adult sponsors as a means of helping celebrate the vessel's 175th anniversary.

Guests registered at a Boston motel where special group rates had been obtained for them. Then followed a walking tour of Boston's famed Freedom Trail in the old city. Stopping at the State House the group was personally welcomed by the Governor of Massachusetts.

In the evening there was a dinner at the motel hosted by the head of the motel chain and afterwards bus-loads of guests left for The Boston Pops Orchestra Concert which was Navy Night with the entire house bought out by New England Navy people.

The Constitution was ready for sea the next morning, manned by a navy crew wearing ceremonial uniforms in the style of those worn by seamen and officers in historic times. The visitors arrived by bus from their motel and thoroughly enjoyed the two-hour cruise into Boston harbor which was well-covered by newspapers and television nationwide.

Following the cruise the young people and their sponsors were guests at a luncheon at a famous Boston fish restaurant and then visited Plymouth Rock. The final event of the day was a traditional New England clambake at a seaside resort at which the First District U.S. Naval Band played both march tunes and dance music.

At the breakfast the following morning, the final event, guests heard a talk by a rear admiral who was retiring after forty-five years service and who told what the Navy had meant to him.

The entire program was conducted at no cost to the government. Transportation to Boston was given by sponsors in each state. Guests paid their own hotel bills. Everything else in Boston was provided by generous friends of the Navy.

Response was excellent consisting of many letters of thanks, the best media coverage in history both in Boston and in home areas of visitors and nationally, and of a welcome for navy recruiters into many new areas.

6. PASSING A SCHOOL BOND ISSUE AFTER TEN FAILURES

After ten repeated failures to pass a school bond issue which would end half-day sessions in a junior high school, the resultant bad publicity began to affect property values and business in a smaller midwestern suburban town of about 6,000 voters. The problem began to be seen as one which not only affected parents of children in school but all others as well.

A public relations firm in a nearby large city was retained to analyze aggregate voting data and other background information, write a plan and train volunteers to execute it. The first step was an opinion survey to uncover how district residents felt about the school system and the bond issue itself.

Before the campaign surfaced publicly, strong support was obtained from the town's business community including real estate people, from elected officials and from senior citizens. It was realized that this would be necessary to show that the issue affected more than just the children and their parents. Endorsements and such participation would neutralize criticism.

The second step was to enlist as many people as possible as volunteers. In a small community the mass media such as newspapers and broadcasting are helpful, but the real work of getting people to the polls and of convincing neighbors is done individually. Eventually about 2,700 people volunteered their help in typing, driving, conducting coffees, mailing brochures and in other ways. They were from all segments of society and included those with children in school and those who did not have children in school. Ads appeared in the local weekly newspaper and the last ad before the election was a full page listing 470 individuals and organizations supporting the bond issue.

Another opinion poll, taken after publicity for the vote had been underway for some weeks, showed that most residents were well aware of the school situation and its meaning.

After heavy publicity of all types the bond issue finally passed 3,125 to 1,976. About 18 percent of the residents had been active in the campaign to achieve this result.

7. A DETROIT BANK FIGHT SLICK SWINDLES

In 1974 Detroit Bank & Trust Company decided to help its customers and other citizens save their money by not falling victim to swindlers, thus performing a needed public relations service. During the next two years there was a great response including not only articles in local newspapers and broadcasts on local television and radio stations, but also feature stories in distant metropolitan newspapers, in national magazines and on national television. In addition, speakers from the bank made dozens of talks upon the subject to Detroit area service clubs and similar groups.

There were several reasons for the response. The program was launched just as the Christmas season began and this is one of the prime times for swindlers. It also came at a time of business recession when many people were struggling to make ends meet and thus were prey for sharp operators who seemed to offer a quick solution. The old, standard con games seem to go on year after year.

The bank's accounting department engaged in considerable research before launching the series. Some of the frauds had come to their attention before; local police were able to supply others; but the remainder took calls to police departments, banks, and Better Business Bureaus all over the United States. As part of its effort the bank issued a small booklet describing nine of the most common swindles and what to do about them. They were:

1 *The charge card overcharge* Dishonest store employees sometimes set the imprinter to record $15 or a $5 charge card sale, even though the handwritten amount is properly $5. The machine will then bill for $15 and the employee steals the rest. The way to avoid this is to compare handwritten and imprinted amounts

Figure A-3   An assistant vice president of Detroit Bank and Trust Company explains a scheme used by swindlers to the host of a television talk show in that city and displays a phony wad of bills used to lure a victim. Because of its wide interest interviews were given on many stations. Courtesy Dennis Clark, Visual Impact Productions.

before signing a charge card slip and to keep all slips and reconcile them against your bill each month.

2 *Stolen checks* Checks should be guarded like money and so should cancelled checks and statements. Cancelled checks reveal your signature to forgers. Also, when you get your cancelled checks back from the bank each month be sure to examine them promptly to see that they match the statement and report any errors at once.

3 *The bank examiner scheme* Many older people fall for this ancient swindle. A con man obtains bank account and other personal information about his or her victim by peering over her shoulder while he or she is writing a transaction slip in a bank lobby or by rummaging through a wastebasket. Then when the victim arrives home she gets a call from someone claiming to be a "bank examiner." The phony examiner explains that a bank employee is suspected of being a thief by altering withdrawal slips and asks the victim's help in trapping the guilty employee.

The "plan" requires that the victim withdraw money from the bank. The cash will then be marked and compared to the withdrawal slip. Any difference will "prove" that the employee has altered the figures on the withdrawal slip and is pocketing the extra money. After the victim makes the withdrawal, the phony bank examiner arrives at the victim's home, flashes a false I.D., marks the money, and leaves with it to return to the bank. He is never seen again nor is the money.

To prevent this many banks ask their tellers to inquire of senior citizens withdrawing large sums of money. The biggest defense, however, is keeping your financial affairs to yourself, tearing up any faulty transaction slips, and not withdrawing money on the request of strangers. Report anyone claiming to be a bank examiner to the police or the the bank at once. Under no circumstances will a real bank examiner, FBI agent, or other official ever request you to withdraw money from your bank account for any reason.

4 *Money to a screaming woman* One common ruse involves a seemingly hysterical woman who rushes to a victim's door claiming that her son has just been injured in an auto accident and needs a blood transfusion and she has no money. She wants $5 or $10 and the names of others who might help her. Such names will then be used with the first victim's implied endorsement to get more money. On a good day such a scheme has been known to collect $500. The best answer is to check with the police, your own doctor, or the Red Cross first.

5 *The pigeon drop* This is such an old trick that it seems impossible that it keeps on going. The answer is, perhaps, that there are always new people who haven't yet heard of it.

A typical scheme (although there are many timely variations) involves a con man approaching his mark and engaging her or him in idle conversation. Then confederate rushes up, excited over having just found an envelope containing $30,000 in cash. Also in the envelope is a note saying that the money was a payoff for a big drug deal. The two discuss if the money can be returned. One con man says he will call an attorney friend for advice. Over the phone the

Be Sure the Yuletide Laugh Isn't on You

WHILE YOU'RE PICKING gifts to make this Christmas jolly, keep in mind that it's also the season to be wary.

Con artists find that the prevailing aura of good will provides a rare opportunity to fleece the unsuspecting.

That is the warning from two experts on the tactics of professional swindlers. William J. Kalmar and David J. Westhoff, officers of the Detroit Bank & Trust, keep a close watch on the trend in such scams. Among their examples of prevalent Christmas swindles—

"Hot" bargain jewelry. This is the big season for the con artist who sidles up to an unwary shopper and whispers that he has a "hot" diamond ring or bracelet for sale at bargain-basement prices. With furtive glances over his shoulder, the

Con artist offers "hot" jewelry.

swindler will try to convince his victim that he is talking to an actual thief with stolen merchandise he wants to unload quickly. If the shopper succumbs, he will probably discover that his "hot" buy is actually a cool piece of worthless glass.

Mail-order offers. Responding to a Christmas ad by an unknown mail-order firm may be equally risky, the bankers say. Some such companies do not have sufficient inventories to fill demands placed on them, or the ability to process in a short time thousands of Christmas orders. Furthermore, the companies may not even be in business. "There are literally hundreds of crooked individuals who place advertisements in magazines and newspapers at Christmastime for products or services that do not exist," they warn. Before sending a check, it is often better to query the local Better Business Bureau.

Unsolicited "gifts." During the yuletide season, hundreds of worthwhile organizations send unsolicited small gifts

through the mail, along with requests for donations. So do a growing number of less scrupulous groups. Send a donation to the charitable organization if you wish, but keep in mind that you are not legally obligated to either pay for or return the unsolicited item.

Phony Santas. Most street-corner Santa Claus characters are obviously soliciting for the Salvation Army or other

Free-lance Santa Claus at work.

legitimate charitable groups. But there are some each year who are simply con men dressed up like Santa, ringing a bell and asking contributions from passing shoppers.

Free-lance salesmen. Strangers often appear in office buildings this time of the year, selling items like Christmas cookies, pen-and-pencil sets, or pots and pans. While many are legitimate salesmen, some use the sale of such products as a ruse to gain entry to an office. Once inside, their game is to pilfer wallets, purses, small clocks and other personal items from the desks. More and more office buildings now keep out all such self-employed salesmen.

Unethical clerk doctoring a credit-card charge slip.

Christmas credit. The use of credit cards also offers the unscrupulous salesperson the opportunity for extra income during a heavy shopping season. If a shopper chooses a $5 gift, for example, the employe may set the imprinter to record $15 on the top right-hand corner of the charge slip. Then, even though the handwritten amount is $5, the charge slip will be processed for an extra $10 and will go undetected unless the shopper looks at the slip carefully before signing. In another ploy, the crooked salesperson will prepare two slips to charge to the buyer's account—one for the correct amount and a second for a fraudulent amount. Later, he will forge the signature from the first slip onto the second, and take either the cash or merchandise home. The recommended solution: Save those receipts and reconcile the store account at month's end.

A fragrant ripoff. Shopping-center parking lots are said to be the favored locale of a seasonal swindle involving cut-rate perfume. Here, the con artist offers the shopper a bottle that he says is a chemically perfect copy of an expensive, name-brand perfume, at greatly reduced prices. After giving him a whiff from an actual bottle of the expensive perfume, he sells him a bottle whose label is a carefully misspelled version of the famous product, which he passes off as a perfectly legal copy made by a local chemist. With luck, the purchaser may get a watered-down version of the original. But more often than not, he will wind up with a bottle of colored water.

The $13.95 goose. One of the most frequent capers carried out at this time of the year, the bankers say, is the unsolicited c.o.d. package. A truck resembling a standard delivery van pulls up in front of a home, and the driver—probably uniformed—comes to the door with a package addressed to the next-door neighbor. He reports that the neighbor is not at home, and asks, "Would you mind accepting the package?" He explains that it contains a perishable item and that the neighbor would have to endure long lines of people in order to pick it up. This can be avoided, he adds, if you will give him the $13.95 required for the c.o.d. If you fall for it and give him the money, he departs; the neighbor later denies ordering any such thing. When the package is opened, it contains something worthless—sometimes what appears to be the remains, appropriately, of a cooked goose, the bankers report.

Figure A-4 National publicity resulted from the "Slick Swindles" public relations effort, and shown in this page from a *U.S. News and World Report* article.

so-called attorney says she sees no reason why the cash should be returned since it was obtained illegally but suggests waiting a few days to see if the police are investigating. The con man then suggests to the victim that each of them put up $5,000 as a guarantee of good faith and then split the money when they see the attorney again in a few days.

At the second meeting they drive to the attorney's office building and one con takes the supposed $30,000 upstairs. When he returns he says that the attorney wants to speak to each one of them alone and each puts in $5,000 as a guarantee. The victim is sent up first but there is no such attorney's office and when he returns his "partners" are gone and so is his $5,000. (The $30,000, of course, never existed except as a few bills on the outside of cut paper.)

This scheme is so transparent that it seems no one would fall for it but it dates back at least 400 years and succeeds because of ignorance and greed. Few legitimate transactions require cash.

6   *Over-ring on sales* A dishonest store clerk can take advantage of customer carelessness by over-charging or short-changing. Count your change, be sure the amount charged agrees with your sales slip, and have a rough idea of what your total bill will be and how much change you should receive.

7   *The $12.95 brick* A person dressed as a delivery person comes to the victim's door with a package addressed to a neighbor. He says the neighbor is not at home and asks the victim to pay $12.95 C.O.D. on the package—explaining that it will save the neighbor a trip downtown or to the Post Office. When the neighbor arrives home and they open the package (which the neighbor had not ordered) it contains only a brick. To avoid this accept only prepaid packages or ones that you have been specifically asked to by your neighbor.

8   *Home improvement schemes* People offer to fix a roof just because they happen to be in the neighborhood, or to mend a driveway, or to inspect a furnace and then find that it is a fire hazard which must be remedied immediately.

Check out unknown contractors with references or the Better Business Bureau, obtaining competing cost estimates. Be sure a contract contains all of the promises of the salesman. Never sign a completion certificate until all of the work has been done to your satisfaction.

9   *Postal fraud* There are all sorts of schemes. One of the meanest is when swindlers watch for death notices in newspapers and then send bills for nonexistent merchandise to the family. Often, since they cannot be easily checked, these are paid. Others include orders for nonexistent products, chain letters and offers to trace family trees. The main protection is to be suspicious. Check the Better Business Bureau before ordering from an unknown firm.

One of the biggest problems that law enforcement officers face is that it is estimated that two out of three victims are too embarrassed to report their losses.

Appendix B

Fourteen Do-it-yourself Public Relations Problems

The following cases cited were all actual occurrences, though occasionally names have been changed. Consider that you are the public relations head for the organization concerned and decide what you would do to solve each of the problems posed.

PROBLEM CASE 1. THE BURNED-OUT PLANT

What would you do if a sudden fire destroyed 80 per cent of your plant plus all sales records? That was the problem faced by A-to-Z Electric Batteries, Inc., of Bridgeville, New Jersey, on Sunday morning, December 1, 1955.

Not only did the main plant burn completely in the overnight fire, but in addition, the laboratory, office, and all sales records, orders, and correspondence were destroyed. A-to-Z, Inc., had no way of knowing what orders were on its books or what had been shipped.

The management decided to stay in business. Besides the problems of replacing equipment and leasing new quarters, there were two main public relations problems:

1 Preventing cancellation of orders by assuring customers that their orders would be filled promptly, and thus discouraging them from turning to other sources of supply.

2 Informing employees that they would be needed back at work as soon as possible, thus maintaining a valuable skilled labor force without which work could not have been resumed.

The problem was intensified by the fact that the fire had been spectacular, had been witnessed by thousands, and had received superb coverage in words and pictures on all the news media of the entire metropolitan area. Rumors that A-to-Z, Inc., would never resume business were perhaps started by competitors. Management estimated that it would take about three days to salvage some batteries which had escaped the blaze and which could be utilized to fill the most immediate orders, and several months of slower-than-normal production before the plant could be fully restored.

Questions

What would you do to solve the immediate public relations problems?
What about the longer-range problems?
Is there any way in which this disaster can be turned into an asset?

PROBLEM CASE 2. THE SUMMER THE WATERWORKS BROKE DOWN

The Riverton Suburban Water Company served scores of thousands of people in a rapidly growing area surrounding a large city which had its own municipal water plant. There was no shortage of water, since the company's main pumping plant was on one of the largest rivers in the United States; but in one drought year its service broke down badly.

There were several reasons. New houses were being built at a dizzy pace in the area served. Automatic washers, air coolers, swimming pools, and many other household uses boosted water consumption inordinately, and the drought forced much lawn and garden watering. A conservative management had been unwilling to face the costs involved in expansion and had tried to make inadequate mains, booster stations, and reservoirs do more than they could.

The results were disastrous. From 4 P.M. until 9 P.M. daily, all during the late summer, many homes in higher sections of the area had no water at all; others suffered from low pressure. Fire chiefs issued warnings of dire consequences. The company was forced to plead for cooperation, asking citizens not to wash cars or water parched lawns. When water pressure was increased, old mains broke and caused miniature floods. The catastrophe was particularly maddening to customers, since water rates had always been higher than in the neighboring big city (which had an actual surplus of water all through the drought) and since the river, the source of Riverton Suburban Water Company's supply, was at a normal summer level. An outcry arose that the company should be taken over and put into public hands.

The management of the company was changed. With fall rains in September the situation eased, and the management said to its newly hired public relations counseling firm, "Now what should we do?"

Questions

What are the immediate steps to be taken?

Much physical work must be done on the company facilities before next summer. By then good service should be restored, but improved supply for every householder is not absolutely certain, since home building is very rapid. How do you face this problem?

Be sure to think of *all* the publics involved.

PROBLEM CASE 3.   CLOSING DOWN AN OIL REFINERY

Long-established industries become a part of a community and of their employee's lives, especially in smaller towns which are much dependent on them. The better the plant's employee and community public relations programs the more this is so.

Yet there is no way in which a business which has become unprofitable can be forced to continue at a loss to its owners or in which an unprofitable division of a generally successful corporation can be expected to long continue as a drain upon the whole operation if there is no prospect of its future success.

This is what happened in Marion, Kansas. For many years the Midwestern Company oil refinery employing about 100 people in this town of 8,000 about 100 miles from Kansas City had been a mainstay of the town which had only a few other small industries and depended mainly upon rural farm trade.

But nothing lasts forever. Increasingly the refinery became uneconomic as nearby oil production declined, pipelines went elsewhere and consumption shifted to the rapidly growing cities. The final blow came when the development of new refining methods caused the Midwestern Company to decide that expensive new machinery should be installed in an existing plant that it had nearer to Kansas City where it could be operated at full capacity and nearer to the main points of sale. The Marion refinery could not be modernized competitively with other oil companies so it was decided to close it as soon as the new equipment nearer Kansas City was installed and tested. This would be in about six months and after that the company would have no further use for the 200 acre refinery at the edge of Marion. Some of the machinery could be dismantled and sold for scrap. There were only a few small buildings otherwise on the site which was fenced and had good railway and highway access.

Only a few of the employees would be needed at the Kansas City area plant which was much more efficient. Room for a few more might be found in other company operations in other states if they were willing to move.

As public relations director of Midwestern you were told about this decision as soon as it was made, about six months in advance, and asked to prepare a plan for handling the situation. It was important to make the necessary closing as painless as possible both for employees and the community because there had been some ill will in the past about Midwestern in Kansas and because the public was upset by a recent rise in oil prices which was being exploited by politicians. Poor handling could affect sales and governmental contracts.

In addition, the company had a real concern about the consequences of its actions. They had been in Marion a long time. The establishment of a plant is not a guarantee that it will stay there forever if not profitable, but over the years personal ties had been formed which meant that everything that could be done within reason should be explored. A good plan of action and then of communication would have to be devised rapidly.

Questions

What can be done for the employees? Remember that this is an old plant in a small town and that many of them have been here for a long time and will not find it easy to sell their homes and move. How should they be told?

What can be done to assist the town? What aid can Midwest bring to the situation which the people of Marion could not muster for themselves?

Can a way be devised to help the town which will also help Midwest employees? What is the town's responsibility to help itself?

PROBLEM CASE 4.   MOVING A RAILROAD HEADQUARTERS

The offices of the Great Southwestern Railroad for many years had been located in a large city in the Midwest in rented quarters in a large downtown office building. At the same time the company had maintained a smaller regional office in a much smaller Texas city.

The railroad's business was highly competitive, since the same area was served by several other lines as well as by truck and air competition; the management therefore decided that it would be more efficient to centralize headquarters in the smaller Texas city, where a much smaller passenger and freight staff could do all that was needed, and to avoid the rental of large metropolitan offices. In fact, a new building, much roomier and better planned, could be built in the smaller city at a considerable saving.

The problems were:

1 Moving the 150 central-office employees, most of whom had lived all their lives in the Midwestern big city, owned their homes, and could hardly imagine living in a "hick town."

2 Keeping the good will of other people in the big city, which was the main eastern terminus of the railroad and a major source of freight and passengers.

3 Gaining ready acceptance for a large group of new people in the smaller Texas city which already had its established social and business patterns. Lack of welcome could seriously affect the morale of your long-established headquarters group—most of whom you wanted to keep because they would be hard to replace. The influx of so many new people at once would also pose some housing, school and public utilities problems.

Questions

How should the news be broken to employees? The new host town? The city from which you are departing?

How can you make the change easy and attractive to employees? Who will be likely not to want to go? What should be done for them?

How can you assure a genuine welcome in the new town? A minimum of opposition in the large city from which you are moving?

PROBLEM CASE 5. MAKING A NEW BUILDING MEMORABLE

The Jacobs Pen Company had an international reputation as a manufacturer of fine writing instruments and despite the competition of cheap ball point pens (which it also produced and marketed under other names) prospered. It was located in a pleasant small city about 60 miles away from an eastern metropolis served by an interstate highway and airline service.

The company itself had been established for many years and its factory-headquarters in the center of the small city had become completely outgrown. It lacked parking space for employees, the neighborhood had run down, the stream upon which it was situated was likely to flood, and the buildings were unimpressive. So the management bought forty acres at the edge of town, a rolling partly wooded site near an intersection of the Interstate highway, and decided to move. It was still within the city limits so no public relations problem was involved there and employees could drive to it more easily.

As soon as the board of directors had agreed to the move the president called you in and said in effect:

"There'll be a lot of manufacturing and operational advantages to building a new plant. But we ought to be able to get something more out of it than just that. We ought to think bigger than just our own people and this town because, after all, we sell all over the country and the world. What can we do to make this plant memorable not only here but also in the big city an hour's drive away and to some extent all over the country? I don't mean to spend a pot full of money. After all, we'll need all we've got just for the building itself. But with a little ingenuity we ought to be able to think of something that would not only make news now but would keep on coming for years. You're in public relations. What do you say?

Questions

What *do* you say? It can't cost too much, ought to be related closely to your business, and ought to last.

Imagine, if you lived in the large city 60 miles away, what would impress you about a new pen company building if you heard about it? What would be likely to make you remember it and drive by sometime?

PROBLEM CASE 6.   PERSUADING LOCAL PEOPLE TO INVEST

The United Electric Company generates and sells power in a large Midwestern state. Some years ago it was part of a large national holding company which was dissolved and split up into smaller state organizations, with the original stockholders each getting shares of the successor organizations. Now it wishes to increase the number of its stockholders in the state area which it serves. There are several reasons:

1   To organize influential local groups who have a financial stake in the company and who therefore will be sympathetic to its problems.
2   To raise funds locally from people who can best see the company's needs and opportunities.
3   To establish a better two-way channel of communication between the company and its public by being home-owned as well as home-operated.

The immediate goal of the company is to get 50 per cent of its stock held within the state in which it operates.

Question

How would you suggest organizing this campaign?

PROBLEM CASE 7.   THE DEFUNCT DEPARTMENT STORE

In New York City at one time a large department store, a branch of another large store in another eastern city, fell behind the times because of poor location and changing trade patterns; it ran downhill and eventually was closed.

When it died, a famous firm of public auctioneers was called in to sell its stock in liquidation at the best prices possible. When the auction staff began to tramp through the acres of vacant corridors, they were amazed. The estimated book value of the goods was several million, but in tradition they turned up such items as an old Mack truck, forty-five tapestries of great age, ancient royal banners, clothing dummies of the early 1900s, and a family of stuffed polar bears donated by an Arctic explorer in 1928.

The auctioneer quickly decided that public interest would determine the success of this venture; he hired the services of a public relations firm to create interest in the short time before the auctions were scheduled.

Question

As the head of that public relations counseling firm, what would you do?

PROBLEM CASE 8. MERGING A BOY'S SCHOOL AND A GIRL'S SCHOOL

Several years ago economic necessity forced the merger of Xavier (boys) and Loretto (girls) high schools located in a large midwestern city of more than a million people. The combined school was located in the Loretto building which with some additions was quite adequate to handle the new student body.

Both schools had been long established with strongly loyal alumni groups. Xavier had had an outstanding prep football team headed by the same coach for twenty years and was widely known to sports fans and sports writers.

Loretto had attracted girls from well-to-do families, many of whom were prominent socially.

In the merger it was planned to drop the Xavier football program and coach since the Loretto building did not have a practice or playing field and bleachers or a suitable indoor work-out area. Basketball would be retained and the reduced athletic program would feature both girl's and boy's sports.

The names of both of the schools would be dropped because they were so firmly established by sexes and the new school would be named St. Michaels. The principal, however, would be a sister Anne who had formerly been head of Loretto and the assistant principal would be the former Xavier principal. Numbers of faculty members would be dropped. The boards of the two schools would be combined and gradually reduced as their terms expired.

It was realized that all of this would produce a hubub. Dropping the football program and dismissing the coach (who could be counted to kick loudly) would anger the male alumni and draw bad press publicity. Diluting the strong social image of the former Loretto high school would not be popular. Coeducation in general would not appeal to some more conservative parents. And the economic reasons given for the action might cause some to conclude that the school's days were numbered anyway.

This was important, because the school would continue to depend upon student tuitions for its existence (as it had before). Any substantial drop in enrollment might well close the combined organization for good.

The problems seemed so complex that before any announcement was made the advice of a prominent public relations counselor in the city was requested. He happened to be a Xavier graduate himself and knew the background well.

Questions

What would you advise in this situation?

How, and in what ways, should the news be broken? What special attentions should be paid to each concerned public?

What steps might be taken to attack the problem positively and to work for an increase in students next year?

PROBLEM CASE 9.   A BANK ANNIVERSARY PROGRAM

The Mountain States National Bank of Denver, Colorado, will celebrate its 100th anniversary next June. That means it is almost as old as Colorado which only became a state in 1876 following a post-Civil War gold boom there. Denver also has a century of lively history in which the bank has been a participant, having received deposits and loaned money to miners, railroad builders, farmers, merchants, airlines and truckers.

Although "new" by eastern American standards, Denver grew up quickly (as did San Francisco, for example) and a considerable number of its people have lived there for several generations. It has produced a literature of its own and is the chief trading and banking center of several western states.

Mountain States is the second largest and second oldest bank in Denver. Its rival, First, passed its 100th birthday several years ago and utilized the occasion for heavy newspaper and TV advertising and a book on its 100 years. Now it's going to be your turn.

Question

What can Mountain States do that will be more newsworthy and of more lasting benefit to the community than its competitor did?

PROBLEM CASE 10.   THE JUNIOR COLLEGE MILLAGE VOTE

Westport is an industrial city of about 60,000 people about 30 miles away from a larger, more prosperous, manufacturing city of 300,000 and not close to any other major population centers. It is surrounded by a good farming area and the total county population is about 100,000. The main industries in Westport are a paper manufacturing company, a chemical plant, office furniture, and a plant making small gasoline engines. The city has not grown much in recent years. Because of national competition its industries have not been expanding, attempts to attract new business have not been very successful, and an increasing number of its young people have gone to the nearby 300,000 population city or to other parts of the country seeming to offer greater opportunities.

About a dozen years ago progressive citizens of Westport felt that the city should have a two-year community college. A new high school had been completed leaving the old high school in the center of town and with some remodeling it could serve. One argument for establishing a community college was that it would offer a low-cost chance for young people to begin college without having to leave home. Another was that it could be strongly shop oriented and supply good craftsmen for local industries and services from those seeking no more than two years education. After a vigorous campaign and some opposition from older citizens who did not want higher property taxes and from local industrialists for the same reason, the vote carried and Westport Community College came into being.

Now the problem is that it has been too successful and needs more operating money. Enrollment has grown from a few hundred to a few thousand. Classroom and shop facilities are inadequate despite daytime and evening operation. Class sizes have mounted. Teachers have become unionized and demand more pay and smaller classes. But the town's business development has been only moderate. Fortunately, the community college is supported on a county-wide basis, so the continuing decline of downtown Westport where the college is located does not have any direct effect except that it makes it more inconvenient to reach for many people and there are some security problems.

Your job is community relations director of the college. You have no staff. The one newspaper in the town has given the college good coverage in the past and supported its establishment but its attitude toward higher taxes has become increasingly hostile so it cannot be counted upon the endorse a tax increase. There is one television station in town but two-thirds of the audience probably listens to the two television stations in the neighboring larger city. There are two small radio stations.

Unionization of the teachers has resulted in some loss of public support and friction between the Board and teachers makes a bad press. The attitude of the industries is doubtful. They certainly do not favor more taxes and some are of marginal profitability. Yet the chemical plant and the paper mill contain individual management people who were for the establishment of the school and who still feel kindly toward it. Retail business downtown has so decayed and dispersed and gone into national chains as to offer no leadership or aid. Most of the old-money families in town have developed homes and interests elsewhere and it is hard to find community leadership.

Questions

You have about six months to work. The first question is strategy: Should you try to engage in an all-out ballyhoo campaign (assuming you can marshall the support and funds)? Or would it be smarter to use interior lines of communication to organize your support without arousing the opposition? How could this be done?

Would it be better to have the vote at the time of a major general election when other big issues of a state and national nature are on the ballot or on an off-date when only minor local matters are involved?

Then, how do you organize your forces?

PROBLEM CASE 11.   PROMOTING A SHOPPING MALL

Using both private and city funds a large new mall was constructed at the edge of a downtown area of a large western city but failed to draw customers. There were several reasons:

Because of its location many people confused it with the nearby decayed center of the city where there had been no retail stores for several years. It lacked identity of its own.

For the same reason, many people feared to visit it because of security apprehensions.

Habits are hard to change. People tend to continue to go where they have been in the habit of going unless there is some good reason to change.

Many people seemed to think that the new mall was a curiosity place such as a "gas light" area. It did have these attractions but was also a serious place to shop, having two major regional chain department stores in it.

Business was so poor that the entire venture began to slip. At that point more experienced public relations people were called in.

Question

What might be done?

PROBLEM CASE 12.   NOVA SCOTIA TOURISM

Nova Scotia, the most Atlantic province of Canada, has many attractions for tourists from the crowded northeastern part of the United States. It can be reached by driving or by car ferry from several northern New England points. It has an interesting seacoast of wooded hills and harbors and old towns. There are several historical points such as the fortress of Louisburg.

Nova Scotia is also noted for its fishermen and their deep sea fast schooners, including the famous old ship "Bluenose" which has been carefully preserved from an earlier era.

The problem for Nova Scotia is how to get its share of American tourists. Advertising, of course, is used as well as publicity releases and photos to travel editors and others. Films and booklets are distributed.

Question

Something else is needed—some action which would draw attention to the province and make news. What might it be?

PROBLEM CASE 13.   LOCKING THE CAR BEFORE IT IS STOLEN

No one likes to have his car stolen—even if it should be insured. The insurance companies don't like it either, because the more cars that are stolen the more claims they have to pay and the lower their income. Police departments are also against car theft.

One of the biggest single causes of car theft is the careless leaving of keys in parked cars—something that only the owner can prevent. It is estimated that perhaps a third of car thefts could be prevented by locking the car and its doors and then taking away the key. Many of these spur-of-the-moment thefts are by juveniles who steal a car to joy-ride—often ending in an accident or a jail sentence and criminal record.

Question

How would you go about getting public cooperation in a campaign to lock cars? Assume that you are working on a city-by-city basis with an individualized program in each place.

PROBLEM CASE 14.   ENCOURAGING PUBLIC
APPRECIATION OF ARCHITECTS

Good architecture is a matter of public concern because everyone has to look at attractive or ugly buildings. The appearance of a city is the sum total of its buildings as well as of its site, streets and parks.

Architects have a professional as well as a personal interest in the promotion of good architecture—and the employment of qualified architects to design buildings. The results of their work are quite public so in trying to obtain general appreciation of architecture the local city chapters of The American Institute of Architects frequently use public relations methods.

Questions

If you were the president of your local city chapter of the AIA what are some of the ways in which you might call attention to good examples (and bad) of local architecture?

How would engaging in such a service personally benefit members of the AIA who took part?

Index